Unless Recalled Earlier
DATE DUE

OCT 18 1991			
JUL 14 1995			
AUG 18 1995			
DEC 20 1995			

DEMCO 38-297

YEATS, FOLKLORE, AND OCCULTISM

Also from Unwin Hyman

THE ART OF FAILURE
Conrad's Fiction
Suresh Raval

BACKGROUNDS FOR JOYCE'S DUBLINERS
Donald T. Torchiana

LADY CHATTERLEY
The Making of the Novel
Derek Britton

POUND'S CANTOS
Peter Makin

THE WASTE LAND
Grover Smith

YEATS, FOLKLORE, AND OCCULTISM

Contexts of the Early Work and Thought

Frank Kinahan

The University of Chicago

Boston
UNWIN HYMAN
London   Sydney   Wellington

© Frank Kinahan, 1988

This book is copyright under the Berne Convention. No reproduction without permission. All rights reserved.

Unwin Hyman Inc.
8 Winchester Place, Winchester, Mass. 01890, USA

Published by the Academic Division of
Unwin Hyman Ltd,
15/17 Broadwick Street, London W1V 1FP, UK

Allen & Unwin (Australia) Ltd,
8 Napier Street, North Sydney, NSW 2060, Australia

Allen & Unwin (New Zealand) Ltd in association with the Port Nicholson Press Ltd,
60 Cambridge Terrace, Wellington, New Zealand

First published in 1988

Library of Congress Cataloging in Publication Data

Kinahan, Frank.
  Yeats, folklore, and occultism: contexts of the early work and thought / Frank Kinahan.
  p. cm.
  Bibliography: p.
  Includes index.
  ISBN 0–04–800062–0 (alk. paper)
  1. Yeats, W. B. (William Butler), 1865–1939—Knowledge—Folklore, mythology. 2. Yeats, W. B. (William Butler), 1865–1939—Knowledge—Occultism. 3. Folklore in literature. 4. Mythology, Celtic, in literature. 5. Occultism in literature. 6. Folklore—Ireland.
  I. Title.
  PR5908.F64K55   1988   87-32603
  821'.8—dc19   CIP

British Library Cataloguing in Publication Data

Kinahan, Frank.
  Yeats, folklore and occultism: contexts of the early work and thought.
  1. Yeats, W. B.—Criticism and interpretation.
  I. Title.
  821'.8   PR5907
  ISBN 0–04–800062–0

Typeset in 10 on 11 point Bembo
Printed and bound in Great Britain by
Billing & Sons Ltd, Worcester

We sometimes call him "melancholy," and speak of the "melancholy" of his poems, and I know not well why, unless it be that we mistake the pensiveness of his early verse, a pensiveness for noble things once had and lost, or for noble things too great not to be nearly beyond hope, for his permanent mood, which was one of delight in the beauty of noon peace, of rest after labour, of orchards in blossom, of the desire of the body and of the desire of the spirit.

W. B. Yeats, 1896

*For my parents,
poets too*

Contents

Preface	page	xiii
Acknowledgements		xix
Abbreviations		xxi
1 Sincerity and the Early Thought and Work		1
2 The Moon upon the Tide: Yeats and the Philosophy of Irish Fairylore		41
3 This Monotony of Happiness: "The Wanderings of Oisin"		85
4 Words of Power, Language of Art		126
5 Natural Ideals: Yeats and the Walled Garden		171
6 Aftermaths		217
Appendix		233
Selected Bibliography		237
Index		249

Preface

Lloyd R. Morris was perhaps the first critic to argue for a radical disjuncture between the spirit of Yeats's early work and that of his later, the precedence his by virtue of the fact that his *The Celtic Dawn* (1917) was written at a time when Yeats's career was finally far enough along to tempt division. Of the pre-1900 poetry, Morris said that "Yeats's unique contribution to poetic feeling lies in [the] dream-like, haunting, other-world spirit that his poetry evokes" (p. 52), a spirit based in "Yeats's disbelief in the life of actuality, and his conviction that the life of dream is the life of reality" (p. 55). Against this stands the "later work", and Morris's claim that Yeats was gradually turning his back on states of pure dream was to be reaffirmed by many a later reader: "In his later work he has dwelled less often in the land of the imagination, and more frequently dealt with reality" (pp. 85–6).

Inasmuch as Morris was burdened by the disadvantage of assessing a career that was still very much in progress, it is surprising how long views like those advanced in *The Celtic Dawn* remained in currency. Though the details of the formulation were to vary from critic to critic, a striking of the average would have produced a picture of a career that comprised three basic phases. The early work, ran the argument, was that of a man in flight from the world he lived in, a lover of worlds beyond. An older Yeats reversed those priorities, came back to basic touch: decided for the earth. The middle work built the bridge between the first and final phases; in it there began to emerge an artist who, as Morris had it, dwelt "less often" in the world of the imagination, and "more frequently" dealt with reality.

Inevitably, this appealingly symmetrical vision would begin to succumb to more complex descriptions of the Yeats canon; and when the reaction began to form, it took the prevailing views of the early career as its most frequent target. For one example, it is by now more than twenty years since Edward Engleberg, taking his cue from an essay written by Allen Tate more than twenty years earlier still, put into plain terms what readers before him had sometimes hinted at: that "Yeats simply never was the total romantic or aesthete that provides critics with a label for his 'early period'".[1] And other critics have offered readings of individual poems that are in accord both with Engleberg and with the bias of the readings offered herein. The fairy lyrics, "The Wanderings of Oisin", and the Rose poems will all provide centers of attention in the pages to follow;[2] and there will be no quarrel here with the comments of (for instance) David Daiches, who correctly sensed that "The Stolen Child" was a poem that imaged a "warm, familiar, human world" that is "rashly given up" by the child of the title in exchange for "something cold and inhuman",[3] or with those of Dwight Eddins and Daniel Albright, whose interpretations of "The Wanderings of Oisin" have shown them in sympathy with Daiches,[4] or with those of William H. O'Donnell, who has extended readings like these to cover central lyrics such as "To the Rose upon the Rood of Time".[5]

Yet, despite the accuracy of analyses like these, the book on Yeats's artistic beginnings is far from closed. For one thing, it remains to be shown that readers like those named above have managed to touch not simply the centers of specific poems, but the underlying attitudes of the early work as a whole; and the early work is an extensive body of poetry and prose that, taken *en bloc*, has never been assessed as thoroughly as it could have been. For another, it even now needs to be shown that this assessment of early Yeats is the more correct one. In 1971, Eddins observed that critical opinion had "of course" swung "completely" away from the "extreme" early position that was content to label the young artist as an aesthete and let matters go at that.[6] Correct on many another count, Eddins is wrong on this one. More recent books from major presses continue to argue that "Yeats's earliest work" betrays "a tendency to flee into dreams", while "in the first decade of the twentieth century...he was able to admit more of reality into his work",[7] a point of view with which *The Celtic Dawn* would have been in entire agreement. And the most recent book to take the early career as its focus describes the poems on the sidhe and the Rose in terms directly opposed to those of Daiches or O'Donnell or, for that matter, those of the chapters to follow. "The Stolen Child" it sees as grounded in an impulse towards "escapism"; and if it admits that the author of the Rose poems may be described as a man "aware of the dangers he courts", it none the less describes the poems themselves as "mystical, escapist".[8]

Readings like these cannot be lightly dismissed. They make it clear that the critical consensus that Eddins spoke of is by no means complete; and this lack of consensus in turn suggests that the recent attempts to revise the long-standing view of Yeats's early career have not been as persuasive as criticism might like to think. A majority of critics once assumed that Yeats's youthful works were mystical, escapist; a majority of critics now assumes that they were not. The school that viewed the young Yeats as escapist had some excellent arguments to advance, as have the critics who have taken this received opinion and recommended a full turn. But neither side has advanced an argument that might fairly be called conclusive. Recognizing that no discussion of Yeats's complex work and thought is likely to contain final words, these chapters none the less aim to show that there are compelling reasons why the critical pendulum should be swinging in the direction that it is, and conclusive reasons for a new and more widespread consensus.

In sum, this book focuses on Yeats's work as it appeared between the beginning of his career and the mid-1890s. It assumes that the early poetry and prose, for all its technical flaws, is the product of a sensibility less refined but every bit as intricate as that of the more mature artist; and its opening reference point is Yeats's emphatic 1921 claim that "our intellects at twenty contain all the truths we shall ever find" (*Au* 189). If that remark proves accurate, then these works of a man in his twenties should by rights reveal themselves as turning upon precisely the same kinds of tensions that made the later work so rich, and thereby reveal themselves as an integral part of a body of writing that was from start to finish of a single piece.

With subject matter and argument thus defined, there remains a brief word to be said about critical approach.

Even as readers of the early verse have tended to focus more on particular poems than on a body of poetry, so the early work as a whole has generally been regarded in isolation from the forces that shaped it;[9] and this is perhaps the primary reason why the spirit of these writings was so often misassessed. It would be hard to lay too brisk an emphasis on the fact that early Yeatsian concerns that later came to seem uncommon were standard topics of discussion among the men and women that a younger artist knew and the manifold sources he drew on. No strange choices, the sidhe and the Rose were rather the natural subject matter of a man who had been deeply marked by two movements that were coming to fruition as Yeats came into his twenties. The first of these was the revival of interest in Irish legend and folklore; the second was the revival of interest in occultism and practical magic.

To assign these two movements pre-eminence in the growth of Yeats's thought is only to follow his lead. In 1904 he asserted that the "stories" and "old epic fragments" that the Irish revival had made available in English had been "the chief influence of my youth" (*UP2* 328); and a dozen years later he wrote of how the "form of meditation" he had learned from his studies in magic had been "the intellectual chief influence on my life" from the time he was in his mid-twenties "up to perhaps my fortieth year" (*Mem* 27). A later stage in this work will discuss how Yeats could name both these diverse interests as the "chief" influence on his formative years and yet feel that he had in each case spoken the truth. But for the purposes of this preface, two briefer points will serve.

The first is that the young poet's researches into folklore and occultism were voluminous. As early as 1889 he declared that he had worked his way through "most, if not all, recorded Irish fairy tales" (*UP1* 139); and in the 1902 draft of *The Speckled Bird* he had Michael, his fictional portrait of the younger man he had been, claiming to have read "all the old magical books he could find" (*VSB* 58). If these ambitious claims are valid – and a retracing of the paths Yeats cut through his early readings will make it plain that they are – then studies thus wide in scope could not have helped but have a profound impact on the early poetry and prose; and apart from its concern with reinforcing a given overview of Yeats's career, the primary goal of this work is to measure how profound that impact was.

The second is that a reading of Yeats's work in its primary contexts must lead to the conclusion that Yeats spoke rightly when he named folklore and occultism as the primary influences on his emerging thought, and that his researches in these areas therefore bear the chief share of responsibility for having moulded the early works into the angular shapes that they took.

The method of the present book, then, is contextual; and, because its original aim was to take Yeats at his word, or at least not to dismiss his claims until they had been put to an adequate test, the central contexts considered here are those of folklore and magic, and the central emphasis is on the effect that his widespread rangings into ancient stories and old magical books had upon his early thought and work. Inasmuch as I will be relying on the early versions of these poems and tales – less perfected, more revealing – I should emphasize at the start that there will be less stress than usual laid upon technical inadequacies: partly because the imperfections are obvious when they appear, and partly because they have often been stressed at length, but most of all because these chapters are as interested in what Yeats was attempting as in what his early works achieved. In a sense this is an experiment in recreation, a test of whether following Yeats's labyrinthine crossings through his known sources can give a reader an idea of what the poet was thinking as he pondered the blank page. Thus regarded, as if from the inside out, these works emerge as more complex and more interesting than most reports would have had us believe; and if it be objected that folklore and magic were but two of the many influences on the young Yeats, and that a relocation of his writings in other of their contexts might reveal those writings to be more interesting still, we can only nod assent and ask a blessing on all future studies of influence. The areas of Yeats's concern that go unremarked herein would have repaid consideration; but life is short, and this book is already long, and Yeats's folklore sources were unmistaken in their claim that "if one was to count all the threads in a coat, it would never come into the tailor's hands".[10]

The introductory chapter surveys the central sources of the early poetry, the ways in which Yeats went about trying to bind these varied interests together, and the ways in which the revivals of interest in magic and Irish folklore encouraged him towards his search for unity.

Chapter 2 examines the early essays and lyrics that grew out of Yeats's excursions into Irish folk and fairy lore; chapter 3 looks at "The Wanderings of Oisin", chapter 4 at the poetry and prose that center on the symbol of the Rose. The argument in each case is that, far from positing the supernatural world as an ideal state, Yeats saw it as incapable of satisfying the complex needs of man. The argument resumes in chapter 5, a reading of those of the early works that center, not on the supernatural, but on the images of the warmer human hearthside and the sheltering natural world: images that best epitomize the motivating spirit behind Yeats's early enquiries into realms both supernal and mundane.

Chapter 6 discusses the ways in which and reasons why these favored early images – the sidhe and the Rose on one hand, home and nature on the other – had by the mid-nineties been banished from the poetry or, if not banished, altered to suit a maturing artist's steadily maturing vision.

Notes to Preface

1 Edward Engleberg, "'He too was in Arcadia': Yeats and the Paradox of the Fortunate Fall", in *In Excited Reverie*, eds A. Norman Jeffares and K. G. W. Cross, p. 90. Allen Tate's "Yeats's Romanticism: Notes and Suggestions" was first published in *The Southern Review* for winter of 1942; it is now more readily available in *The Permanence of Yeats*, eds James Hall and Martin Steinmann, pp. 97–105.
2 As regards the early poems, the appendix lists the tables of contents of *The Wanderings of Oisin and Other Poems* (1889) and *The Countess Kathleen and Various Legends and Lyrics* (1892), and compares them with the tables of contents of the *Poems* of 1895 and *W. B. Yeats: The Poems* (1984). It also shows which early poems Yeats abandoned, which titles he altered, and the new order he assigned his early lyrics when he prepared them for the "collected" edition of 1895.

Throughout this work, all citations from Yeats's published writings will come from the first editions in which the passages in question appeared; but whenever possible, page references will direct the reader to more accessible reprints. Thus citations of "The Wanderings of Oisin" are from *The Wanderings of Oisin and Other Poems* or the *Poems* of 1895, while page references are to the *Variorum Poems*. The bibliography provides a full list of editions used.
3 David Daiches, "The Earlier Poems: Some Themes and Patterns", in *In Excited Reverie*, p. 54.
4 Cf. Eddins, *Yeats: The Nineteenth Century Matrix*, pp. 67–76, and Albright, *The Myth Against Myth: A Study of Yeats's Imagination in Old Age*, pp. 54–116.
5 William H. O'Donnell, "Yeats as Adept and Artist: *The Speckled Bird*, *The Secret Rose*, and *The Wind Among the Reeds*", in *Yeats and the Occult*, ed. George Mills Harper, pp. 68–9.
6 Eddins, op. cit., p. viii.
7 Brenda Webster, *Yeats: A Psychoanalytic Study*, pp. 1, 2.
8 M. C. Flannery, *Yeats and Magic: The Earlier Works*, pp. 30, 87.
9 Of the notable exceptions to this claim, the most notable is Thomas F. Parkinson's *W. B. Yeats, Self-Critic: A Study of His Early Verse* (1951; reprinted 1971), which superseded previous work on the early poetry and remains the best book in the area. As will become evident, the present work's disagreement with Parkinson centers on his continuing claim that the young Yeats used his knowledge of "Celtic and occult lore" to express his "conviction that the natural world... is to be spurned and the eternal world... is to be embraced" (pp. 18–19).

Among more recent books, Harold Orel's *The Development of William Butler Yeats: 1885–1900* (1968) offers a helpful general survey of the early career; Eddins's *Yeats: The Nineteenth Century Matrix* (1971) examines the relationship between Yeats's early poetry and that of his predecessors in England, Ireland, and France; Frank Hughes Murphy's *Yeats's Early Poetry: The Quest for Reconciliation* (1975) accurately resumes the argument that Yeats was seeking to resolve "warring antinomies" into a "universal harmony" (p. 61); and Thomas L. Byrd's *The Early Poetry of W. B. Yeats: The Poetic Quest* (1978) sets out to demonstrate that Yeats was "searching for the true reality that exists behind the apparent cleavage between what we see as natural and spiritual" (p. 89).

Finally, Allen R. Grossman's provocative *Poetic Knowledge in the Early Yeats* (1969) comes closest to the present work in its attention to Yeats's manifold uses of his arcane sources; but Grossman's focus is on *The Wind Among the Reeds* rather than the earlier poetry and prose.

Ensuing chapters and notes will express my many debts to these and other critics.

10 Patrick Kennedy, *The Fireside Stories of Ireland*, p. 107.

Acknowledgements

Describing the genesis of 1894's "The Cap and Bells", Yeats said that "'The authors are in eternity'" (*VP*, p. 808); and I must confess that there were times when I thought I would join them before the present project was completed. My debts are many, and of long standing.

My thanks to John Boyd, F. X. Connolly, John McGrath, Paul Naumann, and A. O. Wlecke – friends in a first hard springtime – for contributing unaware. To Bruno Bettelheim for sharing his knowledge of the difference between the dark endings of Irish tales of the sidhe and the generally more benign resolutions of the fairytales that have come down from England and continental Europe. To Ronan Murphy and Anne O'Gara for keeping a needful eye on my use of Irish. To Allen G. Debus for his detailed remarks on late nineteenth-century views of Paracelsus, and to Wendy O'Flaherty for her notes on my remarks about the rise of interest in comparative mythology in the Europe of the 1880s and 1890s. To John Killeen and John Loughnane for their help with matters topographical, and to James McGarry for his company and guidance in Sligo and environs. To David and Mary Kinahan Ockay for their assistance in running down occult sources that would otherwise have remained out of reach. To Daniel Kinahan for lending a keen ear. To Christopher Urrows, fine chronologer. To Jason Sommer for his conversation and his cutting of tape in Dublin, and to Ted Hickey and Brian McCabe for "knowing a man who could get that done" when I had given up hope of finding one. To the Humanities Division of The University of Chicago, particularly W. Braxton Ross, Jr, and Karl J. Weintraub, for aid with travelling and typing expenses when aid was badly needed. To Edward O'Shea and M. H. Thuente for sharing their knowledge. To Rosemary Camilleri and Bronac McKibben for extensive technical help. To the library staffs of Harvard University, the National Library of Ireland, the Newberry Library, the New York Public Library, Queen's University Belfast, University College Dublin, and The University of Chicago. To Allen Fitchen for incisive editorial advice. To mentors, colleagues and friends: William Alfred, Merlin Bowen, Robert Ferguson, Elizabeth Helsinger, Jerome McGann, Edward Rosenheim and Richard Strier, each of whom saw a part or all of the manuscript when it was in its earlier stages and helped set it back on course. To yet another colleague and friend, Peter Blayney, for his assistance with the diagrams in the fourth chapter. To the Institute of Irish Studies at Queen's University Belfast for providing me with a home base in 1987. To my research assistant, Lisa Dickler, in part for a sense of humor that often helped to restore my own vanishing sense of perspective, and in part for her rapid, efficient limning of varied esoterica. To Warwick Gould, who was kind enough to offer an extended commentary on what appeared to be a completed version of this book, and exacting enough to observe that it was not yet complete. And to the staff of Unwin Hyman for abundant help over a long haul.

My more particular thanks to John V. Kelleher, Donald Torchiana, William Veeder and Anne Butler Yeats, each of whom will I think understand me when I say that what I owe can neither be briefly acknowledged nor soon repaid.

Finally, to Mary O'Connell and Caitlin O'Connell Kinahan, who need to know how rightly I appreciated their learning of patience, and how grudging a teacher I was.

For permission to quote from the works of W. B. Yeats, I wish to thank Macmillan Publishing Company (New York) and A. P. Watt Ltd (on behalf of Michael B. Yeats and Macmillan London Ltd).

As regards individual works, I wish to thank Oxford University Press for permission to quote from *The Collected Letters of W. B. Yeats*, Vol. I, eds John Kelly and Eric Domville; McClelland and Stewart (Toronto) for permission to quote from *The Speckled Bird, With Variant Versions*, ed. William H. O'Donnell; and Columbia University Press for permission to quote from the two volumes of *Uncollected Prose by W. B. Yeats* (copyright Richard J. Finneran, 1977). Vol. I of *Uncollected Prose* was edited by John P. Frayne, Vol. II by John P. Frayne and Colton Johnson.

Finally, I wish to thank a number of sources for assistance with the illustrations. The drawing of the Rose Cross Lamen (Ch. 4 and cover) has been reproduced from *The Golden Dawn*, ed. Israel Regardie; the diagram of the Paths on the Tree (Ch. 4) is reproduced with the permission of the estate of R. G. Torrens; the photograph of the Celtic cross at Ahenny, Co. Tipperary (cover), is reproduced with the permission of Rosemary F. Hanley; and the 1889 portrait of Yeats by Henry Marriott Paget (cover) is reproduced with the permission of the Ulster Museum, Belfast.

Abbreviations

Citations from the more frequently used primary and secondary sources will appear in abbreviated form in the text proper. In cases in which an early first edition has subsequently been reprinted, page references are to the most recent edition cited below.

A   Books by Yeats

Au	*Autobiographies* (London: Macmillan, 1955).
CL1	*The Collected Letters of W. B. Yeats*, Vol. I, eds John Kelly and Eric Domville (Oxford: Clarendon Press, 1986).
CP	*W. B. Yeats: The Poems*, ed. Richard J. Finneran (London: Macmillan, 1984).
CPl	*The Collected Plays of W. B. Yeats* (London: Macmillan, 1960).
CT	*The Celtic Twilight. Men and women, dhouls and fairies* (London: Lawrence and Bullen, 1893). Revised and expanded as *The Celtic Twilight* (London: A. H. Bullen, 1902). Reprinted as *The Celtic Twilight* (New York: New American Library, 1962).
E&I	*Essays and Introductions* (New York: Macmillan, 1961).
Ex	*Explorations* (New York: Macmillan, 1973).
FFT	*Fairy and Folk Tales of the Irish Peasantry* (London: Walter Scott, 1888). Reprinted in *Fairy and Folk Tales of Ireland* (Gerrards Cross: Colin Smythe, 1977).
IFT	*Irish Fairy Tales* (London: T. Fisher Unwin, 1892). Reprinted in *Fairy and Folk Tales of Ireland* (Gerrards Cross: Colin Smythe, 1977).
Let	*The Letters of W. B. Yeats*, ed. Allan Wade (London: Rupert Hart-Davis, 1954).
LNI	*Letters to the New Island*, ed. Horace Reynolds (Cambridge, Mass.: Harvard University Press, 1970).
Mem	*Memoirs*, ed. Denis Donoghue (London: Macmillan, 1972).
Myth	*Mythologies* (New York: Macmillan, 1977).
UP1	*Uncollected Prose by W. B. Yeats*, Vol. I, ed. John P. Frayne (New York: Columbia University Press, 1970).
UP2	*Uncollected Prose by W. B. Yeats*, Vol. II, eds John P. Frayne and Colton Johnson (London: Macmillan, 1975).
VP	*The Variorum Edition of the Poems of W. B. Yeats*, eds Peter Allt and Russell K. Alspach (New York: Macmillan, 1966).
VPl	*The Variorum Edition of the Plays of W. B. Yeats*, ed. Russell K. Alspach (New York: Macmillan, 1966).
VSB	*The Speckled Bird, With Variant Versions*, ed. William H. O'Donnell (Toronto: McClelland and Stewart, 1976).
VSR	*The Secret Rose: Stories by W. B. Yeats: A Variorum Edition*, eds Phillip L. Marcus, Warwick Gould and Michael J. Sidnell (Ithaca, NY: Cornell University Press, 1981).

B Books by Yeats's Sources

AC	Lady Wilde's *Ancient Cures, Charms, and Usages of Ireland* (London: Ward and Downey, 1890).
AL	Lady Wilde's *Ancient Legends, Mystic Charms, and Superstitions of Ireland* (London: Ward and Downey, 1888).
BTF	Hyde's *Beside the Fire* (London: David Nutt, 1890).
EB	Sinnett's *Esoteric Buddhism* (London: Trübner and Co., 1883).
FL	Croker's *Fairy Legends and Traditions of the South of Ireland* (London: John Murray, 1834).
FSI	Kennedy's *The Fireside Stories of Ireland* (Dublin: M'Glashan and Gill, 1870).
GD I	Regardie's *The Golden Dawn: An Account of the Teachings, Rites and Ceremonies of the Order of the Golden Dawn* (St Paul, Minn.: Llewellyn Publications, 1978). Four volumes combined in one. (First published as individual volumes by The Aries Press, Chicago, 1937–40.)
GD II	*The Golden Dawn*, Vol. II.
GD III	*The Golden Dawn*, Vol. III.
GD IV	*The Golden Dawn*, Vol. IV.
Hist I	O'Grady's *History of Ireland: The Heroic Period* (London: Sampson Low, Marston, and Rivington, 1878).
Hist II	O'Grady's *History of Ireland: Cuculain and his Contemporaries* (London: Sampson Low, Searle, Marston, and Rivington, 1880).
IF	O'Hanlon's *Irish Folk Lore* (Glasgow: Cameron and Ferguson, 1870).
IPS	William Wilde's *Irish Popular Superstitions* (Dublin: J. McGlashan, 1852).
IU I	Blavatsky's *Isis Unveiled*, Vol. I (New York: J. W. Bouton, 1877).
IU II	Blavatsky's *Isis Unveiled*, Vol. II (New York: J. W. Bouton, 1877).
IW	McAnally's *Irish Wonders: the Ghosts, Giants, Pookas, Leprechawns, Banshees, Fairies, Witches, Widows, Old Maids and Other Marvels of the Emerald Isle* (London: Ward, Lock, and Co., 1888).
LFIC	Kennedy's *Legendary Fictions of the Irish Celts* (London: Macmillan and Co., 1866).
L&S	Lover's *Legends and Stories of Ireland* (New York: D. and J. Sadlier and Co., 1872).
MFI	Curtin's *Myths and Folk-Lore of Ireland* (New York: British Book Centre, Inc., 1975).
MWB	Hartmann's *Magic, White and Black* (New York: Theosophical Society Publishing Department, 1904).
T&S	Carleton's *Tales and Sketches, Illustrating the Character, Usages, Traditions, Sports and Pastimes of the Irish Peasantry* (Dublin: James Duffy, 1845).
TOS I	*Transactions of the Ossianic Society* (1853), Vol. I (Dublin: John O'Daly, 1853).
TOS IV	*Transactions of the Ossianic Society* (1856), Vol. IV (Dublin: John O'Daly, 1859).
TSD I	Blavatsky's *The Secret Doctrine*, Vol. I (London: The Theosophical Publishing Society, 1908).
TSD II	Blavatsky's *The Secret Doctrine*, Vol. II (London: The Theosophical Publishing Society, 1908).
TSD III	Blavatsky's *The Secret Doctrine*, Vol. III (London: The Theosophical Publishing Society, 1897).

Abbreviations

Note to Reader

When using these abbreviations in the main text, we have followed a convention that differentiates between abbreviations referring to Yeats's own works and those abbreviations that refer to books by Yeats's sources. We hope that this will assist the reader.

Books by Yeats are referred to as: (*CT* 100), (*FFT* 96), (*Mem* 25), i.e. there is no lower-case p. (representing "page") inserted before the numeral that indicates the page number.

Books by Yeats's sources are referred to as: (*AL*, p. 20), (*FL*, p. 43), (*MWB*, p. 107), i.e. the lower-case p. has been inserted before the page number.

[1]

Sincerity and the Early Thought and Work

> With Irish literature and Irish
> thought alone have I to do.
>
> The mystical life is the centre of all that I
> do & all that I think & all that I write.
>
> And what of her that took
> All till my youth was gone?

Late in 1921, playwright Gordon Bottomley wrote to Yeats: "Your 'Four Years' is newly arrived from Dublin, and I am enjoying again your story of years that must, when we are all dead, seem extraordinarily rich and fruitful."[1] Bottomley's reference was to *Four Years [1887–1891]*, the volume of memoirs published by Cuala in December 1921 and later included in *Autobiographies*; and whatever effect this brief span of time may have had on his contemporaries, there is no denying that these were extraordinarily rich and fruitful years for Yeats. "It is curious how one's life falls into definite sections", he wrote in 1934 (*Let* 820), and these four years were among the cuttings he had in mind. In the *Autobiographies* Yeats specifically identified 1887 as a year in which he was "at a most receptive age" (*Au* 183), and it was in that year and the years immediately following that virtually all of his lasting obsessions first came calling at his door. The young poet publishes his first book of poetry; the young lover meets Maud Gonne; the occult revival moves into high gear, and a man who had already begun to probe into occult theory becomes a practicing magician; the revival of interest in Irish fairy and folklore reaches a new peak, and Yeats joins Douglas Hyde (1860–1949) as one of its two most eloquent proponents.

Vocation, chosen mate, country, and form of belief: these are universal areas of concern. But Yeats's interest in these areas was distinguished by his felt need to join them together. A prefatory overview of the early work and thought needs to consider first the motive forces behind this keenness for merger, and then the ways in which the thought of his times encouraged

Yeats to believe that a merger might be effected, and then a young man's sometimes rebuffed and sometimes successful attempts to bring that merger about in his life and in his art.

Yeats's development as an artist was a relatively steady one, steady at least in the sense that he had no *annus mirabilis*. But if we were seeking to locate a year in the early career that might be described as pivotal, 1887 would emerge as a prime candidate. Yeats had several good reasons for settling on 1887 as the first of the four years that he singled out for notice in his *Autobiographies*. It was in 1887 that he completed the first full draft of "The Wanderings of Oisin", most ambitious of the early poems, and that his shorter poems first began to appear in other than Irish outlets. The appearance of Lady Wilde's *Ancient Legends* in the same year not only marked the end of a long hiatus of general interest in Irish folklore – the last full-length collection in the area had been John O'Hanlon's derivative *Irish Folk Lore* (1870) – but presaged the appearance of the numerous other collections that would appear on the scene between 1887 and the mid-nineties; and in 1891 Yeats gave Wilde's work its due when he placed it first on the list of plantings that had since grown into "the harvest-time of folk-lore" (*UP1* 187). Moreover, it was in May of 1887 that the Yeats family, having once again moved from Ireland to London, finally settled into the house in Eardley Crescent in Earl's Court. This was the same month in which Madame Blavatsky returned to London, taking up residence in Norwood; and it was in 1887 that the Blavatsky Lodge of the Theosophical Society was founded in London, and in 1887 that Yeats began an affiliation with Blavatsky that would continue through late 1890. Finally, it was "in May or June 1887" – so Yeats recalled in 1921, though the accuracy of these dates has often been called into question[2] – that a young Irish poet who had come again to London was "initiated" into "a society which sometimes called itself... 'The Hermetic Students'". His introduction to the society had come through MacGregor Mathers (1854–1918), the society's "governing mind" (*Au* 183); and within a year of what Yeats recalled as the date of his initiation, the society was formally to incorporate as the Order of the Golden Dawn, the most influential Western magical order to surface in the course of the past century. The Golden Dawn made Yeats into a practicing adept, and so confirmed him in a decision he had arrived at in years when both he and the Order were in their formative stages: "four or five years ago", he told John O'Leary in the oft-cited letter of 1892, he had "decided deliberately" that, "next to [his] poetry", magic was to be "the most important pursuit of [his] life" (*CL1* 303).

At the age of two-and-twenty, then, Yeats was already well along the path to the discovery of his lasting objects of heed. Here are all but one of the central foci of the early poetry – magic, Ireland, and poetry itself – and Maud Gonne was shortly to make the fourth. An ancient countryside and a dark art, a hard craft and a beautiful woman: few men could have imagined a bond among all four, and no man but Yeats would have spent so many long years trying to forge one. That he made the attempt is the surest proof that his most settled early conviction was his belief in the need for sincerity.

By the time it took its place near the center of Yeats's critical vocabulary, the concept of sincerity had already earned a prominent place on the nineteenth-century literary scene; indeed, "by the 1860s, the term was so far from needing justification that it could be raised explicitly to the dignity of a fundamental principle for literary creation".[3] Patricia M. Ball has traced the rise of the concept from its tentative origins in Wordsworth through its assumption of a central place in the writings of Walter Pater;[4] and had she chosen to continue her history into the twentieth century, no writer would have suited Ball's purposes better than Yeats. Born in the 1860s, the Irish writer was the last major poet to subscribe outright to the belief in sincerity that his Romantic and Victorian forebears had formulated.

When a writer has persuaded his readers to a constant expectation of complexities, he runs the risk of having his more straightforward statements either too subtly assessed or paid too scant a heed; and it may be the very directness of Yeats's remarks on sincerity, his implied assumption that his audience will share his easy familiarity with the term, that has kept criticism from paying any but a generalized attention to the concept. Consider, for instance, the forthright observations offered by Yeats in his early (1901–8) series of essays on the Irish dramatic movement. Herein the sincere artist emerges as a man who has the courage to give an honest voice to his own deepest thoughts and feelings, and talent enough to give those thoughts and feelings their precise expression. The artist's lot is the recording of "one man's vision of the world, one man's experience" (*Ex* 115), Yeats writes, the iteration of those "dreams and daily thoughts" that are peculiarly his own (*Ex* 116). Whatever opposition he encounters, he must insist upon this "right of the individual mind to see the world in its own way" (*Ex* 229), since not only his own but "all" art "is founded upon personal vision" (*Ex* 194); and he must make certain that his work expresses that vision precisely, conveys "exactly what [he] think[s] and feel[s]", since otherwise "all" his art will be "oratorical and insincere" (*Ex* 199). Whether the truth he is bound to reveal be palatable or otherwise, then, the man of real "sincerity" must "be as incapable of telling a lie as Nature" (*Ex* 117), and not only when delineating his own thoughts and feelings but when describing the world around him; though the public may protest, Yeats argued, the artist must picture life "as it is, not as we would have it be" (*Ex* 117).

This is not a complex set of principles, nor was it in any sense original with Yeats. Before the future poet had ever published a poem, his father had persuaded him that, without "sincerity", his work would never be of "the best";[5] and as late as 1918 J. B. Yeats was still claiming that his contribution to his famous son's growth had been largely a question of helping him rid himself of "*insincerity*".[6] Resisting his father's influence on many another count, Yeats went along with him on this one;[7] in this debate, after all, the elder Yeats had the better part of a century on his side. A wide range of nineteenth-century artists and critics had argued that sincerity was the *sine qua non* of the serious artist; and though their use of the term was varied, certain among them offered definitions of sincerity that were all but identical with Yeats's. For the Irish poet, a sincere work of art was one that expressed what was "personal" to the artist (*Ex* 115), and expressed it not only with unremitting honesty but with that "precision" (*Ex* 123) that alone was the trademark of "perfect sincerity" (*Ex* 122). Thus too Walter Pater, who, writing early in 1889, spoke of "sincerity" as the issue of a "perfect fidelity to one's own inward presentations, to the precise features of the picture within", and who shored up J. B. Yeats's claims for a connection between personal sincerity and the poet's chance for greatness by observing that, without sincerity, "profound poetry is impossible".[8] In Ball's summary of Pater's view, "sincerity" translates into

> a strenuous artistic effort to reach and record the encounter of the individual self with the actual world and with its own inner world, an exacting process of discovery and specific, experiential assessments.[9]

Yeats would gladly have embraced that passage as a description of his own intents, not only in its substance but in its choice of terms. Ball speaks of a process of "discovery", and of "experiential" assessments that derive from the encounter of the "individual" with the "world"; and in 1906 Yeats was to describe poets as "men who were content to express the sensations and experiences which they themselves received, being face to face with the world". The poet, he added, must be concerned "above all" with "the realities of experience" and "the pursuit of the one central reality of them all": the "discovery" and the "representation in poetry" of himself (*UP2* 343).

It is not surprising that Yeats and Pater should have been in so close an accord in this matter; it was to Pater that the Yeats of the early nineties "looked consciously" for his artistic "philosophy" (*Au* 302) and, in all likelihood, it was primarily from Pater that he took the details of the philosophy whose importance J. B. Yeats had been preaching. But for the purposes of a general introduction to the concerns of the early career, identifying the sources whence Yeats derived his ideas about sincerity is less important than determining what he made of the sources he drew on; and what he made of the concept of sincerity was a touchstone for his life and work.

It was in his second published article that Yeats praised the work of Samuel Ferguson for its "sincerity" (*UP1* 90), and it was forty-five years later on that he argued that it was Joyce's willingness to listen to whatever might be "sounding and echoing in the depths of his own mind" that explained the "heroic sincerity" of Joyce's ongoing work (*E&I* 405). Dating respectively from 1886 and 1931, these references bracket many a reference of a like kind.[10] And though the writers he singled out for praise over the years differed widely in talent and achievement, to Yeats's eye they were none the less joined by a common thread: sincerity, that insistence on being "true to himself absolutely" without which no artist could produce work that would be what the Yeats of 1892 called "*the best of its kind*" (*CL1* 289).[11]

Though the young artist had his moments of self-doubt, there can be no question about his lifelong determination to create works that would be considered the best of their kind; and it is this determination that most fully explains his permanent concern with making his work "an honest witness" (*UP1* 374) to his thoughts and feelings. In 1895 he claimed that a poem that gives "the true history of an emotion" has "done all we have the right to demand" (*UP1* 374); let the artist strive "to give sincere expression" to his moods, and he will have been the faithful servant of "the only sincerity literature knows of".[12] In later years Yeats would recall how thoughts like these had come to be the ground from which his own early work had built up, how he had chanced on the "discovery" that the business of the artist was giving voice to his "emotions exactly as they came to [him] in life", delineating "the actual thoughts of a man" (*Au* 102–3). He would also recall what he felt had been at stake: a man who had mastered language, and who could locate a compelling subject matter, and who was able to "be sincere", might well become a "great poet" (*Au* 103). These thoughts would alter little with the years. In a 1912 letter to his father, for instance, Yeats discussed the difficulties involved in making one's work "emotionally sincere", and then explained why the artist must none the less make the effort:

> It is always such a long research getting down to one's exact impression, one's exact ignorance and knowledge. I remember your once writing to me, that all good art is good just in so far as it is intimate. It always seems to me that that intimacy comes only from personal sincerity (*Let* 568).

But knowing that sincerity was a necessary precondition of "all good art" was considerably easier than making one's work sincere. It was a simple enough thing to advise other writers of the need to cleave to their own, or to praise them for having had the wisdom to do so. Thus the young Yeats could tell orthodox believer Katharine Tynan that her work was at its "best" when it took her "religious feeling" as its theme (*CL1* 119), or could argue that, since W. T. Horton was profoundly committed to mysticism, it was at those moments when his art expressed his "spiritual purpose" that it acquired that "sincerity" that characterized his drawings at their "best",[13] or could admonish a young Irishwoman, a would-be poet, to take "Irish legends and places" for her subject matter and setting. The reason for this, he explained, was that she needed to write on what was "nearest and most interwoven with [her] life" if she hoped to make her verses "sincere" (*CL1* 131). In each of these cases Yeats was preaching a doctrine of sincerity brought down to particulars: a mystic should write of mysticism, an Irishwoman of Ireland. The theory was simple and clear, so much so that the fledgling artist wondered why the sincere body of work that he had imagined himself as crafting was not as fine as his expectations had promised (*Au* 103). A consideration of the subject matter of the early work helps to clarify the reasons for his frustration.

Though he was always to be a ruthless student of his own personality, even a mature Yeats had trouble getting down to his "exact" impression, his "exact" ignorance and knowledge; and the Yeats of the eighties and early nineties, anxious as he was to record precisely what he thought and felt, labored under the added burden of being too young "even to know" what his real thoughts and feelings were (*AU* 103). The premise he had settled on was that a story or poem should evoke its author's deepest interests; but when it came to transforming theory into practice, the problems that he encountered were twofold. The first was that his interests were too numerous. In 1916 he recalled himself as having "had as many ideas" at about age twenty "as I have now"; but, he added, "I did not know how to choose from among them those that belonged to my life" (*Au* 83). The difficulty here, then, was one of self-definition: a necessary process for the artist who was sincere in the Yeatsian sense of the term, since only what "belonged to his life" was to be the subject matter of his work. The second difficulty was that, once a growing self-knowledge had enabled him to winnow out his mere opinions, the sincere writer had the additional task of taking the various home truths that remained and joining them into one. Why this further check? Yeats's fullest explanation comes in 1919's "If I were Four-and-Twenty", the essay in which he set out to analyze the dilemma that had fronted him in his formative years as an author.

In the late eighties, Yeats wrote, he had "had three interests: interest in a form of literature, in a form of philosophy, and a belief in nationality" (*Ex* 263). To complete the list, he need only have added Maud Gonne; and he might also have added that, since poetry and occultism, Ireland and Maud Gonne were destined to become his central interests, they were also destined to become his primary subject matter. Many another young artist might have faced such richness with delight; but to an apprentice bent on sincerity this multiplicity of interests was disheartening. Yeats was convinced that any interest central enough to be called a "conviction" needed to have a man's "whole character" behind it (*Ex* 263), but could see no clear way of giving his "whole" character over to each of several interests, particularly when "none" of the interests in question "seemed to have anything to do with the other" (*Ex* 263). On the one hand, he was conscious of profound attractions that were taking his heart in what appeared to be different directions; on the other, he was certain that a great artist must find his themes in that to which he had given his heart sincerely, and hence undividedly. What he needed to do, then, was to combine the fragmentary gleams of his vision into what a later poem calls one inextricable beam. The connections among them could not be forced, since a forced connection would for a surety be insincere; nor would a series of merely intellectual linkings suffice, since the intellect was but one of the aspects of a man's "whole character" – and, for the young Yeats, a lesser aspect at that. The solution would have to come from a deeper source; and, as if unbidden, come the solution did. Yeats recalled the sudden revelation thus:

> One day when I was twenty-three or twenty-four this sentence seemed to form in my head, without my willing it, much as sentences form when we are half-asleep: "Hammer your thoughts into unity". For days I could think of nothing else, and for years I tested all I did by that sentence (*Ex* 263).

Thereafter follow the lines, cited in part above, in which he recounts his central interests and his early doubts about their compatibility, and then comes his description of how, despite his doubts, the three eventually blended into the kind of "single conviction" on which a sincere prose and verse could be based:

> None of these seemed to have anything to do with the other, but gradually my love of literature and my belief in nationality came together. Then for years I said to myself that these two had nothing to do with my form of philosophy, but that I had only... to keep from constraining one by the other and they would become one interest. Now all three are, I think, one, or rather all three are a discrete expression of a single conviction. I think that each has behind it my whole character (*Ex* 263).

The basis of this syncretic vision was Yeats's unstated assumption that the personality of the sincere man comprised a kind of magnet; it would draw towards itself nothing for which it lacked a natural affinity, and all the interests thus attracted would necessarily have common elements in their composition. To relate these "main interests one to another", then, the "cultivated man", the man of "character", needed only to continue to develop until his maturing perception had revealed the hidden ways in which his gathered "varied interests" had been no more than variations on a single covert theme. Nor could there be any doubt that these interconnections would surface: one needed "only to be" – key to it all – "sincere" (*Ex* 263).

The concept of sincerity thus occupied a central place in Yeats's personal system, with other aspects of his life and thought turning slow orbits around it. It formed the underpinnings of his later ideas about unity of being: a term he had first learned from his father, who had spoken of the need to make oneself like "a musical instrument so strung that if we touch a string all the strings murmur faintly."[14] It helps to explain why so much of Yeats's poetry is Yeatsian self-presentation, since he saw "sincerity" in an artist as requiring him to present "a picture of the soul of man, and not of his exterior life" (*UP2* 297), and a picture of his own soul in particular: it was the artist's honest "digging in the deep pit" of himself that could "alone produce great literature" (*UP2* 307). Sincerity was also the factor that determined the degree of an artist's "orig[i]nality", or so Yeats asserted in 1889 (*CL1* 131); and in this case too he was echoing the elder Yeats, who five years earlier had told his son that the greatest works of art were those "to which went the hardest thoughts", and that it was this sort of intense self-scrutiny that was not only "the secret of sincerity" but "the secret of originality" as well.[15] This is the same set of principles advanced by the poet in 1903, when he wrote that Irish artists had need "of more precise thought" and "of a more perfect sincerity" if they expected to produce work that expressed "a new discovery of life" (*Ex* 122). In later essays Yeats would explain this connection between sincerity and "newness" (*Ex* 263) in greater detail; since "every man's character" is "peculiar to himself" (*Ex* 263), he would argue, the poet who is able to remain "utterly" himself has the chance to produce a unique body of work, work that "shows us the world" as if "we were Adam and this the first morning" (*E&I* 339). Sincerity may not make the artist popular – indeed, a vision that is at once practical, honest, and new is more likely to be met with "opposition" (*Ex* 193), or even with "riot" (*Ex* 230) – but the artist who creates out "of his sincerity" will be, for a certainty, "different" (*Mem* 250).

Interesting in their own right, Yeats's strivings after sincerity are yet more interesting for the light they shed on the poet's habits of mind, the particular tilt of his vision. In 1888 he told Katharine Tynan that he had put his very "life" into his poems (*CL1* 93); and it was his insistence on being sincere that determined which aspects of his life those poems centered on, and that serves to explain why Yeats could make statements that appear to contradict each other outright and yet feel that he had not contradicted himself at all. In September of 1891, for instance, he told the readers of *The Boston Pilot*: "With Irish literature and Irish thought alone have I to do" (*LNI* 137–8). The comment reads as if built to wall out all but a solitary guest. Yet a scant ten months later Yeats was telling John O'Leary that it was rather "the mystical life" that was "the centre of all that I do & all that I think & all that I write" (*CL1* 303), and from 1889 onwards he had been telling whoever would listen of the woman to whom he had given "all" till his youth was gone (*VP* 315). Since Ireland and Maud Gonne and occultism were at the center of the early thought, they could not have helped but take their places at the center of the early work; and it was the sincerity of his attempt to hammer his thought into unity that pushed the young writer towards his stance of regarding these varied interests as if they were one and the same, and thence towards his belief that each of them had all of himself behind it.

But it is relatively easy for an imaginative man to wed his central concerns through his emotions, and it is something else again when he tries to effect the same sort of union in his life or art. The process most insistently at work during Yeats's early career is a process of slow cajolery, with the writer constantly introducing his wary interests one to another, insisting to each in the absence of the others that they would all be good friends once they got to know each other better. The majority of the early works might thus be described as attempts at matchmaking, efforts to blend several foci into a single unified theme: the Rose poems, for instance, wherein Yeats attempts the intricate feat of adopting the voice of a man who is at one and the same time a poet and an Irishman, a lover and an occultist. There is a sense in which the varied writings this book will discuss fall into either of two categories: works in which a young artist's endeavor to see all his obsessions through the same lens enabled him to juxtapose his deep concerns in striking combinations, and works in which precisely the same habit of mind drove him towards a yoking together by violence. Of the lyrics that belong in the latter grouping, "The Rose of Battle" will later come to serve as an apt illustration: here is Yeats determined to speak as an Irish poet, and here is Yeats no less determined to speak as an occultist, and here is a poem in which the enforced blending of these different voices makes for hodgepodge. But if his convictions about sincerity could at times work to the poet's detriment, they more often worked to his advantage; and there is one aspect of those convictions with which this book will have no quarrel. Wherever we rank Yeats among this century's major writers, there is no denying that there has been no writer in this century quite like him. Barely launched on his long career, he told Katharine Tynan in 1888: "I think you will be right to make your ballad Irish, you will be so much more orig[i]nal – one should have a speciality. You have yours in Ireland and your Religion" (*CL1* 66). He had his own specialities in a devotion to literature and a belief in nationality, in a hidden form of philosophy and his love of a remarkable woman. And he was right. They would make him original.

There is nothing new in the observation that the young Yeats was embarked on what Richard Ellmann once called the search for unity.[16] But long after Ellmann's accurate remarks, there remains a widespread impression that Yeats's quest was largely the product of one man's idiosyncratic need to arrange it all in one clear view (*VP* 633), and what has often been lost to sight is that it is precisely those points at which the young author seems at his most idiosyncratic that mark him at his most derivative. Yeats's debts to the folklore and occult revivals have by now been well documented.[17] But there has been considerably less commentary on what he owed to the two movements taken in conjunction, and too little detailed analysis of the correspondences between Yeats's apparently singular thought and the singular thought of his times.

Ellic Howe's *The Magicians of the Golden Dawn* (1972) speaks of the late 1880s as a time "when there was a noticeable expansion of interest in occultism", surface tremors so palpable that they could only have come about as the result of "something like an underground explosion" (p. xxiii). If this remark errs at all, it does so on the side of understatement. It was in the late eighties that the Theosophical Society began to regain the popularity and membership it had lost in the aftermath of its 1885 investigation by the Society for Psychical Research,[18] and it was in the late eighties that the Golden Dawn was founded and saw its membership flourish.[19] The year 1886 witnessed the first extended translation into English of the writings of the legendary Éliphas Lévi (1810–75), the French magus generally credited with having done most to create the climate of interest that enabled the occult revival to come about in the first place.[20] A year later Franz Hartmann would follow his earlier *Magic, White and Black* (1884), most readable of the early explanations of the central doctrines of Theosophy, with *The Life of Philippus Theophrastus Bombast of Hohenheim* [*Paracelsus*], a compilation and commentary that afforded English readers a chance to acquaint themselves with the theories of a man whose works had not been readily accessible in English since the end of the seventeenth century. This was also the year in which a London reader could first have laid his hands on the revised and expanded version of C. W. King's *The Gnostics and Their Remains* (1864, 1887), or on the third edition of Hargrave Jennings's two-volume *The Rosicrucians: Their Rites and Mysteries* (1870, 1879, 1887), or on A. E. Waite's *The Real History of the Rosicrucians*: all of them works that had a greater or lesser part to play in the final shaping of the Order of the Golden Dawn, but all of them overshadowed by the appearance in the same year of the Mathers translation of *The Kabbalah Unveiled*, the book to which the doctrines of the Order would be most directly indebted. The year to follow marked a further unveiling. Blavatsky's magnum opus had been advertised for a long time. Her two-volume *Isis Unveiled* (1877) had been a beginning, an obscure promise of a future explanation; and she had found her promoter in A. P. Sinnett (1840–1921), who had turned out a popular book in his *The Occult World* (1881), and a less popular but more revealing book in his *Esoteric Buddhism* (1883), and an apologia for the heterodox life and thought of his mentor in his *Incidents in the Life of Madame Blavatsky* (1886). When the first two volumes of Blavatsky's long-awaited *The Secret Doctrine* (1888) finally appeared on the scene, then, the spirit among Theosophists was a spirit of anticipation. In 1888, Yeats was a Theosophist.

As following chapters will indicate, there are occult works not named above that also left their mark on Yeats and his writings; and the named books sometimes left great marks, and sometimes left no more than trace elements. But whatever their individual impact, their combined promise had a strong pull on a young man who "did not think [he] could live without religion" (*Au* 26). When his father's "unbelief" (*Au* 25) and the skeptical bent of late Victorian thought conspired to deprive him of "the simple-minded religion of [his] childhood" (*Au* 115), they thereby cast him adrift on the fitful subterranean tides of the eighties. At twenty years of age, he was cut off from orthodoxy and in search of a substitute belief; and the times were breeding substitute beliefs with regularity, forms of faith that pledged to overmatch their pale traditional alternatives. Theosophy, said *The Occult World*, aimed to teach those "universal ideas" that "touch[ed] man's true position in the universe in relation to his previous and future births, his origin and ultimate destiny; the relation of the mortal to the immortal, of the temporary to the eternal, of the finite to the infinite" (p. 150). To this *Esoteric Buddhism* added that the "secret doctrine" is "a mine of entirely trustworthy knowledge from which all religions and philosophies have derived whatever they possess of truth" (p. vi), and that it proclaims "the absolute truth" about both "spiritual things" (p. vi) and "Nature, Man, the origin of the Universe, and the destinies towards which its inhabitants are tending" (p. viii). In like fashion, the Golden Dawn (the phrases cited are from the introduction to *The Kabbalah Unveiled*, though Mathers borrowed much of what he had to say from an earlier and more obscure source[21]) would claim to have found in the cabala a means of elucidating the "Supreme Being, His nature and attributes", the "Cosmogony", the "destiny of man and angels", the "nature of the soul", the "nature of angels, demons, and elementals", the "import of the revealed law", and the "equilibrium of contraries" (p. 15). These are ambitious aims, but other of Yeats's sources were to define the fundamental goals of Theosophy and Rosicrucianism in terms more inclusive still. "Magic", said *The Real History of the Rosicrucians*, "is that great and hidden wisdom which discovers the interior constitution of everything" (p. 205). The epigraph to *The Secret Doctrine* (Vol. III) put the same case more simply: "The end is omniscience."

Yeats came to all this as a hungry man to table. In search of a system diversified enough to accommodate his own diversified thought, he found in occultism tempting shapes of belief, slants of thought as angular as his own. In the late eighties and early nineties, the particular target of magic's scorn was material science; *The Secret Doctrine* (Vol. I), for instance, repeatedly insisted that, between the end of the eighties and the end of the nineties, "there will be a large rent made in the Veil of Nature, and materialistic Science will receive a death-blow" (p. 671).[22] Yeats too felt the "inquietude of the veil" (*Myth* 309) – in the late nineties he described the belief in its imminent parting as "a characteristic of our times" (*Myth* 309) – and he likewise agreed with Blavatsky that material science was irrevocably on the wane. In 1889 he set down his conviction that the "new little boat of science" was destined to be "shipwrecked", while "the great galleon of tradition" would sail on as it had sailed "always" (*LNI* 204). The year 1905 brought the same affirmation, though Yeats's terms were considerably more tentative: "the scientific movement is ebbing a little everywhere", he wrote, and he declared that Ireland, where the scientific movement "has never been in flood at all", might well become the first country "to recover after the fifty years of mistake" (*Ex* 197). And a decade later, long after it had become clear that science had paid no heed to the gauntlet thrown down by occultism, the poet could still rightly claim that the "new research" that had been going forth in the late eighties had come about largely as a "reaction from popular science", and that it was his sympathy with and participation in this reaction that had first made him feel that, somewhere in a living underground, he "had allies" for what was rapidly becoming his own "secret thought" (*Au* 89).

Though Yeats was often to quarrel with his fellow theosophists and occultists, his youthful involvement in occult societies once gave him allies indeed, and the alliance had begun as any genuine alliance begins: with a sense of a common enemy. Yeats railed against science, reserving his most specific invective for John Tyndall (1820–93) and T. H. Huxley (1825-95), whom he "detested" (*Au* 115); magic railed against science, not coincidentally reserving its most specific invective for "the Tyndalls and Huxleys of the day" (*IU* I, p. 271 n.), damning in one breath "the indifference of Huxley, the jocularity of Tyndall" (*IU* I, p. 233).[23] Magic's bias, moreover, was not only anti-scientific but anti-rational, and on this count too it found a kindred spirit in a young man who considered intellect "impure" (*Au* 188). Though they had their disagreements in other areas, Yeats's fellow magicians were in complete accord in their descriptions of the late Victorian period as a time when "the Intellect only has been cultivated & that, at the expense of the

Intuitional";[24] and the occult texts of the time were no less vehement in their insistence that this order of priorities needed to be reversed. "Intellectual learning is an artificial thing", said Hartmann's *Paracelsus*, "but wisdom is the realisation of truth within the soul" (p. 169). "Wisdom", in fact, had "nothing" to do "with the action of the intellect" (pp. 241–2); true understanding came only "from the soul, for the soul is the substance of life" (p. 223).

Yeats wedded himself to magic, then, not only as an individual – a man in search of romance,[25] and of a counterbalance to a parent's scorn,[26] and of a system of faith that matched the "fanaticism" of his own (*Au* 79) – but as a member of a movement. His 1897 analysis of how the movement had come about in the first place – as a "reaction against the rationalism of the eighteenth century", mingled "with a reaction against the materialism of the nineteenth century" (*E&I* 187) – took its cues directly from the volumes of curious lore he had pored through by the time he made the claim. Nor was there anything unique in his analysis of what lay at the movement's heart. Like all of the major occult texts published during the poet's young manhood,[27] *Paracelsus* had affirmed the primacy of the soul over the intellect. When the Yeats of 1892 told O'Leary that he had always "considered my self a voice of what I beleive [*sic*] to be a greater renais[s]ance – the revolt of the soul against the intellect – now begin[n]ing in the world" (*CL1* 303), he was writing as a child of the times.

Alliances expect victories: witness Yeats's description of the occult revival as a "revolt" and "a greater renaissance". In the decade to follow he would continue to argue that "this age of criticism is about to pass", and that an age of "revelation" was "about to come in its place" (*E&I* 197), or to speak in more general terms of "the change that is coming upon the world" (*E&I* 51). He had bulwarks for his thought. Theosophy had taught him that man had begun his earthly career as a spiritual being, and that he had thereafter declined by degrees towards the material, and that he was now once again beginning to resume the place he had held to begin with: "evolution", Blavatsky wrote, traced a progress "from the ethereal down to the semi-ethereal and purely physical", after which it began to run its course "upward again" towards spirituality (*TSD* I, pp. 703, 704). Statements like these are the only screen on which certain of Yeats's early comments can be brought into sharp focus; take, for example, the otherwise elusive passage in which he affirms that

> we are, it may be, at a crowning crisis of the world, at the moment when man is about to ascend, with the wealth he has been so long gathering upon his shoulders, the stairway he has been descending from the first days (*E&I* 192).

That statement came in 1898, when Yeats could still find reason to share the assurance of his magical "schoolmates" (*E&I* xi) that "the most significant and important feature of the present remarkable epoch is, unquestionably, the revival of Occult Science and Mystical, or Esoteric, Philosophy", and that "it may be confidently anticipated" of "the revival we are witnessing now" that "the success attained will far surpass any yet achieved".[28] Similar predictions of a coming triumph may be found in literally every work that the occult revival generated; indeed, it was its steady expectation that a new and better day was imminent that gave the Order of the Golden Dawn its name.[29] But if neither the Order nor the revival that spawned it was destined to last, they were destined to leave lasting marks; and the most notable marks that they left were on the thought and work of Yeats.

Deeply committed to occultism, and just as deeply convinced that the poet needed to take his subject matter from his areas of deep commitment, Yeats was speaking in all sincerity when he told O'Leary that the mystical life was the center of all that he did and thought and wrote. But while we cannot lay too heavy a stress on the importance of occultism to the young artist, it is no less necessary to insist that he did not intend his reference to the mystical life as an exclusive reference to magic. By the time he wrote to O'Leary, his central interests were already well into their wary dance towards merger. A consuming interest in its own right, magic also seemed to bear a strong resemblance towards folklore; folklore, in its turn, seemed to have much in common with magic. And if the connection between the two areas seemed to be forced, it was not Yeats who had forced it. The voice that had told him to hammer his thoughts into unity had been made up of many whispers, muted cries that filled the air around him.

Yeats arrived in his early twenties at a time when two compelling movements were emerging side by side. He rode them both, and he would often have had good reason for wondering how distinct they were to begin with. Magic, for instance, spoke of how every man had an "astral body" or "double", a "phantasmal duplicate" (*IU* I, p. 360); folklore spoke of the fetch, fetches being the "Doubles" of men (*IF*, p. 40), their "supernatural fac-simile(s)".[30] Theosophy asserted that "Air Elementals" were "the wickedest things in the world" (*TSD* III, p. 594); folklore asserted that, of all the spirits that "haunted the lonely places of Ireland", "air-demons" were "most dreaded by the people".[31] Nor was there much to choose between magic's more general comments on the elementals and the descriptions of the sidhe put forth by Irish fairylore. Occultism alluded to beings able to take on "forms and configurations subjected to numerous variations" (*IU* I, p. 332), fairylore to beings owning the "power of taking on many forms" (*IPS*, p. 125). Occultism suggested that these shape-changers might be "the invisible antitypes" of "men [yet] to be born" (*IU* I, p. 310); Yeats's own *Fairy and Folk Tales* avowed that "these creatures of whim" might well be "human souls in the crucible" (*FFT* 11). Occultism pictured the elementals as "always striving" to ally themselves with man, "seeking a share of his particular privilege of immortality, which has been denied to them";[32] fairylore pictured the sidhe as envious of the fact that "mortals are certain of immortality", while they themselves "must die without hope of regaining heaven" (*AL*, p. 132). Occultism spoke of two orders of elementals, one "gentle as messengers between earth and heaven", the other "of horrible malignity" and "hostile as fiends to men";[33] fairylore spoke of two orders of sidhe, one "a gentle race that loves music and dancing", the other a tribe that had "obtained power from the devil, and [was] always trying to work evil" (*AL*, p. 73). Both magic and folklore, moreover, agreed that there were places on earth where the ancient belief in the omnipresence of spirits had carried down to the present day, countries wherein "the 'old times' are just like the 'modern times'" (*IU* I, p. 599). Blavatsky, for instance, imagined an Asia "full of mystics" from "one end to the other", a primeval tract in which "belief in a spiritual world full of invisible beings who, on certain occasions, appear to mortals objectively, is universal" (*IU* I, p. 603). These were words that Yeats could have written, though he would have been speaking of folk that he knew. "The Irish peasant believes the whole world to be full of spirits" (*LNI* 203), he noted in 1889, and later affirmed that, among the peasants with whom he had spoken, the belief in "what I can but call spirits" appeared to be as universal as it was in the landscape sketched by Blavatsky. "'There is no man mowing a meadow'", a man in Galway had told him, "'but sees them at one time or another'" (*E&I* 42).

To another reader of signatures, correspondences like these might have seemed no more than coincidental or, perhaps, too trivial to merit more than passing notice. But to Yeats they pointed to the existence of a direct connection between a folklore that he loved and an esoteric lore that he had decided to make his "constant study" (*CL1* 303). In making that connection, he had direct encouragement.

The poet's attempt to hammer magic and folk art into unity can only be fully apprehended when relocated in the context that tempted Yeats into the forge. When, for instance, the Yeats of 1889 made his extravagant claim that "the earliest poet of India and the Irish peasant in his hovel nod to each other across the ages, and are in perfect agreement" (*LNI* 204), he was speaking as a man who knew what Theosophy had to say about a universal belief in spirits, and who knew what Irish folklore had to say on the same theme, and who had persuaded himself that the resemblances between the stories told by a mystical Irish peasant and a mystical Indian poet implied a "perfect agreement" between the storytellers. And when, a decade later, he wrote that folk beliefs were "touched with a shadow of old faiths, that gives them a brotherhood with magic" (*UP2* 167), he was doing no more than rejoining his voice to what had been a general chorus in his youth.

When Yeats first took up the folktale, folklorists were actively "on the gad after" (*FFT* 6) the primal religion;[34] when he first took up his studies in magic, occultists – men and women who saw themselves as having revivified the primal religion – were investigating the folktale. The Theosophical Society actively encouraged its members to study folklore, declaring that studies of the kind could lead to the recovery of "long-lost but important secrets".[35] Blavatsky had explained to her followers that a discovery of the "hidden meaning" of fairytales would take the intuitive reader back to an understanding of the "first principles of nature" (*IU* II, p. 406). It was the fairytale that preserved the "profound religion of our forefathers" (*TSD* I, p. 458), she said, and it was thus that a careful perusal of "popular superstition and folk-lore" could help the neophyte further his knowledge of the "secrets" that belonged to the beginnings.[36] The folklorists whose work Yeats read in the eighties were in wholehearted agreement with this claim, noting that a "diligent study of the ancient myths, legends, and traditions of the world" would serve to revivify "information respecting the early modes of thought prevalent among the primitive race", information that would enable the student of the folktale "to reconstruct the first articles of belief in the creed of humanity" (*AL*, p. 2).³⁷ Given the precise correspondence between these and other of his occult and folklore sources, it is no surprise that Yeats should have come to perceive these two central areas of his interest as hovering over the same central target. He had already discovered a body of indigenous Irish tales that were simultaneously "altogether new" (*UP2* 125) and among the "most... ancient" in Europe (*UP1* 350);³⁸ and the folklorists' claims for a resurrected Irish folklore found a selfsame mate in the claims advanced by the proponents of magic, a discipline that, as A. P. Sinnett argued, was "new for us, though so old in one sense" (*OW*, p. xiv), a "primeval doctrine" that had been "newly disclosed" (*EB*, p. xvi).

Old doctrines, new disclosures. Between his twentieth and thirtieth years Yeats found himself wrapped up in both writing and folklore and magic. Each of the three made strong claims on his attention, and those claims were the stronger for appearing to be the same. In the late eighties, for instance, Yeats knew a woman living in London, a flamboyant older woman whose reputation as a conversationalist kept her rooms filled with callers. With "her imagination" full of "folk-lore" (*Au* 175), she had set out

> to rescue from degradation the archaic truths which are the basis of all religions; and to uncover, to some extent, the fundamental unity from which they all spring.³⁹

To all appearances this was a precise description of Lady Wilde (1820–96), whose receptions Yeats attended simply "to hear her talk" (*LNI* 76), who had at her disposal "everything in the way of" folk charm or "fairy tale" (*LNI* 78), and who had set out to bring together the old tales that

> still remain at the base of all thought and all creeds; broken fragments of the primal faith... the echo of which still vibrates through the legends, the songs, the poetry, and the usages of every people on the face of the earth (*AL*, p. 126, and see *AC*, p. 97).

But Yeats was referring, not to Lady Wilde, but to Madame Blavatsky (1831–91), who had "'become the most famous woman in the world by sitting in a big chair and permitting'" her guests to talk (*Au* 180), and who, moreover, claimed familiarity with "every ancient folk-lore" (*TSD* II, p. 29). The Yeats who came across Wilde's assertion that "the numerous myths and legends of the nations of the earth" bore "so striking a conformity to each other" as to "point to a common origin" (*AL*, p. 2) already knew Blavatsky's description of those ancient religious monuments that, though built in different lands and ages, none the less presented "such features of resemblance that it seems impossible to escape the conviction that they were built by peoples moved by the same religious ideas" (*IU* I, p. 561); and when *Ancient Legends* told the poet that the dedicated student of folklore had an opportunity to reconstruct mankind's first articles of belief, it told him nothing he had not already learned from occultism. What 1877's *Isis Unveiled* (Vol. II) had "desire[d] to prove" was that "underlying every ancient popular religion" was "the same ancient wisdom-doctrine, one and identical" (p. 99).

Yeats's tendency to associate the figures of Wilde and Blavatsky should be taken for what it is: one of many possible examples of his predisposition to wed folklore and magic. But it is more to the point to note that, when Yeats began to make those connections, all the evidence he had available to him suggested that the connections were there to be made. Folklore spoke to him of "primal faith" and "primitive unity" (*AL*, pp. 126, 127), magic of "archaic truths" and "fundamental unity" (*TSD* I, p. viii). It was not only through the folktale that the "broken fragments" of the "primal faith" might be reassembled (*AL*, p. 126), since one could also look to the cabala as the medium through which the "broken mirror" of the "universal faith" might be restored.[40] Yeats also learned early on that the guardians of the ancient wisdom that he sought had "been a race apart", who because of their isolation had been able to carry on "with a perfect continuity" the "traditions" that had been "handed down to them by their predecessors". Yet scarce a man knew they even existed: "all this time the stream of civilization, on the foremost waves of which the culture of modern Europe is floating", had "been wholly and absolutely neglectful"[41] of this "long-sealed ancient fountain"[42] of knowledge. Here was a typical nineteenth-century portrait of Irish folklore and the Irish peasant, whose geographical isolation on "this island prison of the Atlantic" (*AL*, p. 299) had cut him off from the wider movements of history, and thereby fixed him as a keeper of ancient traditions:

> The swift currents of thought that stir the great centres of civilization and impel the human intellect on its path of progress, have never reached [the Irish peasantry]; all the waves of the centuries drift by their shores and leave them unchanged (*AL*, p. 188).[43]

But the description of the "race apart" appeared in Sinnett's *The Occult World*, the book that had first impelled Yeats's friend and magical ally, Charles Johnston, to the serious study of magic; and the description applied to occultists.

Folklore, magic, poetry: all conjoined. Barely twenty years of age, Yeats wondered whether "whatever the great poets had affirmed in their finest moments" might not be "the nearest we could come to an authoritative religion" (*Au* 90); but folklore offered to reveal the primal religion; and magic claimed to *be* the primal religion, "the universally diffused religion of the ancient and prehistoric world" (*TSD* I, p. 18). "All good poems are fruit of the Tree of Life" (*UP2* 301); but folklore, Yeats had learned, could lead a man "under the wall of Paradise to the roots of the trees of knowledge and of life" (*CT* 128); and magic was the "science which leads to the highest goal of the highest knowledge, to the real tasting of the Tree of Life" (*OW*, p. 148). "The holy Kabala" was Yeats's "bible" (*CL1* 379), or so he said early in 1894; but late in 1893 he had observed that folklore "is at once the Bible, the Thirty-nine Articles, and the Book of Common Prayer" (*UP1* 284); and early in his life he had come to look upon great poetry "exactly" as others look upon "the scriptures" (*VSB* 247). Poetry, he had rightly told O'Leary, was to be the most important pursuit of his life (*CL1* 303). But he was just as insistent about his debt to occultism, "the intellectual chief influence" on his early years (*Mem* 27). And in this regard his interest in magic was not to be distinguished from his interest in folklore, which he also called "the chief influence of my youth" (*UP2* 328); nor were either to be distinguished from Maud Gonne, who was "of course" the "chief" of the interests owned by Yeats in the nineties (*Mem* 73).

Inevitably, the presence of Yeats's beloved on the list of his "chief" influences and interests was to mean that his attempts to gather those interests into unity would meet with mixed results. But his studies in folklore and occultism had encouraged him to believe that these two areas at least might be successfully blent, and his efforts to blend them were unremitting. In search of a pathway into the ancient wisdom that could make his own work wise, the young artist had been encouraged to believe that the path of the folklorist and the path of the magician led by different ways into the same ancient grove; and the discovery was prompted not only by his readings but by personal experience. In the company of his uncle, George Pollexfen, he put into practice what he had learned from MacGregor Mathers about the use of magical symbols as a means of calling up visions. The visions evoked by the two men proved to be familiar ones. Yeats had come across them, or so he felt, in the stories told by Irish cottagers who knew nothing of magic at all, countrymen who were the unwitting priests of a primal religion, and who therefore subscribed to "a tradition of belief older than any European Church, and founded upon the experience of the world before the modern bias" (*Au* 265). Since he was himself "search(ing) for a tradition", he studied "the visions and thoughts of the countrypeople", and "soon discovered" that their visions "were very like those" he had "called up by symbol" (*Au* 265). Given this coincidence between his own experiments and the written supporting testimony of his fellow magicians and folklorists, it was inevitable that Yeats should have come to identify his interests in folklore and the occult as directly as he did. In various of his later writings his joining of the two is direct, as when he eventually came to speak of his magical studies as part "of a folk-lore that has perhaps been handed down for generations".[44] But the more subtle and sure sign of the conjoining of these two chief interests in his mind is his inclination to use a vocabulary more usually associated with one area when talking about the other. Thus, for instance, the old man from Wicklow whom AE had once described to him became a "peasant visionary" (*CT* 39), folk artist and mystic combined. "My object was to find actual experience of the supernatural" (*Au* 400): this could serve as a description of the experiments Yeats conducted as a member of the Theosophical Society's Esoteric Section or the Golden Dawn's Inner Order, but is rather an account of what he hoped to discover when he went "from cottage to cottage collecting folk-lore" in Galway (*Au* 399). And Madame Blavatsky: a mercurial woman who had been, and might again have been, described in any number of ways. When Yeats searched for words that could locate her for his reader, his mind gravitated towards a telling phrase. Their first meeting took place in the house in Norwood. One of her followers "sat in an outer room to keep out undesirable visitors", says Yeats, and "I was kept a long time kicking my heels. Presently I was admitted and found" an "old woman in a plain loose dark dress", a "sort of old Irish peasant woman" (*Au* 173).

One of the tales Yeats came across in his folklore readings helps explain how the young magician could look at the founder of Theosophy and perceive an old Irish peasant woman sitting in her place. In an early review of Lady Wilde's *Ancient Cures* (1890), the poet sought support for a point he was making by relating the tale of "an Irish peasant" who one morning went out to the hills to hunt, and

> saw a deer drinking at a pool, and levelled his gun. Now iron dissolves every manner of spell, and the moment he looked along the barrel he saw that the deer was really an old man changed by wizardry (*UP1* 173).

In his first[45] meeting with Madame Blavatsky, Yeats placed her between his sights and saw a woman very like the "old peasant woman"[46] from Ballysadare who had sung old songs to him before he left for England (*VP* 90, 797); and the iron that dissolved the spell was Yeats's conviction that the seeress in London and the folk artist from Sligo had, in their different ways, a similar kind of wisdom to impart. Folk tales were mystic tracts; when properly meditated upon, in fact, images from Irish folklore would become "a part of a mystic language", "true symbols" that, like the symbols of magic, held the promise of "strange revelation" (*VP* 800). Revelation was what Yeats sought in Irish folklore; it was what he sought in magic. Sligo and London were equal way-stations on his youthful mystic odyssey. He took leave of Ballysadare to seek out an old Irish peasant woman in Norwood.

Back in London in autumn of 1891, Yeats wrote to George Russell in Dublin. He told his fellow occultist that Maud Gonne was to be initiated into the Order of the Golden Dawn "tomorrow" (*CL1* 266), and added that

> the next day she goes to Paris but I shall see her on her way through London a couple of weeks later – she promises to work at the Young Ireland League for me this winter. Go & see her when she gets to Dublin & keep her from forgetting me & Occultism (*CL1* 266).

It is indicative that Yeats should have needed only two sentences to conjoin Ireland,[47] magic, and Maud Gonne. But it is still more indicative that he should have felt the need to call on Russell to serve him as a go-between.

By the time Yeats met Maud Gonne, he had already begun the process of gathering his earlier two obsessions into the net of his imagination; the first words in the first note to 1888's *Fairy and Folk Tales*, for instance, refer the reader to the similarities between Irish folk belief and the beliefs espoused by "occultists, from Paracelsus to Elephas [*sic*] Levi" (*FFT* 287). But the third of his constant loves persisted in leaping over the cords. The young poet was perplexed: not simply because he loved a woman who constantly refused to wed him, but because those refusals cried in the face of careful planning. Maud Gonne shared his secret thoughts on Ireland and occultism; to Yeats she seemed a destined companion, natural mate. But no lure he could think of had made her his, and Yeats did not know why. The retrospective explanation for his bafflement is simpler than anything a young lover could possibly have come up with. Being very much in love with Maud Gonne, he had dreamt her into wholehearted agreement with himself. She, being very much her own woman, was not about to allow herself to be imagined into unity.

Yeats's first meeting with Maud Gonne (30 January 1889) took place only several months after Maud Gonne's first meeting with Michael Davitt (1846–1906),[48] and the difference between the first impressions she left on the two men has a clear light to shed on Yeats's early habits of mind. When she interviewed Davitt in 1888, she came speaking the language of revolution; she had sought Davitt out, she told him, to find out how her energetic love of Ireland might find its most practical use. But Davitt was deeply skeptical about the sincerity of her offer – he thought she was a *provocateur* sent to goad him into statements that the English might later use against him – and the obvious point to be made here is that Davitt had good reason to be skeptical. In years to come Yeats's beloved would prove herself the patriot she had claimed to be in 1888; but when she was in her early twenties the vast bulk of her work for Irish causes still lay ahead of her, and her Irish credentials looked forged. Born in England of English parents, daughter of a colonel in an English garrison in Ireland, the young woman who put Davitt on his guard had achieved early notice as a Dublin Castle debutante and had spent as much of her early life outside of Ireland as in. It would have been more natural to size her up as a woman on the English side of things than as an Irishwoman, let alone a fiery hand, and Maud Gonne herself understood that Davitt had just cause for suspicion. The founder of the Land League had thought she was a "spy", she wrote in *A Servant of the Queen*, and, in an intriguing afterthought, candidly admitted that she "didn't blame him" for thinking as he did (p. 91).

It is against assessments like these – the suspect image that Maud Gonne presented to Davitt and, more tellingly, the suspect image she could imagine herself as presenting – that Yeats's initial reaction to his Irish phoenix must be judged. Two days after he first laid eyes on her he wrote a letter to John O'Leary, and when he wrote of Maud Gonne he showed none of Davitt's qualms: "She is very Irish" (*CL1* 137). Here Yeats was telling O'Leary what O'Leary wanted to hear; the eminent Fenian had played a major part in the conversion of Maud Gonne to the Irish cause, and Yeats's letter would have served to confirm the success of his mentor's recruiting efforts. But there are other reasons why Yeats's measurement of his new acquaintance should have differed so sharply from Davitt's. The older man had been taught prudence; Yeats was still learning enthusiasm. Davitt was not in love; Yeats had been mastered utterly. If Maud Gonne said she was part of the movement, that was good enough for him; for that matter, he wrote on 3 February 1889, "if she said the world was flat or the moon an old caubeen tossed up into the sky I would be proud to be of her party" (*CL1* 140–1). Finally, and most centrally, Yeats could not have thought of Maud Gonne as being anything *but* an Irishwoman. In 1889, already pledged to Ireland, he also finds himself pledged to a "very handsome" and "very clever" young woman (*CL1* 137). He needs to make a match, and he makes it in a stroke. Davitt's hesitations notwithstanding, Maud Gonne was "very" Irish.

Yeats's early linking of his country and his chosen woman would deepen into direct identification as the years passed; in a 1910 entry in his private journal, for instance, he speaks of how he thinks of her "as in a sense Ireland, a summing up in one mind of what is best in the romantic political Ireland of my youth" (*Mem* 247). Nor did he have any difficulty tying her to his love of folk and fairylore. "There was an element in her beauty that moved minds full of old Gaelic stories and poems" (*Au* 364); indeed, she seemed the embodiment of the beauty of which the old tales spoke, and from the time Yeats met her "the paradise where... [he] imagined... the people of faery to live seemed to draw nearer".[49] Thus were two of the poet's chief early interests naturally conjoined. What remained to Yeats was the working of a more oblique piece into the puzzle, the uniting of Maud Gonne with magic.

In the early stages of their acquaintance Yeats was to discover that Maud Gonne, like himself, "never doubted the existence of spiritual forces surrounding us".[50] *A Servant of the Queen* speaks frankly of its author's youthful gift for seeing "things invisible to most" (p. 83); she was given to prevision, clairvoyance, and clairaudience, and was later – most notably during her spiritual marriages (1898–9 and 1908–9) with Yeats – to meet with success in the practice of astral projection as well. Like Yeats, she tended towards belief in reincarnation, nursing a private hope for the early rebirth of the child, dead in infancy, whom she had borne to Lucien Millevoye in the early nineties;[51] and her natural inclination towards magical theory and practice led her, as it led the poet, to associate herself with the more prominent occult societies of the day. It was through Yeats that she was introduced to Madame Blavatsky, whose *Isis Unveiled* she had already read on her own;[52] and it was at Yeats's urging that she joined the Order of the Golden Dawn in November 1891. She remained a member long enough to pass through the initiations for the Order's first four degrees; but she resigned when she began to suspect (Yeats protesting the contrary) that the Order had its roots in Freemasonry, the Royal Art that was to her mind one of the central underpinnings of the British Empire.[53] When she told Yeats she had resigned, she notes in *Servant of the Queen*, the poet was "very disappointed" (p. 249).

Yeats was indeed very disappointed when Maud Gonne left the Golden Dawn, and he had reason to be. His energies had been exhausted on coalition; and when his loved one left an occult order for Irish reasons, his attempted synthesis of his three fundamental interests was showing all the signs of coming undone at the seams. But if it was easier to hammer one's thoughts into unity than it was to mould one's life, Yeats was not one to stop trying. Maud Gonne's political qualms about the Order had not effaced her sympathies with spiritism – Yeats's retrospective portrait was of a woman who continued to seem "to understand... all my spiritual philosophy" (*Mem* 61) – and from 1897 to 1899, and periodically thereafter, she collaborated with the poet in the writing of the rituals for his projected Castle of the Heroes. As Yeats envisioned it, the Castle was to house an Irish equivalent of the Order of the Golden Dawn; and for "ten years" of the younger artist's life his "most impassioned thought was a vain attempt to find philosophy and to create ritual for that Order" (*Au* 254). That unequivocal remark needs to be given a fuller weight in surveys of Yeats's early life and career. A project to which a man gives a decade, and to which he devotes his "most impassioned" thought, is a project that might safely be labelled (as Yeats himself labelled it) an "obsession" (*Mem* 123). The Castle of the Heroes represents the longest-lived, and in many ways least successful, of Yeats's attempts to bond all of his early obsessions, to set them singing as one with a single roof above them.

The specifics of Yeats's plan for his new mystical Order began to take shape while he was visiting Douglas Hyde at Ratra in Roscommon in April 1895. While staying with Hyde he paid a visit to nearby Lough Key, setting for the old tale of Una MacDermot, the "Una Bhán" of the well-known traditional song. The story of her frustrated love for the prideful MacCostello (her father's objection to the match, and his enforced isolation of his daughter from her suitor, led to the deaths of the lovers and their burial side by side) had come down from the seventeenth century. Yeats wanted the details of the history for a story he was planning,[54] and in the course of his search for those details he also found, by happenstance, an island home for his Castle of the Heroes.

Una Bhán and her lover were buried on Trinity Island in the southwestern reaches of Lough Key; but the site of her confinement by her father had been Carraig Mhic Diarmada, MacDermot's Rock, in the southeast corner of the lake. Most of the small area of Carraig Mhic Diarmada is occupied by a small castle, built in the early 1800s and abandoned shortly thereafter; but the history of the island reached back far beyond the nineteenth century. From the late seventeenth century until the time of Yeats's visit, both MacDermot's Rock and the estates adjoining Lough Key had been in the possession of the King family, descendants of that Sir John King whose son, Edward, was destined to be memorialized as Lycidas. And an Irish literary history hovered around the island still more closely than an English. From the twelfth through the seventeenth centuries Carraig Mhic Diarmada and the lands around Lough Key had been the site of the stronghold of the MacDermots, a widespread powerful family who ensured their praise by scribes' pens by serving as patrons of the scribes. The most highly praised among them was Ruaidhri Mac Diarmada, whom *The Annals of Lough Cé* recall as having offered school invitations to the poets of Ireland on several occasions in the mid-sixteenth century. It was at his invitation, according to the *Annals*, that in 1540 "the poets and ollaves of Erinn came to the seat of the hospitality and generosity of the province of Connacht", the gathering taking place on "the Rock" in "the smooth-flowing Loch-Cé";[55] and it was through his beneficence that some "twelve hundred cows, and ten saddle horses", stolen for the purpose from another clan, "were given to the professors and poets of Erinn" in 1549, and all this "in one day".[56]

It is unlikely that Yeats was familiar with the colorful history of the Rock in smooth-flowing Lough Key on the spring day in 1895 when he first set foot on "'Castle Rock', an island all castle" (*Au* 253); but in the days immediately following his visit, he would have found his guides to the traditions that had gathered around the island in the family of Douglas Hyde. The last man to live in the castle had been Hyde's father, Arthur, and Hyde himself knew Lough Key and its legends thoroughly; it was "Hyde's account" (*Au* 253) of the legend of Una in 1893's *Love Songs of Connacht* (pp. 51–61) that had brought Yeats to the lake in the first place. Here, then, was what could only have impressed Yeats as a "romantic" place (*Au* 253): an island that had attracted other Irish poets in other more distant centuries, and the site of the love story that had given rise to the song that Hyde's *Love Songs* described as the most widely-known work of its kind among native-speakers in Ireland (p. 47). What Yeats was planning to do was to bring a second pair of celebrated lovers to the same scene, and the Castle of the Heroes was the means through which he hoped to accomplish his end.

In retrospect it is clear that Yeats evolved the scheme for the Castle primarily with Maud Gonne in mind, and that the scheme came about in good part as an alternative to his failed attempt to enfold his beloved in his occult activities through their shared membership in the Order of the Golden Dawn. It was not simply the Masonic connection that had driven her out of the Mathers group, but the fact that, expecting high romance, she had rather felt herself "oppressed by the drab appearance and mediocrity of [her] fellow-mystics".[57] Yeats knew his beloved well enough to understand why she would be disenchanted with a group she had assessed as being both Masonic and bourgeois; he also knew her well enough to know that he would find it easier to persuade her into an occult order that grounded its rituals in the symbols and myths of Ireland, and that welcomed into its midst, not the drab and mediocre, but a select few who had earned the right to cross the threshold of a secluded mysterious castle[58] that none but heroes could enter. And Maud Gonne was indeed deeply tempted. She not only worked regularly with Yeats when the project was still in its planning stages, but retained vivid memories of the enterprise even into her seventies. Her memoir of Yeats in *Scattering Branches* (1940), for instance, accords a central place to what had once been their shared plans for a refuge "in the middle of a lake, a shrine of Irish tradition where only those who had dedicated their lives to Ireland might penetrate";[59] and late in 1943 she recalled that her last words with the poet had likewise centered on the Castle. The time was late summer of 1938; the place was Riversdale in Rathfarnham, the snug domestic setting that would prove to be Yeats's last home in Ireland. As their visit drew to its close, Yeats "startled me by saying suddenly, 'Maud, you and I should have built the Castle of Heroes, when I come back we might do it still'". "Willie never returned" from that last winter in France, she added, "and if he had we were both too old to make that dream materialise, but I was surprised and very happy that he remembered it."[60]

It is most unlikely that even a younger Yeats and Maud Gonne could have made "that dream" materialize, could have transformed a romantic little island in Roscommon into the home base for what the Yeats of 1898 felt would become "a great movement" (*Let* 293). But impractical as the venture may have been, it would be wrong either to underestimate its importance to the poet and his beloved, or to balk at Yeats's claim that the idea consumed him for years. All the available evidence, particularly letters to and from the poet and his own private journals, suggests that he expended considerable time and energy on the Castle in the late 1890s and early 1900s, and not simply time and energy of his own. He set his fellow magicians to devising rituals for the new order, his fellow writers to revising the rituals thus devised, his fellow artists to the creation of designs, and his fellow seers (Maud Gonne most of all) to seership;[61] and with their help and "a great deal of work" of his own, he had his "Magical Rites... sketched... out in their entirety" (*Let* 364) by early 1902. In the absence of any direct comment by Yeats himself, a reader can only speculate as to why the poet abandoned the specifics of a project that he saw as approaching completion. In its lengthy summary of Yeats's manuscript drafts of the Castle rituals, Virginia Moore's *The Unicorn* intimates that part of the problem lay with the rituals themselves, that what Yeats meant to be magical rites too often came out as something nearer to tone poems (pp. 78, 81). This is an accurate judgment; and when MacGregor Mathers ceased his help with the Castle rites after the Golden Dawn schism of 1900, an artist who had been striving to make his ceremonies beautiful lost the one ally who could best have helped him make them efficacious as well. This was a harsh blow; but there was a worse defection to come. Though Yeats had finished outlining his rites by 1902, his correspondence from 1903 onwards makes little mention of the Castle. It was in February of 1903 that John MacBride married Maud Gonne.

It had been his "desire for a fair woman" (*Mem* 59) that had led Yeats to redouble his efforts for Ireland, to become a man who "wished to found societies and to influence newspapers" (*Mem* 59); and the same motive force was behind his plan for the castle on Lough Key. "Politics", after all, "were merely a means of meeting, but" his collaboration with Maud Gonne on the Castle "was a link so perfect that [it] would restore at once, even [after] a quarrel, the sense of intimacy" (*Mem* 125). Yeats knew that he "could not influence" his beloved's actions in the public arena, but was none the less convinced that he "could dominate her inner being" (*Mem* 124). The Castle was designed to give him his chance to dominate. Since his "own seership was... inadequate" for the devising of magical rites, he would perforce need to make use of her greater talent for "clairvoyance" to produce a ritual that "was to be Maud Gonne's work and mine" (*Mem* 124). The spiritual intimacy thus engendered – "there would be, as it were, a spiritual birth from the soul of a man and a woman" (*Mem* 125) – would in turn engender a physical intimacy whose absence, by the late nineties, had become an "unendurable torture" (*Mem* 125) for the poet. Maud Gonne "entirely shared" his ideas for a magical Irish order, Yeats wrote in retrospect, "and I did not doubt that in carrying them out I should win her for myself" (*Mem* 125). He had felt no different in the years when the scheme had been preparing, as for instance in the late 1897 letter in which he had bound together in a single breath Maud Gonne and "the Celtic movement" in "its more mystical development" (*Let* 287). It was on Carraig Mhic Diarmada, old home of poets and lovers, that it was all to come together. They would lie down in the bed of Diarmuid and Grania, and the bed would be strewn with roses.

But the Castle never came to be, and the central reason why Yeats abandoned it was that he had miscalculated in thinking that it would serve his private goals in a way that the Golden Dawn had not. Her work on the Irish rites did indeed bring Maud Gonne closer to the poet; but it did not bring about the lasting union he had hoped for. Written during the same years that the plans for the Castle were forming, the various drafts of *The Speckled Bird* (1896–1902), with their portraits of "Michael" and "Margaret" and the "order of the Grail", afford an unobstructed line of sight into what Yeats had in mind for himself and his co-worker and their Castle of the Heroes. Yeats envisioned an order that would be the issue of Maud Gonne's work and his own; Michael thought that "supernatural guidance" had sent him Margaret to be his magical "fellow-worker" (*VSB* 42). Yeats did not doubt that his plans for the Castle would enable him to win his loved one for himself; Michael thought that the order of the Grail would make it possible for him to show Margaret the true spiritual "way", and thereby to "win her love" (*VSB* 52, 187). Finally, it was after Maud Gonne's marriage that the poet's visionary plot for Castle Rock was sent into abeyance; and it is at the moment that Michael discovers that Margaret will not be his that his vision of the Grail starts to die. He has just finished reading the letter in which she tells him of her recent and (to him) unexpected marriage; he looks "at the papers on his table", his "diagrams" and "emblematic patterns", magical "notes" and records of "dreams written down on waking" – all the materials on which he had been planning to build his new rituals. And suddenly "the dream that [had] made them beautiful and wise and mysterious had faded, for he had always worked for Margaret's eyes" (*VSB* 209). The "great work" he had undertaken for the Order had been "all for her" (*VSB* 84), he declares, and when he visits Margaret after her marriage and she asks him about his plans for "the order", he tells her that he is "not thinking about it, that he half thought of giving up the idea" (*VSB* 97). Yeats's feelings about the Castle ran in the same vein. It was not that the poet and his fictive counterpart failed to take their beliefs in occultism seriously, but that each of them was possessed by an obsession that cut even deeper. Said Michael: "'My work, the life the undying ones have set before me, my own soul, are all nothing beside a passion and beside a woman.'" (*VSB* 215). Said Yeats: the Castle was "an obsession more constant than anything but my love itself" (*Mem* 123). When Margaret left Michael, when Maud Gonne went from Yeats, the Order and the Castle went with them.

A discussion of the Castle of Heroes carries past the period in Yeats's life with which this book is most directly concerned, but it might justly be claimed that there is little distinction to be drawn between what Yeats hoped to achieve through the Castle and what he had been trying to achieve in the years before he ever set eyes on Lough Key. Between the mid and late eighties he had given himself over to literature and magic, Ireland and Maud Gonne, and from the time he made those commitments he had set out – sincerely – to make them into one. The Castle was his flawed attempt to bring together in his life those fixations that he had long since been trying to bring together in his work.

Later chapters will discuss the specific ways in which the early works set out to fuse obsessions; this introduction might conclude with the more general observation that, in Yeats's art no less than in his life, his focus on his deep concerns was unrelenting. Aside from the earliest lyrics and verse–dramas, there is scarce an early work in prose or verse that does not draw, directly or indirectly, on Yeats's knowledge and experience of those preoccupations he had numbered as his "chief". "Fergus and the Druid" (1892), for instance, weds its author's selective readings about the backgrounds of the Red Branch king with his knowledge of the occult doctrines that testified to the possibility of achieving a "sudden remembrance of all one's past incarnations".[62] "The Two Trees", also published in 1892, was written to Maud Gonne, but though it advertises itself as a love poem it finds its most direct gloss in magic.[63] So too do early lyrics such as the recondite "The Poet pleads with the Elemental Powers" and, less expectedly, the misleadingly simple "When You are Old".

Presented with the basic facts about these last two poems, a reader unfamiliar with either of them might well expect them to bear a marked resemblance to each other. Both were first published in 1892; both were written to Maud Gonne; both take their central images from occult sources. Yet the existence of affinities like these only serves to underscore how different these lyrics are. Here it will be enough simply to suggest a point that later chapters will elaborate: that Yeats's early use of the magical tradition is at its most effective when the private voice of the magus is subsumed by the more public voice of the artist, and at its least effective when the voice of the magus supersedes that of the poet. "The Poet pleads with the Elemental Powers" clearly falls into the latter category; it fails because Yeats allowed the arcane to dominate its foreground, and in the process hid the human thought of his poem all too deep for retrieval. The poem was much rewritten between 1892 and 1898, but at no point in its progress did it bid the reader welcome. The final version of the opening stanza typifies the poem's drift:

> The Powers whose name and shape no living creature knows
> Have pulled the Immortal Rose;
> And though the Seven Lights bowed in their dance and wept,
> The Polar Dragon slept,
> His heavy rings uncoiled from glimmering deep to deep:
> When will he wake from sleep?

It would be impossible to achieve a full understanding of these lines without a direct knowledge of Yeats's researches into magic. We could not entirely apprehend the reference to the "Powers whose name and shape no living creature knows" except by further reference, in this case to occultism's vision of a "World of Incorporeal Being... wherein the Intelligences... have neither shape nor name" (*TSD* I, p. 624). Nor could we comprehend the "Seven Lights" without an awareness of what occultism alternately called the "Seven Lights" (*TSD* I, p. 145) or "seven creative Rishis" (*TSD* I, p. 233) or "Seven Builders" (*TSD* I, p. 521) or "seven... Governors" (*TSD* II, p. 247 n.). Nor, for that matter, could we unravel the meaning of the stanza as a whole without knowing that these two groups of demigods – one greater, one less – were imaged by occultism as being at war over the fate of man, and that the former of the two – Yeats's unnamable "Powers", magic's unnamable "Intelligences" – were said to have won through. It was they "who had broken, countless aeons before, through the 'Seven Circles,' and thus 'robbed' them of the Sacred Fire": so said Blavatsky (*TSD* II, p. 84). It was they who had broken through the circling "Seven Lights", and thus "pulled the Immortal Rose": so said Yeats's poem. What the first stanza of this lyric is trying to invoke, then, is an esoteric version of the myth of Prometheus; reduced to their essentials, these lines describe the moment at which a guarded secret wisdom first became available to mankind.

Whatever his abilities, a poet who asks his readers to track him down alleys as dimly lit as these is simply demanding more than the reader can supply. The backgrounds of the opening of this poem, as of its other two stanzas, are far more convoluted than even the above discussion might indicate.[64] Yet the skeleton on which these elaborate trappings have been hung is simple enough in its outlines, as simple in its way as that of "When You are Old". "The Poet pleads with the Elemental Powers" opens with a description of the moment when man took on awareness. The second stanza describes the growth in "care" that a growth in knowledge brings, a concern that is here directed particularly towards "her I love" (*VP* 174). In the final stanza, this attitude of troubled vigilance gives rise in turn to the poet's closing plea to the rulers of the elements to keep watch over his loved one. This is not the everyday stuff of a love poem – invoking the protection of the spirits who controlled the elements was a practice of the Golden Dawn[65] – but neither is it a theme that needed to be adorned from heel to throat. Still less convincing was Yeats's attempt to root his poem in an Irish context, as when in 1894 he titled the second published version of the poem "A Mystical Prayer to the Masters of the Elements, Finvarra, Feacra, and Caolte", a resolute superimposition that betrays a too resolute frame of mind.

But if his quest for synthesis sometimes persuaded Yeats into a dogged forcing of connections, the same search more often generated work in which the poet's central interests forged evocative links that rang true. A poem that is generally liked but rarely praised aloud, "When You are Old" provides an antidote to the young poet's plea to the elementals; it evolves into an effective lyric precisely because it abandons an esoteric foregrounding in favor of a readily accessible theme that is lit up from behind by the unspoken.

Written a few weeks before Maud Gonne's initiation into the Golden Dawn in autumn of 1891, "When You are Old" takes the cue for its opening stanza from Ronsard's seductive *"Quand Vous Serez Bien Vieille"*. Thereafter the two poems part company, not simply in spirit but in imagery. Ronsard concludes his poem by enjoining his reluctant "Hélène" to gather the rosebuds. Yeats's appeal to his Helen is of a decidedly less earthy kind; and an understanding of these differences depends upon an understanding of Yeats's second quatrain, the point at which his poem veers away from Ronsard to find a voice of its own.

Here quoted as it appeared in *The Countess Kathleen and Various Legends and Lyrics*, the second stanza of "When You are Old" read much as it reads now:

> How many loved your moments of glad grace,
>   And loved your beauty with love false or true,
>   But one man loved the pilgrim soul in you,
>   And loved the sorrows of your changing face.

"Changing face" was a skilled choice. It looks back to the first stanza's image of the woman nodding by the changing light of the fire; it looks ahead to the woman's old age, and declares that she will remain well loved no matter how physical beauty may change. Thus do image and theme build in harmony. But these tight internal resonances do not serve to explain how Yeats came to light on the image in the first place, the process by which a toiling writer came to his artful finding. The silent working mind behind these lines is that of a man who was simultaneously an artist and a magician; and the poem took the direction that it did because a dedicated artist was searching for a phrase, and a no less dedicated occultist was able to suggest one.

From the time he had met Maud Gonne, Yeats had seen her as a woman burdened with a "soul that... seemed... incapable of rest" (*Mem* 47). Hence an image like that of the "pilgrim soul" came naturally to the author of this love song.[66] But, striking as it is, the image was worn coin when Yeats first came across it. It appears in virtually all of the major occult tracts that were published or privately circulated in the final quarter of the nineteenth century, and in each of its uses the phrase refers to the spiritual principle in man, the undying "pilgrim" whose task it is to traverse the many rounds of incarnations that the spirit must undergo before it can achieve release from the earth. The argument of "When You are Old", then, was that there was only "one man" among the "many" who loved Maud Gonne for her beauty who was also capable of loving her for her everlasting spirit; but there was more to the argument than that. Searching out readier images for its concept of the pilgrim soul, occultism had decided on a pair of heavenly bodies that, like the spirit, traversed a continual round: the moon came to serve as a symbol of the female pilgrim, the sun of the male. Once Yeats had arrived at his equation between magic's pilgrim and the restless soul of his beloved, then, the image pattern of the rest of his poem all but completed itself. "Pilgrim soul" carried him directly on to the image of the "changing face" – of the moon, of the woman – and the two images working in tandem served to generate the poem's suggestive final stanza, wherein "Love" – imaged here as the male principle and, implicitly, as the sun – "paced upon the mountains far above,/And hid his face amid a crowd of stars". The setting of the sun behind the mountains, the rising starlit sky are allusive emblems of love's steady wane, emblems that came out of an occult tradition to carry a poem that began as an adaptation on to a conclusion that was very much its own.[67]

"When You are Old" thus demonstrates both Yeats's reliance on the magical tradition as a source of ready images and his ability to adapt those images to his own more artistic usages; in its quiet way, it is less a demonstration of the constancy of his love for Maud Gonne than of the sincerity of his need to hammer his thoughts into unity. Seeing Ireland and magic and Maud Gonne as forming the nexus of all that he did and thought, he saw it as necessary that they form the nexus of all that he wrote as well. Inasmuch as the great artist was great in proportion to the degree of his sincerity, the poet could escape mediocrity only by writing well of what he knew best. It was this attitude that led Yeats to his heady – and, ultimately, inaccurate – 1892 claim that, "had [he] not made magic [his] constant study", *The Countess Kathleen* would "have [n]ever come to exist" (*CL1* 303), and that led him to abide by his long-standing conviction that the play was based on Irish legend even after he had found conclusive evidence that its plot had a "French source" (*Let* 346). He said such things out of psychic necessity. Occultism and Ireland were what he knew best. He had written *The Countess Kathleen*. A lasting work of art can only grow out of what is closest to the artist. Thus: *Kathleen* had its base in magic, *Kathleen* was – as its 1892 subtitle asserted – "An Irish Drama" (*VPl* 2). To have claimed less would have been to deny the play's sincerity and, by extension, its validity as a work of art.

In sum, what Yeats was up to in this early play was an attempt to will baseless contexts into realities. But to dismiss these tendencies as exercises in self-deception would be to ignore the paradox that obtains in cases of the kind: that Yeats was deceiving himself in order to be true to his image of the manner of man that he was. Both the early works and their author's remarks about them are riddled with what might precisely be called confusions. At times his attempts to make his work sincere pushed him towards contrived unions: of love and occultism in the inflated lyric on the elemental powers, of occultism and Ireland in his comments about the genesis of *The Countess Kathleen*. But he was more often able to resist the impulse to impose his will upon his imagination; and when his several voices rise naturally as one, their concert takes him far towards what he would later call perfection of the work. Unlike *The Countess Kathleen*, a love song like "When You are Old" actually is a better work than it could have been had Yeats not made magic his constant study; and in this it is characteristic. From the lesser lyrics through the ambitious expanse of "The Wanderings of Oisin", the most intriguing of the early works declined to deal independently with love or magic or Ireland; and so did Yeats. Literature was his vocation; his avocations were Ireland, occultism, and Maud Gonne; and, to paraphrase Frost, his object in living was to unite his avocations and his vocation, even as his eyes made one in sight. Being sincere, he would not have had it otherwise; remaining sincere, he became the great poet that a youthful poet had imagined into reality.

Notes to Chapter 1

1 Cf. R. J. Finneran *et al.*, *Letters to W. B. Yeats*, Vol. II, p. 404.
2 It has by now been conclusively established that Yeats's initiation into the Golden Dawn took place on 7 March 1890. Yet Laurence W. Fennelly has rightly noted the care the poet took to tabulate his involvement with occultism (see G. M. Harper, ed., *Yeats and The Occult*, p. 288); and while it appears nearly a third of the way through the *Autobiographies*, the reference to "May or June 1887" (*Au* 183) comprises the first specific date in the volume. Whether his memory was right or wrong, then, Yeats saw his initiation as a landmark to be fixed as precisely as he could. If his recollection was correct – and it seems unlikely that he would have been out by nearly three years in a matter of this kind – then the fact that he was introduced to "The Hermetic Students" by Mathers (*Au* 183) can only imply that the Society was a precursor of the Golden Dawn, and there is indeed evidence to suggest that the Golden Dawn existed in an embryonic form as early as 1887. In his *The Secret Rituals of the Golden Dawn*, for instance, R. G. Torrens cites a pamphlet, ostensibly written by Order co-founder W. Wynn Westcott, which gives 1887 as the founding date of the Isis-Urania Temple (p. 222). Order historian Israel Regardie likewise accepts 1887 as the date of the Order's inception (*GD* I, p. 21). Finally, Torrens's *The Golden Dawn: The Inner Teachings* hints at the existence of a precursor to the Order proper with its reference to "the first branch" of the Order, "The Order of the Companions of the Rising Light of the Morning – the Golden Dawn in the Outer" (p. 194). Yeats may well have had such a group in mind when he noted that the society he remembered joining in 1887 "had a different name among its members" (*Au* 183).
3 Cf. Patricia M. Ball, *The Central Self: A Study in Romantic and Victorian Imagination*, pp. 158–9.
4 ibid., pp. 152–65.
5 J. B. Yeats made this claim in a letter written to Edward Dowden (7 January 1884). Cf. Joseph Hone, *W. B. Yeats: 1865–1939*, p. 43.

6   So the poet's father wrote to Isaac Butt Yeats; the letter (28 January 1918) is cited in William M. Murphy's *Prodigal Father: The Life of John Butler Yeats (1839–1922)*, p. 485.
7   Certainly the concept of sincerity should be numbered among the more readily identifiable of the ideas Yeats had in mind when, in February 1910, he told his father that he had noticed "with some surprise how fully my philosophy of life has been inherited from you in all but its details and applications" (*Let* 549).
8   Cf. Walter Pater's "Wordsworth", an essay first published on 27 February 1889, and later reprinted in his *Essays from 'The Guardian'*, p. 102.
9   Ball, op. cit., p. 161.
10 For Yeats's more direct references to the sincerity of individual artists, see his remarks on Douglas Hyde (*CL1* 99, *UP1* 255), John Todhunter (*LNI* 190), J. J. Callanan (*UP1* 151), Charles Kickham (*UP1* 161), Rose Kavanagh (*CL1* 245), Ellen O'Leary (*LNI* 126–7), Thomas Davis (*CL1* 287), Maud Gonne (*LNI* 149, *E&I* 249), James Clarence Mangan (*A Book of Irish Verse*, p. xxii), Arthur Symons (*UP1* 374), George Russell (*UP1* 380), Edmund Spenser (*E&I* 357), George Fitzmaurice (*Let* 495), John Synge (*E&I* 339, *Mem* 250), Walter Pater (*E&I* 236), Dora Sigerson (*Let* 648), Ezra Pound (*E&I* 405), the men and women on whom the young Abbey Theatre had pinned its hopes (*Let* 311), the tellers of Irish folktales (*UP1* 327) and, of course, folk art itself, a body of work that affords no room whatever to that which is "insincere" (*CT* 128).

It is appropriate that Irish names dominate this eclectic list, since the form of sincerity that Yeats most consistently preached was intimately linked to homeland. "One's nation" is "the only thing one knows even a little of", he wrote in 1888 (*LNI* 174); nor can the remark be written off as the product of youthful enthusiasm, since 1906 found him reaffirming that "no man knows more of the world" than the "countryside where he was born and bred" (*UP2* 347). Since sincerity demanded that the artist write of topics he knew to the bone, Ireland for Yeats was an inevitable subject matter. If there can be "no great literature without nationality" (*LNI* 103–4), then "Ireland is the true subject for the Irish" (*LNI* 90); thus, should "an Irish writer" stray away "from Irish themes and Irish feeling", in "almost all cases" he will create nothing more than "alms for oblivion" (*LNI* 103).
11 Yeats repeated the claim in 1922, when he observed that the man of genius was perforce a man of "sincerity" (*Au* 109); and four years later he added that it was the "sincerity" of "the Great Masters" that accounted for the "genius" of their work (*UP2* 470). To be sure, Yeats never claimed that sincerity in an artist could alone guarantee success. But he was candid about his preference for a poetry that made an attempt to "build up from the ground" to the work of writers who, however great their technique, relied upon an "insincere literary language" (*Let* 322): better a "sincere naivety" than even a famous poem that "never once moves with an emotional life", and whose entire thrust is therefore "insincere" (*Let* 325). And if sincerity did not ensure greatness, it was at least true that greatness was impossible without it. As early as 1888 he was insisting on the need to avoid the "insincerity" of writing "on other men's truth" (*CL1* 48); the writer who does not take his "own thoughts" as his topic, he told Katharine Tynan, will go "down into that whirlpool of ins[i]ncerity from which no man returns" (*CL1* 117).
12 Cf. *A Book of Irish Verse*, p. xxii.
13 From Yeats's Introduction to Horton's *A Book of Images* (London: The Unicorn Press, 1898), pp. 15, 14. The Introduction has since been reprinted in part in an

article by George Mills Harper and Richard J. Finneran, in George Mills Harper, ed., *Yeats and The Occult*, pp. 201–3.
14 *Autobiographies* (190). For an elaboration of the idea, cf. J. B. Yeats's distinction between "character" and "personality" in his *Early Memories: Some Chapters of Autobiography*, pp. 28–9.
15 J. B. Yeats made the connection between sincerity and originality in the 1884 letter to Dowden (Hone, op. cit., p. 43). Within a few years his son was to make the same connection in a letter to Lily White, when he observed that writing about familiar legends and landscapes "helps orig[i]nality and makes one's verses sincere" (*CL1* 131).
16 Ellmann, *Yeats: The Man and the Masks*, pp. 118 ff.
17 The more recent research on Yeats and folklore will be detailed in the notes to Chapter 2. For concise summaries of the major researches on Yeats and occultism, see *Anglo-Irish Literature: A Review of Research*, ed. Richard J. Finneran (1976). Rightly noting that few readers "have a clear understanding of [Yeats's] almost lifelong occult activities and their relationship to his achievement" (p. 313), Finneran is justly critical of works that should have taken account of those activities but did not (pp. 232–3, 295, 296, 302). For summaries of the major Yeats criticism published since the mid-1970s, see pp. 85–153 of *Recent Research on Anglo-Irish Writers* (1983), also edited by Finneran. The volume surveys all available criticism published up to 1980, and also a number of items published in 1981.

Readers interested in the general backgrounds of the poet's forays into the hidden art might well begin their investigations with the works of George Mills Harper and Ellic Howe, but should not overlook Francis King's *The Rites of Modern Occult Magic* (1971). Sometimes inaccurate but generally informative, this volume was first published in 1970 under the more accurate title of *Ritual Magic in England: 1887 to the Present Day*. The documents of the Order are now most readily available in the 1978 reprint of Israel Regardie's *The Golden Dawn: An Account of the Teachings, Rites and Ceremonies of the Order of the Golden Dawn*, which collects four volumes under one cover. Supplemental Order materials may be found in King's *Astral Projection, Ritual Magic and Alchemy* (1971), which includes a number of documents not previously published; and for versions of the Outer Order rituals as they existed before the Golden Dawn schism of 1900, see R. G. Torrens's *The Secret Rituals of the Golden Dawn* (1973). Torrens had earlier offered a summary of Order theory and practice in his *The Golden Dawn: The Inner Teachings* (1969).

Of works that do not center specifically on Rosicrucianism, the study most relevant to the present work is M. C. Flannery's *Yeats and Magic: The Earlier Works* (1977). See too the Spring 1981 issue of *Studies in the Literary Imagination*, which is wholly devoted to the occult and philosophical backgrounds of Yeats's work and thought. Finally, any future study of Yeats and ancient tradition will need to take account of James Olney's *The Rhizome and the Flower: The Perennial Philosophy – Yeats and Jung* (1980). This provocative study of the pre-Socratic and Platonic traditions sheds a diffuse but important light on Yeats's debt to occultism, a discipline that could accurately be described as the shadowy brother of neo-Platonism.

18 The Society's negative report on Madame Blavatsky, published in December 1885, so undermined the credibility of Theosophy that, when Yeats first met Blavatsky, she told him that she had only "three followers left" (*Au* 173). But the resilient popularity of occultism in the London of the 1880s enabled the Blavatsky group to recoup its losses in short order;

when Yeats next met with her, he recalled, she was "surrounded by followers" (*Au* 174).

19 For a summary of the rapid growth in Order membership, cf. Harper's *Yeats's Golden Dawn*, p. 12. Harper's comments are based on figures gathered by Ellic Howe.

20 The translation in question was A. E. Waite's *The Mysteries of Magic: A Digest of the Writings of Éliphas Lévi* (see "Lévi, Éliphas", 1886). For evidence of Yeats's early (no later than early 1888) familiarity with this volume, see the summary of the unpublished findings of Thomas L. Dume in James Lovic Allen's "Life as Art: Yeats and the Alchemical Quest", in the Yeats issue of *Literary Imagination*, pp. 24–6. Yeats would also have known Lévi's work through his membership in the Golden Dawn; Mathers's *The Kabbalah Unveiled* had described the French magus as a "great philosopher and Qabalist" (p. 17), and Lévi's theories appear broadcast in the Order rituals.

21 Compare Mathers's comments on the cabala with the precisely similar remarks offered by Christian D. Ginsburg in *The Kabbalah*, pp. 86–7.

22 Blavatsky's timetable was specific; writing in the late eighties, she asserted that the veil would part "between this time and 1897" (*TSD* I, p. 671). For similar observations, cf. *TSD* I, pp. 27, 702, and *TSD* III, p. 488. It was this claim of Blavatsky's that Yeats recalled himself as having disagreed with. An unnamed member of the Society had told him "'that all spiritual influx into the Society will come to an end in 1897 for exactly one hundred years'". "I knew the doctrine", Yeats writes, "and it made me wonder", for "influx of some kind there must always be" (*Au* 182).

23 Yeats's case against Tyndall and Huxley is well known; but it should also be noted that the majority of his critical comments are concentrated in the section of the *Autobiographies* entitled "Four Years: 1887–1891", the years when he was formally involved with Theosophy. This was appropriate, since it was largely from Theosophy that Yeats learned to despise Huxley and Tyndall and the school of thought they were said to represent. Blavatsky's *Isis Unveiled* (Vol. I) is a particularly rich source of invective. For its hatred of Tyndall, cf. pp. xxii, 14, 57, 86–7, 135, 189, 273, 314–15, 396, 418, 439; of Huxley, pp. 15, 74, 120–1, 193–4, 223, 251, 408, 416, 473; of the two men taken together, pp. 43, 85, 232, 242, 248, 249, 250, 256, 336, 340. The *Autobiographies* generally blend the two men into a single symbolic figure, and here too Yeats may well have taken his lead from Theosophy; compare Blavatsky's more characteristic litanies against the two scientists (*IU* I, pp. 233, 271 n., 417) with their counterparts in "Four Years" (*Au* 115, 125, 157, 168, 173, 190).

24 *Letters to W. B. Yeats*, Vol. I, p. 20. The letter came from W. T. Horton.

25 Yeats's commitment to occult theory and practice was joined by a frank delight in the trappings of the movement; and when his disagreements with Blavatsky led him to leave her "romantic house" in London in his wake (*Au* 181), he had already taken up with an occult group in London that was more romantic still. Waite's *Real History of the Rosicrucians* had noted that the "'poetry and romance'" of "'every European country'" were "'deeply indebted to the Rosicrucians for many a fascinating creation'" (pp. 1–2). Like other occult apologists of the time, Waite would have included masterworks such as *Le Roman de la Rose* and *Divina Commèdia* in his bibliography of influence; but his claim was not wholly an exaggeration, since Rosicrucianism had in fact caught not a few distinguished literary eyes. The opening canto of Part I of Butler's *Hudibras*, for instance, had attributed "Rosycrucian" (1. 545) learning to Ralph, the Squire (11. 457–622). The year 1712 had brought the Rosicrucians a

prominent notice in *The Spectator* (No. 379, 15 May 1712); and Pope had nodded bemusedly towards Rosicrucianism in his 1714 dedication to "The Rape of the Lock" (1712, 1714), and had borrowed the supernatural "Machinery" for the final version of his poem from the Abbé de Villars's *Comte de Gabalis* (1670), itself a work that had commanded wide attention because of the mysterious death of its author. The next major ripple of literary interest came towards the start of the nineteenth century, first in Godwin's *St. Leon: A Tale of the Sixteenth Century* (1799), and then in Shelley's imitative *St. Ervyne; or, The Rosicrucian* (1811), and later in De Quincey's "Historico-Critical Inquiry into the Origin of the Rosicrucians and Free-masons" (1824). Writers such as Butler, of course, were having fun at magic's expense; but as a general rule, public notice of the Rosicrucians contained poetry and romance aplenty. For an illustrative passage from a literary source, see Bulwer-Lytton's lengthy description of the Rosicrucians' "mystical Fraternity", a "glorious sect" whose "tenets and powers have never been more than most partially explored", in the popular *Zanoni* (1842), pp. 78, 77. For similar observations from nineteenth-century occult sources, see particularly *Zanoni*, pp. vi, 113, 114, 185; Lévi's *The History of Magic*, pp. 351–4, 358–9; Jennings's *The Rosicrucians: Their Rites and Mysteries*, Vol. I, p. ix; Vol. II, pp. 143, 144, 157, 218, 220; *Isis Unveiled*, Vol. I, p. 64; Vol. II, p. 380; *The Gnostics and Their Remains*, pp. 423, 428; *The Real History of the Rosicrucians*, pp. 22–3, 405; *Astral Projection, Ritual Magic and Alchemy*, p. 91. Like other members of the Order, Yeats was much taken by this pervasive air of mystery. Like the lodgings of Blavatsky, the Mathers residence at Stent Lodge in Forest Hill impressed him as "a romantic place" (*Au* 185); and like Blavatsky herself, Mathers too seemed "a figure of romance", a latter-day "Faust" (*Au* 183, 187).

26 Seeking to explain the sporadic but widespread swerves towards the magical tradition during the past hundred years, Mircea Eliade's *Occultism, Witchcraft, and Cultural Fashions* (1976) speaks of a condition of revolt, a desire "to go beyond one's parents'... world of meanings" (p. 92); and certainly this was a major motive force for Yeats. The *Literatim Transcription of the Manuscripts of William Butler Yeats's The Speckled Bird*, for instance, has Michael describing his growing interest in the spiritual world as having come about "more and more" as a reaction to his "father's indignant skepti[cism]" (p. 312); and in this case it is safe to identify the poet's fictional character as his personal spokesman. Conscious of deep-ranging differences between his father's cast of mind and his own, and conscious too of his "father's influence upon [his] thoughts" (*Au* 64), Yeats found in occultism a sanctuary that his father's eloquent lack of reverence could not penetrate. When it came to occultism, he wrote in 1892, his father could only argue "out of the immense depths of his ignorance as to everything that I am doing & thinking" (*CL1* 303). An immense sense of self-satisfaction resonates in that sentence, and Yeats had good reason to be satisfied. "It was only when I began to study psychical research and mystical philosophy", he wrote, "that I broke away from my father's influence" (*Au* 89).

27 The anti-rational bias of occultism was unmitigated. Theosophy spoke of the mind as the spirit's "greatest enemy" (*TSD* III, p. 60); Westcott asserted that "the main object" of the Golden Dawn was "the development of the Spiritual sides of our natures in contradistinction to the purely intellectual" (*Astral Projection, Ritual Magic and Alchemy*, p. 101). For late nineteenth-century occultism's views on the primacy of the soul over the intellect, see particularly *The Rosicrucians: Their Rites and Mysteries*, Vol. I, p. 89; Vol. II, pp. 168, 172,

237; *Isis Unveiled*, Vol. I, pp. 409, 425, 433, 434, 467, 486; Vol. II, p. 636; *Magic, White and Black*, pp. 29, 47, 113, 146, 213, 255; *Paracelsus*, pp. 143 n., 161 n., 169, 174, 223, 241–2, 267, 270, 274–5; *The Secret Doctrine*, Vol. I, p. 31 n.; Vol. II, pp. 77–8, 314–15; Vol. III, pp. 331, 592; *The Golden Dawn*, Vol. II, pp. 209, 281; Vol. III, pp. 178, 273.

28 The remarks are Edward Maitland's; cf. *The Virgin of the World* (1885), pp. ix, x.

29 The Order held that "the rising of the Sun of ineffable light" was imminent (*GD* II, p. 290), and in this regard Order members were of a single mind with other occultists of the time. For the more salient remarks on the matter, cf. *Isis Unveiled*, Vol. I, pp. 119, 494, 613, 622; Vol. II, p. 369; *The Occult World* (1881), p. 149; *Incidents in the Life of Madame Blavatsky*, p. 321; *The Real History of the Rosicrucians*, pp. 3, 93; *The Kabbalah Unveiled*, p. 1; *The Secret Doctrine*, Vol. I, pp. 27, 38 n.; Vol. II, pp. 77–8, 838, 842. The 1897 edition of *The Occult World* reflected Blavatsky's belief that 1897 would prove the final year of the major spiritual influx; therein Sinnett observed that the hidden spiritual Masters of the Theosophical Society were "more disposed to be communicative at this moment than they have been for a long time past" (p. 174), and that "the dawn of psychic truth has begun to brighten our sky from several directions at once" (p. 207).

As the title of his *The Celtic Twilight* suggests, Yeats confidently expected the coming dawn to break sooner in Ireland than elsewhere; and his studies in magic had lent support to his expectations. Occultism's brief against the intellect was based in part on its feeling that the spirit world visited only those minds that had become like "tranquil and clear water" (*TSD* III, p. 420); and Yeats saw the minds of his countrymen as having a unique potential for achieving just such a tranquility. "Images form themselves in our minds perpetually as if they were reflected in some pool", he wrote in 1902, "we can make our minds so like still water that beings gather about us that they may see, it may be, their own images, and so live for a moment with a clearer, perhaps even with a fiercer life because of our quiet" (*CT* 87).

30 Banim, John, *Peter of the Castle; and, The Fetches* (Dublin: James Duffy, 1866), p. 203.

31 Cf. P[atrick] W[eston] Joyce's "Fergus O'Mara and the Air-demons", reprinted in *FFT* 341. As M. H. Thuente notes in her "List of Sources" of the poems and tales in *FFT* and *IFT*, Yeats found this obscure story of Joyce's in the volume called *Good and Pleasant Reading* (Dublin: Gill, 1886). Cf. *FFT* xix.

32 Cf. Jennings's *The Rosicrucians: Their Rites and Mysteries*, Vol. I, p. 248. Jennings's second volume contains a long discussion of the elementals and the question of salvation (pp. 202 ff.), the same topic that Irish folklore so often addressed in the case of the sidhe. Certain strands of Irish folk belief held that the sidhe were fallen angels, and spoke of their ability to transform themselves in ways that would enable them to lure men into their realm; and *The Rosicrucians* (Vol. II) likewise noted that certain among the fallen angels had been permitted to reappear on earth (pp. 251–5), and that the more "malific" of the spirits had the power to take on "lovely forms" in order to entrap mortals (pp. 184, 185).

33 Bulwer-Lytton, *Zanoni*, p. 194.

34 In context, Yeats's remarks about folklore and the primal religion take the form of a disclaimer; the introduction to *FFT* praises the collectors of Irish folklore for having "made their work literature rather than science, and [having] told us of the Irish peasantry rather than of the primitive religion of mankind, or whatever else the folk-lorists are on the gad after. To be considered scientists",

he adds, "they should have tabulated all their tales in forms like grocers' bills – item the fairy king, item the queen" (*FFT* 6). But the objection here was to the "scientific" bent of mind, not to the theory of primal religion. Yeats was describing Irish fairylore as an expression of ancient religious beliefs within a few weeks of the publication of *FFT* (*UP1* 137), and stated his case for "fables and fairy tales" as the living remnants of "once famous religions fallen into ruin" still more directly in February 1890 (*LNI* 101). Moreover, late in 1890 he explained that the above-cited remarks from the introduction to *FFT* had not been intended as a protest against scientific theories of folklore *per se*, but against folklore studies that were "merely" scientific (*UP1* 174). His ideal folklorist would combine the best traits of scientist and artist. Thus in 1890 he praised the work of Hyde as being "quite as accurate as any 'scientific' person's rendering", but at the same time full of "subtle imaginative sympathy" (*UP1* 174); and in the same year he described Curtin's *Myths and Folk-Lore of Ireland* (1890) as probably "the most careful and scientific work on Irish folk-lore yet published", and worthy of respect because it grew out of a "science of folk-lore" that rejected tabulation in favor of remaining "imaginative" (*LNI* 101).

35 The admonition that occultists should study folklore was written into an early charter of the Theosophical Society; cf. Sinnett's *Incidents in the Life of Madame Blavatsky*, p. 184.

36 ibid., p. 184. Blavatsky, who was no doubt the primary author of the Society charter, offers the same observation about the value of "popular folk-lore and traditions" in *The Key to Theosophy*, p. 48.

37 For the clearer comments on the primal religion in other of Yeats's folklore sources, cf. Lady Wilde's *Ancient Cures* (1890), pp. 1–4, 97–8, 106, and more particularly Hyde's *Beside the Fire* (1890), pp. xxxvi–xli. For a more generalized discussion of the idea, cf. Curtin's *Myths and Folk-Lore of Ireland* (1890), pp. 21–8.

Yeats found further confirmation of the primal religion theory in sources both scholarly and occult. His more orthodox authorities would have included Goblet d'Alviella's *The Migration of Symbols* (1894). Though the author of *Migration* had his doubts about the theory, he noted the tendency of his fellow comparative mythologists to speak of a "profound primitive wisdom" of which "all the religious practices [of] antiquity" were but "the disguised or disfigured reflection" (p. 4); and he thus indirectly helped to confirm the long-standing claims of occultism, which likewise held that all religions were the "children of one common parent, the Wisdom Religion" (*TSD* III, p. 308). For a concise summary of magic's position in the matter, cf. *The Key to Theosophy*, pp. 4–11. For similar claims in other prominent occult sources, see particularly *The History of Magic*, pp. 28–9, 247, 248; *Isis Unveiled*, Vol. I, pp. 271, 444, 561, 573, 580; Vol. II, p. 470; *The Occult World* (1881), pp. 4, 134, 139, 157, 172; *Esoteric Buddhism*, p. vi; *The Virgin of the World*, p. x; *The Gnostics and Their Remains*, pp. 216, 272, 417; *The Secret Doctrine*, Vol. I, pp. viii, xxi, 14, 18, 20, 27, 28, 328, 364, 381, 457, 719; Vol. II, pp. 810, 818 n., 838, 839, 842; Vol. III, pp. 166, 176, 178, 211, 236, 308; *The Occult World* (1897), p. 161. Yeats, of course, was particularly interested in locating the primal religion in Ireland, and here he had the support not only of his folklore sources but of works such as John Rhys's *Celtic Heathendom* (1888), which argued that the mythologies of the Celts, Teutons, and Greeks "all represent in their way the same primaeval Aryan myth" (p. 622). Comments like these form the backdrop against which the poet undertook his visits to Irish cottages, where he hoped to discover "a tradition of belief older than any European Church, and founded upon the experience of the world before the modern bias" (*Au* 265). "I do not think the Church is necessary to me – I have my own spiritual life and a form of faith so old that the form of the Church is but of yesterday beside it. My mass is the daily rising and setting of the sun", says Michael in *The Speckled Bird* (*VSB* 34); and the remark reflects basic Yeatsian assumptions about the primal faith as it existed in vestigial form in Ireland. Thus 1897's "The Celtic Element in Literature" not only alludes to the Celts as being closer to the primal religion – the "beliefs of ancient times in Europe" – than any other European country (*E&I* 185), but specifies why Michael's faith should center on the rising and setting of the sun: the sense of the mystery of nature shared by the Irish and Welsh, Yeats notes, "is but the ancient religion of the world, the ancient worship of Nature" (*E&I* 176).

38 Yeats's description of Irish legend and folklore as simultaneously "most ancient" and "altogether new" was grounded on the correct assumption that the Ireland of the middle and late nineteenth century had at its disposal a deep body of indigenous myths that, for reasons cultural and historical, had reclined for years in the quiet dark, and that had only recently begun to come to general notice. Here were works that were "eternally young for all their centuries" (*Ex* 217); and here, therefore, was a chance for Ireland's writers to create works that were "old with words and thoughts and reveries handed down for ages" but that none the less belonged "to Ireland and youth" (*LNI* 191). Yeats's most dogmatic statement on the matter came in the spring of 1893, when he spoke of how Ireland's "exceptional opportunity" to give its ancient national materials new voice had perhaps left it standing "alone... among the nations" (*UP1* 275, 273).

39 *The Secret Doctrine*, Vol. I, p. viii.

40 *The History of Magic*, pp. 28–9, 29. Since this work was not published in English translation until 1913, Yeats would not have been directly familiar with Lévi's reference to the broken mirror of the primal faith. But the phrase might safely be cited as representative, since Lévi's view of the cabala as the repository of the primitive religion was shared by virtually all of the poet's occult sources.

41 *The Occult World* (1881), p. 17.

42 ibid., p. 139.

43 For similar comments in other of Yeats's folklore sources, cf. Lady Wilde's *Ancient Cures*, pp. 3–4, and D. R. McAnally's *Irish Wonders* (1888), p. 189.

44 Later revised by Yeats, this observation originally appeared in the typescript of the Dedication to *A Vision* (1925). For details, cf. *Yeats's Golden Dawn*, p. 198, n. 84.

45 Though the reference in *Au* to an "old Irish peasant woman" postdates Yeats's first meeting with Blavatsky by many years, he was describing her as an "old peas[a]nt woman" as early as 1889 (*CL1* 164).

46 The "old peasant woman" (*VP* 90, 797) from Ballysadare is a familiar figure: the "little old woman in a white cap" (*CT* 82) from whom Yeats gathered the "old song" (*VP* 90) that became the basis of "An Old Song Re-sung" (now "Down by the Salley Gardens"), and who would later sing and translate for him the "old Gaelic ballad" (*VP* 803, 804) that inspired 1893's "The Host of the Air".

47 It was in autumn of 1891 that Yeats was putting his ambitious plans for the Young Ireland League into practice. For his summary of the League and its purposes, cf. *UP1* 206–8 and *CL1* 266 ff.

48 The precise date of Maud Gonne's meeting with Davitt has not been established. The present text follows a chronology suggested by Nancy Cardozo's *Lucky*

Eyes and a High Heart: The Life of Maud Gonne (pp. 57, 58, 71) rather than the vaguer dating in Samuel Levenson's *Maud Gonne: A Biography of Yeats' Beloved* (p. 44).

49   As it appears on p. 70 of the *Literatim Transcription of the Manuscripts of William Butler Yeats's The Speckled Bird*, this sentence describes Michael's reaction to his growing love for Margaret.

50   *A Servant of the Queen*, p. 256.

51   *CL1* summarizes the known facts about her son, George, who was born in January 1890 and died of meningitis in July 1891 (*CL1* 489). According to Yeats, it was after a conversation with George Russell that Maud Gonne came to believe that the soul of a child who had died in infancy could reincarnate immediately (*Mem* 48); and Russell's was a standard theosophical theory, expressed most succinctly in *Esoteric Buddhism* (pp. 120–1).

52   Cardozo, op. cit., p. 45.

53   At the time of Maud Gonne's resignation from the Order, the debate about the links between Rosicrucianism and Freemasonry was a lively one among occultists. Yeats would no doubt have argued that the Golden Dawn had set out to rescue Rosicrucianism from its debasements by Masonry; Maud Gonne would no doubt have countered with the claim that it was Rosicrucianism that had given rise to Freemasonry in the first place; and the prevailing historical arguments, scattered and speculative as they were, would have been on her side. For the views on the matter that obtained at the time, see particularly *The History of Magic*, p. 382; *Isis Unveiled*, Vol. II, p. 349; and *The Gnostics and Their Remains*, pp. 392–3. For a somewhat more detached overview, cf. *The Rites of Modern Occult Magic*, pp. 25–8.

54   First published in 1896, the story is now known as "Proud Costello, Mac-Dermot's Daughter, and the Bitter Tongue" (*Myth* 196–210, *VSR* 61–81). Yeats's original source for the story, Hyde's *Love Songs of Connacht*, had offered other and more straightforward accounts of the death of Costello (pp. 57, 153); Yeats fixed on the most romantic versions (pp. 55, 57, 152), and embellished them with details (*Myth* 209–10, *VSR* 80–1) of which Hyde makes no mention.

55   *Annals of Lough Cé*, Vol. II, p. 327. My thanks to James McGarry for first calling my attention to this source.

56   ibid., pp. 355, 357.

57   Maud Gonne, op. cit., p. 247.

58   The idea of a Castle of Wisdom was widespread both in Rosicrucian literature and occult literature in general; and it would not be stretching the point to claim that Yeats later found in Thoor Ballylee a functional equivalent for the Castle of Wisdom that he had once hoped to found on Lough Key. In the later drafts of *The Speckled Bird*, the Castle of Heroes appears as the "castle of the Grail" (*VSB* 80, 203, 204, 205), and Michael projects Margaret as the "queen" of his new "little kingdom" (*VSB* 188): he asks her "if she would like to be a queen, and she began to speak of the palace she would build if she were" (*VSB* 25). In thus attributing the idea of the palace to Margaret, *The Speckled Bird* reflects Yeats's own perception of the Castle project; so anxious was he to confirm Maud Gonne's participation in the scheme that he at one point suggested that the idea had originated with her rather than him. Cf. the early 1898 letter to George Russell, in which the poet writes that "Maud Gonne has seen [a] vision of a little temple of the heroes which she proposes to build somewhere in Ireland... and to make the centre of our mystical and literary movement" (*Let* 295).

59 Stephen Gwynn, ed., *Scattering Branches*, p. 23.
60 The remark appears in a late 1943 letter to Ella Young; the letter is cited in Levenson's *Maud Gonne*, pp. 394–5.
61 Volume I of *Letters to W. B. Yeats* finds Mathers working on rituals (p. 34) while his wife worked on designs (p. 51), George Pollexfen working on visions (pp. 46–7), William Sharp helping to revise the rites (pp. 54, 84), Maud Gonne assisting with visions and commenting on her agreement with Yeats's "divisions of the ceremonies" (p. 82), and George Russell lending a hand with designs and with probings of Celtic mythology (pp. 90–1, 97). For a summary of the preparations for the writing of the Castle rituals, and of the rituals themselves, cf. Moore's *The Unicorn*, pp. 68–82.
62 As described in *The Key to Theosophy*, the condition in which one was able to summon up all of his past incarnations was known as *Samma Sambuddha* (p. 363). Occultism thus furnished Yeats with a precedent for the visionary moment that overtakes Fergus at the end of the poem; but it should be noted that he had found just the same precedent in his readings in Irish source materials. "Fergus and the Druid" finds Fergus asserting that his past lives had cast him in the roles of "slave", of "king", and of "A green drop in the surge, a gleam of light/Upon a sword, a fir-tree on a hill" (*VP* 104); and one likely source of his recollections is *Celtic Heathendom*, which Yeats read shortly after its publication in 1888 (*CL1* 115) and which recounted the famous tales of Celtic prophet-bards such as Taliessin, who claimed to have been "a word, a book, a bridge, a coracle, a sword, a drop in a shower", and Amorgen, who testified to his experiences as "the wind and the wave, a loch on the plain, a spear, a tear of the sun" (p. 549). The same page of the Rhys volume would have informed the young poet that the druid was able to "take any form he like[d], and command the elements according to his will"; and while there is no firm proof that Yeats had Rhys directly in mind when writing "Fergus and the Druid", it is at least suggestive that the figures of the shape-changing druid and the man who recalls his past lives should be juxtaposed as directly in *Celtic Heathendom* as they are in Yeats's poem.

Of the known sources of "Fergus and the Druid", the most direct was Ferguson's "The Abdication of Fergus MacRoy", which Yeats referred to directly in 1886's "The Poetry of Sir Samuel Ferguson – II" (*UP1* 91–2) and alluded to, though not by name, in the May, 1899 issue of *Beltaine* (*UP2* 161). Yeats also named Ferguson as one of the central sources of his vision of Fergus in a note to 1899's *The Wind Among the Reeds* (*VP* 813); but in later years he was to claim that, when he wrote the early poems on Fergus, he "only knew" the character from his readings in "Mr. Standish O'Grady", and that he had allowed his imagination to deal "more freely with what I did know than I would approve of to-day" (*VP* 814). His dropping of the reference to Ferguson can only be explained as a lapse in memory, in part because he had demonstrably known Ferguson's "Abdication" no later than 1886, but more so because not even the freest of imaginations could have transformed the Fergus pictured by O'Grady into the dreaming king envisioned by Yeats. Indeed, while Yeats's Fergus describes the druid as the "most wise of living souls" (*VP* 102), the Fergus that appears in O'Grady's *History* spends much of his time inveighing against the druids and their "lying magic" (*Hist* I, p. 168) and "idle lore" (*Hist* II, p. 249). For the most expressive anti-druidic diatribe to be found in a known Yeats source, see all of Fergus's long speech in the first volume of the *History*, p. 168.

Yeats also identified O'Grady as the probable source of his portrait of Cú Chulainn and Fand "walking among flaming dew" in 1896's "The Secret Rose", and here too his memory betrayed him. His source had been *Celtic Heathendom*. For details, see my "A Source Note on 'The Madness of King Goll'", in *Yeats Annual*, Vol. 4 (London: Macmillan, 1986), p. 193. Rhys may also have had his part to play in the shaping of 1897's "The Blessed" (*VP* 166–8), yet another of the early works that attempts to locate an occult event in an Irish context. With its reference to blessedness as the product of drunkenness, the poem is referring to the effects of the soma-cup. Yeats would first have heard of this miraculous brew in the work of Blavatsky, who mentioned it frequently (*IU* I, pp. xl–xli, 157; *IU* II, pp. 91 n., 117; *TSD* II, p. 524; *TSD* III, pp. 124 n., 282 n.) and who described it as "the ambrosia of Secret Wisdom" (*TSD* III, p. 245). Thereafter, he would have found confirmation of Blavatsky's remarks in *Celtic Heathendom*, wherein soma emerges as an elixir that makes "wise men or poets, of those who have drunk of it", and that "is said to untie the poet's tongue" (p. 297); as "the origin of poetry and wisdom" (p. 298), it gives men "the dreams of poets and the visions of prophets" (p. 672) – precisely the effect it is said to produce in "The Blessed". For Yeats's most direct reference to the drink, see his remarks on "soma-drinking priests" (*E&I* 469).

63 To the many sources of "The Two Trees" that have already been adduced, we might add *The Secret Doctrine* (Vol. II), which speaks of how "the Tree of Knowledge, in the Paradise of man's own heart, becomes the Tree of Life Eternal" (p. 621), and of "the Tree of Knowledge, whose fruits give Life Eternal and not physical life alone" (p. 622). Blavatsky had also referred to man as "the container of the Eden in which grows the Tree of Knowledge of good and evil" (*TSD* II, p. 214), while Hartmann's *Magic, White and Black* had described the Rose Cross as "the full-grown Tree of Life and of Knowledge", which every true Rosicrucian "carries deeply buried within his own heart" (p. 280). While there is no direct proof that any or all of these passages served as a direct source of "The Two Trees", there is an evident resemblance between their imagery and the image of the "holy tree" (*VP* 134) of Yeats's opening stanza; and the "ravens of unresting thought" that appear in the second verse (*VP* 136) likewise have a counterpart in "The Ravens of Death", which the Golden Dawn had numbered among the adverse spirits who inhabited the Tree of Life in its malign aspect (*GD* I, p. 163). As a conscious salvo in the gathering revolt of the soul against the intellect (*CL1* 303), the poem clearly sides with the "higher intuitive intellect", the Golden Dawn's "Watcher within" (*GD* III, p. 273), as opposed to the analytic mind, the barren "Watcher without" (*GD* III, p. 273).

64 In the eclectic language of Theosophy, the nameless shapeless ones – the purer spirits – are known as the Agnishvâtta; in cabalistic terms, they would have their counterparts in the residents of the Briatic world. The Seven Lights, on the other hand, were known to Theosophy as the Barhishad: cabalistically, the dwellers in the Jetziratic world, the world below Briah. For a gloss on the distinction between the Agnishvâtta and the Barhishad, cf. *TSD* II, p. 81; and see the same volume for discussions of why the Agnishvâtta have no shape (p. 82), and of why they rather than the Barhishad occupy the place of Prometheus in the occult schema (pp. 83, 99), and of how apt the Promethean comparison is (p. 430).

For discussion of why "the Seven Lights bowed in their dance and wept" (*VP* 174), cf. Blavatsky's description of how "the seven Planetary Gods... danced around [the sun] the sacred circular dance, the symbol of the rotation of the planets" (*TSD* III, p. 316). The Seven Lights weep because, like the sidhe of Irish folklore, they exceed man in power but not in potential; once man receives the gift of divine wisdom, here symbolized by Yeats's "Immortal Rose", he has the potential to become a being superior to the Seven Rishis themselves. For elaboration of this idea, cf. *TSD* II, p. 254; and for Blavatsky's most specific comments on the Seven Lights and their analogues in other mythologies, cf. *TSD* III, pp. 327-8.

As regards earlier versions of the poem, the original first stanza describes how "the crimson Rose" was stolen from "God's garden" (11. 1–2); and one possible source of the image would have been Waite's *Real History*, which not only spoke of God's garden but identified the idea of stealing the paradisiacal Rose as a widespread mythological belief (pp. 11–12).

Finally, the 1898 note to the poem speaks of how "certain old mythologies" imagine the "Seven Lights" and "the Dragon" as "encircl[ing] the Tree of Life" (*VP* 174), images so widespread in Yeats's occult sources that it would be pointless to speak of "The Poet pleads with the Elemental Powers" as reflecting any one source in particular. For general occult background on the Polar Dragon and the Seven Lights, cf. *TSD* I, p. 438; on the Polar Dragon and the Tree of Life, cf. *TSD* I, pp. 434–42, 721. Blavatsky also offers an image of the Polar Dragon as stretched across the universe (*TSD* II, p. 372) in coils (*TSD* II, pp. 373, 531), its body "luminous" (*TSD* II, p. 427); and it may be possible to hear in these latter references an echo of Yeats's "Polar Dragon" with its "heavy rings uncoiled from glimmering deep to deep" (*VP* 174). The Golden Dawn also drew on the imagery of the Seven Lights (*GD* IV, p. 222), Polar Dragon (*GD* IV, pp. 221, 231, 236), and Tree of Life (*GD* IV pp. 231, 305), while Theosophy spoke of how the "Spirit of God" – in one branch of theosophical symbolism, the Universal Serpent – sleeps "before each new "Creation"" (*TSD* II, p. 530) – a theory that would appear to be lurking in the background of Yeats's description of the Polar Dragon as sleeping when the Promethean moment arrives (*VP* 174).

65 For a description of one such invocation, cf. R. G. Torrens's *The Golden Dawn: The Inner Teachings*, p. 188.

66 The image recurs in the 1897–8 drafts of *The Speckled Bird*, with Michael referring to Margaret as "a pilgrim crying of dim and distant things" (*VSB* 133).

67 The equation between the sun and the male principle is clearer in later versions of the poem; as it appeared in 1892 and 1895, the lyric left open the possibility that Love was fleeing from both lovers rather than from the woman (*VP* 121). For a brief definition of the Pilgrim Soul, cf. *TSD* I, p. 45 n.; for further elucidation of the concept, cf. *Comte de Gabalis*, p. viii; *Isis Unveiled*, Vol. I, p. 328; *Virgin of the World*, p. 98; *The Secret Doctrine*, Vol. I, pp. 198, 229, 288; Vol. II, pp. 266, 768–9; Vol. III, p. 374; *The Key to Theosophy*, pp. 167, 182, 351; *The Golden Dawn*, Vol. IV, p. 212. For a variant of the images of sun and moon, in which the journey of the pilgrim through its rounds of incarnation is compared to the journey of a comet through space, cf. *TSD* I, pp. 224, 269.

[2]

The Moon upon the Tide: Yeats and the Philosophy of Irish Fairylore

When in 1888 Ernest Rhys set the young Yeats to collecting the fairy and folktales of the Irish peasantry for publication, the folklore that would come to be what Yeats called the "chief influence" (*UP2* 328) on his youth already had a varied history behind it. For all practical purposes, it was Thomas Crofton Croker's elegant and surprisingly comprehensive *Fairy Legends and Traditions of the South of Ireland* (1825–8) that first stirred the Irish folktale from its hidden sleep. Like the majority of his nineteenth-century successors in the field, Croker (1798–1854) was less a folklorist than a literary man with a deep interest in folklore; and his literary bias was to turn his *Fairy Legends* into recastings rather than recordings, thus rendering them more the work of an individual than the words of the storytellers themselves. In his later and more studious collection of tales, *Beside the Fire* (1890), the more diligent Douglas Hyde (1860–1949) cast a baleful retrospective eye on the work of Croker and, for that matter, of most of the rest of the nineteenth-century folklorists who had followed in Croker's path.

> It is not devoid of interest to watch the various garbs in which the sophisticated minds of the ladies and gentlemen who trifled in such matters, clothed the dry bones [of the stories they had collected]. But when the skeletons were thus padded round and clad, although built upon folk-lore, they were no longer folk-lore themselves, for folk-lore can only find a fitting garment in the language that comes from the mouths of those whose minds are so primitive that they retain with pleasure those tales which the more sophisticated invariably forget (*BTF*, pp. xvi–xvii).

Arch though they are, these remarks make for an accurate description of the tendency of the literary school of Irish folklore – in the nineteenth century, by far the dominant school – to prettify the rude. But what Hyde rightly perceived as a defect in a work like *Fairy Legends* had been a virtue when the book first appeared. The grace that Croker lent to the stories he had collected had indeed reft them of their original flavor. But it had also gained for those stories a wide and immediate audience – the first printing of *Fairy Legends* sold out within a few days – and, in the process, had touched off an interest in a folklore that had been lying more or less dormant until Croker's volumes appeared.[1] Popularizers may not serve a cause, but they often serve a purpose; and though his criticisms of *Fairy Legends* and its heirs were accurate, Hyde was himself working out of a climate of interest that Croker had in large measure originally helped to create.

The middle years of the nineteenth century saw various learned journals[2] and a wide variety of full-length books taking up the theme that *Fairy Legends* had announced. The work went on intermittently, with brief periods of sustained interest followed by lapses of silence; but all of it, calm and momentary turbulence alike, was a gradual preparation for a cresting of the wave. It was in the late 1880s that the Irish folktale began to rise towards full prominence among readers,[3] and it came into prominence then because the climate for its reception was by then finally right. By the late 1880s the hunt for the hidden Ireland was moving towards full cry. The Gaelic Union had already gathered into its general sphere of influence the more dedicated of the men who would go on to form the Gaelic League in July of 1893; the Gaelic Athletic Association had begun to harness the emerging interest in traditional games. Language, music, and games were three of the more prominent trophies that the nationally minded were actively promoting. A fourth, and for a young writer like Yeats the most important, was the folktale.

In June of 1894 Yeats described "the recent revival of Irish literature" as "very largely a folk-lore revival, an awakening of interest in the wisdom and ways of the poor, and in the poems and legends handed down among the cabins" (*UP1* 326).[4] He had earned his right to speak out on the matter; he had by then become not only the leading figure in the literary movement but, in the company of Hyde, one of the most prominent proponents of the folklore revival – and, for that matter, one of its first. Yeats as a young man had a remarkable knack for anticipating trends. The "moment of supernatural insight" (*Au* 199) that impelled his 1891 prediction of the coming literary revival is the best-known instance of this ability; and though he made no equally striking prediction about the revival of interest in folklore, the publication of his *Fairy and Folk Tales of the Irish Peasantry* in September 1888 was to prove one of the earliest harbingers of a renewed and radically expanded Irish interest in tales told beside the fire. There was no writer on whom the revival he helped to create would leave more intriguing marks than it did on Yeats himself.

In 1889 Yeats claimed to have read "most, if not all" of the recorded Irish fairytales that had been translated into English (*UP1* 139). Though he was talking about a body of work that by then numbered thousands of pages, he was not overstating his case. Within a brief span of time he had mastered all the Irish fairylore and folklore to which an English-language reader could gain access; and the sheer breadth of his acquaintance with his materials is the first thing that makes a survey of his relationship to the Irish fairy tradition a troublesome undertaking.

The second and more crucial difficulty is that Yeats not only read these works but put them to uses that were at once extensive and complex. If it were possible to gather under one cover all the early writings based on his researches into fairylore, the book would be a long one. His annotated anthology of *Fairy and Folk Tales* was shortly to be joined by his anthology of *Irish Fairy Tales* (1892), and these two editions would in turn be joined by the varied tales that Yeats himself collected and published in his own *The Celtic Twilight* (1893, 1902). There are also all the many early essays and stories and reviews that detailed Ireland's variegated views of the dim kingdom and its inhabitants; there are early plays like *The Island of Statues* (1885) and *The Land of Heart's Desire* (1894); there are the early fairy lyrics, several of which Yeats later dropped from the canon. It is the overall thrust of this expanse of work that the present chapter will discuss, with "The Wanderings of Oisin" being reserved for discussion in the chapter to follow. The central concerns of both chapters will be not simply with Yeats's borrowings from his Irish sources – a topic much treated of late[5] – but with the ways in which he modified what he borrowed to suit his own views and purposes. Earlier writers on the sidhe had been hard pressed to explain the complex relationship that obtained between the sidhe and their mortal neighbors. In his early writings, Yeats was to echo the various basic accounts they had offered, and then to extend the philosophy of Irish fairylore by proffering a new and more sophisticated explanation of his own.

Yeats listed his folklore "authorities" in the endnotes to *Fairy and Folk Tales* and *Irish Fairy Tales*, and the lists were long ones. Croker and his nineteenth-century successors: William Carleton, Samuel Lover, Patrick Kennedy, Fr John O'Hanlon, D. R. McAnally, Jeremiah Curtin, Douglas Hyde, Sir William and Lady Wilde, and more. Perhaps the simplest way of sifting all this material into intelligibility is to begin with the book of Irish folklore that the Yeats of the late eighties himself most admired.[6] "The best book" since the seminal work of Croker, he called it in 1888 (*FFT* 7). By 1892 his cautious early praise of Croker had given way to outright distrust, but his admiration for the other book remained; *Irish Fairy Tales* described it as "the most poetical and ample collection of Irish folk-lore yet published" (*IFT* 299). This was Lady Wilde's *Ancient Legends* (1887).

Ancient Legends contains a recurring phrase that epitomizes the broadcast attitude of ambivalence that Irish fairylorists had towards the Irish fairies: it speaks of the sidhe as having power over men "whether for good or evil" (*AL*, pp. xii, 29, 38, 72, 143, 257). In drawing on that phrase, Lady Wilde was echoing the wariness of her predecessors in Irish folklore studies, at least four of whom had used the same or similar words to describe a fairy kingdom that refused to be firmly defined.[7] She was also skirting an issue that neither she nor her predecessors ever did manage to resolve: whether the good or evil aspect of the fairies was dominant. On this topic *Ancient Legends* changes face almost from page to page. The fairy is

> a bright and beautiful creation, only living for pleasure, music, and the dance, and rarely malignant or ill-natured, except when their dancing grounds are interfered with, or when they are not treated with proper generous consideration in the matter of wine (p. 128).

Yet

> it is on Fridays that the fairies have the most power to work evil; therefore Friday is an unlucky day to begin work, or to go on a journey, or to have a wedding; for the spirits are then present everywhere, and hear and see everything that is going on, and will mar and spoil all they can, just out of malice and jealousy of the human race (p. 210).

At the same time,

> the fairies are born aristocrats, true ladies and gentlemen, and if treated with proper respect are never in the least malignant or ill-natured (p. 143).

But if they are "never" in the least malignant, it is also true that man is

> never to trust the fairies, for with all their sweet words and pleasant ways and bright red wine, they are full of malice and envy and deceit, and are always ready to ruin a poor fellow and then laugh at him, just for fun, and for the spite and jealousy they have against the human race (p. 267).

The same spirit of contradiction marks the discussions in *Ancient Legends* of more particular types of fairy activity. Lady Wilde's remarks on glamouring provide a background against which an early Yeats poem like "The Stolen Child" may be re-examined with happy results, but a confused background it is. The general description of the lives that stolen mortals live in fairyland runs in an apparently familiar mainstream of happily-ever-after:

> Their friends mourn for them as dead with much lamentation, but in reality they are leading a joyous life down in the heart of the hill, in the fairy palace with the silver columns and the crystal walls (pp. 132–3).

But the problem with this plain statement is that the specific stories of glamouring that *Ancient Legends* retells do not really support it. Wilde recounts a handful of glamouring stories that wrap up happily (pp. 64–7, 88–9, 106, 248–50, 258), but in the final analysis they are small fish running against a dark tide. The antidote to her remarks about silver columns and crystal walls comes with remarks like this:

> [The fairies] have no objection to offer to mortals the subtle red wine at the fairy banquets, which lulls the soul to sleep and makes the reason powerless. The young men that they beguile into their fairy palaces become their bond-slaves, and are set to hard tasks (p. 259).

The joyous life down in the heart of the hill clearly has its hidden side. Other of the *Ancient Legends* describe how the sidhe use savage force in their attempt to steal a young woman (pp. 30–2), or glamourings that conclude in the sudden and violent death of the mortal stolen (pp. 73–4, 75–6, 76–8, 80, 231). In one case the fairies torture a young boy to death by beating him and by gradually cutting off his breath (pp. 46–7); in another they beat the parents (pp. 229–31). Stolen mortals who manage to make their way back to the human world often re-emerge in hideous form, sometimes as decaying corpses (p. 91); or the sidhe will grow tired of a glamoured young woman as she begins to age, and send her back, "old and ugly", to her earthly companions (p. 114). At one point Lady Wilde refers to a kidnapped mortal as a "victim" (p. 128); at another she calls the practice of glamouring "evil" (p. 229); at a third she describes it as the work of an "evil spirit" (p. 78). The *Ancient Legends* testify to the accuracy of her word choice.

There are basically two reasons for these inconsistencies. The first is that *Ancient Legends* was Lady Wilde's anthology, but William Wilde's collection. In reviewing *Ancient Cures* (1890), her second book of folk and fairylore, Yeats describes how both her books came into being. William Wilde, he writes, had "collected a vast bulk of tales and spells and proverbs", and then

> threw all his gatherings into a big box, and thence it is that Lady Wilde has quarried the materials of her new book... I heartily wish they had been better and more scientifically treated, but I scarce know whom to blame: Lady Wilde, Sir William Wilde, his collectors, or the big box (*UP1* 170).[8]

This was diplomatic on Yeats's part, since *Ancient Legends* was manifestly a patchwork. Its stories are drawn from numerous and widely divergent local traditions. The book can claim in one breath that the fairies are never malignant, and in another that they are full of malice, because Lady Wilde either did not bother or simply had not been afforded the opportunity to discriminate among the varied traditions on which she was drawing.

The second reason for the inconsistencies cuts deeper. The confusion that characterized *Ancient Legends* in 1887 was a new bud on a gnarled bough. Virtually every Irish fairylorist, whether predecessor or contemporary of Wilde, was likewise uncertain about whether the sidhe were agents of good or evil or both; Yeats himself could speak in the same sentence of the "horrible doings" of a fairy tribe that was itself "innocent and graceful and kindly" (*UP1* 181). There are a number of ways of resolving inconsistencies like these; and even amid the difficulties she faced, Lady Wilde would light on several of them.[9] If the fairies are workers of both good and evil, she said, then there must be two kinds of fairies:

> there are two parties amongst the fairy spirits, one a gentle race that loves music and dancing, the other that has obtained power from the devil, and is always trying to work evil (*AL*, p. 73).

The merit of this Christian solution lies in its accessibility: there was ample precedent for the idea that forces of absolute good and forces of absolute evil were both at work in the world. That said, it should be added that adopting a manichean view of faery raised more problems than it solved. For one thing, the idea went too far; the Irish folk tradition out of which Wilde was working simply furnished too little hard evidence that the sidhe were in the habit of consorting with the devil. In discussing Wilde's idea of fairy demonism in his own *Fairy and Folk Tales*, Yeats asserts that "no other Irish writer gives this tradition" (*FFT* 48). This was not entirely true, since several earlier Irish writers whose work Yeats knew had at least glanced towards what John O'Hanlon called the "intimate relations" between "demonology and fairyism".[10] Nor did Yeats himself entirely reject the manichean view. In his *Irish Fairy Tales* he would adapt the two-party theory described by Wilde to his own purposes, couching it more gently:

> Irish Fairies divide themselves into two great classes: the sociable and the solitary. The first are in the main kindly, and the second full of all uncharitableness (*IFT* 383).[11]

But while "sociable" and "solitary" come closer to describing the nineteenth–century Irish view of the sidhe than do "gentle" and "demoniac", neither Wilde's formulation nor Yeats's tempering of it was completely satisfactory. The second and more troublesome problem with the manichean explanation was that it failed to cover the known facts. *Ancient Legends* spoke of two distinct faces of faery; but the Irish fairytales on which Wilde and Yeats based their observations more often spoke of but a single face, and said that it could smile or frown at will.[12] There was need for a second and more comprehensive hypothesis than the idea of two tribes, and here too Wilde would propose one. The sidhe were by and large good neighbors, she argued, "and ready enough to help any one they like"; but, she adds, they are "often very malicious if offended or insulted" (*AL*, p. 91), in which cases "their vengeance is swift and sure" (*AL*, p. 105). Unlike the idea of demonism, this proposition had the advantage of a clear and tangible base in Irish fairylore. The stories of fairy vengeance that Lady Wilde recounts find hundreds of counterparts elsewhere in Irish fairytales. *Ancient Legends* was on solid ground when it described the fairies' resentment of any maltreatment by mortals (pp. 57–9), or any intrusion on their privacy (pp. 114–15), or the putting up of a building on one of their accustomed pathways (pp. 234–5), and their particular resentment of men whom they regarded as ungenerous or overly thrifty (pp. 46–7, 49–52, 97, 142–3). This was a sensible way of accounting alike for the smiles and frowns of the sidhe, and again Yeats follows the lead; when the fairies do someone an injury, he asserts in *Irish Fairy Tales*, "it is nearly always deserved" (*IFT* 384).

Here the matter might have come to rest, the ambivalences of fairydom been neatly resolved, were it not for that single troubling phrase: nearly always. The vengeance theory covered more cases more satisfactorily than did the idea of good and evil factions, but it did not cover them all. It did not cover those more arbitrary occasions when the sidhe ruined a man and then laughed at him, "just for fun" and for "spite" (*AL*, p. 267) or "just out of malice and jealousy of the human race" (*AL*, p. 210). Clearly the face that smiled or frowned at will could also sometimes frown at random. There was active hatred here. On what strange cause?

Most of the fairylorists whose work Yeats studied eventually address the question of where the sidhe originated. Yeats had his choice of explanations, and in his *Fairy and Folk Tales* he chose to follow, sometimes word for word,[13] the account offered by William Wilde's *Irish Popular Superstitions* (1852). Yeats's version:

> Who are they? "Fallen angels who were not good enough to be saved, nor bad enough to be lost," say the peasantry. "The gods of the earth," says the Book of Armagh. "The gods of pagan Ireland," say the Irish antiquarians, "the *Tuatha De Danān*, who, when no longer worshipped and fed with offerings, dwindled away in the popular imagination, and now are only a few spans high" (*FFT* 11).

There were varying theories about why the sidhe had fallen from heaven in the first place. *Ancient Legends* grouped them with the rebellious angels, and said they had been cast out of heaven as a punishment for their pride (pp. 256–7). But a theory at once more widespread and more complex held that they had remained neutral during the battle between the armies of Michael and Lucifer. The archangel's triumph landed the satanic forces in hell. The neutral angels – "not good enough to be saved, nor bad enough to be lost" – fell at the same time, but because they had taken no active part in the revolt they did not fall as far. Soft earth stopped their descent; and the earth has had fairies since. It is the second of these two accounts that *Fairy and Folk Tales* draws on; and though Yeats would later come to see the sidhe almost exclusively as the descendants of the Tuatha Dé Danaan, in *Fairy and Folk Tales* he was more inclined to view them as heaven's refugees than as "gods of the earth" or the dwindled remnant of Ireland's former rulers.[14] "There is", according to his introduction to that volume, "much evidence to prove them fallen angels" (*FFT* 11).[15]

To understand what it meant to see the fairies as fallen angels is to come a fair way towards understanding Yeats's early attempts to formulate a philosophy of Irish fairylore. This pantheology had its niceties. Adoption of the idea that the sidhe were divine castoffs brought with it adoption of a corollary: that the sidhe were no friends of man. And it was from meditation on man's last end that the corollary derived.

If there were shadings of opinion about where the sidhe had come from, there was outright disagreement over where they would end up. That they would remain on earth until the end of earthly time was certain, but eternity was a troubler. When it came to the question of what the judgment day would bring for beings neither good enough for heaven nor bad enough for hell, Yeats's sources were divided. William Wilde said that the Irish peasantry "believe that God will admit the fairies into his palace on the day of judgment" (*IPS*, p. 125), but in this opinion he was more or less alone. His wife said that the sidhe would simply vanish on "judgment day, when they are fated to pass into annihilation, to perish utterly and be seen no more" (*AL*, p. 256). In *The Fireside Stories of Ireland* (1870), Patrick Kennedy (1801–73) claimed that their ultimate fate was "uncertain" (p. 131), and William Carleton (1794–1869), in *Tales and Stories of the Irish Peasantry* (1845), agreed (p. 72).[16] But in his earlier *Legendary Fictions of the Irish Celts* (1866), Kennedy had declared that the sidhe would probably end up with Satan's armies after all – they "all live in fear of utter condemnation at the Day of Judgment" (p. 97) – and in this he had the support of Crofton Croker, whose *Fairy Legends* at one point flatly described the sidhe as "damned" (p. 28).[17]

Despite these divergences of opinion, Yeats's sources were agreed on at least one foreboding element of the issue: that the fairies' suspicion that they might not – or conviction that they would not – be saved had made them the foes of man. Lady Wilde's summary of the matter might fairly be taken as typical. The fairies

> remember that they were once angels in heaven though now cast down to earth, and though they have power over all the mysteries of Nature, yet they must die without hope of regaining heaven, while mortals are certain of immortality. Therefore this one sorrow darkens their life, a mournful envy of humanity: because, while man is created immortal, the beautiful fairy race is doomed to annihilation (*AL*, p. 132).

The Irish peasants may fear the sidhe, but according to Lady Wilde they never offer them worship: "for they look on the Sidhe as a race quite inferior to man" (*AL*, p. 39). Contrariwise, the fairies "look on mortals as of much higher race than themselves" (*AL*, p. 73). Here, then, was a third and more complex way of accounting for the malice of the sidhe, a means of explaining why the faces glancing out at man from the "happy" other world sometimes frowned without apparent provocation, and sometimes did more than frown. Kennedy puts it directly: "Their dislike of the human race arises from envy of [human] destiny, which they regard as the filling of the heavenly seats lost by themselves" (*LFIC*, p. 97). "Their proceedings towards man", he adds, are "of a capricious, if not baleful character, and their interference in human affairs [is] deprecated by all right-minded and timorous people" (*LFIC*, p. 84). Even William Wilde, the lone salvationist among Yeats's authorities, recognized that the only thing preventing the sidhe from attacking man still more directly was their hope that good behavior might leave them eligible to rejoin the elect: "were it not for this ... they would strike or enchant men and cattle much more frequently" (*IPS*, p. 125). And Carleton pushed the same idea to an unequivocal conclusion. It is fortunate for man that the sidhe are uncertain about the possibility of salvation, he writes, since "nothing but their hopes of salvation prevent them from at once annihilating the whole human race" (*T&S*, p. 72).

In 1902 Yeats found a man near Kiltartan who sided with Carleton; he told the poet that the sidhe "have the hope of heaven or they wouldn't leave one on the face of the earth" (*UP2* 275). But in the eighties his place in the dispute about the last end of the sidhe was basically in accord with views like those espoused in the *Ancient Legends* that he then admired. Like Lady Wilde, he held that the fairies "must die without hope of regaining heaven" (*AL*, p. 132), and that immortality was a privilege reserved for mortals. So says the fairy song that appeared in the 1885 verse play *The Island of Statues*, the final scene of which Yeats reprinted in the first edition of *The Wanderings of Oisin and Other Poems*:

> A man has a hope for heaven,
> But soulless a fairy dies,
> As a leaf that is old, and withered and cold
> When the wint'ry vapours rise. (*VP* 643)

And for Yeats, as for Wilde, the consolation of the sidhe comes with their knowledge that until their demise they are to "have power over all the mysteries of Nature" (*AL*, p. 132).

> So let us dance on the fringed waves,
> And shout at the wisest owls
> In their downy caps, and startle the naps
> Of the dreaming water-fowls,
>
> And fight for the black sloe-berries,
> For soulless a fairy dies,
> As a leaf that is old, and withered and cold
> When the wint'ry vapours rise. (*VP* 644)

Elsewhere in the same volume, specifically in the early lyric titled "The Priest and the Fairy", Yeats follows the lead of tales like that told by Patrick Kennedy, who had written that "sometimes [the fairies] experience a slight hope that their place may not be with Satan and his angels". At moments like these they press "holy and wise mortals", generally priests, "to give judgment on their case" (*LFIC*, p. 97). Kennedy follows this prefatory comment with a folktale in which a country priest, returning from a sick call, loses his way in a darkened field and is overtaken by the sidhe. One of their number asks him if the fairies have a chance for salvation, and promises to reward an affirmative answer. The priest is at first afraid; but when he recovers the courage to speak, he asks the sidhe if they "adore and love the Son of God", and "receive[s] no answer but weak and shrill cries, and the rushing of wings" (*LFIC*, p. 99). The wings bear their sad owners away, and the priest makes his way back home.

Tales of this type were too common a feature in nineteenth-century Irish folklore[18] for a reader to claim the Kennedy version as the primary model for "The Priest and the Fairy". What may be said is that the narrative progress of both the Kennedy story and the Yeats lyric is the same. Kennedy sets his tale in an isolated field; Yeats sets his in the isolated "heart of the woodland" (*VP* 728). Both story and poem describe an interchange between a priest and the sidhe. In both, a fairy asks about the chances of the sidhe for salvation, and promises to reward a positive response; the priest is afraid to speak, then answers in the negative; and the sidhe vanish. More to the point, in both story and poem the sidhe are told that they will die "soulless". But the spirit of playful mockery that charges Yeats's poem leaves open the question of whether the belief about the last end of the fairies that Yeats's priest voices is a belief that the poet shares. The priest as rendered here is less Kennedy's holy and wise mortal than a figure of fun; the poem would be anti-clerical if it were serious. It made its first and final appearance in the first edition of *The Wanderings of Oisin and Other Poems* in January 1889, and two months after its appearance Yeats published an essay that made it sound as though belief in the soullessness of the sidhe was indeed the property of the priests alone. "In Ireland", the essay runs, the sidhe

> have been permitted by the priests to consult them on the state of their souls. Unhappily the priests have decided that they have no souls, that they will dry up like so much bright vapour at the last day (*CT* 106).

Here it becomes necessary to see the young Yeats as engaged in a wary negotiation with his source materials, sorting through his predecessors' views of the supernatural world of the sidhe, rejecting or modifying certain of those views even as he continued to echo certain others. It was not simply the priests who had "decided" that the sidhe lacked souls. In March 1890 Yeats echoed his 1885 assertion that "soulless a fairy dies", this when he described the sidhe as "nations of gay creatures, having no souls; nothing in their bright bodies but a mouthful of sweet air" (*UP1* 173). And in June 1889, three months after the essay describing the priests' "unhappy" belief that the sidhe would dry up like bright vapour at the last day, a piece by Yeats in the *Scots Observer* detailed a view of the fairies' last end that was precisely the same as the view that he had attributed to the priests. Here the young fairylorist is describing the fairy habit of stealing children or newlyweds:

> Sometimes a new-wed bride or a new-born baby goes with them into their mountains; the door swings to behind, and the new-born or the new-wed moves henceforth in the bloodless land of Faery; happy enough, but doomed to melt out at the last day like bright vapour, for the soul cannot live without sorrow (*CT* 80).

In this Yeats is once again following the line of thought that declared that the sidhe would neither be saved nor damned but simply "doomed to annihilation" (*AL*, p. 132). It is worth establishing that he did, since acceptance of that basic premise carries with it acceptance of a number of ominous derivations. Central among them was the notion that the sidhe, heaven's door shut against them, despised the race for whom that same door would one day swing open, and cast themselves as Cain against man's Abel. Their acts of jealous vengeance against their human neighbors ranged from the simply mischievous to the flatly sadistic; and no action of their devising was more finely wrought with malice than the practice of glamouring, since in glamouring they had found a means of destroying man's soul. As John O'Hanlon's *Irish Folk Lore* (1870) had it, the glamoured mortal was forever "condemned to endure... all the vicissitudes of a constrained exile from both earth and heaven" (p. 43). To allow yourself to be glamoured, then, was to conclude a Faustian bargain. You purchased life in the heart of the hill; but you were thenceforth doomed, like the sidhe themselves, to disappear on the last day. Otherworldly misery loved its mortal company, and bought it with alms for oblivion.

Not that the alms lacked appeal: on the contrary. The Irish folk tradition included a good number of stories in which mortals were glamoured by force, but what is by far the more typical story has the sidhe luring men into their domain with promises of unending joy and wealth beyond measure. *FFT* includes a good example of the type, the anonymous "Loughlea (Lake of Healing)" (pp. 185–9).[19] A young man finds himself "before a most elegant palace built with jewels, and all manner of fine stones". Out of the palace issue "a hundred ladies and gentlemen, as fine as any in the land". Their leader tries to persuade the young man to join them by telling him that he can "stop here and live in a palace". When the young man declines the offer, the leader raises the stakes: "Here you can walk through gardens loaded with fruit and flowers." Again the offer is declined, and again a more attractive offer succeeds it. The appeal in this case is to the impoverished young man's empty belly: "Here you can eat and drink of the best." But again the man demurs, declaring his preference for the poorer but more familiar life he has always led; and the sidhe are forced to return him to the earth (*FFT* 188–9).

In its main elements the story is a common one. The general run of nineteenth-century Irish fairylore agreed that the sidhe had no ultimate power over mortals strong enough to resist their enticements, and the mode of enticement – "here you can eat and drink of the best" – is likewise typical. But straightforward as the story may be, it raises delicate problems. That there were two faces of faery was clear. It was also clear that there was need for an explanation that could comprehend both faces at once. The two-tribes theory held that the faces were distinct, masks benign and malicious respectively; the vengeance theory argued that there was but a single face, and that it smiled except when provoked; the view of the sidhe as fallen angels implied that the one same face could smile or frown as it chose. In his early prose and verse, Yeats glanced towards each of these accounts; but what he came to realize was that none of the three could account for a face that smiled in order to mask a frown. Here you can live in a palace, said a smiling host, Come in that you may be damned. There was something subtler and more insidious going on here than any reference to vengeance or fallen angels could explain; there was need of a fourth, a subtler and more insidious, hypothesis. Yeats's early work contains one.

Yeats had probably read Keats's "Lamia" while still in his adolescence, but for a certainty he had read it no later than early 1889. His earliest published reference to the poem comes but a single sentence after his above-cited remarks on the glamouring of "new-wed" brides or "new-born" children, remarks which themselves describe a lamian phenomenon: glamoured souls are "happy enough, but doomed to melt out at the last day like bright vapour" (*CT* 80). The Keats reference follows immediately thereafter:

> Somewhere about the beginning of last century appeared at the western corner of Market Street, Sligo,... not a palace, as in Keats's *Lamia*, but an apothecary's shop, ruled over by a certain unaccountable Dr. Opendon. Where he came from, none ever knew... He was dressed all in black, the same as [his] cat, and his wife... dressed in black likewise... The black doctor cured many people; but one day a rich patient died, and cat, wife, and doctor all vanished the night after (*CT* 80–1).

The sidhe and their kidnapped mortal companions melt away like vapour; Dr Opendon and his lamian retinue "vanish". There is a clear subtextual connection here between Yeats's use of the lamia theme and his view of the fairy kingdom, a connection that when pushed to its conclusion yields up the fourth and most comprehensive means of accounting for the dual countenance of the dim kingdom. Confronted by the fact that fairyland showed a pair of apparently contradictory faces, Yeats's early writings on the sidhe would resolve the contradiction by suggesting that one of the faces was false, and that the false face was the smiling one: the face of the lamia. The radiant welcome extended to man by the sidhe masked a threat to man by its radiance.

The work of Keats was the vehicle through which Yeats most directly suggested the connection between the lamia motif and the hidden philosophy of Irish fairylore, but he had by no means needed to turn to English Romantic poetry in order to make that connection. In regarding Keats's picture of an illusionary palace, he could only have rediscovered a variant of images that he had already come across dozens of times in his researches into Irish folklore, a folklore filled with vanishing acts. Wilde's *Ancient Cures*, for instance, told Yeats the tale of a young man who, like Yeats's own Oisin, had been glamoured by a woman of the sidhe who wanted him for her husband. When the young man's family managed to effect his rescue through a countercharm, "the form of the fairy bride seemed to melt into the sunset", even as Lamia "vanished",[20] and "the whole scene passed away like a mist" (p. 114). For Yeats there was nothing novel in this comparison of the sidhe to passing mist. Several years before the publication of *Ancient Cures*, Croker's *Fairy Legends* had told him the story of "Diarmid Bawn, the Piper", the title character of which meets a fairy troop, does them a service and earns a reward, whereupon the fairies "vanished like the mist of the mountain" (p. 359). But if Yeats did not find the image original, he surely found it affective. He improvised on Croker's version of it in January 1889, when he told the readers of his essay on "Irish Fairies, Ghosts, Witches, etc." that if a man takes his eyes off a lepracaun "the creature vanishes like smoke" (*UP1* 135); and in that same month "The Priest and the Fairy" averred that the cleric of the title lost sight of his sad visitor when the "fairy vanished from his sight" like "a wreath of smoke in wind-blown flight" (*VP* 730). March 1889 uncovered a somewhat darker image of evanescence, when in reviewing D. R. McAnally's *Irish Wonders* (1888) Yeats asserted that

> Celtic fairies are much like common men and women. Often the fairy-seer meets with them on some lonely road, and joins in their dance, and listens to their music; and does not know what people they are till the whole company melts away into shadow and night (*UP1* 139).

By July of 1891 he was willing to reveal Sligo's Biddy Hart as one of the sources of this sort of view of the sidhe, and to assert that the palaces of the sidhe were as ephemeral as their occupants. Biddy Hart

> will tell you of peasants who met the fairy cavalcade and thought it but a troop of peasants like themselves until it vanished into shadow and night, and of great fairy palaces that were mistaken, until they melted away, for the country seats of rich gentlemen (*IFT* 302).

And it was another old woman from Sligo, Ballysadare's "little old woman in a white cap" (*CT* 82), who first told Yeats the local legend of how

> a young man going at nightfall to the house of his just married bride, met in the way with a jolly company, and with them his bride. They were faeries, and had stolen her as a wife for the chief of their band. To him they seemed only a company of merry mortals. His bride, when she saw her old love, bade him welcome, but was most fearful lest he should eat the faery food, and so be glamoured out of the earth into that bloodless dim nation, wherefore she set him down to play cards with three of the cavalcade; and he played on, realizing nothing until he saw the chief of the band carrying his bride away in his arms. Immediately he started up, and knew that they were faeries; for slowly all that jolly company melted into shadow and night (*CT* 82).

Yeats first published this story in June of 1889, but the well-known poem he based on it – originally "The Stolen Bride", now "The Host of the Air" – did not appear in print until November of 1893. In its earliest versions the lyric transformed the image of "shadow and night" into a fading cloud:

> O'Driscoll got up from the grass,
> And scattered the cards with a cry,
> But the old men and dancers were gone,
> As a cloud faded into the sky.

But by the time the poem reappeared in 1899's *The Wind Among the Reeds* the ambiguous diction of those last two lines had disappeared, and the image of vanishing mist had once again come to the fore:

> O'Driscoll scattered the cards
> And out of his dream awoke:
> Old men and young men and young girls
> Were gone like a drifting smoke. (*VP* 145)[21]

In sum, it is clear that the association of images of evanescence with the sidhe – perhaps most beautifully when the fairy woman of "The Song of Wandering Aengus" ran and "faded through the brightening air" (*VP* 150) – forms part of a general pattern in Yeats's early work; and it is no less clear that the same association formed part of the general pattern of the Irish folktales that Yeats had made so central an object of his study. When in one of his notes to 1888's *Fairy and Folk Tales of the Irish Peasantry* he cautioned his readers that it "is to be remembered" that "the form of an enchanted thing is a fiction" (*FFT* 135), he was building on warnings like that issued by William Carleton in 1845. Carleton's *Tales and Stories* had informed Yeats that the sidhe had the power to take "a rude and ragged cave or a barren rock", and "by anointing your eyes with the oil of fiction, present it to you as a lordly palace, bedecked with light, beauty, and magnificence" (p. 370). Yeats and Carleton, moreover, were not the only Irish writers to discuss these delusive seats of kingship, any more than they were the only writers to discuss the false face of the Irish fairy kingdom. In the work of Carleton, Yeats found a generalized description of the world of the sidhe as lamian; elsewhere he would find the same idea given concrete expression in stories. One of many Irish tales of a like kind, William Wilde's "Lamia" was the story of Biddy Mannion.

As Wilde's *Irish Popular Superstitions* has it, Biddy Mannion is a young woman who gives birth to a son after a year of marriage. At the same time the fairies find themselves in need of a wetnurse for a newborn prince of the sidhe. They abduct the young mortal woman and bring her to a "'big house'... with trees growing all round it" and "a beautiful garden". Here she is greeted by a "polite" and "grand looking gentleman dressed all in scarlet". This king of the sidhe leaves her briefly alone, and she meets a mortal woman who had been glamoured earlier on. The woman is full of regret at being forced to live in the fairy kingdom, and warns Biddy Mannion that she too will be lost if she eats or drinks while within the palace. The king returns, and brings Biddy in to meet the fairy queen, "a darling, fine-looking lady" who is surrounded by her court, "a power of quality" dressed in brilliant red gowns and standing within a hall containing a table "laid out with all sorts of eating" (pp. 132, 133, 134). After Biddy finishes nursing the fairy prince, the king invites her to eat. She refuses, and her refusal breaks the charm. The queen tells her that she may go home, but before she leaves the king anoints her eyes with an ointment that clears her sight. And

> no sooner had he done so than she found herself in a frightful cave where she couldn't see her hand before her. "Don't be any ways afeard," says [the king]; "this is to let you know what kind of a people we are that took you away. We are the fallen angels that the people up above upon the earth call the fairies;" and then after a while she began to see about her, and the place was full of dead men's bones, and had a terrible musty smell; and after a while he took her into another room where there was more light, and here she found a wonderful sight of young children, and them all blindfolded, and doing nothing but sitting upon *pookauns* (p. 134).[22]

In the story of Biddy Mannion and the many[23] stories like it, the benign and malevolent aspects of faery merge in the face of the lamia. And here the lamia theme emerges in the single most threatening form that Irish folk belief admitted: the use of a compelling but finally illusory beauty to dazzle unwary mortals and guile them into oblivion. The word used to describe this process – "glamouring" – is itself lamian, since the glamour is only apparent. Another of Yeats's sources, Kennedy's "The Fairy Cure" (*LFIC*, pp. 117–21), takes but a single phrase to fix the lamian world of the sidhe precisely in place. Like Biddy Mannion, the woman in "The Fairy Cure" has been kidnapped by the fairies to serve their queen, in this case as midwife. She arrives at the fairy palace, and

> in the hall she was surprised to see an old neighbour, who had long been spirited away from the haunts of his youth and manhood, to the joyless, though showy life of the Sidhe caverns (*LFIC*, p. 118).

"Joyless, though showy" sums it up concisely. In the fabulous caves of the sidhe, beauty nestles in the lap of terror.

Whatever else may be said of this sort of world, it is safe to say that it is not solely the home of a folk whom William Wilde had earlier described as dancers by the streamlet's bank (*IPS*, p. 12). Nor is it a happy residence for the mortals whom the sidhe manage to entice inside. Shortly before recounting the story of Biddy Mannion, Wilde quotes without contradiction another old story in which glamouring is said to be the work of "demons" (*IPS*, p. 126). Thirty-six years later, his wife would elaborate the idea:

> The Sidhe look with envy on the beautiful young human children, and steal them when they can; and the children of a Sidhe and a mortal mother are reputed to grow up strong and powerful, but with evil and dangerous natures. There is also a belief that every seven years the fairies are obliged to deliver up a victim to the Evil One, and to save their own people they try to abduct some beautiful young mortal

girl, and her they hand over to the Prince of Darkness (*AL*, p. 7: cf. also pp. 38, 39, 40, 77, 90).

Vestiges of beliefs like these crop up randomly in Yeats's work of the period. Both the early and present versions of "The Wanderings of Oisin" refer to "glamours by demons flung" (*VP* 50), and Father Hart in *The Land of Heart's Desire* warns Maire Bruin against the sidhe in terms that are directly reminiscent of Wilde's:

> ... they are the children of the fiend,
> And they have power until the end of Time,
> When God shall fight with them a great pitched battle
> And hack them into pieces. (*VPl* 187)

And when his warning fails and Maire Bruin is taken, the priest describes the sidhe as "evil spirits [who] snatch their prey/Almost out of the very hand of God" (*VPl* 210). But if Yeats was interested enough in the idea put forth by the Wildes to put it to his own use on occasion, when he came to comment on the idea itself he not only felt obliged to qualify Lady Wilde's remarks but lapsed in recollection of precisely what she had said:

> Lady Wilde gives a gloomy tradition that there are two kinds of fairies – one kind merry and gentle, the other evil, and sacrificing every year a life to Satan, for which purpose they steal mortals. No other Irish writer gives this tradition – if such fairies there be, they must be among the solitary spirits (*FFT* 48).

This is far from an openhanded acceptance of the idea of fairy demonism, and Yeats's unwillingness to credit Wilde's claim fully is symptomatic of the fact that even his youthful views of the supernatural kingdom were to prove more sophisticated than those of his sources. If he hesitated over Lady Wilde's description of the sidhe as demoniac, he also hesitated over Carleton's above-cited vision of their residences as nothing more than "a rude and ragged cave or a barren rock" bedecked. He had that passage from Carleton in mind when, in October 1890, he wrote that "some say" that glamoured mortals "are happy enough", while

> others will have it that they are always wretched, longing for their friends, and that the splendour of the fairy kingdom is merely a magical delusion, woven to deceive the minds of men by poor little withered apparitions who live in caves and barren places. But this is, I suspect, a theological opinion, invented because all goblins are pagans. Many things about fairies, indeed, are most uncertain (*UP1* 177).

As with his early 1889 remarks about the priests' belief in the fairies' lack of souls, Yeats is here attempting to undermine a negative view of the sidhe by putting it in the mouth of "theological opinion". He is also implying that Carleton, like William Wilde with his stories of "frightful caves" and Kennedy with his unqualified comments on "joylessness", had portrayed the world of the sidhe in terms too black and white. They and other nineteenth-century Irish fairylorists had espoused a lamian tradition that held that the fairy kingdom seemed to be all beauty but was in fact all ugliness. Though the lamian reading of fairyland was the most complex of the several explanations that his sources had held out to him, Yeats none the less saw even this vision as somewhat too easy; and his unique contribution to the Irish fairy tradition came when he took a fairylore that had sketched in black and white and extended it through colors more subtle. He borrowed images from earlier writers in the field for his use – passing mist, drifting smoke – but his sense of the uses to which the theme of the lamia might be put was different from that of his predecessors. The lamian world that his early work describes is a world whose beauties are dangerous but real, and a world that poses a threat to man considerably more complex than a display of dead men's bones might suggest. It is in this world that a lyric like "The Stolen Child" moves; and a reading of this lyric in its contexts will thereby help to clarify the singularity of Yeats's relationship to the folk tradition that informed so much of his early work, a tradition he both mastered and advanced.

Fairy and Folk Tales of the Irish Peasantry was the first full book to have the name of Yeats attached to it. It opens with a diversified assortment of fairystories, then moves on to a section specifically devoted to changelings, the human-seeming semblances that the sidhe leave behind to disguise their theft of a mortal. Though "The Stolen Child" is not directly about a changeling, it was at the end of this section that Yeats chose to locate it. The effect of this placement was to turn the lyrics and tales with which he precedes his poem into warning signals, guideposts that point the reader towards tone. The tone thus revealed shades towards darkness. There are several stories of glamouring in the opening pages of *Fairy and Folk Tales*, and they all conclude unhappily. The work of Samuel Ferguson (1810–86) contributes two poems, "The Fairy Thorn" and "The Fairy Well of Lagnanay". The first, a poem that had some part to play in the shaping of the Celtic twilight,[24] advertises itself as a "tale of sorrow". It deals with the visit of four young women to a nearby place of fairy resort, where the "fairest of the four" is stolen against her will by the sidhe; her three companions, "wild" with "terror", pine away and die shortly thereafter (*FFT* 41–3). The second poem is likewise a "tale of woe"; it describes the theft of a young woman who visits a fairy well in the company of her sister, and concludes with a "pray'r" that no other mortal may meet a like fate (*FFT* 21–3). J. J. Callanan's "Cusheen Loo" goes a step further; his "song of fear" comes from within the fairy palace itself, and is sung by a young bride who sees her confinement by the fairies as the result of "a hateful spell" (*FFT* 37–8). And the poem that remains the most widely anthologized of Irish fairy verses, William Allingham's "The Fairies", opens Yeats's anthology by detailing an unhappy journey both There and Back Again. In Allingham's view of the matter, there are solid reasons why mortals daren't go a-hunting for fear of little men. The fairies

>   stole little Bridget
>   For seven years long;
>   When she came down again
>   Her friends were all gone.
>   They took her lightly back,
>   Between the night and morrow,
>   They thought that she was fast asleep,
>   But she was dead with sorrow.
>   They have kept her ever since
>   Deep within the lake,
>   On a bed of flag-leaves,
>   Watching till she wake. (*FFT* 13–14)

How direct an influence "The Fairies" had on "The Stolen Child" remains an open question, but the thematic connection between the two is evident. The Irish fairylore in which Yeats had steeped himself takes a dim view of the fate of glamoured mortals. The narratives Yeats selected for inclusion in *Fairy and Folk Tales* take a precisely similar view; so too does the Allingham poem that Yeats chose to place first in his collection. It is possible that "The Stolen Child" does otherwise, but it is not likely. Both Yeats's poem and Allingham's deal with kidnapped children; and if Bridget, "dead with sorrow", is not a sister to Yeats's "solemn-eyed" young boy, she is at least his close relation.

More immediately relevant – if only because more proximate – to "The Stolen Child" is the story in *Fairy and Folk Tales* that immediately precedes it. Letitia MacLintock's "Jamie Freel and the Young Lady", a tale-type of which Yeats found variants in several of his folklore sources,[25] recounts how the young Donegal man of the title meets the sidhe in a ruined castle on Halloween night. The sidhe are plotting to fly off to Dublin to steal a young woman from her house off Stephen's Green. They invite Jamie to join them, and fairy horses carry them to the successful theft in Dublin. On their way back to Donegal, Freel asks the fairies to allow the young lady to ride with him for a while; and as soon as they have set her on his horse he drops down from the sky and lands in front of his mother's house. Enraged by the loss of the girl, the fairies strike her dumb.

Jamie eventually restores her speech, marries her and becomes a rich man; but the malicious actions of the sidhe in the meanwhile are enough to make a reader take a closer survey of their actions in the poem by Yeats that follows. Early critical reaction to "The Stolen Child" typically described the poem as the work of "an imagination which is seeking out an escape from the world of everyday realities",[26] and noted that its "exquisitely romantic refrain" revealed "the literally escapist side of Yeats's early pathetic manner".[27] Remarks like these followed the lead of the well-known observation offered by Yeats himself. Revising his work as a prelude to the appearance of *The Wanderings of Oisin and Other Poems*, he wrote to Katharine Tynan:

I have noticed some things about my poetry, I did not know before, in this process of correction, for instance that it is almost all a flight into fairy land, from the real world, and a summons to that flight. The chorus to the "stollen child" [sic] sums it up – That it is not the poetry of insight and knowledge but of longing and complaint – the cry of the heart against neccesity [sic] (*CL1* 54–5).

But as the poet observed in another context, it is many years before one can believe enough in what one feels even to know what the feeling is (*Au* 103). Yeats was not always his own best exegete, and the letter to Katharine Tynan came from a young man who was hearing his work too closely to be able to tell all its resonance. Taken in isolation, the chorus to "The Stolen Child" may indeed fit its author's description of it as a summons to flight. But the poem as a whole confutes the image presented by the refrain. The version of the poem that appeared in *The Wanderings of Oisin and Other Poems* is in its essentials the same as that which appeared in *FFT*. Its first three stanzas oppose the apparent happiness of the fairy world to the apparent sorrow of the mortal realm.

> Where dips the rocky highland
>   Of Slewth Wood in the lake,
> There lies a leafy island
>   Where flapping herons wake
> The drowsy water rats;
> There we've hid our fairy vats
> Full of berries
> And of reddest stolen cherries.
> Come away, O human child!
> To the woods and waters wild
> With a fairy, hand in hand,
> For the world's more full of weeping than you can
>   understand.
>
> Where the wave of moonlight glosses
>   The dim grey sands with light,
> Far off by furthest Rosses
>   We foot it all the night,
> Weaving olden dances,
> Mingling hands and mingling glances
>   Till the moon has taken flight;
> To and fro we leap
>   And chase the frothy bubbles,
>   While the world is full of troubles
> And is anxious in its sleep.
> Come away, O human child!
> To the woods and waters wild
> With a fairy, hand in hand,
> For the world's more full of weeping than you can
>   understand.
>
> Where the wandering water gushes
>   From the hills above Glen-Car,

> In pools among the rushes
>   That scarce could bathe a star,
> We seek for slumbering trout,
>   And whispering in their ears
>   We give them evil dreams,
> Leaning softly out
>   From ferns that drop their tears
>   Of dew on the young streams.
> Come, O human child!
> To the woods and waters wild
> With a fairy, hand in hand,
> For the world's more full of weeping than you can
>   understand.

Had "The Stolen Child" stopped here, the poem would have been no more than a mellifluous nod in the direction of enchantment. But the fourth and concluding stanza describes the world that the boy lives in, and that world is diametrically the opposite of what the first three stanzas would lead the reader to expect. It is neither a world of weeping, nor "full of troubles", nor "anxious in its sleep"; these, it is worth remembering, are the words of the sidhe themselves, and the sidhe are notorious liars. Clearly they are lying to the boy. The first three stanzas are addressed to him directly – "the world's more full of weeping than you can understand" – and in these the fairies invite him to leave man's woe behind and come and join the dance. But in the final stanza they are speaking, not to the boy – here the world is more full of weeping than "he" can understand – but among themselves, and are therefore speaking more candidly. Once the boy has made his decision to join them, their description of the "weeping" world from which they are taking him undergoes a keen transformation:

>   Away with us he's going,
>   The solemn-eyed –
> He'll hear no more the lowing
>   Of the calves on the warm hillside,
> Or the kettle on the hob
>   Sing peace into his breast,
> Or see the brown mice bob
>   Round and round the oatmeal chest.
> For he comes, the human child,
> To the woods and waters wild
> With a fairy, hand in hand,
> For the world's more full of weeping than he can
>   understand.

Given the warm description of human ways that precedes it, it is impossible to take that final line at face value. The sole appropriate spirit for the speaking of it would be one of jubilant irony: The sorry young fool believed us. The boy does not in fact understand the fairies' claim that his world is full of weeping. But while the sidhe are bent on persuading him that he is simply too young to be able to comprehend the dark underside of life, the real reason why he does not understand the mournful human picture being held up to his notice is that it is not a picture he recognizes. The world he inhabits, and from which he is about to be stolen, is a world of the warm hearthside, protective, marked by a glad domesticity. Out of context, the middle lines of the last stanza –

> He'll hear no more the lowing
>   Of the calves on the warm hillside,
> Or the kettle on the hob
>   Sing peace into his breast –

describe a kind of dying. And a reading of them in context confirms them as the epitaph they are.

Yeats shared with the Irish folklorists on whose work he drew a belief that glamoured mortals were dead men. In the already cited *Scots Observer* essay, which appeared in print at about the same time (June 1889) as the above version of "The Stolen Child" (January 1889), he had asserted that glamoured souls were doomed to vanish on the day of judgment. In the meanwhile, said the same sentence in which that judgment appeared, they would be "happy enough": no more. The reason for the qualifier was a belief that was widespread in Yeats's folklore sources,[28] and a belief that Yeats himself subscribed to: that anyone taken by the sidhe spent the time between now and the last day in a kind of limbo. So the piece in the *Scots Observer* goes on to suggest. Having made his general remarks about the sad fate of the kidnapped, Yeats moves on to particular examples. The first of these is the tale of the goodlooking Mr Ormsby, who fell mysteriously ill and died. His wife knew who had taken him, and what manner of place they had gone to. "She knew well where he was", she said, "and it wasn't in heaven or hell or purgatory either" (*CT* 81). They dance all day who dance among the sidhe; but the dancers in the "bloodless dim nation" (*CT* 82) are pale shades, and humans who step to their tune abandon both the joys of life in this world and all hope of happiness in the next.

In short, those who conclude their bargain with the sidhe conclude a bad bargain. Yeats's description of glamoured souls as being happy enough is a description that might also apply to the fairy world as it appears in "The Stolen Child". It is by no means clear that the world that the sidhe inhabit is a place of pure ingenuous joy. The same fairies who lie to the boy about life in his own world are relentlessly coy when describing life in the world they would entice him to. They play in invisible pools, "pools among the rushes"; their vats are "hid" on a "leafy" island; and they dance beyond mortal vision, "far" off by "furthest" Rosses. There is quite literally more going on here than meets the human eye. Certain of Yeats's other early works suggest what that something might be.

The leafy island that lies "where dips the rocky highland / Of Slewth Wood in the lake" is Innisfree, and "The Stolen Child" is only one of several early works by Yeats in which the sidhe manage to lure a mortal onto the lake isle. In May of 1893 he published a lyric that identified Innisfree as the place where grew "The Danaan Quicken Tree", the "mournful" tree that the narrator of this "bitter tale" of Yeats's identifies as "a poison to all men" (*VP* 742–3). The slightly later story of "The Cradles of Gold" catalogues the sad fate of Whinny Hearne, who from her home on the shore of Lough Gill has a vision of "cradles of gold hanging between the trees and bushes on a little island that is under Sleuth Wood" (*UP1* 414). The following night she is taken by the sidhe, and remains among them until her brother-in-law faces down the fairy king whose servant she has become and extracts his promise that the woman will be released in a month's time. And so she is, but with a touch reminiscent of the fairies' treatment of the glamoured woman in "Jamie Freel"; from the time Whinny Hearne returns to the world, "her voice" is "low and her touch chill" (*UP1* 418).[29]

What early works like these would suggest, then, is that the leafy island to which the sidhe would entice the stolen child is a place that mortals visit at their peril. So too the sands of Rosses. The narrator of "The Danaan Quicken Tree", who after his visit to Innisfree leaves his human "service all undone" (*VP* 743), and Whinny Hearne, her voice low and touch chill, suffer the loss of their human vitality. But visitors to Rosses stand to lose something more. "Further Rosses is a very noted fairy locality", notes Yeats in the *Fairy and Folk Tales* in which "The Stolen Child" appeared, and therefore a place of "danger". Fall asleep there and wake to damnation:

> There is [on Further Rosses] a little point of rocks where, if anyone falls asleep, there is danger of their waking silly, the fairies having carried off their souls (*FFT* 289).

Unwary visitors to Innisfree suffer a decline in their human joy; and for the "solemn-eyed" stolen child, the decline has already begun. Unwary visitors to Rosses may suffer the loss of their souls; and it is this danger that the stolen child faces, and this danger that the sidhe so masterfully conceal. When they tell the child about the grief of life by his hearthside, they lie; and when they provide information about life in the waters and the wild, the information they provide is oblique. The process at work here, in short, is a process of seduction. The sidhe represent a threat to the boy; but the only overtly threatening note in the 1889 version of the poem is their admission that they give "evil" dreams to the dumb fish. And by 1895 even that much candour has disappeared. In all versions of "The Stolen Child" that appeared from 1895 onward, the "evil" dreams have become "unquiet". Lifted out of context, the shift from "evil" to "unquiet" has the effect of making the sidhe seem less malign. Looked at in the light of Irish fairylore, however, the switch has the effect of making their enticement of the boy more insidious rather than less. The threat to the child is greater because more successfully masked. "Evil" might have frightened him off; "unquiet" will not. And the boy goes.

"The Stolen Child", then, is a poem that describes a danger that has sense enough to keep its mouth shut until its hidden aims are accomplished, a danger decked out to allure. In this regard the poem is a Yeatsian variation on one of the dominant motifs of nineteenth-century Irish fairylore: the lamia motif, the grin of malice masked by a face smiling welcome. But there is more than a category to be quarried from this identification. A re-placing of the poem within the Irish fairy tradition, as Yeats understood that tradition, makes for several gains in understanding. Two among them are paramount.

The first is that a reading of "The Stolen Child" as lamian provides a means of resolving the contradictions that, in other possible readings, might threaten to unbalance the poem. In the poem's refrain the fairies present the human world as a sorry place; in the final stanza they describe it as happy. There are contradictory faces here, but the contradiction disappears in light of the poem's suggestion that one of the faces is false. To see the sidhe for the lords of deception that they are, and to see their happy other world as genuinely enticing but ultimately fatal to man, is to acknowledge that there is little really glamorous about their glamouring of the human child and, in the last analysis, nothing finally ambiguous about the poem itself. Admitting the reality of the dangers that the sidhe represent will in turn confirm the fact that the sympathies of "The Stolen Child" ultimately come to rest with the warm earthly hillsides and the kettles on the hob. The sidhe misrepresent this world to the boy in order to attract him to their own. What they will do with him once they have him there is uncertain, but his prospects are not promising. It is not apparent that the fairies who give evil dreams to the helpless trout have planned a blither reception for the equally helpless human; and if Yeats did not fully share Lady Wilde's belief that glamouring was a demoniac exercise, he none the less saw it as something just next. "Witches... receive their power... from evil spirits" and are "always feared and hated", he wrote, "the spells of the witch... smell of the grave" (*FFT* 133, 134). And glamouring, said the author of "The Stolen Child", was a "most malicious habit", a "habit worthy of a witch" (*IFT* 383).

The second and more central advantage to locating the poem within its Irish context is that its context helps to locate the general impulse that underlies a good number of Yeats's early poems. When we consider all the early writings that deal with man's relationship to the supernatural world, it becomes apparent that the influence of that world upon Yeats's youthful life and work was precisely that of the moon upon the tide. At times its strong pull draws him out towards mystic depths; then the influence wanes, and an earthly counterpull brings him, as it brought Oisin, back to the shores on which the frailer tents are pitched. This is not to say that the Yeats of the late eighties and nineties ever doubted the existence of the world beyond; indeed, the argument that the poet's views of the sidhe were more intricate than those of his predecessors depends upon the argument that Yeats not only believed in a world of the spirit but saw its pull as genuinely compelling. The fairies who tempt the human child promise him vats of berries, and promise waves of moonlight; and the greatest danger that confronts the child is that they are capable, if they choose, of making those promises good. Yeats may not have seen the world of the sidhe as wholly joyful, nor again as a fit home for the heart of man. But he did see it as beautiful; and it is in this above all that he differed from the earlier

Irish fairylorists who saw the land of faery as lamian in a more obvious sense of the term. Writers such as Carleton, Kennedy and the Wildes saw the attractions of faery as dangerous because illusory. Yeats saw them as dangerous because real. In "The Stolen Child" he shadowed forth a fairy world that owned attractions more spectacular than any the mundane world might offer, and described a pull of faery that, like the draw of the tide, was strong beyond the power of the child to resist it. What the boy was too young to realize was that tides can kill: that those who let themselves be drawn out towards an otherworldly beauty must drown to the beauty that the eye rests on daily. It is not wise, as Yeats noted in his instructive short essay on "The Eaters of Precious Stones" (1893), to seek "after beautiful and wonderful things with too avid a thirst" (*CT* 101). Unlike the boy in the poem, the author of "The Stolen Child" cast his lot with a happy world closer to home. It was not as flamboyant as faery; but its beauty was as substantial as the hearthside, and you did not need to barter eternity to take a seat by the warmth. Among the other things that the last verse of Yeats's lyric accomplishes, it summons the reader back to a simple worship of the day.

Far from positing the fairy world as an ideal, then, Yeats's early writings on the sidhe – whether prose, poetry, or drama – suggest his hesitancy to give himself over wholly to the supernatural world and his ultimate choice for a world whose workaday sounds sing peace into the breast. The backgrounds for his preference find a rich illustration in the interwoven text and contexts of "The Man who Dreamed of Faeryland".

Yeats considered this lyric one of the best of his early poems; so did the critical W. E. Henley (*Au* 129, *Mem* 39); and such perceptive critics as Edward Garnett, reader for Fisher Unwin, said that it might well be the very best of them all (*CL1* 247). There was no significant revision of the poem until the *Selected Poems* of 1929, and with good reason; of all the early poems, only "The Two Trees" and "The Wanderings of Oisin" achieve an internal balance as tight as that to be found here. A good share of this formal coherence is apparent simply on the level of narrative. Each of the four stanzas of the poem contrasts the limitations of human life or feeling with the less restricted lives of the supernatural island-dwellers. The first stanza opposes the love of the dreamer for a mortal woman to the immortal loves of the inhabitants of the islands, and the emphasis on a specific detail like the "silken dress" lends to his human love a localized, transient quality that makes it seem a poor substitute for a love that time cannot touch. His lack of money likewise comes off poorly in comparison to the bounty of the island, and again specific detail is the vehicle through which Yeats stresses earthly limits; this second stanza declares that the dreamer might have known, at best, "some prudent years". The third stanza contrasts his human anger with the calm of the lonely folk beyond, his longing for a surrounding grave with the "gentle feeling" that "wraps them like a fleece". And the final stanza knits the central images of the poem into cohesion. The dreamer was trapped on the seashore, bound between earth and ocean. The sea prevented him from reaching the islands of the sidhe; but if he left the shore and turned inland, abandoned his search for transcendence, he would find that the only alternative to immortality is oblivion, the grave below a Cope's Mountain[30] that lies against the sky like a cairn. Laid to rest there at last, he is reminded by the worms that spire about his bones that the earth–ocean tension that harried him into the grave has no share in the islanders' existence, that their oceans are calm and the bounty of earth adorns them: " ... none may feel the power of squall and wave,/And no one any leaf-crowned dancer miss."

Every stanza, moreover, balances every other stanza. The juxtaposition of the fourth line of each enables the poem to build precisely towards climax, and other and similar repetitions enhance the sense of inevitability that attaches to the poem's conclusion: the use of "at last" as motif, for instance, or the balancings of the final line of each stanza. In 1892, the poem read as follows:

> He stood among a crowd at Drumahair,
>   His heart hung all upon a silken dress,
>   And he had known at last some tenderness
> Before earth made of him her sleepy care;
> But when a man poured fish into a pile,
>   It seemed they raised their little silver heads
>   And sang how day a Druid twilight sheds
> Upon a dim, green, well-beloved isle,
> Where people love beside star-laden seas;
>   How Time may never mar their fairy wovs
>   Under the woven roofs of quicken boughs; –
> The singing shook him out of his new ease.
>
> As he went by the sands of Lisadill,
>   His mind ran all on money cares and fears,
>   And he had known at last some prudent years
> Before they heaped his grave under the hill;
> But while he passed before a plashy place,
>   A lug-worm with its gray and muddy mouth
>   Sang how somewhere to north or east or south
> There dwelt a gay, exulting, gentle race;
> And how beneath those three times blessed skies
>   A Danaan fruitage makes a shower of moons
>   And as it falls awakens leafy tunes; –
> And at that singing he was no more wise.
>
> He mused beside the well of Scanavin,
>   He mused upon his mockers. Without fail
>   His sudden vengeance were a country tale
> Now that deep earth has drunk his body in
> But one small knot-grass growing by the rim
>   Told where – ah, little, all-unneeded voice! –
>   Old Silence bids a lonely folk rejoice,
> And chaplet their calm brows with leafage dim,
> And how, when fades the sea-strewn rose of day,
>   A gentle feeling wraps them like a fleece,
>   And all their trouble dies into its peace; –
> The tale drove his fine angry mood away.

> He slept under the hill of Lugnagall,
>   And might have known at last unhaunted sleep
>   Under that cold and vapour-turbaned steep,
> Now that old earth had taken man and all:
> Were not the worms that spired about his bones
>   A-telling with their low and reedy cry,
>   Of how God leans His hands out of the sky,
> To bless that isle with honey in His tones,
> That none may feel the power of squall and wave,
>   And no one any leaf-crowned dancer miss
>   Until He burn up Nature with a kiss; –
> The man has found no comfort in the grave.

The most obvious thing about these verses is that they combine with the verses of "The Stolen Child" to make up a poetic atlas of Sligo. Slish ("Slewth") Wood, Rosses Point, Lissadell, Toberscanavan – the small village, now all but gone, whose name Yeats shortens to "Scanavin" above – and Lugnagall are all located in that county, and the waterfalls of Glencar and the market town of Dromahair are just across the border in County Leitrim. And in the poem itself this local geography turns functional. Yeats sets his dreamer to tracking down the clue provided him on the sands of Lissadell - that the "gentle race" of his dreams dwells "somewhere to north or east or south" – by sending him to the four points of the compass in the course of his search: Lissadell in the west, Dromahair in the east, Toberscanavan in the south, and Lugnagall in the dead cold of the north. His comprehensive journey may echo what Yeats knew to be the Irish folk belief that invoking the points of the compass was an effective countercharm against enchantment by the sidhe, or again against Druidic spells – the island that calls the dreamer out of human contentment is a land of "Druid twilight" – but if the dreamer is attempting this kind of invocation, he is attempting it in vain.[31]

Aside from the proximity of their settings, both "The Stolen Child" and "The Man who Dreamed of Faeryland" center on a mortal trapped between pull and counterpull. The young boy of the fairy lyric moves solemn-eyed through emotional limbo, caught between his own peaceful home life and the pull of the waves of moonlight. The man who dreamed finds himself on the verge of attaining human happiness in the form of love and financial security, but is called away at the critical moment by the voice of the world beyond. No writer other than the young Yeats would have picked such uncommon singers.

The vehicles of the several epiphanies that the dreamer experiences are all unattractive, and grow more so as the poem progresses: from dead fish to lugworms to a knot of grass to the worms of the grave. The temptation is to take this to mean that the poem takes a skeptical stance towards the transcendent world by depicting the heralds of that world as repellent; but it would be most uncharacteristic of the early Yeats to indulge himself in an irony so blunt. It may be more to the point to note that the fish, the lugworm, and the grass knot are all symbolic of the state in which the human dreamer finds himself. In his *Autobiographies* Yeats wrote that "it is a natural conviction for a painter's son to believe that there may be a landscape that is symbolical of some spiritual condition" (*Au* 74), and spiritual conditions are what the landscapes of the early poems express. Yeats's early uses of the images of ocean, seashore, islands and inland will be the object of more detailed discussion in a later chapter, but for a discussion of "The Man who Dreamed of Faeryland" it is enough to mention the more general sense of the symbols. In Yeats's broadest use of it, the ocean is that which stands between man and the possibility of transcendence; it puts the islands of the sidhe beyond the dreamer's reach, even as time and old mortality prevent a man from reaching beyond natural bounds. Seashores and lakesides, in turn, become symbolic midpoints between the immortal islands and the narrow graves that lie inland. Privileged mortals like Oisin are allowed to depart the shore and travel out towards the lands of the ever-living. A more typical fate is that of the dreamer, who wanders the shores as Oisin did but whose wishful rovings are fated to carry him away from the waves and back towards the buried dark.

The geography of the poem in question makes clear how completely its title character vacillates between earth and ocean. The first stanza finds him in an inland market, the second on the seashore; the third stanza combines the earth and water images by placing him at an inland well. The final stanza discovers him bound up in the single image of earth, and it would be natural to expect this to indicate that the antinomies of earth and ocean, mortality and transcendence, have been resolved for the man by the hard fact of death. The poem's final ingenuity is that they have not, with the inescapable graveworms plaguing the dreamer with reminders of the island that he never managed to reach. The verbs Yeats chooses to describe their voice show a maturing craftsman's care. The earlier messengers – the fish and the lugworm – "sang"; but the knot of grass "told", and the worms are "a-telling". What youth hears as poetry, age hears as prose; and corroborating evidence of the steady decline in the dreamer's condition comes with his gradual cessation of movement. He begins the poem among a market crowd; and the movement implied in that scene finds additional reinforcement in the lack of movement implicit in the scene's otherworldly counterpart, since the image of "star-laden seas" in the first stanza is an image of seas that are motionless. Their appearance here hints at what the rest of the poem will confirm: that the fairyland that this lyric describes is a place marked most of all by inertia, sighing on the grass. The dancers who appear in the last few lines of the poem are apparently the only island-dwellers willing to lift a limb; the rest is stillness. As the next chapter will argue, this lack of significant motion will prove one of the most telling characteristics of Yeats's early visions of the islands in the west; the portraits of fairyland that frame the descriptions of both the dreamer and Oisin might aptly be described as still lifes, and the island-dwellers are still because the lands they inhabit are static.

The stillness in which the human dreamer will conclude is different from the kind of quietude in which the sidhe rest content. The motion that served as a backdrop to his situation in the first stanza carries over into the first line of the second, but by now the man is alone. The third stanza discovers him alone and motionless; the fourth locates him in a final immobility, and assigns him ultimate companions which are worse than none at all. And the progress from "sang" to "told" to "a-telling" serves a further function here, suggests a final bitter drop, since it announces that the man's frustration will be present tense forever. Emblematic as they are of what should be the finality of death, the worms that do the telling are not associated with the water over which the course to the eternal islands runs; but the earlier three messengers, like the dreamer himself, are linked with both water and earth. The fish have been taken out of their element and brought inland to be sold, and the first stanza specifically identifies them with the dreamer by noting that they are "in a pile" while setting him among a crowd. The amphibious lugworm lives in the sands of the seashore. The knot of grass, itself of the earth, rests on the rim of a well. And it is the sad fact of these divided existences that prompts in the dreamer his vision of a better world. Fish, lugworm, and earth knot call up their own contrasts, much like the "things uncomely" of 1892's "The Lover tells of the Rose in his Heart". Being part of both earth and ocean, they belong wholly to neither; they are intermediaries, and as intermediaries they remind the dreamer of his own intermediate situation. He is unable to reach the transcendent world; but the persistent call of that world prevents him from finding joy in the things of the earth.

It has been said of the poem on the dreamer that it embodies Yeats's "old theme of a nostalgia for the world of phantasy and dream",[32] that it defines a movement "away from the things of this world to the things of the spirit".[33] These remarks come from insightful critics, but even so they skirt the central point. If Yeats's early writings did no more than express a single-minded urge towards escape, one could say as much of their themes and there let the matter rest. But it is rare that any work by Yeats can be pinned down by a single sentence. Like so many of the works of Yeats's maturity, the early fairy lyrics draw their energy from the clash of contrasting visions. They speak directly of the attractions of the spiritual world, and no less directly of the counterpull of home; but their active centers are imbedded neither in the one place nor the other, but exactly in that turbulent hidden place where the two streams meet. "The Stolen Child" remains an interesting poem, not because it praises the beauty of one world and laments the inadequacies of the other, but because of the tensions that ensue when an unearthly beauty begins to lure a boy away from the promise of a peaceful life among his own kind. "The Man who Dreamed of Faeryland" turns on the same tension. The song that lured the boy is the song that lures the dreamer, and its effect on him is even more self-evidently destructive than the fairies' influence on the child. Thematically, the poem turns on the word "had", which carries the force of "would have": "His heart hung all upon a silken dress,/And he had known at last some tenderness", "His mind ran all on money cares and fears,/And he had known at last some prudent years". Lines like these do express an old theme of nostalgia; but as Yeats himself asserted, the sense of regret that marks these verses derives from the fact that "vague idealisms & impossible hopes... blow in upon us to the ruin of near & common & substantial ambitions" (*CL1* 380). The dreamer, like the child, would have found contentment close to home. But the transcendent world intruded; and when the spirits seek a man out for their own, it is to carry him off to limbo or mock him into the grave.

It is not only in their settings and themes that "The Stolen Child" and "The Man who Dreamed of Faeryland" are allied, since both poems also have a firm and specific base in Yeats's Irish folklore sources. Yeats's predecessors in folklore studies described the dreamer years before Yeats's poem did: as early as 1825, for instance, when Croker's *Fairy Legends* told of how a young man, fairy-stricken, "used to walk the whole day by the ditch side, talking to himself, like as if there was some one along with him" (p. 84). Twenty years afterwards Carleton would define the fatal consequence of this sort of aimless unwilling drift, though the man he described was to find his haunted sleep in Scotland rather than in Ireland:

> He appeared to be what the Scotch call *fey* – that is, to act as if he were moved by some impulse that leads to death, and from the influence of which a man cannot withdraw himself (*T&S*, p. 62).

The equivalent of "fey" in Irish fairylore is "blasted" or "stricken"; and when in 1887 Lady Wilde pictured the effect on a man of the fairy "blast" or "stroke", she also anticipated the appearance several years thereafter of the man who dreamed of fairyland. "When a person becomes low and depressed and careless about everything," she wrote, "as if all vital strength and energy had gone, he is said to have got a fairy blast" (*AL*, p. 200); and if Yeats's stricken dreamer dies untimely, it is because Yeats knew, from his readings in Wilde and elsewhere, that men and women who have been subjected to the blast generally go to their graves shortly after.[34] Elsewhere *Ancient Legends* described the undesirable effects of acts of spiritual carnality, the offspring of which are severely handicapped:

> The children of the sidhe and a mortal mother are... passionate and wilful, and have strange, moody fits, when they desire solitude above all things, and seem to hold converse with unseen spiritual beings (p. 91).

The human dreamer, with his strange, "moody" fits ("The tale drove his fine angry mood away"), his steadily increasing solitude, and his tendency to "seem" to hold converse with unseen beings ("But when a man poured fish into a pile,/It seemed they raised their little silver heads/And sang... "), was no literal child of the sidhe, but certainly Yeats perceived him as their spiritual son. The description of fairystruck mortals that appears in *FFT* is adapted directly from Wilde: "Those [whom] the fairies love are [not] always carried off – they may merely grow silent and strange, and take to lonely wanderings in the 'gentle' places" (*FFT* 133).

This sentence is in effect an early prose version of the later poem about the dreamer. He grows increasingly more "strange" as the call of faery continues;

he also grows more "lonely". He sets off on "wanderings" that carry him over most of the face of Sligo; and his wanderings lead him, not merely to the lesser "gentle" places, but to precisely those locations that Yeats himself saw as the most fairy-ridden sites in the county he knew best. The settings of the first and fourth stanzas, Dromahair and Lugnagall, comprise a kind of otherworldly parenthesis within which the rest of the poem is set. As the poet noted in the late eighties, Dromahair is held by many to be one of the two "most gentle... place[s] in the whole of County Sligo" (*CT* 32); the other is Drumcliff, the "wide green valley... at the foot of Ben Bulben" (*CT* 92) which is "chokeful of ghosts" (*CT* 96) and which, unfortunately for the human dreamer, adjoins Lugnagall. The beginning and end of this poem, then, find the man as effectively fairy-haunted as a man in Sligo can be; if he leaves the sidhe behind him, it is only to find them lying in wait up the road. What needs to be asked at this stage is why the sidhe have singled him out in the first place. If he is among "those [whom] the fairies love", it would be hard to prove their affection for him from the poem. They dog and haunt him, drive him into an unquiet grave, transform him into what Yeats elsewhere called one of "the children of reverie... whose feet find no resting-place upon the earth", "grief-struck... feeble and worn" (*CT* 52) and, like the other children of reverie, the object of Yeats's "pity" (*CT* 53). This sort of thing is not love's issue. Its source lies elsewhere, and there are a number of paths tracking sourcewards.

The first is Irish fairylore in certain of its specific details. The sidhe torment the dreamer in large measure because his state of mind leaves him vulnerable to their torments. The opening stanza, with its claim that the dreamer would have "known at last some tenderness", makes it clear that he is in love and that his love is likely to be reciprocated; and it is at moments like these that the sidhe are most likely to strike. New-married brides are their more usual targets, but there are any number of Irish folktales in which grooms are glamoured instead. In either case the glamouring almost always takes place just before or shortly after the wedding ceremony: in other words, before the marriage can be consummated. The tales of otherworldly abduction with which Yeats was familiar are buoyed up on a deepbedded current of sexual jealousy. Lady Wilde, for instance, speaks of marriages taking place "despite all the envy and jealousy of the fairies, who maliciously [try] to mar the pleasures of the festival" (*AL*, p. 260). The lyrics by Samuel Ferguson that Yeats included in *Fairy and Folk Tales* give a more graphic expression to the same impulse. Ostensibly stories of glamouring, they are in fact repressed tales of rape; and at times the masking phrases are transparent. Thus the young girl of "The Fairy Well of Lagnanay" visits the well of the title and there "bares her bosom's swell", washes her breasts in the enchanted waters and invites the sidhe attendant on the well to "work their will" (*FFT* 21–2). The young women in "The Fairy Thorn" rendezvous at a fairy hawthorn with "neck and ankle bare", and as the sidhe begin to close in they "lie" down "cowering" and "fling their lovely arms o'er their drooping necks so fair,/Then vainly strive again their naked arms to hide". By the end of the poem the "enchantment lies" "heavy on their senses"; and "the fairest of the four" is taken by force from her companions, and made a thrall of faery lest she become a bride of man (*FFT* 41–2).

The perversity of motive that underlies these acts of malice finds its most direct expression in the mouths of the sidhe themselves. William Wilde, for instance, recounts the troubling case of John Fitzgerald, who in the year 1736 was glamoured from his wedding feast. Fitzgerald, Wilde's story asserts, was the noblest-looking young man then living in Munster: a characteristic note in tales of the kind, since when breaching mortal love affairs the sidhe steal only the young and beautiful.[35] The wedding went off without incident; but during the dance that followed the wedding, Fitzgerald suddenly "clasped his beautiful bride in his arms, impressed a burning kiss upon her lips" (*IPS, p. 123*), *and immediately thereafter fell dead at her feet*. The most notable fairy-seers in the province were summoned in an attempt to "bring him back from fairyland, whither it was universally believed he had been carried" (*IPS, p. 123*). None succeeded, but one among them managed at least to plead the case of Fitzgerald's bride before Cliodhna, the fairy queen of south Munster[36] who had carried Fitzgerald off. Cliodhna "acknowledged the soft impeachment, but peremptorily refused to restore so noble a prize to any mere creature of earth" (*IPS*, pp. 123–4). And when the fairy-seer continued to argue, she put a chill end to the debate. "To marry or wed I will not allow him," said she, "I prefer, even tho' [he be] dead, to have him myself,/Than married to any beauteous maid of Erin" (*IPS*, p. 124).

The situations in which Fitzgerald and Yeats's dreamer find themselves are not precise analogues, but they are close. The Irish fairy tradition holds young lovers more susceptible to the influence of the sidhe than most other mortals; both Fitzgerald and the dreamer are in love, and both of them are marked out of the crowd by the sidhe. The tradition also holds that the sidhe take a perverse delight in preventing mortals from finding happiness in love; and neither Fitzgerald nor the dreamer finds happiness. What they find in its stead is the grave.

This is one of the more direct instances of the way in which Yeats's early work is backgrounded by his close knowledge of Irish fairylore. It also serves to illustrate the trouble that Yeats's dreamer is in; for the etiquette of fairyland is delicate – lips' touch can breach it – and the sidhe have the habit of taking offence at thoughts and actions that a man would find inoffensive. Maliciously shaken out of his doting thoughts about "a silken dress", the dreamer goes walking on the strand of Lissadell, his mind turned now towards "money cares and fears". This state of mind would be too familiar to a fellow mortal to compel anything but a sympathetic nod of recognition. But the sidhe, who dwell in a land where the fruit falls so plentifully that it sets the trees to singing, find in money cares and fears an affront to their less burdened sensibilities. Yeats's poem describes them as "exulting" and "gay"; his sources had referred to them as "free" and "joyous":

> The fairies, with their free, joyous temperament and love of beauty and luxury, hold in great contempt the minor virtues of thrift and economy, and, above all things, abhor the close, hard, niggardly nature

that spends grudgingly and never gives freely. Indeed, they seem to hold it as their peculiar mission to punish such people, and make them suffer for the sins of the hard heart and niggard hand (*AL*, p. 49).[37]

In the story that follows that passage, Lady Wilde details the destruction of an entire family by the offended sidhe. The man who dreamed suffers nothing so comprehensive, if only because the sidhe have already seen to it that he will have no family for them to destroy. He provoked their jealousy by falling in love; he will provoke their contempt by his thrift. His punishment will become their peculiar mission. The "prudent" years he was hoping for will slip through his hands like quicksilver; and it is entirely in accord with Irish fairylore's views of the sidhe that they should.[38]

Frustration of the loving and punishment of the thrifty are common practices of the sidhe, but the third stanza of "The Man who Dreamed of Faeryland" finds its folklore corollary in an offence against the fairies that is both more particular and more obscure. The scene is a holy well at Toberscanavan,[39] one among those "fountains of health and healing which some saint had blessed" (*AL*, p. 236) and to which the Irish faithful still resort[40] to offer worship and pray for cures. The setting, with its blending of earth and water images, continues the pattern of symbolism set up in the opening stanza; but there are other and more specific reasons why the choice of a well is appropriate. Sites of worship, the wells also tended to attract devotees of a less orthodox sort. Lady Wilde describes the strange goings-on at one of them:

> Near the great mountain of Croagh-Patrick there is a lake called *Clonvencagh*, or the Lake of Revenge, to which evil-disposed persons used to resort in order to imprecate maledictions on their enemies. It was the custom to erect monuments round the well by placing on end a long flagstone, and heaping round it a pyramid of sand in order to keep it fixed firmly in its place. Over these pillar-stones certain mystic rites were then performed by the pilgrims, and prayers were said which took the form of the most terrible imprecations (*AL*, pp. 251–2).

There is nothing so macabre going on in the case of the dreamer, but at least he is following a time-honored Irish folk custom in resorting to a well in order to ponder his "sudden vengeance" upon his "mockers". And if Irish folklore suggests one likely reason why Yeats sends the man to a well, it also suggests a reason why this "fountain of health and healing" can have no restorative effect on him. Belief in the power of the wells amounted to an article of faith among the peasants; *Ancient Legends*, for instance, claimed that "there is no superstition stronger in Ireland than a belief in the curative power of the sacred wells that are scattered over the country" (p. 236). But the tradition also held that only the untroubled heart could take advantage of what the wells offered. Thus Wilde's account of the destruction of an Irish monastery by English troops, and the subsequent departure of the monks:

> When the monks, broken-hearted and beggared, were leaving their beautiful home, one of them kneeled down and prayed to God for forgiveness of his enemies. Immediately a well of pure water sprang up where the monk had knelt; and the water even to this day is held by the people to have the power to cure all diseases, if the soul of the patient, as he drinks of the well, is free from all malice and the desire of revenge upon those who may have injured him (*AL*, p. 225).

This is not a description of the well that the dreamer visits, but it does describe the frame of mind in which he pays his call. A pilgrim to a private lake of vengeance, he comes to the well of Scanavan seeking retribution on those who may have injured him. This is not prudent, since to visit a holy well with an unholy end in mind is to commit an act of desecration that invites stern punishment. The folk beliefs that Yeats found recorded in Lady Wilde decreed only that a man with a mind for revenge must depart from a holy well unrestored; but a passage he had come across in John O'Hanlon's *Irish Folk Lore* went an ominous step further.

> Since the Druidic times, Irish spring wells are said to have been invested with some sacred character. To desecrate a holy spring is considered profanity... Severe chastisement is believed to be visited oftentimes on the wanton delinquent (p. 149).

It cannot be said that the man who dreamed suffers severe chastisement "oftentimes" after his dark meditation in Toberscanavan, simply because what he suffers is final. The desire for revenge that he expresses by a spring well in Sligo is desecration; and the consequence is quick.

The voice that interrupts the dreamer's reverie in this third stanza is the least common of all the uncommon voices in the poem, the "little, all-unneeded voice" of "one small knot-grass growing by the rim" of the well. It is strange enough when the dumb fish speak, but the land where the grass gives tongue is not a land where men may walk at ease. Enchantment is at work here; and the Irish folktales that Yeats pored over had described several kinds of grasses that were sacred to the sidhe, bits of charmed knotgrass that mortal feet brushed at their peril. There is, for instance, the

> fairy grass, called the *Faud Shaughran*, or the "stray sod", and whoever treads the path it grows on is compelled by an irresistible impulse to travel on without stopping, all through the night, delirious and restless... And those who fall under this strange influence are utterly unable to pause or turn back or change their career (*AL*, p. 183).

And there is also

> the *Fair-Gortha*, or the "hunger-stricken sod," and if the hapless traveller accidentally treads on this grass by the road-side, while passing on a journey, either by night or day, he becomes at once seized

with the most extraordinary cravings of hunger and weakness, and unless timely relief is afforded he must certainly die (*AL*, p. 183).

To follow Yeats closely through his extensive readings in folklore is to find that his sources of information on the sidhe are like a beam of light, with Yeats's imagination a prism through which the beam filters. When it re-emerges transformed into the writings themselves, the light has become several, rainbowed in a way that the original beam was not. But it is also more diffuse, and this diffusion makes it difficult to prove the presence in a given work of an influence whose presence the reader may none the less strongly sense. One cannot prove that enchanted grasses like the *Faud Shaughran* or *Fair-Gortha* are the specific rays of light that come to colorful new life on the rim of a well in Sligo. But, that said, it is worth suggesting that Yeats had something very like the enchanted grass in mind, that the small knot-grass of "The Man who Dreamed of Faeryland" grew out of his deep and generalized knowledge of even the shadier nooks of the Irish folk tradition. For one thing, the idea of enchanted grass appeared in a good many of the works in which he had steeped himself: not only in Lady Wilde, but in Carleton, Kennedy, O'Hanlon.[41] More to the point, the belief that the wrath of the sidhe will descend on mortals who make contact with the charmed earth helps to complete the pattern of the poem. The first two stanzas detail offences by the dreamer against the sidhe; the third stanza thus becomes the proper home for the third and final offence, fairydom's proverbial doombringer.[42] Finally, and most to the point, the effect that Irish folklore pictures the enchanted grass as having on mortals is the same effect that the voice of the grass knot has on the man who dreamed. Yeats's folklore sources here provide a means of explaining why Yeats chose the image of the knot-grass in the first place. It furthers the earth–water image pattern announced early on in the poem, but other and less curious images would have served the same purpose: Yeats's much-used image of an island in a lake, for instance. The mind does not naturally gravitate towards fantastic images of earth clumps on well rims; and when an image so strange is forthcoming, it is a safe assumption that its source lies in part somewhere outside the individual mind. The dreamer is a driven man, his feet insistent, restless. He has an appetite for the extraordinary, cravings too deep for relief to find them. He must certainly die. At Scanavan he heard the grass speak. The likeliest source of all this strangeness is a fairylore that held that certain grasses were strange.

The particulars of Irish fairy belief, then, afford several possible reasons for the tormenting of the dreamer by the sidhe. But a recollection of the broader pages of that same tradition is enough to make it clear that the sidhe, once they have a given man in sight, need no specific excuse to set off in his pursuit. They are jealous of human love, contemptuous of human thrift. On these counts the dreamer offends, and for giving offence he is punished. If this is not just, it is at least intelligible. Not so the malice revealed in stanza three. The sign that would warn a man off the grass should at least be visible. Yet the enchanted grass gives no warning, nor does it discriminate. It affects those who have offended the residents of faery; it affects those who have not. This is both arbitrary and excessive. Then again, so are the sidhe.

That they are provides a second and more general way of accounting for the pain they inflict on man. Irish fairylore is filled with stories in which the sidhe act meanly because they feel like acting meanly, and men become their targets because they like man not at all. The stolen child was innocent and a victim; and from a mortal perspective, the man who dreamed has done nothing that would merit the radical punishment that descends on him. In this respect both child and dreamer owe their existence to Yeats's knowledge of the wider and more treacherous implications of Irish fairylore. And there is one further element of that lore that filters down into both poems. The boy is lost to the hillsides; the man dies. It is the lamia that destroys them both, the extended hand that shines so bright with welcome that they never notice the hard glint hidden in the sleeve.

Ancient Legends gives a number of lamia stories, and one of them rehearses the "The Man who Dreamed of Faeryland" four years before the poem was published. The story concerns a young Aran Islander who falls asleep in a field on a Friday evening. The sidhe carry him off to a palace that Biddy Mannion would have had no trouble recognizing, "a beautiful hall, where a banquet was laid out" on a table "covered with fruit, and chickens, and young turkeys, and butter, and cakes fresh from the oven, and crystal cups of bright red wine" (p. 74). The prince of the sidhe, with "a red sash round his waist, and a gold band on his head", reaches out a warm hand: "Sit down with this pleasant company," he says, "and eat with us; you are welcome." In the next sentence those familiar smiles appear as if on cue: "And there were many beautiful ladies seated round, and grand noblemen, with red caps and sashes; and they all smiled at him and bade him eat" (p. 74). Frightened, the young man refuses and asks to be let go. "Not at least till you taste our wine," the prince says "with a friendly smile". A "beautiful" lady fills one of the cups with bright wine and hands it to the man, "and he could not help himself, but drank it all off without stopping; for it seemed to him the most delicious draught he ever had in his whole life" (p. 74). The sequel is as bitter as immediate, for

> no sooner had he laid down the glass, than a noise like thunder shook the building, and all the lights went out; and he found himself alone in the dark night lying under the very same hayrick where he had cast himself down to sleep... So he made his way home at last; but the taste of the fairy wine burned in his veins, and a fever was on him night and day for another draught; and he did no good, but pined away, seeking the fairy mansion, though he never found it any more. And so he died in his youth, a warning to all who eat of the fairy food, or drink of the fairy wine; for never more will they know peace or content, or be fit for their work, as in the days before the fairy spell was on them, which brings doom

and death to all who fall under the fatal enchantment of its unholy power (p. 74).

"The Man who Dreamed of Faeryland" is a poem that arises directly out of an Irish folklore in which characters like the man who dreamed abounded. Yeats gave the figure its most expressive shape, but only by refining models that lesser writers had worked from the clay years before. His poem would inspire copies in its turn. In his *The Flight of the Eagle* (1897), Standish O'Grady took a cue from Yeats's verses when he described a

> youth wandering unconsoled o'erladen with the burthen of his thoughts, rapt with visions, tormented by the gods, a stranger in his own household, scorned by those whom he cannot scorn, outcast from the wholesome cheerful life of men.[43]

As a gloss of "The Man who Dreamed", this passage is instructive. It is easy enough to trace the ascent of the figure of the fairy-stricken man from Croker through Carleton through Wilde through Yeats to O'Grady. O'Grady's tormented young man is a model of a type; so is Wilde's fevered young man from Aran; so is Yeats's haunted young man from Sligo. The taste of faery burns in his veins. He is shaken out of ease. A fever is on him night and day. He searches after faery; he never finds it. He does no good, but pines away. Alone and little loved, he dies without having known peace or content, a stranger in his own household, buried under a Lugnagall whose name Yeats took to mean the Steep Place of the Strangers (*Myth* 183).[44] And the man has found no comfort in his grave, not even the cold comfort that Eden's heirs claim as sorry birthright. In 1866 another of Yeats's folklore sources, Patrick Kennedy's *Legendary Fictions of the Irish Celts*, spoke of "the indescribable wretchedness of the too rash and too curious mortals who would tear asunder the veil that divides the visible from the invisible world" (pp. 176–7). The book was thus describing both Wilde's young man, and O'Grady's, and Yeats's. There is a beguiling world out there – its wine is bright, its islands dim and green – but doom and death greet all who fall under the fatal enchantment of its unholy power. This is true in Wilde's story; it is true in Yeats's poem. The most accomplished of Yeats's early writings on the sidhe are not an expression of longing for life in a perfect other world, but an exegesis of the woe that too great a longing for perfection must engender. Their theme, as "The Eaters of Precious Stones" has it, is that all who seek too avidly after a beauty charged with wonder will lose "peace and form and bec[o]me shapeless and common" (*CT* 101). "When it is spring with us, the trees are withering" There, and "when it is summer with us, the snow is falling" There, "and maybe when it's night with us, it is day with" Them: "to be sure", says the wise Fool in the later play *The Hour-Glass*, "does not everybody with an intellect know that?" (*VPl* 585). Yeats's earlier writings on the sidhe say the same. It is better to stay at home. There is this world and there is an alluring other world, but the two elements are forever at variance.

Notes to Chapter 2

1. Ireland aside, Birgit Bramsbäck has noted that Croker's book "appears to be the very first collection of oral tales to have been gathered in the British Isles". Cf. "William Butler Yeats and Folklore Material", in *Hereditas*, eds Bo Almqvist, Breandán Mac Aodha and Gearóid Mac Eoin (Dublin: The Folklore of Ireland Society, 1975), p. 62.
2. *The Folk-lore Record*, which in 1883 became *The Folk-lore Journal* (Yeats cites both names), the proceedings and transactions of the Kilkenny Archaeological Society, and the *Transactions of the Ossianic Society* are the works Yeats singles out for commendation in his endnote to *FFT* (p. 294). As the name of the group suggests, the short-lived but influential Ossianic Society actually centered its attention more on legends and hero tales than on folktales; and Yeats drops his reference to their transactions in the endnote to *IFT*.
3. As witness the difference between the lists of recommended readings supplied by Yeats at the end of 1888's *FFT* and 1892's *IFT*.

    The endnote to *FFT* lists eleven full-length books as primary folklore sources: in the order in which Yeats names them, one book each by Croker, Lady Wilde, Sir William Wilde, D. R. McAnally, Fr John O'Hanlon ("Lageniensis"), and Samuel Lover – then four books by Patrick Kennedy, and one by William Carleton. Nine of these eleven were published in 1870 or earlier, and five of those nine – Lover's *Legends and Stories of Ireland* (1831), Carleton's *Traits and Stories of the Irish Peasantry* (1830–3), and Kennedy's *Legends of Mount Leinster* (1855), *The Banks of the Boro* (1867), and *Evenings in the Duffrey* (1869) – are not properly works of folklore at all, but works of fiction or biographical reminiscence that contain a few stories or anecdotes based on folktales or beliefs. Moreover, the four books published in or before 1870 that might conceivably qualify as studies in folklore were published over intervals: first Croker's *FL* in the mid-twenties, then William Wilde's *Irish Popular Superstitions* (1852), Kennedy's *Legendary Fictions of the Irish Celts* (1866) and O'Hanlon's *Irish Folk Lore* (1870).

    The corresponding list in *IFT* is longer. Its thirteen titles include (in order) Croker, two books by Lady Wilde, William Wilde, McAnally, O'Hanlon, Jeremiah Curtin, two books by Hyde, and the same four books by Kennedy. This was more legitimate. The works of Carleton and Lover are now no longer listed as authoritative folklore sources; somewhat more correctly, *IFT* relegates them to the position of books that contain "much" folklore (p. 388). More to the immediate point, the spate of enthusiasm for folklore that surfaced in the late eighties and early years of the nineties had enabled Yeats to update his list of authorities radically: of the thirteen books so described, six had first been published between 1887 and 1890. The least significant of the six was unquestionably the Irish–American McAnally's *Irish Wonders* (1888), a book Yeats rightly took to task for its "sham picturesqueness" (*UP1* 139). But the other five – Lady Wilde's *Ancient Legends* (1887) and *Ancient Cures* (1890), Curtin's *Myths and Folk-Lore of Ireland* (1890), and Hyde's *Leabhar Sgeuluigheachta* (1889) and *Beside the Fire* (1890) – were deserving of the attention the poet paid them, and gave him warrant for his proclamation that a folklore revival was indeed in progress. "There has been published in [the past] three years as much Irish folk-lore as in the foregoing fifty", he wrote in early 1891, this is "the harvest-time of folk-lore" (*UP1* 188, 187).
4. For similar affirmations of the interrelationship between folklore and the literary revival, see *UP1* 368 and *UP2* 152.

5   As recently as 1975 Bramsbäck could accurately note that "there is... no full-scale comprehensive investigation of the rôle played by folklore in the Yeats canon"; cf. "William Butler Yeats and Folklore Material", in *Hereditas*, p. 57. The Bramsbäck article also contains a valuable list of the Irish sources (folklore and otherwise) that Yeats is likely to have drawn on (pp. 65–8). Certain of these sources have yet to be explored; but Bramsbäck herself has helped to fill the gap she spoke of with her valuable *Folklore and W. B. Yeats: The Function of Folklore Elements in Three Early Plays* (1984). A still more comprehensive investigation of the area may be found in M. H. Thuente's *W. B. Yeats and Irish Folklore* (1981), and here I wish to acknowledge my immediate debts to both this book and its author. I should also make it clear that, since the focus of the present work is less on Yeats as folklorist than on his uses and interpretations of folklore materials, these chapters will be using the term "folklore" in what the Bramsbäck essay calls its "wide sense" (p. 60). For a more technical discussion of the term's range of meanings, see *W. B. Yeats and Irish Folklore*, pp. 47–8 and 80–2.

My other general debts should also be noted here. Edward Hirsch has offered a concise overview of the young Yeats's relationship to folklore in his "'Contention is better than loneliness': The Poet as Folklorist" (*Genre*, Winter 1979), and Kevin Danaher has located folklore in the context of the literary revival as a whole; see "Folk Tradition and Literature" (*Journal of Irish Literature*, May 1972). Regrettably, Danaher puts his case much too strongly when he says that Yeats merely "dabbled in folk lore" (p. 71). A more wide-ranging view of the matter is available in Thomas Flanagan's "Yeats, Joyce, and the Matter of Ireland" (*Critical Inquiry*, Autumn 1975); herein Flanagan explores both Yeats's complex relationship to the peasantry and their lore and Joyce's staunchly opposite attitude.

In more specific studies in the area, perhaps the most constant focus has been on Yeats's uses of traditional Irish airs in his work. Here, see particularly Colin Meir's investigation of *The Ballads and Songs of W. B. Yeats: The Anglo-Irish Heritage in Subject and Style* (1974); Michael Yeats's fine "W. B. Yeats and Irish Folk Song" (*Southern Folklore Quarterly*, June 1966); the detailed discussion of the impact on Yeats of the rhythms of Irish speech and song in Seán Lucy's "Metre and Movement in Anglo-Irish Verse" (*Irish University Review*, Autumn 1978); and G. S. Fraser's "Yeats and the Ballad Style" (*Shenandoah*, Spring 1970). Fraser's discussion of Ferguson's "Cashel of Munster" as it bears on Yeats's work (pp. 177–8) anticipates the similar discussion in Austin Clarke's "Gaelic Ireland Rediscovered: The Early Period", in *Irish Poets in English*, ed. Seán Lucy (1973), p. 32; and Fraser's comparison of George Fox's version of "The County of Mayo" to Yeats's "The Curse of Cromwell" (p. 186) anticipates David R. Clark's remarks on the same matter in his "Yeats: 'Out of a People to a People'" (*Malahat Review*, April 1972). Clark's article is not directly about Yeats and folklore, but does discuss the ways in which the older Yeats turned back to traditional Irish rhythms and melodies in order to write "in as near to folk fashion as he could manage" (p. 32).

Finally, for an overview of nineteenth century attitudes towards the folklore of the peasantry, see *Views of the Irish Peasantry 1800–1916*, eds Daniel J. Casey and Robert E. Rhodes (1977). Of the many excellent essays in this volume, those that most often glance towards Yeats are Alf MacLochlainn's "Gael and Peasant – A Case of Mistaken Identity?" (pp. 17–36), James MacKillop's "Finn MacCool: The Hero and the Anti-Hero in Irish Folk Tradition" (pp. 86–106), Maurice Harmon's "Cobwebs before the Wind: Aspects of the Peasantry in Irish

Literature from 1800 to 1916" (pp. 129–59); and John Unterecker's evocative "Countryman, Peasant, and Servant in the Poetry of W. B. Yeats" (pp. 178–91). See too John C. Messenger's valuable bibliography of researches in the area, pp. 203–17.

Works to which this book is more specifically indebted will be cited in individual notes.

6   As will become clear, those of Yeats's earlier writings that have their base in folklore or fairylore owe a greater debt to Wilde's *Ancient Legends* than to any other individual source. Hyde's *Beside the Fire* would later replace *AL* in Yeats's affections, with Yeats referring to it as late as 1900 as "the one quite perfect book of Irish folklore" (*UP2* 218).

7   In their *Ireland: its scenery, character, etc.* (1841–3), Mr and Mrs S. C. Hall observed that the fairies have the power to assume "any form they please; and they often do so both for benevolent and mischievous purposes" (Vol. III, p. 241). In 1845 Carleton's *Tales and Stories* claimed that "the fairy... is supposed to be a singular mixture of good and evil, not very moral in its actions or objects, often very thievish, and sometimes benevolent, when kindness is least expected from it" (p. 73). In 1870, O'Hanlon's *Irish Folk Lore* echoed Carleton: "An intermixture of good and evil balances their actions and motives; and their passions are often vindictive, as their inclinations are frequently humane and generous" (p. 37). For similar observations about the sidhe, see Kennedy's *The Fireside Stories of Ireland* (1870) for remarks about their "good or evil dispositions" (p. 131), and Lady Wilde's echoings of her *AL* in its sequel, *Ancient Cures*, pp. 2, 59, 155. The description of the sidhe as having power "for good or ill" appears as recently as 1977 in E. Estyn Evans's "Peasant Beliefs in Nineteenth-Century Ireland", in *Views of the Irish Peasantry*, p. 48.

8   The big box was not the only quarry that Lady Wilde worked. Her description of the Salmon of Knowledge, for instance, came directly from O'Hanlon's *IF* (*AL*, pp. 182–3; *IF*, pp. 244–5), and her remarks on the way in which the poets of ancient Ireland obtained the gift of prophecy came from the same source (*AL*, pp. 217–18; *IF*, pp. 243–4). This failure to credit verbatim borrowings was by no means unique to Wilde. The descent of sentences and paragraphs from author to author was one of the more constant features of nineteenth-century Irish folklore; as later notes will show, Yeats himself did not hesitate to work passages from earlier writers into his own notes on the sidhe and the folk and their ways.

9   We cannot say as much of most of her predecessors in the area. William Wilde's *Irish Popular Superstitions*, for instance, had also presented the contradictory views of the sidhe, but had made no attempt to resolve them. A typical passage from *IPS* is one which comprehends the positive and negative aspects of the middle kingdom in a single breath: thus the fairies

> are looked upon by us from beyond the Shannon, as the great agents and prime movers in all accidents, diseases, and death, in "man or baste"; causing the healthfulness and fertility of seasons, persons, cattle and localities (p. 120).

For similar remarks from known Yeatsian sources, see Carleton's *T&S*, pp. 72–3, and O'Hanlon's *IF*, p. 32.

10 O'Hanlon's remarks appear in *IF*, p. 165. Lady Wilde stretched her claim about the sidhe as demoniac to cover the changelings they left behind them, "imp[s] of Satan" (*AC*, pp. 153–5, and see pp. 155–7). Croker's *FL* lent implicit support

to the description; it refers to glamouring as the work of "the devil" (pp. 40, 48–9). Yeats had also come across the assertion in Standish O'Grady's *History of Ireland* (Vol. II) that medieval Christianity had regarded the Tuatha Dé Danaan, forebears of the sidhe tribe, as "devils" (p. 84) or "demons" (p. 256 n.); and in McAnally's *IW*, which Yeats read just before the publication of *FFT*, he found a portrait of Satan's attendance at the revels of the sidhe (pp. 21–2).

Descriptions of the sidhe as satanic were later to make inroads into Yeats's own prose. In 1893, he referred to the fairies as the children of Adam and the wife of Satan (*UP1* 316); and nearly ten years later he noted a Galway tradition that described the sidhe as the "children of Satan" himself, adding at the same time that in his own view of the matter they were probably "children of Pan" instead (*CT* 61).

11   Yeats's division of the sidhe into two tribes took its cue from Lady Wilde, but his description of those tribes as "sociable" and "solitary" derived from the work of O'Hanlon and McAnally. For details, see my "Armchair Folklore: Yeats and the Textual Sources of *Fairy and Folk Tales of the Irish Peasantry*", in the *Proceedings of the Royal Irish Academy*, vol. 83c (1983), p. 257 and note. For help in the preparation of this and other articles, as also in the preparation of this book, I wish to thank Anne Yeats for her courteous permission to examine her father's personal library, currently housed in her home in Dalkey.

12   In later years Yeats would find more substantial support for the two-tribes theory, both in his own invocations of the sidhe (*UP1* 246–7) and in the more traditional notion that the good and evil fairy tribes were the descendants of the good and evil tribes that had ruled ancient Ireland (*UP2* 226, 271).

13   In writing his commentaries and notes for *FFT* and *IFT*, Yeats frequently drew upon his folklore sources and generally failed to credit his direct appropriations. For a fuller accounting, see my "Armchair Folklore", op. cit., pp. 255–67.

14   For some of the more direct among Yeats's later identifications of the sidhe with the Tuatha Dé Danaan, cf. *UP1* 137, 165, and *UP2* 226, 271. *UP2* also describes the sidhe as descendants of the "great gods of an earlier time" (161) or of "magicians" (221), both of which descriptions fit the Danaan tribe.

15   Yeats was referring to the sidhe as fallen angels as late as 1921 (*VP* 433). His known sources include numerous discussions of the theory; cf. particularly Croker's *FL*, pp. 23–8; Carleton's *T&S*, p. 72; Kennedy's *LFIC*, pp. 142–3; O'Hanlon's *IF*, p. 164; and Wilde's *AL*, p. 89. For an interesting variant, in which the fallen angels are transformed into "birds of beautiful plumage", see *LFIC*, pp. 338–9. Kennedy's description of the "Island of the Birds" on which these outcasts dwell may have influenced Yeats's description of the Island of the Living in "The Wanderings of Oisin".

For comments or discussions about the sidhe as "gods of the earth", cf. *AL*, pp. 142, 234, 248, 256, and, more particularly, *FFT* 287. This theory too had a strong attraction for the young occultist, since it enabled him to identify the sidhe with the elementals.

16   *Traits and Stories of the Irish Peasantry 1830–3* was the only work of Carleton's mentioned in Yeats's endnotes to *FFT* and *IFT*. But the Carleton materials that Yeats included in these volumes came, not from the *Traits*, but from the lesser-known *Tales and Sketches, Illustrating the Character, Usages, Traditions, Sports and Pastimes of the Irish Peasantry* (1845), the short title of which was *Tales and Stories of the Irish Peasantry*.

17   On the same page, be it noted, Croker quotes without comment the "mediaeval notion" that the "question of [the fairies'] ultimate salvation was left uncertain" (*FL*, p. 28). For further speculations on the uncertain fate of the sidhe, cf.

O'Hanlon's *IF*, p. 37; Wilde's *AL*, pp. 38, 96, 132, 256 and *AC*, p. 76; and McAnally's *IW*, pp. 92–3. *Irish Wonders* adds a note to the effect that one of the duties of the sidhe is to escort human souls to heaven (p. 96); and in commenting on this observation of McAnally's, Yeats pictures the sidhe as returning from heaven "disconsolate like the poor earth-bound creatures they are" (*LNI* 194).

18 Yeats included a variant of the type, Croker's "The Priest's Supper", in *FFT* 18–21.

19 The original title of this story was, simply and with a difference in spelling, "Loughliagh". Yeats found it in *The Dublin and London Magazine* (London: James Robins and Co.) for 1825, pp. 352–4. For the sources of the other materials in Yeats's anthology, see M. H. Thuente's "List of Sources" in *Fairy and Folk Tales of Ireland* (1977), pp. xvii–xxi.

20 Cf. Keats, "Lamia", Part II, l. 306.

21 "The Host of the Air" owes other debts to Yeats's readings in Irish folk and fairylore. It has perhaps already been noted that the final stanza of Yeats's poem echoes the final stanza of William Allingham's "A Dream", which Yeats reprinted in *FFT* (119). Yeats:

> But he heard high up in the air
> A piper piping away,
> And never was piping so sad,
> And never was piping so gay. (*VP* 145)

Allingham:

> And first there came a bitter laughter,
> A sound of tears the moment after;
> And then a music so lofty and gay,
> That every morning, day by day,
> I strive to recall it if I may. (*FFT* 119)

The Yeats poem is about a troop of the sidhe, Allingham's about a procession of ghosts. But what is more to the point is that both Yeats and Allingham are working out of a specifically Irish view of the vagaries of the other world. The final lines of Yeats's poem affirm that a mournful melody beautifully played can become a catalyst of gaiety, and in this respect they anticipate the dominant theme of the much later "Lapis Lazuli". But the lines also look back to Yeats's earlier description of faery as a world whose residents are "happy" but "doomed" (*CT* 80); and the source of this vision was Irish folklore. For another source of "The Host of the Air", cf. Croker's story of Davy Roche's meeting with the sidhe (*FL*, pp. 85–6), reprinted by Yeats in *FFT* (165).

22 Wilde's note to the passage reads: "*Pookauns*, mushrooms, fairy-stools, or puff-balls; the term is applied to all the family of fungi" (*IPS*, p. 134 n.). But *púcán* means a pouch; the word for mushroom or toadstool is *beacán*, while the word for puff-ball is *bolgán*. My thanks to John V. Kelleher for his comments on the uses and misuses of Irish by Yeats and his sources, and no less for his invaluable criticisms of this book in its earlier stages.

23 They are many indeed. For stories or observations that fit the pattern, see the following of Yeats's known sources: Kennedy's *Legends of Mount Leinster*, pp. 177–80; his *LFIC*, pp. 106–10, 116–17, 232–5; his *Evenings in the Duffrey*, pp. 340–3; Lady Wilde's *AL*, pp. 7, 73–4, 87, 260–3, 264–7; and her *AC*, pp. 141–4.

For stories or comments about disappearing castles, see Croker's *FL*, pp. 283–5, 468–76, 478–85; Kennedy's *LFIC*, p. 66, and his *FSI*, pp. 87–91; and Hyde's *BTF*, pp. 91–103. For tales of false fairy treasures, see Croker's *FL*, pp. 113–16, 117 n., 403–18; Kennedy's *LFIC*, pp. 106, 109, 142; Wilde's *AL*, pp. 53–5, 78–80, 88, and her *AC*, pp. 144–7. Croker's *FL* contains a descriptive note that nicely summarizes the belief that treasures wrung by mortals from the sidhe almost invariably turn out to be illusory (p. 420). This pattern of disappearance is so persistent a feature in the Irish folktale that Yeats's sources usually express surprise when the pattern is broken; *LFIC*, for instance, describes how a man manages to win a hundred pounds while gaming with one of the sidhe, and then goes out of its way to observe that, when the man examined the money the following day, it "did not turn out to be withered leaves" (p. 257).

For tales of vanishing treasure recorded by Yeats, see *UP2* 235, 269, 271; for some of his more direct personal uses of the image, see *The Green Helmet* (*CPl* 233, 238). Perhaps his most powerful evocations of the image of the vanishing "great house" are in "The Curse of Cromwell" (*VP* 580–1) and again in *Purgatory* (*CPl* 681–9).

24 Thus Austin Clarke: "A.E. once told me that 'The Fairy Thorn', an Ulster ballad by Ferguson, had fascinated both Yeats and himself, and was indeed the real origin of the Celtic Twilight." Cf. "Gaelic Ireland Rediscovered: The Early Period", in *Irish Poets in English*, p. 32.

25 The more notable analogues include "Manus O'Mallaghan and the Fairies", in *Royal Hibernian Tales*, pp. 40–5; Kennedy's "How John Hackett Won the French Princess", in *FSI*, pp. 137–9; Lady Wilde's "The Stolen Bride" and "Ethna the Bride", in *AL*, pp. 27–9 and 42–5; and Hyde's "Guleesh na Guss Dhu" (Guleesh of the black foot), in *BTF*, pp. 104–28.

26 V. K. Narayana Menon, *The Development of William Butler Yeats*, p. 14.

27 B. L. Reid, *William Butler Yeats: The Lyric of Tragedy*, p. 62.

28 The concept of fairyland as limbo comprises an evident blending of the folk and religious traditions. Folk belief held that children who were stillborn or who died shortly after birth had been taken by the sidhe, who felt that an unchristened child would have as little chance of reaching heaven as themselves. As Carleton noted, "Everyone knows that the power of fairies in Ireland is never so strong, nor so earnestly put forth, as in the moment of parturition, when they strive by all possible means to secure the new-born infant before it is christened" (*T&S*, p. 122). The Church, in turn, taught that children who died before they could be baptized went to limbo rather than to heaven: hence the equation of fairyland and limbo in Irish folk belief. "Writers on Irish superstitions", says O'Hanlon, "represent unbaptized children as sitting blindfolded within fairy moats, the peasantry supposing such souls [to] 'go into naught'" (*IF*, p. 86). This is the tradition to which Wilde gave concrete expression in his story of Biddy Mannion, with its vision of young children blindfolded and "doing nothing but sitting upon *pookauns*" (*IPS*, p. 134).

29 "The Cradles of Gold" also bears on "The Stolen Child" in that it was the temporary home of another early poem about glamouring, the untitled lyric afterwards called "The Unappeasable Host". Cf. *UP1* 415–16 and *VP* 146–7.

30 Though both local usage and the Ordnance Survey permit Yeats's reference to the hill of Lugnagall, the "hill" is in fact Cope's Mountain; Lugnagall is a townland at its foot. There would have been several reasons for Yeats's choice of "Lugnagall" over its more precise counterpart. Lugnagall sounds better; it scans better; it completes the pattern that dictates that place names in the poem be names that derive from Irish rather than English; and, as the end of

this chapter suggests, the English translation of the Irish name suits Yeats's thematic purposes in a way that "Cope's Mountain" could not have.

31 Carleton gives a good example of one such charm (*T&S*, pp. 136–7), as does Lady Wilde (*AL*, p. 42). A description of the charm's effectiveness against Druidic spells appears in Kennedy's *Evenings in the Duffrey*, p. 230.

32 Menon, op. cit., p. 14.

33 John Unterecker, *A Reader's Guide to William Butler Yeats*, p. 82.

34 The belief that the stroke precipitated death was widespread in Yeats's sources; see, for instance, Wilde's *AL*, pp. 68, 233, and see the same source for Wilde's other comments on the "blast" or "stroke" (pp. 231, 234). The description of this phenomenon that Yeats offers in *FFT* appears to have been influenced by Croker's *FL*, which affirmed that "the term 'fairy struck' is applied to paralytic affections [sic], which are supposed to proceed from a blow given by the invisible hand of an offended fairy" (p. 88). Yeats: "when the fairy strikes anyone a tumor rises, or they become paralyzed. This is called a 'fairy blast' or a 'fairy stroke'" (*FFT* 133). The description of paralysis as the result of a stroke has since passed into common usage.

35 Thus the thefts referred to in this chapter: of the "goodlooking" Mr Ormsby (*CT* 81), or of "the fairest of the four" in "The Fairy Thorn". Yeats refers to the preference of the sidhe for the more handsome among mortals in a number of his essays, most directly in "The Prisoners of the Gods": "Next after a young child and a woman in childbirth, a young, handsome and strong man is thought in most danger. When he dies about his marriage day he is believed to die, I think, because a woman of 'the others' wants him for herself" (*UP2* 80). The description of the man as "strong" is indicative; a central strand of the Irish fairy tradition held that, without the aid of a living mortal, the sidhe could accomplish nothing that required physical strength.

36 A misprint in *Letters to the New Island* has Yeats referring to Cliodhna as "queen of the monster fairies" (*LNI* 199), a mistake he would not have made. For a description of a fairy-seer who succeeded in overcoming Cliodhna, see "Cliona of Munster" in Kennedy's *FSI*, pp. 133–5. Kennedy lends support to the idea that sexual jealousy was a major motive force behind the fairies' glamouring of mortals by describing Cliodhna as Irish folklore's equivalent of Calypso or Circe.

37 For similar comments by Wilde, cf. her *AL*, pp. 142–3, and *AC*, p. 75.

38 Lady Wilde's claim that the sidhe hold it as their "peculiar" mission to punish the tight fist is a claim to which Yeats's other sources lent solid support. For the stories Yeats read on the theme, see particularly Carleton's *T&S*, pp. 77–84; Kennedy's *LFIC*, pp. 54–7; Hyde's *BTF*, pp. 148–53; the anonymous tale of "The Blacksmith" in *Royal Hibernian Tales*, pp. 98–105, and its close analogue in Gerald Griffin's *Tales of the Jury Room*, pp. 236–69 and p. 268 in particular.

39 Toberscanavan – "the well of the fine shingle", according to James Mc-Garry's *Place Names in the Writings of William Butler Yeats* (p. 80) – appears to have taken its name from the public well that stood near what was then the center of the village, on the road that led from Toberscanavan to Collooney. The well is still in use, its waters having since been diverted to a less prominent location on the other side of the road. But even when it was more in evidence, the well owned no associations of a sort that would have made it an appropriate site for a visit by Yeats's dreamer. The context of this poem points to a holy well as the dreamer's place of resort; and the likeliest location for Yeats's third stanza is the Well of Bride. Yeats knew the well both firsthand and from a description in Archdeacon Terence O'Rorke's *History, Antiquities, and Present*

State of the Parishes of Ballysadare and Kilvarnet, in the County of Sligo, p. 241. The well was located just north of Toberscanavan and just off the Collooney road, and was locally famous for its curative powers. It remained in use until its destruction in a storm in 1974.

40 For an account of the continuing popularity of holy wells in Dublin and environs, see E. Estyn Evans's excellent "Peasant Beliefs in Nineteenth-Century Ireland", in *Views of the Irish Peasantry*, p. 44.

41 Kennedy discusses the idea of "hungry grass" in his *FSI*, p. 170, and adds that Carleton had once described the superstition in a story. Though Kennedy does not name it, the story was "The Rival Kempers" (*T&S*, pp. 70–84); the reference to hungry grass therein describes it as an insidious form of fairy vengeance.

> Whenever a meal is eaten upon the grass in the open field, and the crumbs are not shaken down upon the spot for [the fairies'] use, there they are sure to leave one of their curses, called the *fair gurtha*, or the hungry-grass; for whoever passes over that particular spot for ever afterwards is liable to be struck down with weakness and hunger; and unless he can taste a morsel of bread he neither can nor will recover (p. 73).

Yeats was well acquainted with this tale of Carleton's, having excerpted it for both *FFT* and *IFT* (pp. 74–6 of the story became *FFT*'s "Paddy Corcoran's Wife"; pp. 76–7 and 77–84 became, respectively, "The Fairies' Dancing Place" and "The Rival Kempers" in *IFT*). He was also familiar with the description of hungry grass offered by O'Hanlon, though a comparison of the O'Hanlon and Carleton passages makes it clear that O'Hanlon – whose *IF* regularly drew on other authors' work without citation – was for the most part simply echoing the Carleton passage cited above (*IF*, p. 126). For another reference to hungry grass in a known Yeats source, cf. Kennedy's *Evenings in the Duffrey*, p. 399.

42 For specific references by Yeats to the "third call" of faery, see *UP2* 78, 79.

43 O'Grady told Yeats that the "young man" that the passage in *Flight of the Eagle* described "was meant" as "a description of" Yeats himself (*Mem* 59); and of all Yeats's early writings, none dovetails more precisely with the O'Grady passage than the poem that describes the dreamer. For the passage itself, cf. O'Grady, *Flight of the Eagle* (1897), pp. 255–6.

44 He was wrong, according to McGarry: "Lug Na nGall, the hollow of the strangers... 'Lug' means hollow." (*Place Names*, p. 68.) But it seems clear that Yeats chose Lugnagall as a fit place for the burial of the dreamer in part because of the association of its name with "strangers". There would have been little reason else for choosing this site instead of (say) Drumcliff churchyard under Ben Bulben, particularly since there is no indication that Lugnagall owned a burial ground.

The choice of Lissadell as the location of the second stanza is likewise suggestive. The proximity of Lissadell House would itself be enough to set the man who dreamed musing on his comparative poverty. But Yeats was also aware of the folk belief that a sighting of the sidhe could result in physical blindness – he describes that belief in an essay of his own (*UP2* 169), and found stories about it in his early folklore sources as well – and may have had that belief in mind when he sent his dreamer to the sands of a Lissadell whose name, in Yeats's own rendering of it, meant the fort or "Liss of the Blindman" (*UP1* 390).

[3]

This Monotony of Happiness: "The Wanderings of Oisin"

"The Man who Dreamed of Faeryland" describes what happened to a mortal who never reached the islands of the blessed. Its complement is "The Wanderings of Oisin", which describes what happened to a man who did.

The poem opens shortly after the fighting of the battle of Gabhra. Nicholas O'Kearney, whose introduction to and translation of the old Irish poem on the battle formed part of Yeats's background reading for his poem, set the date of the battle in AD 283 and claimed that it marked the "final overthrow and dissolution"[1] of the powerful Fenian clans. So strong had the Fenians become that no woman in Ireland could be given in marriage unless she first asked three times whether any of the Fenians wished to claim her for his own; if any did, she was required to marry him instead (*TOS* I, p. 43). This particular Fenian privilege was put to its sternest test when the king of Ireland, Cairbre, gave permission for his daughter – Sgeimh Sholais, or "Beauty of Light" – to wed an Irish prince. The Clanna Baoisgne – the Leinster Fenians – demanded that Cairbre pay them twenty ingots of gold as recompense for having usurped their right to claim the hand of any engaged woman. Cairbre saw in the challenge a chance to put an end to the despotism of this independent clan, and called on the still loyal Fenians of Connacht to come to his aid. The ensuing battle pitted the Clanna Baoisgne and their allies against a royal army led by the Fenians of Connacht. The contest lasted but a day, but the carnage was immense. The Leinster Fenians, led by the warrior bard Oisin and his strong son Oscar, lost all but three thousand of an army of twenty-one thousand men, and Oscar himself was killed. Cairbre's forces fared better without faring well: this Pyrrhic victory witnessed the survival of only sixteen thousand of his twenty-eight thousand soldiers.[2]

The opening lines of the 1889 version of "The Wanderings of Oisin" describe the exhausted remnant of the Leinster leadership in unsuccessful pursuit of a deer in the hills above Lough Leane, largest of the lakes of

Killarney.³ Their hunt is interrupted by the appearance of Niamh, who identifies herself as the daughter of the king of the Land of the Young, traditional name for the Elysium of Irish legend. Like all "maidens who take the [love] initiative in Irish tales", she cites a hero's fame as the motive force behind her visit to mortal lands⁴ and invites Oisin to join her in leaving those lands behind. He takes a sad leave of his fellow warriors, mounts her fairy horse and finds himself riding out over the ocean waves towards the Island of the Living.

The first of the three islands he visits is to all appearances a place of unalloyed joy, with its ever-young inhabitants giving themselves over to pleasures endlessly repeated. His alliance with Niamh affords Oisin an opportunity to make an eternal home amid their happiness; but when one day the staff of a broken war-lance washes onto the fairy shores, a reawakened nostalgia for the Fenians and battle shakes his dormant feelings of "human sadness" (*VP* 25) from their sleep and tells him the time has come to leave. He and Niamh mount the horse once more and cross the ocean to the Island of Victories, antithesis of all that the first island stood for. The island is surmounted by a huge black castle; its sole inhabitants are a "dusk[y] demon" (*VP* 39) and his captive, a young woman in chains. Resolved to free her from the island, Oisin cuts the chains and goes off to do battle with the demon. Like the battle of Gabhra, this fight too lasts an entire day, largely because Oisin's sad adversary is protean, taking on the shapes of a fir tree and a drowned corpse even as they fight. Oisin finally kills him, or so it seems, and after throwing the body into the ocean rejoins Niamh and the apparently liberated captive for a feast that lasts three days. On the morning of the fourth day the demon re-emerges from the sea; their battle is joined again, with precisely the same result. Like the unending loves on the Island of the Living, this cycle of battle, seeming victory, feasting, and battle renewed promises to continue *ad infinitum*; but the waves bring a second messenger from mortal shores, this time a beech bough. Its appearance reminds Oisin of the earthly forests the Fenians had rejoiced in and, his heart again grown "sore" (*VP* 44) with memories of his mortal companions, he determines to remain on the island no longer. His repetitious struggles prove to have been in vain. As he and Niamh take their leave, they hear the demon, alive once more, singing in a distant monotone. His song asserts his ability to outlast the transient emotions of man, and hints – the poem does not reveal specifically what happens to her – that the woman Oisin sought to free is the demon's captive once more.

If love and war are the themes that dance attendance on the first two islands, the third is marked by its very lack of attitude. Its gigantic residents live in a valley surrounded by a barely penetrable forest of enormous trees; and neither lust nor rage intrudes on their eternal sleep. One of them holds a branch hung with bells, a branch so venerable that even the *seanchaidhthe* tell of it in their recitations.⁵ The sound of the bells keeps the giants asleep, and Oisin and Niamh succumb to the same music. Their slumber ends when a weary starling from mortal lands drops onto the island. Reminded for a third time of the world he left behind, feeling "once more" in his heart "the ancient sadness of man" (*VP* 54), Oisin decides to revisit the Fenians in his original island home. A tearful Niamh agrees to his departure, but tells him that during his absence he must not touch the earth. The horse carries him back to Ireland, and he discovers that what had seemed to him brief sojourns on each of the three islands have taken a century apiece. The Fenians are long since dead, and St Patrick and his priests ride herd on a new race of weaklings. He turns back towards Niamh, and has almost reached the ocean when he sees two men struggling under the weight of a sack of sand. Pity drives him to reach down to take the sack, but as he hurls it forward the girth of his saddle snaps; his feet touch the ground; his three hundred years of grace descend on him in an instant, and he is transformed into an old man on the edge of death. The poem, which from its start takes the form of an interchange between St Patrick and the now aged Oisin, concludes with the saint's attempt to persuade the pagan swordsman that he must turn Christian to avoid the damnation visited on his fellow Fenians. Unregenerate, Oisin proclaims his preference for hell, where his war songs will rouse the Fenians to battle with and victory over the devils of Christianity.

The variety of this plot stems in part from the fact that Yeats drew on varied sources in the course of designing his poem. The bulk of these sources have since come to light,[6] the most central among them being Michael Comyn's *Laoidh Oisín ar Thír na nÓg* ("The Lay of Oisin on the Land of Youth"). Perhaps the last Fenian lay to have been composed, the poem dated from the first half of the eighteenth century and had been translated by Bryan O'Looney for the Ossianic Society in 1856 (see *TOS* IV). Yeats follows O'Looney's translation up to the point at which Oisin and Niamh depart for the islands of the sidhe; but from that point on, "The Wanderings of Oisin" and its original generally part company. The first fairyland in the Comyn poem is the "Land of Virtues". It is here that Oisin does battle with a giant named Fomhor Builleach, whose only resemblance to the dusky demon pictured by Yeats is that he too has a female captive, the daughter of the king of the "Land of Life". Oisin kills the giant, and he and Niamh depart for Tir na nOg, the "Land of Perpetual Youth", of which her father is king. They live there three hundred years, at the end of which time Oisin decides to pay a final visit to his mortal friends before returning to live in the Land of Youth forever. He returns to Ireland, finds that the Fenians are dead, and is on his way back to Niamh when he meets a group of men struggling to move a large flag of marble. They ask for his help; he reaches down and hurls the marble forward, but as he does so his foot touches the ground and he becomes an old man.

Certain of the alterations Yeats effected are manifest. The original mentions three realms – the Land of Virtues, the Land of Life, and the Land of Perpetual Youth – though Oisin and Niamh actually visit only two of the three. The Land of Perpetual Youth becomes Yeats's Island of the Living; the Land of Virtues becomes his Island of Victories. The Land of Life does not figure in his poem, but he substitutes for it the Island of Forgetfulness. The transformation of the Land of Virtues into the Island of Victories was effected in part with the aid of O'Looney's notes and introduction to his translation of Comyn. O'Looney felt that the "Lay of

Oisin" had erred in designating the land in which Oisin fights the giant as the Land of Virtues. "The 'Land of Virtues,'" he writes, is "a country not mentioned in any other copy of this poem that I have seen" (*TOS* IV, p. 250 n.). His description of the true nature of that land lends a roundabout credence to Yeats's decision to replace Virtues with Victories:

> In the "Land of Virtues," or as some call it, the "Land of Victories," (but the latter name I suppose to be a mis-translation, as I have never heard of a battle or strife in this country); it is all peace, tranquility and happiness. As there is no conflict there can be no victory – and there is no virtue to be desired which is not to be had on entering this country! (*TOS* IV, pp. 230–1).

And indeed it does seem strange that the land that the "Lay of Oisin" describes as a battlefield should be called by the name of virtuous. Yeats does not imitate the incongruity. The title he borrows from O'Looney is an apter one, apter for its irony. Oisin is not, after all, victorious in the Yeatsian version of the land of victories; the woman he seeks to free remains a captive, and the demon continues with his sad eternal drone.

The original text also helps to account for Yeats's failure to describe the ultimate fate of the demon's captive in detail. The Oisin imaged by Comyn did not know what had happened to her either:

> We prepared ourselves without a stay,
>   And we took our leave of the virgin,
>   We were sorrowful and sad after her,
>   And not less after us was the refulgent maid.
>
> I do not know, O mild Patrick!
>   What occurred to the young princess,
>   Since the day we both parted her,
>   Or whether she herself returned to the Land of
>   Life. (*TOS* IV, p. 257)

But if Yeats in this case decided to remain faithful to his source, in most instances he felt free to modify that source to suit his own purposes. Thus the marble flag of the original becomes a bag of sand in Yeats's adaptation: image more fit, suggesting as it does the burden of mortality that weighs the men down. Yeats knew, moreover, that the image had a precedent in the Irish folktales that had grown up around the figure of Oisin. One William Williams of Waterford had written to the Ossianic Society to describe a local variant of the Oisin legend that he had heard while living in Cork. His letter has Oisin entering Tir na nOg through a cavern near Mitchelstown; the *Transactions* of the Society printed the document directly before the Comyn poem that Yeats drew on. And Williams began thus:

> Oisin went into the cave, met a beautiful damsel, after crossing the stream, lived with her for (as he fancied) a few days, wished to revisit the Fenians, obtained consent at last, on condition of not

alighting from a *white steed*, with which she furnished him, stating that it was over 300 years since he came to the cave. He proceeded till he met a carrier, whose cart, containing a bag of sand, was upset; he asked Oisin to help him; unable to raise the bag with one hand, he alighted, on which the steed fled, leaving him a *withered, decrepid* [sic], *blind* old man (*TOS* IV, p. 233).

Irish folklore and legend were by no means the only foundations on which Yeats raised "The Wanderings of Oisin"; the poem has an equally firm basis in Yeats's occult studies, his readings in theosophy in particular. But the grounding of the poem in works like the *Transactions* was direct, and the *Transactions* were only one of a variety of Irish sources Yeats appropriated. The two volumes of Standish O'Grady's *History of Ireland* (1878, 1880), for instance, furnished "the Fraygarta" (*Hist* I, p. 198), the "sword of Mananān" (*Hist* II, p. 279 n.) that, according to O'Grady, shone "like glittering diamond... and on its starry sides were there graved verses in... Ogham" (*Hist* II, p. 279). It is this weapon that Yeats puts into Oisin's hands before his battle with the demon, "a sword whose wizard shine/Not loaded centuries might vapour. Ran/Deep sunken on the blade's length, 'Mananan!'", this last word written "in Ogham letters" (*VP* 37–8).[7] O'Grady's first volume was also a source of one of the shapes that Yeats has the demon take in the 1895 version of his poem; it was in the *History* that Yeats encountered O'Grady's description of "the Ban-Shee of Lōk Mac Favash" (*Hist II*, p. 229), a protean spectre that continually returns to life after the hero, in this case Cú Chulainn, has killed him. Like Yeats's demon, O'Grady's misnamed "banshee" undergoes three distinct transformations in the course of its encounter with the champion of the Red Branch; and one of the shapes it assumes is that of "a great eel" (p. 208), even as Oisin will find himself lunging "at the smooth throat/Of a great eel" (*VP* 40).[8]

If not direct borrowings, these are at least direct analogues; and the feast that takes place in the aftermath of the battle also has its analogues in known Yeats sources. "The Dragon-Slayer", one of the "most popular" folktales in Ireland and "usually introduced by the successive slaying of three giants by the hero... before he goes on to rescue a princess",[9] is a tale-type whose variants the young Yeats had come across in several of the works of Irish folklore that he read and recommended. The version of the tale that most closely parallels the feasting scenes in "The Wanderings of Oisin", "The Fellow in the Goat-Skin", appeared in Patrick Kennedy's *Fireside Stories*. Herein the hero fights a giant, rests for three days, fights another giant, rests for three days, fights a third giant and then rests once more. The intervals of rest between Oisin's clashes with the demon cover the same length of time – "three days we feasted" (*VP* 43) – and the rewards visited on the two champions are likewise similar. At the end of the Kennedy tale the fellow in the goat-skin wins his most difficult battle to date. Then: "he lay on a settle bed for three days", and had "the princess and all her maids of honour to wait on him, and pity him, and give him gruel, and toast, and tay of all the colours under the sun" (p. 113). So too Oisin, who recalls that at the end of his first day of apparently successful combat Niamh and the demon's prisoner "brought me wine and bread", and

> on the skin supine
> Of wolves, of boreal bears, we quaffed the wine
> Brewed of the sea-gods, from huge cups that lay
> Upon the lips of sea-gods in their day,
> And on the skins of wolves and bears we slept. (*VP* 41)

Yeats's early readings in Irish folklore, then, provide suggestive parallels with his early writings on the events of Irish legend and, for that matter, with his descriptions of non-events as well. A number of likely models for the sleepers on the Island of Forgetfulness have been run to ground; but it would be hard to find a more precise description of these drowsy former warriors, unwilling or unable to speak, than the one Yeats came across in O'Hanlon's *Irish Folk Lore*. As O'Hanlon had it, the "general theory" held that the ancient races of Ireland were now dwelling in Tir na nOg "under some magic thrall; and that adventurous or wrecked voyagers" – in this case a Fenian wanderer and a princess of the sidhe – "had been cast on that fabled land, where they found chieftains and warriors silent or somnambulant, being incapable of giving any information about their past, present, or future state" (p. 294). And the music that keeps them asleep, a music that fills Oisin with "softness", that destroys "the memories of the whole of [his] sorrow and the memories of the whole of [his] mirth" (*VP* 52), has a twin in Lady Wilde's account of the effect that the music of the fairy harp has on those who hear it: they "lose all memory of love or hate, and forget all things... save the soft music of the fairy harp" (*AL*, p. 30).

Nowhere else in Yeats's vision of Oisin does music have so direct an effect on those it reaches, but this is not to say that the musical motif in the poem reaches no further than the Island of Forgetfulness. Sounds gay, or sad, or lulling are the respective properties of the first, second, and third islands; and Yeats's decision to associate each island with a different kind of melody is intriguing, particularly in the light of what his folklore readings had taught him about both the structure of the Irish folktale and the categories into which Irish folk music had traditionally been divided. Pinpointing the moment when a resemblance becomes an influence is a delicate business, more so when we are dealing with a young man who read widely and eclectically and who owned a highly selective memory. But it is hard not to find in the structure of "The Wanderings of Oisin" an echo of the "three thirds of the night" motif, a typical element in the Irish folktale and an element with which Yeats was entirely familiar. When the heroes of the many tales that draw on the motif take their rest at the end of the day's adventures, they agree to divide the coming night into thirds: the first third to be spent in play, the second in sport or in recounting tales of combat, the third in sleep.[10] The activities on (respectively) the Islands of the Living, of Victories, of Forgetfulness follow the same progress; and the different kinds of music that accompany those activities are also evocative, resonant of the "three *styles*" of traditional Irish music, "of all three" of which there are "numerous well-marked examples descending to the present day":

> The *Gen-traige* (gan-tree), which incited to merriment and laughter, is represented by the lively dance-tunes and other such spirited pieces. The *Gol-traige* (gol-tree) expressed sorrow: represented by the *keens* or death-tunes, many of which are still preserved. The *Súan-traige* (suan-tree) produced sleep. This style is seen in our lullabies or nurse-tunes, of which we have numerous beautiful specimens.[11]

Yeats's description of the Island of the Living owns numerous well-marked examples of a music that incites to merriment and laughter. When Oisin and Niamh first arrive on the island, they meet "a band/Of youths and maidens hand in hand,/And singing, singing all together", their song leaving them "laugh[ing] like murmurs of the sea", their joy a "sudden laughter" that "sprang/From all their lips" (*VP* 15, 16). The music on the Island of Victories produces a precisely opposite effect, expresses sorrow. Invincible though he may be, the demon whom Oisin sees for the first time is a mournful figure, "crooning to himself an unknown tongue", singing "in a sad revelry" (*VP* 39). His captive is no happier. Oisin and Niamh hear her song come "swimming sadly down the mighty stair" of the castle, and climb the stair towards the song:

> Crashed on the stones, upon the glimmering stones,
> Our tread, as rose and fell the liquid tones
> Of knitted music. Oft the fond repining
> Flowed on anew, and oft, anew declining,
> Sobbed into silence. (*VP* 32, 33)

Finally, the music of the third island –

> And I gazed on the bell-branch, sleep's forebear, far
>   sung of the Sennachies.
> I saw how those slumberers, grown weary, there camping
>   in grasses deep,
> Of wars with the wide world and pacing the shores of
>   the seven seas,
> Laid hands on the bell-branch and swayed it, and fed of
>   unhuman sleep (*VP* 50–1) –

is, by choice or chance, that of the *súan-traige*, irresistible slumber tune.

However useful a process, discovering what mines Yeats worked is less important than determining what he did with what he quarried. Ellmann observed that Yeats managed to weave his poem into a "very tight web"[12] by paying close attention to the progress of its themes. The same care for structure is evident on the level of narrative as well. Each of the spans of a hundred years concludes with an image that foreshadows the span to come. The lance washed ashore on the Island of the Living calls Oisin off to battle with the demon; and the fact that the lance is broken suggests in advance that the battle will be in vain.[13] The beech bough that prompts him to leave the Island of Victories looks ahead to the immense trees beneath which the inhabitants of the Island of Forgetfulness sleep out eternity. And the earthly starling that calls up memories of Ireland anticipates Oisin himself. The bird drops down exhausted on the giants' island; Oisin is to touch the earth and turn into an "old man, full of sleep" (*VP* 60).

This linking together of the various parts of the poem by images that prepare for subsequent events and settings is but one notable aspect of the poem's structure. Within its formal tripartite division, "The Wanderings of Oisin" falls into five distinct scenes. The first, middle, and last of these are related to battle; they are separated by interludes of love and forgetfulness. The consistency of this pattern is a further indication that the order in which the scenes occur follows a set design, an indication that the steady evolution of Yeats's narrative confirms. When Yeats moved the fight with the maiden's captor from the beginning of the Comyn poem to the middle of his own, he was departing from Comyn's plot in order to better chart his central character's progress from an attitude of defeat to a stance of heroic defiance.

The opening of "The Wanderings of Oisin" prescinds from O'Kearney's remarks on the battle of Gabhra as watershed, a debacle that marked the final breaking of Fenian power. The ruined warriors who ride through the opening lines of Yeats's narrative are unable to bring down even the single weary deer they are hunting. Nor are their hounds much help. Traditionally three thousand in number, they have here been reduced to three; and though the three that remain are those that legend numbers as the pride of the Fenian pack, the frustration of the hunt has even them "lolling their tongues" with fatigue (*VP* 2). Arrived on the scene, Niamh asks the reason for the Fenians' sadness; Fionn's answer speaks of the dead at Gabhra and, more particularly, of the battlefield death of Oscar. His singling out of this one warrior has its explanation. Though the poem does not say so, the stories surrounding the Fenians named Oscar as the greatest of their warriors; "the Invincible" was one of the more characteristic epithets that gathered around his name. His death at Gabhra was to the Fenians what Hector's was to Troy; and Oisin and Fionn, his father and grandfather, had deeper reasons for grief than the rest.[14]

In Yeats's view, then, it is a desperate situation that Oisin leaves behind when he departs the fields of death and sets off with Niamh for the Island of the Living. The time he spends there is primarily a period of necessary convalescence, a renewal of strength among those who are always strong. The Fenians' lack of success in the hunt is juxtaposed with the constant triumph of the island's young warriors; the hall of their king is "all covered over/With antlers and the shaggy skin/Of many a slaughtered forest rover" (*VP* 17). In taking up residence among the undefeated islanders, Oisin resumes his own old habit of victory. Deer no longer elude him:

> Oh, Patrick, on that woody shore
> A hundred years I chased the boar,
> And slew the badger and the deer,
> And flung the joyous hunting-spear! (*VP* 23)

And when at the end of a hundred years he remembers the Fenians, the change in his attitude towards them is telling. There is no mention here of Gabhra or its aftermath; his memories are rather of how the Fenians were "equal" to whatever the battle might send.

> When once beside the shore I stood,
> A sea-worn waif came floating by.
> I drew it forth; the staff of wood,
> It was of some dead warrior's lance.
> I turned it in my hands; the stains
> Of war were on it, and I wept,
> Remembering how along the plains,
> Equal to good or evil chance
> In war, the noble Fenians stept. (*VP* 24)

He has regained the strength he had before the Fenian defeat, and is himself once again equal to good or evil chance in war. His recovery comes none too soon, for his next opponent is to prove even more formidable than the royal army that destroyed the Clanna Baoisgne.

This second and most central of the three battle scenes begins with the arrival of Oisin and Niamh on the Island of Victories and their discovery of the maiden chained in the castle.[15] Oisin's decision to fight the demon traces directly back to the pride and confidence that he managed to recover on the Island of the Living. Both Niamh and, more pointedly, the woman who has a chance to gain her freedom through his intervention attempt to discourage him from doing battle; indeed, the demon's captive urges her "deliverer" (*VP* 34) to leave the island entirely, since "none may fight,/With hope, mine enemy", and the very "demons of the wilds and winds" scream "for fright" when he appears (*VP* 34). Oisin's response to this dark vantage is a response that the weary campaigner whom Niamh first met could not have given:

>   'Nay,' I answered; 'my hands burn
> For battle.'
>   'Fly ye from a thing so dread.
> It brings no shame upon a human head
> To fly a spirit,' Niam weeping said.
> Though from beseeching they desisted not,
> They stirred my spacious soul in me no jot –
>   ... For an answering sign
> I burst the chain. (*VP* 35–6)

The results of this second battle relate directly to the results of the first. Gabhra had ended in complete defeat. The fight with the demon, by comparison, represents a step forward for Oisin, concluding as it does in neither defeat nor true victory. The demon does not relinquish his prisoner, but for all his superior might he never succeeds in overcoming Oisin. Faced with the inevitable resurgence of an undying foe, the fighter from mortal lands might well have given way to the kind of despair the Fenians had felt after Gabhra. But he acquits himself with pride. Inasmuch as he knows that he can never be wholly victorious, his long refusal to leave the field is an act of plain heroism. He concludes by taking on his protean opponent less in hopes of conquering him than in order to test his renewed strength against a superior enemy, and he discovers that his strength is real. The battle of Gabhra had left the Fenians exhausted. But the battle on the Island of Victories, longer by far and far more difficult than the assault by Cairbre's armies, touches a calm pulse:

> ...for a hundred years
> So warred, so feasted we. No dreams, no fears,
> No languor, no fatigue; an endless feast,
> An endless war. (*VP* 44)

Though he fails to destroy his indestructible opponent, he is at the same time putting his strength to a harsh and constant test; and his survivals of those tests enable him to recover his own sense of kingliness. In his second memory of the Fenians he imagines himself walking with Fionn and Oscar beneath the trees of Emain Macha, fortress castle of the Red Branch:

> The hundredth year had ceased.
> I stood upon the stair; the surges bore
> A beech bough to me, and my heart grew sore,
> Remembering how I paced in days gone o'er,
> At Eman, 'neath the beech trees, on each side,
> Fin, Conan, Oscar, many more, the tide
> Of planets watching, watching the race of hares
> Leap in the meadow. (*VP* 44)

Like the battle of Gabhra, the battle with the demon is followed by a period of repose that prepares Oisin for a battle yet to come. The Island of Forgetfulness is the shadow that the first two islands cast, a mimic of their vividness. Of all the three islands, that of the Living is the one on which music is heard most constantly – so continual is its sound that "It seemed to fall from the very flame/Of the great round sun, from his central fires" (*VP* 13) – while the Island of Victories is, above all, a battlefield. The third island too has its music, and its hints of the shakings of earth; but the sound of the bell-branch summons to sleep rather than song, and the armor of the giants lies about them, unused.

> More comely than man may make them, inlaid with silver and gold,
> Were arrow and shield and war-axe, arrow and spear and blade,

And dew-blanched horns, in whose hollows a child of three
  years old
Could sleep on a couch of rushes – round and about them
  laid. (*VP* 49)

Oisin joins them in rest, and his dreams are a direct preparation for his coming encounter with Patrick. As the legends had it, the saint's arrival in Ireland was preceded by three major periods in Irish history: the ascendancy of the Tuatha Dé Danaan, the heroic age of the Red Branch, and the years of Fenian rule. Oisin dreams of all three, and in so doing clears the stage for his meeting with the exemplar of the fourth and final age, that of Christianity. His reverie includes a varied cast. The Tuatha Dé Danaan came back to power after their triumph over the Fomoire at the second battle of Magh Tuiredh, a victory that came about when Lugh, chief among his tribe, slung a stone through the eye of the cyclopean Balor.[16] The eye was so large that it took four men to raise its lid, and Balor's unimpeded gaze could destroy an army; and it is this that Oisin is recalling when he dreams of "Balor, as old as a forest, his vast face sunk/Helpless, men lifting the lids of his weary and death-pouring eye" (*VP* 53). His vision of the Red Branch likewise focuses on characters and events that are central to the Red Branch story: first on "Cuchulin" (*VP* 53), and then on the tragedy of Deirdre. Coveted by the most prominent of the Red Branch kings, Conchobar Mac Nessa, Deirdre fell unwillingly into his hands when Fergus, who had promised her his protection, was unable to make good his promise. Mac Nessa had persuaded Barach, whose hospitality Fergus was bound by tabu to accept, to invite Fergus to a feast, and seized his reluctant loved one once Fergus was out of the way – all this evoked when Oisin's wandering dream fans out to include "Mac Nessa" and "Cook Barach, the traitor" and "Fergus who feastward sad slunk" (*VP* 53). Finally, Oisin's imaging of the third of the major pre-Christian eras – "And by me, in soft red raiment, the Fenians moved in loud streams" (*VP* 53) – is an image that readies its aftermath; the next verses in Yeats's narrative have Oisin waking from sleep, thence to return to Ireland and discover that the era of the Fenians has itself been superseded.

In thus recalling the central actors on a more ancient Irish stage, Oisin has placed himself in a position in which racial memory replaces personal memory. His recollections of his own life are obliterated:

And, man of the many white crosiers, a century there I
  forgot;
That the spearshaft is made out of ashwood, the shield
  out of osier and hide;
How the hammers spring on the anvil, on the spearhead's
  burning spot;
How the slow blue-eyed oxen of Fin low sadly at evening
  tide. (*VP* 52)

He is in a state of semi-trance, has become a blank page on which spirits or men might write their instructions:

> So lived I and lived not, so wrought I and wrought not,
>   with creatures of dreams,
> In a long iron sleep, as a fish in the water goes dumb
>   as a stone. (*VP* 53)

His hundred years' sleep, then, has the effect of neutralizing the strength he had displayed in refusing to succumb to the demon; and it will take a third visitation from mortal shores, this time the appearance of the starling, to make him whole yet again. In this case, the memory of the Fenians that the sight of the starling prompts carries back to the beginning of the poem. In his earlier recollections of his former mates, he had envisioned them going into battle or walking on the grounds of Emain; but now he sees them as they were on the day when he first met Niamh, following their enchanted hounds to the hunt.

> So watched I when, man of the crosiers, at the heel of a
>   century fell,
> Weak, in the midst of the meadow, from his miles in the
>   midst of the air,
> A starling – like them that foregathered 'neath a moon
>   waking white as a shell,
> When the Fenians made foray at morning with Bran,
>   Sgeolan, Lomair. (*VP* 54)

In sum, he has come full cycle. Bowed by the dead at Gabhra, he had recovered his strength on the Island of the Living, and had tested and proved that strength on the island he came to next. His sleep on the third island had brought him memories of a rich heritage. With his own might restored and the memory of the power of his forebears for support, he is ready to be reborn, to balance his former retreat from Ireland with a triumphal return to home.

In later years Yeats came to see "The Wanderings of Oisin" as an anti-progress myth,[17] as in a general sense it is. Oisin's wanderings never come to specific conclusion. At the end of the poem he makes ready to go off once again, to stride into hell or, as Yeats's own retrospective comment on his poem suggested, sail off to another island. But there is a progress of sorts in the poem, and it locates itself in the steady development of Oisin himself. The hero who returns to Ireland is different from the man who left. The concluding section of the poem pictures a man who, after long travail, has regained a grasp on defiance. He finds the men who now inhabit Ireland

> ... weeding or ploughing with faces a-shining with
>   much-toil wet;
> And in this place and that place, with bodies unglorious,
>   their chieftains stood,
> Awaiting in patience the straw-death, crosiered one,
>   caught in thy net –
> Went the laughter of scorn from my mouth like the
>   roaring of wind in a wood. (*VP* 58)

Oisin and This Monotony of Happiness

And it is a mixture of scorn and pity that prompts him to put his own great strength at their service. The beginning of the poem had found him posed in an unproductive sadness, but his sorrow here is a proud one. He sees the men struggling with the sack of sand:

> With sweating, with staggering, they lifted and
>   shouldered a sack full of sand,
> But prone on the pathway, prone struggling, they lay
>   'neath the sand-sack at length.
> Leaning forth from the gem-studded saddle, I flung it
>   five yards with my hand
> With a sob – for men waxing so weakly, a sob for the
>   Fenians' old strength. (*VP* 60)

Nor does his attitude change even after he falls from the horse to touch the ground and feel the years descend. After the battle of Gabhra, he had needed the love of Niamh, help from an outside source, in order to forget his sorrow over the destruction of the Fenians. The situation he encounters upon his return to Ireland should prove a still more forceful catalyst for despair. Former resident of two remarkable worlds, he now has no home at all: the Fenians, more than defeated, are gone from the face of the earth, and he has lost his chance to spend eternity with Niamh in the bargain. Yeats knew versions of the legend in which the arguments of the saint had prevailed, and Oisin had turned Christian after all;[18] and there is ample motive even in Yeats's poem for Oisin to do the same. Yet he refuses to capitulate, and his refusal must be read as proof that he is a mightier man in old age than he had been in youth, his bodily decrepitude serving only to set his defiance in a stronger light and make it seem yet more heroic. The passage from Blake's letters that Yeats quoted often and with admiration has a bearing here, since Yeats's aged Fenian owns a strong resemblance to the aged visionary poet. "I have been very near the gates of death," wrote Blake,

> and have returned very weak, and an old man, feeble and tottering, but not in spirit and life, not in the real man, the imagination which liveth forever. In that I grow stronger and stronger as this foolish body decays.[19]

This is a precise description of Oisin's attitude at the end of his dialogue with Patrick. He is the first of the many old men who troop indefatigably through Yeats's verse, sweeping proud, open-eyed and laughing towards the tomb (*VP* 501). The first few words of his response to Patrick's argument that he must either turn Christian or join the Fenians in hell are an admission of bodily weakness, but the rest of his answer points to a spirit that grows stronger even as his body decays.

> Put the staff in my hands; I will go to the Fenians,
>   thou cleric, and chant
> The war-songs that roused them of old; they will rise,
>   making clouds with their breath

> Innumerable, singing, exultant – the clay underneath
>   them shall pant,
> And demons, all broken in pieces, be trampled beneath
>   them in death.
>
> And demons afraid in their darkness – deep horror of eyes
>   and of wings,
> Afraid their ears on the earth laid, shall listen and rise
>   up and weep;
> Hearing the shaking of shields and the quiver of stretched
>   bowstrings,
> Hearing hell loud with a murmur, as shouting and mocking
>   we sweep.
>
> We will tear out the red flaming stones, and will batter
>   the gateway of brass
> And enter, and none sayeth 'nay' when there enters the
>   strongly armed guest;
> Make clean as a broom cleans, and march on as oxen move
>   over young grass;
> Then feast, making converse of Eri, of wars, and of old
>   wounds and rest. (*VP* 61–2)

The war-songs that Oisin proposes to chant to the Fenians do not appear in Comyn's poem, but other of Yeats's sources had told him what they were. "The *Ross-catha*, or battle-hymn" was "the great war-song to which the warriors marched to battle, and which inspired them with the heroic madness that braved death for victory";[20] indeed, the "composition and recitation of a *Rosg catha* (war ode) was the first step to victory".[21] As both these comments imply, the key word here is "victory". Patrick tells Oisin that the devils of hell are invincible, that "no man may war with the strong spirits wage" (*VP* 62); but then the woman on the Island of Victories had said the same of the demon, and Oisin had been neither dissuaded by her words nor mastered by her captor. There is no apparent reason why he should be apprehensive about a war with hell's armies, inasmuch as earlier in the poem he had shown no fear when confronted with the wrath of God. The heavens had answered his description of Patrick as a "liar and flatterer of the weak" (*VP* 42) with a thunder that terrified Patrick and his priests. But not Oisin:

> Saint, dost thou weep? I hear amid the thunder
> The horses of the Fenians – tearing asunder
> Of armour – laughter and cries – the armies' shock.

His contention that his songs will summon the Fenians to conquer the forces of hell is a credible one because he goes off to the battle armed with an attitude that will not brook defeat. The opening scene of the poem was set in a post-battle atmosphere of desolation. The middle scene dealt with a battle in progress, and this time Oisin was to leave the field unsubdued. The final scene is the antithesis of the first and, like Oisin's three memories of the Fenians, is designed to bring the poem full circle; it is set before a battle rather than after, and Oisin's chant therein is the first step to final victory. From the Connacht Fenians to the demon who cannot be killed to all the legions of hell: his opponents grow more formidable as his wanderings progress, but so does he. The travels that carry him forward to his confrontation with a saint carry his spirit back: to the years when the Fenians, their "old strength" (*VP* 60) still in its youth, had no mere saints to contend with, but itemized kings as their liegemen.

To discuss the structure of "The Wanderings of Oisin" in its relation to the growth of the poem's central character is to come part way towards understanding what Yeats had in mind in shaping his poem's narrative as he did; but to weigh the poem's persistent allusiveness is to sense that Yeats, as so often, had something more than simple narrative in mind. So he himself suggested in the letter written to Katharine Tynan some five months before *The Wanderings of Oisin and Other Poems* was published:

> In the second part of Oisin under disguise of symbolism I have said sever[a]l things, to which I only have the key. The romance is for my readers, they must not even know there is a symbol anywhere. They will not find out. If they did it would spoil the art (*CL1* 98).

This well-known comment may be taken as applying to the poem as a whole, not simply its "second part"; and what is perhaps most interesting about it is that it helps to disclose what it seeks to conceal. In the course of insisting on mystery, Yeats is tipping his hand as to what kind of thing it is that he firmly intends to keep secret.

Yeats's occult sources had several things in common, and veiled diction was prominent among them. Aimed at a dual audience of the initiated and the curious perplexed, the dark works of the eighties sought to straddle the two groups by claiming that they contained concealed wisdom: the wisdom being intended for those with eyes that could see, with the fact that it was concealed covering the skeptics who might question whether anything of substance was really going on here in the first place. The book that exercised so direct an influence on the young Yeats and his friend Charles Johnston, A. P. Sinnett's *Esoteric Buddhism* (1883), asserted that mainline occult works like those of Madame Blavatsky – Sinnett's own Master – employed this "veil of obscurity" out of vigilance: "to wrap the doctrine from careless observation" (p. 208). And the work that ushered in the popular phase of the occult revival in England, Sinnett's earlier *The Occult World* (1881), had noted that "almost all existing occult literature" made use of what Yeats's letter to Tynan referred to as the disguise of symbolism; these works, said Sinnett, had been "rendered purposely obscure by the use of an elaborate symbology" (p. 173).

Sinnett was not exaggerating. Virtually all of the works that the occultists of the eighties came to regard as touchstones claimed to hint at hidden revelations. *Zanoni*, Bulwer-Lytton's immensely popular novel, was a type of the kind. In 1842 Lytton, friend of Éliphas Lévi and Grand Patron of the Societas Rosicruciana in Anglia – the organization whence emerged the founding fathers of the Order of the Golden Dawn – offered the reading public a book of "sibyl leaves, weird with many a dark enigma". The novel achieved a wide currency, gaining a close to canonical status in both the Golden Dawn and the Theosophical Society.[22] The aura of mystery that had contributed so roundly to its success also raised questions about what it was that the book meant, but Lytton refused to be any more specific about his intentions than the author of "The Wanderings of Oisin" would later be about his. His introduction to the novel is couched in the same kind of language that Yeats was to use when writing to Katharine Tynan about his poem. For the general reader, Yeats's poem would simply seem a "romance"; for those who owned the "key" to its symbols it was something quite other. So too *Zanoni*: "It is a romance, and it is not a romance. It is a truth for those who can comprehend it, and an extravagance for those who cannot" (p. ix). Pressed for explanation, Lytton later added an endnote that advised the reader to find what explanation he could. Lytton himself would go no further than to suggest that "beneath the narrative [*Zanoni*] relates, *typical* meanings are concealed", and that hence the novel is to be "regarded in two characters". What the deeper of those two characters might be, it was not for the author to say; he would give "no key to mysteries, be they trivial or important, which may be found in the secret chambers by those who lift the tapestry from the wall" (p. 352).

The similarities in diction here are apparent. Like other occultists before him, Yeats too had written a romance – Lytton's "tapestry" – that veiled a hidden meaning, a secret chamber that could only be unlocked by those who owned the key to Yeats's elaborate symbology. What the letter to Katharine Tynan was hinting at, then, was Yeats's view of "The Wanderings of Oisin" as a work in the occult tradition, a narrative that masked "typical" meanings, a poem to be regarded in two characters. What mystery lay within its secret chambers remains to be determined. Yeats was a man with a profound interest in the occult, and the author of an uncommon poem whose central figure departs this world for a world beyond, there undergoes a series of strange encounters, then returns to the world he had originally taken leave of. Here one needs to ask the most basic of questions: what ought all this to mean?

It ought to mean that what lie hidden in Yeats's poem are his early beliefs about the departure of the soul from earth after the death of the body, the experiences it undergoes in the state it inhabits between its earthly incarnations and, finally, its return to the world it had left once the moment for its rebirth has arrived; and there is ample evidence in both the poem and its occult contexts to indicate that "The Wanderings of Oisin" meant just that.

In years to come Yeats's varied readings would speak time after time of the belief of the ancient Irish in the doctrine of rebirth. He was to come across the concept in Blavatsky's *The Secret Doctrine* (1888), Rhys's *Celtic Heathendom* (1888), Hyde's *Literary History of Ireland* (1899), and the English translation of Arbois de Jubainville's *The Irish Mythological Cycle and Celtic*

Mythology (1903).[23] More tellingly still, he would find in Alfred Nutt's two volumes, *The Voyage of Bran* (1895, 1897), that the legends that set Celtic heroes wandering between this world and Tir na nOg were, like his own poem, parables. In his 1898 review of the *Voyage*, Yeats compliments Nutt for having revealed that tales of this kind illustrated the Celtic belief in the "doctrine of the rebirth of the soul, of its coming out of the happy other world of the dead, and living once more" – a doctrine, Yeats added, that constituted "the most important of all old beliefs" (*UP2* 120, 119). But Yeats had not needed to wait to be instructed by Nutt. He had uncovered the connection between the doctrine of rebirth and the wanderings of Oisin a good decade earlier, and in the same volumes of the *Transactions of the Ossianic Society* whence he had culled his narrative.

Yeats himself pointed to his use of Comyn's "The Lay of Oisin on the Land of Youth" as a source, and it was Yeats too who suggested that he had also drawn on other volumes of the Ossianic Society's *Transactions*. "In the quarrels between the saint and the blind warrior," he wrote, "I have used suggestions from various ballad Dialogues of Oisin and Patrick, published by the Ossianic Society" (*CL1* 176). The allusion to ballad dialogues refers to Volume IV of the *Transactions*, which contains O'Looney's translation of Comyn and a number of similar ballads; and to Volume III, which concludes with Standish O'Grady's "The Lamentation of Oisin after the Fenians";[24] and to Volume I, which consists of Nicholas O'Kearney's introduction to and translation of the Ossianic poem on the battle of Gabhra.

The numerous quatrains of this last poem depict Oisin in the act of describing the disaster at Gabhra to Patrick. He tells the saint of the valiant death of Oscar, his "brave and generous" son, and of how Fionn stood over his grandson's battlefield deathbed in tears. O'Kearney addresses himself to a number of intriguing questions in the course of his introduction. How, for instance, does one account for the fact that the Ossianic poems make the long-dead Oisin a contemporary of St Patrick? How explain Fionn's appearance over the broken body of Oscar, when Fionn himself had been killed some ten years before? (*TOS* I, pp. 10–11)[25]

O'Kearney's answers to these questions were no doubt most suggestive to the young poet who felt so pressing a need to bring Ireland and the occult together in his poetry. O'Kearney explained the reappearance of Oisin by pointing to the very poem by Comyn that became Yeats's primary source, claiming that "this very curious poem... pretty fully elucidates the Irish pagan doctrine of metempsychosis as believed by the druids" (*TOS* I, p. 25), and that Comyn's account of

> the Elysium of the pagan Irish... and of Oisin having returned to life after a lapse of three hundred years or upwards, so as to meet St. Patrick, and narrate the history of Fenian achievements, is, probably, the remnant of history that best explains the doctrine of the transmigration of souls (*TOS* I, p. 21).

It is doubtful, O'Kearney continues,

if St. Patrick ever saw the real Oisin, but only some druid or old *seanchaidhe*, who believed himself to be Oisin revived, in virtue of the druidic doctrine of metempsychosis, or transmigration of the spirit into other bodies (*TOS* I, p. 28).

He accounts for the anomalous appearance by Fionn in a similar manner: when the poem observes that Fionn was thrown into such despair by the death of Oscar that he "never slept a calm sleep,/From that night to the day of his death" (*TOS* I, p. 131), O'Kearney hazards his belief that the phrase "day of his death" is

> a poetic licence and evidently refers to the time when the spirit of Fionn, according to the druidic doctrine of transmigration of souls, should assume mortality in some other shape and character, and revisit the earth (*TOS* I, pp. 132–3 n.).

If O'Kearney's remarks furnished Yeats with a warrant for turning his "romance" on Oisin into a poem that hinted at covert truths, they are none the less too general to have provided the poet with specific ideas for the form that his descriptions of the three islands should take. For those, Yeats needed to draw on what he had already learned about the doctrine of rebirth from his meetings with Mohini Chatterji, his affiliation with the Theosophical Society and, more particularly, his own studies in the works that members and friends of the Society had published. When Yeats began to write about Oisin, he had been a student of theosophy for several years; before he finished his poem, he had met and come under the tutelage of the redoubtable Blavatsky herself. Given his habit of taking his central objects of study and making them over into images and themes, it would be odd not to find stray magical hints glancing through the fine haze of Oisin's wanderings. Suggestions here and there: is Oisin's sleep on the Island of Forgetfulness an echo of Blavatsky's "sacred sleep", a sleep in which visions appear, and in which "the sleeper takes no note of the lapse of time, but upon awakening", however long he may have slept, "imagines he has slept but a few moments"?[26] Does Yeats's poem evoke Blavatsky's theory that before rebirth the soul is suspended in "a flitting spiritual existence", embarked on a "vast, wild journey", and that it is only after its reappearance on "the large and shining planet named the Earth" that it achieves a genuine consciousness of itself, only then that it can truly refer to itself by the "glorious" name of Man? (*IU* I, p. 368). In any event, the reader is barely into Yeats's poem before ideas that are palpably theosophical begin to manifest, as in the early lines that suggest that the souls of men have their origins in "some old star" or in "the twisted moon" (*VP* 19), a concept whose source is the Blavatsky theory that human souls derive from the souls of man's "Lunar Ancestors".[27] Nor – more pointedly – can we read through the poem without being brushed by an idea that resided at the center of Yeats's studies in theosophy, the idea of Devachan.

All of the magical systems with which the Yeats of the mid-eighties was familiar subscribed to the rebirth theory, though different schemas gave the theory different shapes. The version of the doctrine that Yeats drew on for "The Wanderings of Oisin" was the variant espoused by Blavatsky and her followers, more particularly by A. P. Sinnett in the *Esoteric Buddhism* that had drawn Yeats and Johnston into theosophical studies in the first place. Sinnett's volume provides a firm base for the claim that Oisin's wanderings through the three islands are a poeticized version of the journey through Devachan, the shadowy realm in which the soul abides while awaiting its next appearance on earth. Several readers of this poem have noted that Oisin's experiences on the three islands are in many ways an extension of his activities on earth. Aside from his poetic abilities, his greatest claims to worldly fame are his love affair with a woman of the sidhe and his skill in battle; and the first two islands he visits are emblematic of love and war respectively. This would have made ready sense to Sinnett, since Devachan is the "spiritual complement of our earth life" (p. 85). "Between each physical existence", says *Esoteric Buddhism*, "the individual unit passes through a period of existence in the corresponding spiritual world", the conditions of which existence are defined by "the use... which the person in question has made of his opportunities in life" (p. 50). And, more grandiloquently: "that dream-life is but the fruition, the harvest-time, of those psychic seed-germs dropped from the tree of physical existence in our moments of dream and hope" – a fruition that was said to lead to fulfilment, since in Devachan "all unrealized hopes, aspirations, dreams, become fully realized" (p. 77). Thus the soul of a "Devachanee" (p. 79) who while on earth "was passionately devoted to music" would be "continuously enraptured by the sensations music produces" (p. 71).

And thus the propriety of giving over the soul of a man preoccupied with love and war to repeated bouts of passion and conflict. But this still leaves the Island of Forgetfulness; and finding a parallel for Oisin's slumber on the third island in the exhaustion he feels at the start of the poem seems a tenuous business at best. Other readers of the poem have found models for the Island of Forgetfulness in folklore, in tales like those of which the story of the Seven Sleepers is a central type. The analogue is a likely one; but the influence of theosophy is equally as direct, since Sinnett's explanation of the nature of Devachan is also an explanation of why the third island should be the kind of place that it is.

In describing Devachan as "a strange region of dreamy semi-animation" (p. 137), *Esoteric Buddhism* inadvertently hints at the kind of thing Yeats had in mind in his accounts of all three of his islands, and of the third island in particular. Like Devachan itself, the Island of Forgetfulness meets Sinnett's description of a place of "sleep – a peaceful night with dreams more vivid than day, and imperishable for many centuries" (pp. 84–5). It thus fits directly into an overall theosophical schema, since "the Devachanic life" as a whole "is itself a process of growth, maturity, and decline" (p. 87). Sinnett's description of the soul's progress through the afterlife rehearses Yeats's vision of Oisin's headway from island to island and, finally, back to the world of men:

As physical existence has its cumulative intensity from infancy to prime, and its diminishing energy thenceforward to dotage and death, so the dream-life of Devachan is lived correspondentially. There is the first flutter of psychic life, the attainment of prime, the gradual exhaustion of force passing into conscious lethargy, semi-unconsciousness, oblivion and – not death but birth! birth into another personality and the resumption of action (p. 78).

Thus too Yeats's wanderer, who finds the life in him reawakening on the Island of the Living, attains his prime on the Island of Victories, passes into oblivion on the Island of Forgetfulness, and who concludes his sojourn in the supernatural world not with death, but birth: rebirth into the world, the defiant resumption of action.

Yeats had come across these ideas in places other than *Esoteric Buddhism*,[28] and certain of these related sources likewise resonate in his poem. Blavatsky's many remarks about the experience of the soul in the afterlife, for instance, comprise a complicated system when taken in sum; she asserts that the soul is required to revisit the scenes of its past life before it can be born into its next (*TSD* III, p. 247),[29] then – as *Isis Unveiled* had it – "loses all recollection of the past" as the moment of rebirth comes around.[30] Both these concepts suggest the Island of Forgetfulness: the amnesia Oisin succumbs to, for one thing, and for another the vision of the Fenian hunt – last of the scenes of his past life – that comes to him just before his return to the earth. Blavatsky was also the original source of a theory about the spiritual evolution of man, a theory that, like the concept of Devachan, casts its symbolic glimmer through the interstices of Yeats's visionary narrative.

Arguably the strangest of all the central tenets of the Theosophical Society, at once too detailed and too extravagant for ready summary, the idea that the spirit of man was undergoing a slow evolution concerned itself less with the state of the soul between earthly lives than with the question of how many rebirths the individual soul might be subject to. In its most general outline, the theory held that the soul had to pass through seven "rounds" of incarnations before it could attain Nirvana. Each of these seven rounds contained seven "planets", with the soul having to spend lengthy periods of time on each of the seven before it could pass on to the next in line. When it had become sufficiently spiritualized to take its leave of the seventh planet of the first round, it would move on to the first planet of the second: "the furthest forward of the worlds is not a region of finality," said *Esoteric Buddhism*, "but the stepping-stone to the furthest back, as the month of December leads us back again to January" (p. 33). From that first planet the soul would begin yet another round of incarnations, the process ceasing only when its residence on the seventh planet of the seventh round had ended, at which point those souls that had managed the passage through all forty-nine of their planetary visitations would cross over into Nirvana.

In its specific details all this is even more extreme than the above précis makes it seem, but Yeats had had a more than ample chance to sort out its vagaries. The theory had appeared in rudimentary form in the second volume of 1877's *Isis Unveiled* (pp. 455–6). Thereafter Blavatsky or her Master, the enigmatic Koot Hoomi, had relayed the details of the schema to Sinnett, who devoted the bulk of three of the chapters of *Esoteric Buddhism* – "The Planetary Chain" (pp. 29–44), "The World Periods" (pp. 45–65), and "The Human Tide-Wave" (pp. 108–21) – to the idea. So taken with Sinnett's work that he became an instant convert to Theosophy (*Au* 90–1), Charles Johnston went on to excerpt *Esoteric Buddhism* – his particular foci were the sections on Devachan and spiritual evolution – and to work the excerpts up into a lecture for the Dublin Hermetic Society that Yeats helped to found. Once he had delivered the lecture, which may have been written with Yeats's help, he went on to publish it in the same issue of *The Dublin University Review* (July, 1885) that contained the second act of Yeats's *The Island of Statues*.[31] Finally, *The Secret Doctrine*. When Yeats first met Blavatsky in mid-1887 the three volumes that comprise this work had not yet been published, but the writing was all but done. Blavatsky's desk in the house in Norwood, the desk over which she and Yeats first met, held a manuscript that at the time of their meeting had reached a height of three feet.[32] Much of it centered on Blavatsky's exegesis of the theory of spiritual evolution that Sinnett and Johnston had already placed before Yeats's gaze.[33] Given Yeats's early interest in the doctrine of rebirth, an interest to which so many of his early works bear witness, it would be strange to discover that the young man who was writing "The Wanderings of Oisin" neglected a chance to discuss the by now familiar concept of spiritual evolution with the woman who was elaborating that concept in *The Secret Doctrine*. Yeats was to visit with her often and, as his description of her in the *Autobiographies* makes clear, to mark her words with care.[34] Blavatsky, after all, was the fountainhead.

Yeats's acquaintance with the concept of planetary rounds, then, was a familiarity several times reinforced; and "The Wanderings of Oisin" suggests that he put his knowledge to his own poetic use. Blavatsky had described the soul's journey through its seven rounds of incarnations as a "Cyclic Pilgrimage" (*TSD* II, p. 466), while Sinnett had termed it "an endless cyclic progression" (*EB*, p. 215); and, had Yeats been able to have his way, his poem would have concluded with Oisin finishing his first round of cyclic travels, then setting off on yet another, passing "over another sea to another island" (*Ex* 393). Moreover, the theosophical theory held that as the soul continued to evolve spiritually it returned to the same planets time upon time, even as Oisin departs from Ireland, makes the rounds of worlds beyond it and then returns to the country whence his cyclic journey had commenced. Finally, the theory posited that with its completion of each of the seven rounds the soul achieved an increase in spirituality; when (for instance) it returned to the first planet at the start of its second round of incarnations, it did so in a more ethereal form than it had owned when it had visited that same planet in round one. The soul revisits the seven planets "again and again", said *Esoteric Buddhism*, and each time "in higher forms" (*EB*, p. 32):

> Many times does it circle, in this way, right round the system, but its passage round must not be thought of merely as a circular revolution in an orbit. In the scale of spiritual perfection it is constantly ascending (*EB*, p. 34).

And Blavatsky's exposition of the same idea comprises a still more direct parallel to the progress of Oisin, who returns to his original starting point, not simply with his spirit in the ascendant, but with his self-awareness radically increased:

> everything that is evolving returns to the condition it was in at its starting point – *plus*, every time, a new and superior degree in the states of consciousness (*TSD* I, p. 253).

Suggestive as these correspondences are, the argument for a connection between what the young poet knew about Devachan and the concept of spiritual evolution and what he wrote about in "The Wanderings of Oisin" rests on more than semblances. If Yeats's early studies in magic left legible marks on work written much later in his life, it would be heedless to argue that those same readings left no trace on work written at the time when his acquaintance with what he was reading was at its most direct; and the effect of his youthful forays into magic on the handiwork of his maturity is beyond doubt, since several of the notions that the would-be magus stitched into the shady background of his tapestry on Oisin later became a part of the fabric of *A Vision*.

The sources of the ideas Yeats discusses in the first edition of *A Vision* (1925) are many and wide-ranging, so much so that the relation between most of those sources and the book itself might best be described as occasional. But whatever the troves Yeats uncovered later on, his mature speculations about the nature of the afterlife often look back not only towards his own early poem, but beyond it to the occult theories on which the poem was in part based. After bodily death and before its next rebirth, *A Vision* argues, the soul must first relive the most intense events of its past lives. Theosophy, with its claim that the soul "has to revisit, before it incarnates into a new body, the scenes that it left at its last disincarnation" (*TSD* III, p. 247), said no less; nor did "The Wanderings of Oisin" when it sent Oisin off to resume in the afterlife the most typical of the activities he had left behind on earth. A later stage in the schema of *A Vision* finds the soul losing all sense of time and place, and forgetting its past lives completely: so too *Isis Unveiled* (Vol. I), so too the Island of Forgetfulness. And having forgotten its past lives and come to the verge of rebirth, the soul that *A Vision* images arrives at a foreknowledge of the companions with whom it will spend its coming incarnation. This is standard theosophical dogma. In Blavatsky's concise summary:

> As the man at the moment of death has a retrospective insight into the life he has led, so, at the moment he is reborn on to earth, the

Ego, awaking from the state of Devachan, has a prospective vision of the life which awaits him.[35]

It is also the prevision of Oisin, who in his third and last memory of the Fenians pictures the men for the sake of whose future companionship he will renounce heaven itself.

In essence, then, "The Wanderings of Oisin" is a romance that discusses the conflict between an ancient pagan order and the Christianity that takes its place, and a symbolic poem that is neither pagan nor Christian but esoteric; like Comyn's "The Lay of Oisin", it is the remnant of Yeats's early writings that best illustrates his belief in the doctrine of rebirth. This is not to say that the symbolic return to earth enacted in the poem is in complete accord with the tenets of theosophy or *A Vision*; indeed, this occult poem differs from traditional theories of rebirth in one of the most central ways of all. In Yeats's system — or anyone's — a reincarnated soul re-enters mortal life because it has not been sufficiently purified to pass into final transcendence; its return to the world is unwilling. But Oisin sets off for the shores of Ireland of his own accord —

> Till fattening the winds of the morning, an odour of
>   new-mown hay
> Came, and my forehead fell low, and my tears like
>   berries fell down;
> Later a sound came, half lost in the sound of a shore
>   far away,
> From the great grass-barnacle calling, and later the
>   shore-weeds brown (*VP* 57) —

out of love for the sweet lures of earth.

It has been said of "The Wanderings of Oisin" that "the three islands, instead of being a refuge from life, are a symbolical representation of it. Oisin's nostalgia for the life he has left behind him is therefore inconsistent."[36] While the logic here has a compelling feel to it, the question this comment neglects to answer is why a man who has a chance for a share in life itself should be content with a poor bare symbolical representation of it. Like so much of his work, this recondite Ossianic narrative weds Yeats's readings in his Irish sources to his studies in magic. The works he investigated in both areas suggest a number of reasons why life on the three islands must leave Oisin unsatisfied.

The concept of Devachan sheds light not only on the islands themselves but on Oisin's motive for leaving them behind. No nebulous spirit, what survives in Devachan "is the same personality as regards its higher feelings, aspirations, affections, and even tastes, as it was on earth" (*EB*, p. 69). It is unlikely that Yeats's warrior-bard, his inclinations the same in the world beyond as formerly in this, could find a genuine contentment in Devachan's dreamy state of semi-animation, and more particularly because his departure from earth comes while he is yet in his prime. *Esoteric Buddhism* drew a broad separating line between the Devachanic experiences of those who had lived out their lives to a natural term and those who departed from earth before their time had come: for a man to leave life behind

> at a time when all his principles are firmly united, and ready to hold together for twenty, forty, or sixty years, whatever the natural remainder of his life would be, must surely be something different from that of a person who, by natural processes of decay, finds himself, when the vital machine stops, readily separable into his various principles, each prepared to travel their separate ways (*EB*, p. 100).

Those who die before their time find life clinging to them in the afterlife, even as "from [an] unripe fruit the stone can only be torn with difficulty, half the pulp clinging to its surface" (*EB*, p. 100). And this was particularly the case with those "overtaken by death in the consummation, whether real or imaginary, of some master passion of their lives" (*EB*, p. 102). For these "desire remain[s] unsatisfied even after [its] full realization" in the afterlife, and "such personalities can never pass beyond the earth attraction to wait for the hour of deliverance in happy ignorance" (*EB*, pp. 102–3).

That Oisin never passes beyond the earth attraction needs no proof; it would be only a slight exaggeration of the case to claim that, if anything, he never really comes within the gravity field of fairyland. It is only in retrospect that he learns that his sojourn has lasted three centuries; the time he passes while on the islands themselves seems to him no time at all and, though he has been in Tir na nOg for what he takes to be the briefest of spans, it requires only the most trivial of nudges to his memory – a lance, a beech bough, a starling – to set him longing for home. Among those dissatisfied souls who took their leave of earthly life while in the consummation of some master passion – the future avenging of the Fenian defeat at Gabhra – his longing for battle remains unsatisfied even after its realization on the Island of Victories; it is a desire that he can gratify only by returning home and leading his beaten clan to a triumph so remarkable that it will reduce their failure against the mortal armies of Cairbre to a memory. Like that of any other Devachanee, his "real consciousness" has been "all the while growing in strength and vitality" (*EB*, p. 86) in the afterlife, so that he returns to earth with his sense of who he is and what he must do fully restored. And even as he "drop[ped] into [his] befitting place" in the afterlife, so too "when his time for re-birth comes" he "emerges in his befitting place in the world" (*EB*, p. 86) of men, the warrior once more.

The theosophical description of the afterlife is only one of the occult paths into an explanation of Oisin's refusal of eternal life. When Yeats mentioned his hidden intents to Katharine Tynan, the language he used served to locate his poem in the tradition of occult works such as *Zanoni*; but "The Wanderings of Oisin" fits the *Zanoni* mode in more ways than one. Not only do both works admit of being read either exoterically or esoterically: both works express precisely similar attitudes towards eternal life and the necessary conflict between those who live forever and those who dwell in the world. Indeed, it is possible to find in the character of Zanoni – a man who turns magus, and thereby becomes an immortal who has the choice of retaining or forsaking his hold on immortality – attitudes typical of both the immortal Niamh and the renouncer of immortality, Oisin. Like Niamh, Zanoni falls in love with a mortal, only to discover that "companionship with the things that die brings with it but sorrow in its sweetness" (*Zanoni*, p. 71); and when Niamh declares that Oisin's departure from Tir na nOg will leave her to "die like a small withered leaf in the autumn" (*VP* 56), Lytton's undying sage is compelled to join her in the chorus: "the deathless die if they dare to love the mortal" (*Zanoni*, p. 328). The viewpoints he shares with Oisin are in similar accord. Both magician and warrior eventually come to learn that the gift of eternal life, what *Zanoni* calls "this state of abstraction and revery, this self-wrapt and self-dependent majesty of existence", also constitutes "a resignation of that nobility which incorporates our own welfare, our joys, our hopes, our fears" with those of other men (*Zanoni*, p. 220). Those who reject the quotidian world in favor of living forever needs must also "reject all human ties", abandon "what makes up the occupation and excitement of men", forgo the right to "covet, or love, or hate" (*Zanoni*, pp. 315, 316). These are clearly major sacrifices; and Zanoni, like Oisin, decides in the end that the sacrifice is too great and, like Oisin, abjures his hold on everlasting life to return to the world of men, to "go where the souls of those for whom" he will die "shall be [his] co-mates" (*Zanoni*, p. 333). Arrived at a recognition of what constitutes "the true ordeal and the real victory" (*Zanoni*, p. 333), Lytton's adept and Yeats's Fenian alike return to the only world in which true ordeals – and hence "real" victories – are possible.

"The Wanderings of Oisin", then, reflects not only occult theory but prescribed occult attitudes towards what the uninitiated mistakenly regarded as the privilege of life eternal. Source after Yeatsian source iterates a skepticism like *Zanoni*'s. The prototype of the Lytton novel, Godwin's *St. Leon: A Tale of the Sixteenth Century* (1799),[37] pictures a deathless nobleman who comes to regard his discovery of the secret of eternal life as a "fatal legacy" (p. 362) that "cut[s] off [its] possessor from the dearest ties of human existence, and render[s] him a solitary, cold, self-centered individual" (p. 363), "utterly alone in the world, separated by an insurmountable barrier from every being of my species" (p. 465). Shelley's youthful work of homage to *St. Leon*, the fantastic *St. Ervyne; or, the Rosicrucian* (1811), followed its model's lead. One among those "early romances" by Shelley in which Yeats himself detected Shelley's "strong... fascination" with "the traditions of magic and of the magical philosophy" (*E&I* 78), the novel describes a number of characters who aspire to become more than human – and concludes with their violent deaths. And the first volume of Hargrave Jennings's *The Rosicrucians: Their Rites and Mysteries* (1870), a work that reached its third edition as the occult revival began to peak in 1887, spoke out still more directly on matters of the kind: "perpetual youth, and life prolonged, with pleasures infinite", wrote

Jennings, "would, to the deeply thinking man who had risen, as it were, *over* life, ... seem vain" (p. 24).

Implicit in that last comment, which finds an echo many years later in Yeats's description of his three enchanted islands as places of (respectively) "vain gaiety, vain battle, vain repose" (*VP* 629), is a criticism not only of man's misguided aspirations towards eternal youth but of the kind of life that Yeats's island-dwellers lead. Life prolonged, with pleasures infinite, was to the occult way of thinking no fit life for man. Blavatsky's disciple, Franz Hartmann, could have explained why Oisin was bound to tire of perpetual gaiety, battle, repose. Man "crave[s] for change and death", said his *Magic, White and Black* (1884), "to remain always the same would be torture" (p. 61). Blavatsky confirmed the words of her follower. The second volume of *The Secret Doctrine* put the point bluntly: "where there is no struggle, there is no merit" (p. 100), and "woe to those who live without suffering. Stagnation and death is the future of all that vegetates without change" (p. 498). This was plain talk, and Yeats was listening with attention. The argument that death was the fate awaiting those who lived without suffering reappeared in a subtler form in the essay he published only six months after the initial appearance of his poem, when he asserted that "the soul cannot live without sorrow" (*CT* 80). The light this remark sheds on "The Wanderings of Oisin" is direct. If the soul cannot live without sorrow, then the soul of Oisin, in its journey through islands whose inhabitants never "grow sad" (*VP* 22), is a soul that has ceased to live. Blavatsky would have approved Yeats's decision to return Oisin from his otherworldly adventures to his natural habitat, whatever the pain engendered by his homecoming. It is better, says *The Secret Doctrine* (Vol. II), to be "a *conscious*, and hence a *responsible* entity" than to live out eternity in the "unconscious perfection" of passivity (p. 255): better to choose, as Oisin chooses, "the *curse* of *incarnation*" (p. 256). Prometheus was Blavatsky's chosen example of a man who "preferred free-will to passive slavery", and preferred "intellectual self-conscious pain and even torture... to inane, imbecile, instinctual beatitude" (p. 439). Oisin was Yeats's.

In selecting the materials to be included in the section of *Fairy and Folk Tales* that dealt with Tir na nOg, Yeats had a wide variety of viewpoints to choose from. Inasmuch as his folklore readings had differed over the question of whether the sidhe were benign or malignant or a combination of both, it was only natural that they should also differ in their descriptions of the lands in which the sidhe were said to reside. Authors such as O'Hanlon, O'Grady, Lady Wilde and Hyde tended to take the kindly view; in one of the notes he wrote for Yeats's anthology, for instance, Hyde affirmed that "'The Country of the Young'... is the place where the Irish peasant will tell you *geabhaedh tu an sonas aer pighin*, 'you will get happiness for a penny,' so cheap and common it will be."[38] *Fairy and Folk Tales* includes two short pieces among its Tir na nOg materials – "The Legend of O'Donoghue" and "Rent Day", both by Crofton Croker – that are generally in accord with this claim of Hyde's; but it also includes selections that suggest that, so far as Yeats was concerned, there was more going on in the homeland of the sidhe than had met Hyde's eye. What might be going on is most obviously apparent in the Yeats source that came closest to matching Yeats's own careful soundings of the islands in the west, Patrick Kennedy's collection of *Legendary Fictions*.

It is in the section on Tir na nOg that *Fairy and Folk Tales* locates the anonymous story cited in the previous chapter, the tale of the young man who refused the sidhe when they invited him to come and live in their palace. Given what happens in "The Wanderings of Oisin", Yeats's choice of a tale that details a rejection of the Country of the Young is itself provocative. It grows more so when we turn to the analogous narrative that *Legendary Fictions* entitles "The Three Crowns." In this complicated fable, most likely a fusion of related types,[39] three princesses, two of them proud and uncharitable and the third and youngest of them very much the opposite, are engaged to three princes who meet the same description. A fairy spirits the princesses away to Tir na nOg, and the princes go off in pursuit. After assorted adventures, the three princesses and the two evil princes effect their escape; but a trick worked by his brothers leaves the good prince stranded. During his stay in this ostensible paradise, the young prince enjoys "the finest of eating and drinking... and a bed of bog-down to sleep on, and fine walks... through gardens and lawns" (pp. 48–9) – the same kinds of pleasures, in short, that are available to Oisin on the Island of the Living. But the prince's affection for these seductive offerings of the sidhe is no more lasting than Oisin's. Says Kennedy:

> Well, I don't think any of us would be tired of this fine way of living for ever. Maybe we would. Anyhow the prince got tired of it before a week, he was so lonesome for his true love; and at the end of a month he didn't know what to do with himself (p. 49).

The story concludes with the reunion of the prince and princess and their marriage, but his boredom in the interim comes far closer to epitomizing the view of Tir na nOg to be found in Yeats's tale of his Fenian traveller than do Hyde's remarks about buying happiness for a penny. Yeats was later to cite Hyde's comment, and the context in which he cites it itself suggests the difference between Hyde's view of Tir na nOg and his own. It appears in the essay in which Yeats spoke of the soul's inability to live without sorrow. The sentence that immediately follows that observation is the sentence in which Yeats locates the line from Hyde. He is describing the kinds of visitors that Tir na nOg is said to have attracted: "Through... the... doors of that land where *geabhadh tu an sonas aer pighin* ('you can buy joy for a penny'), have gone kings, queens, and princes" (*CT* 80). Oisin is among that royal company, and his creator was suggesting something about Tir na nOg that Hyde had overlooked: that the happiness that could be bought for a penny – the happiness that Hyde himself had described as "common" and "cheap" – was not worth the price of purchase. "I suppose that one tires of all abundant things" (*Let* 546), Yeats wrote later in his life, and the remark holds true of a wide variety of characters: of the magus in *Zanoni*, of the prince in "The Three Crowns", of the Fenian bard in "The Wanderings of Oisin". Kennedy's is again the view that most closely dovetails with Yeats's. *Legendary Fictions* describes Niamh's seduction of Oisin from Ireland, then adds that

> for a hundred and fifty years he enjoyed her sweet society in the Land of Youth below the waters. Getting at last tired of this monotony of happiness, he expressed a wish to revisit the land where his youth and manhood had been spent (p. 240).

What Kennedy had sensibly perceived was the idea that unending play would pall on the human soul as rapidly as any other activity that repeated itself without end, and Yeats would explore the idea still further. To say that the soul cannot live without sorrow is to affirm that the spirit of man feeds on change, whether the change be for worse or better, and that in the absence of change the soul meets the same end as any other living being that lacks its proper food. Both occultism and Irish folklore taught the lesson, and the author of "The Wanderings of Oisin" was an apt pupil.

After its two offerings from Croker and the story of the man who resists the offer of the sidhe, the Tir na nOg subdivision of *Fairy and Folk Tales* rounds off with two brief fragments, one an excerpt from the *Historical Works* of Cambrensis, the other Yeats's edited version of a poem by Gerald Griffin. The Cambrensis excerpt describes a mysterious island that appeared one day off Ireland's coast, and that sank whenever the curious mainlanders tried to approach it by boat, only to pique their curiosity again by resurfacing on the days after it had disappeared, "mock[ing] them "with the like delusion" (*FFT* 191). The stanzas by Griffin are in the same mode. They describe "a shadowy land" that "appeared" on the waves intermittently, a "beautiful spectre" that remained "loveily distant" irrespective of attempts to reach it, a "shadowy isle" that "o'er the faint rim of distance, reflected its smile"; and they are critical of men who, because they "thought" of the island as "a region of sunshine and rest", wasted their lives in vain endeavors to beach on its shores (*FFT* 190). All of this anticipates the description of enchanted Irish islands that Yeats would find in another of the sources he drew on for *Fairy and Folk Tales*, D. R. McAnally's *Irish Wonders* (1888). Flawed attempts at dialect notwithstanding, McAnally wrote that the enchanted island in question

> is not what it seems to be, that is to say, not 'airth an' shtones, like as thim we see, but only a deludherin' show that avil sper'ts, or the divil belike, makes fur to desave us poor disholute craythers (*IW* 70).

The McAnally book came too late to have any influence on the stance of "The Wanderings of Oisin"; but Yeats was familiar with the tradition of vanishing islands, delusive shows built for deceit, several times over. Two of his five Tir na nOg selections for *Fairy and Folk Tales* center on the idea, as does his introductory note to the section. The first of the three paragraphs of this note describes Oisin's journey to Tir na nOg, a land that "neither tears nor loud laughter" have anchored in (*FFT* 179) – it is only after his departure from the islands that Oisin gives way to anything recognizable as tears (*VP* 57) or laughter (*VP* 58) – while the second paragraph runs as follows:

> A Dutch pilot, settled in Dublin, told M. De La Boullage Le Cong, who travelled in Ireland in 1614, that round the poles were many islands; some hard to be approached because of the witches who inhabit them and destroy by storms those who seek to land. He had once, off the coast of Greenland, in sixty-one degrees of latitude, seen and approached such an island only to see it vanish. Sailing in an opposite direction, they met with the same island, and sailing near, were almost destroyed by a furious tempest (*FFT* 179).

Obscure even for Yeats, filled with miscitations that probably came from his cramped handwriting, the reference here is to *The Tour of the French Traveller M. De La Boullaye le Gouz in Ireland, A.D. 1644*. The English version of this volume, published in London in 1837, was a book Yeats had come across while readying *Fairy and Folk Tales* for the press, the likeliest reason for his having come across it being that the editor of the English edition was the versatile Crofton Croker. *The Tour* offered a comprehensive description of "the Enchanted Island" of *O'Brazile*, a name that Irish folklore frequently treats as synonymous with Tir na nOg; and like the paragraph from Cambrensis and the poem by Griffin, *The Tour* pictures islands of the kind as places that seem solid enough from a distance, but that vanish when men try to reach them. "To those possessing strong imaginative powers," *The Tour* adds, the notion of vanishing islands "presents an ample field for romantic fiction."[40]

So it does. In his fairy lyrics Yeats had taken the ingenuous views of the sidhe presented by his folklore sources and filtered them through his own more complex sensibility, had – in Maud Gonne's apt phrase – dressed the sidhe in "new clothes".[41] In "The Wanderings of Oisin", Yeats's strong imaginative powers would refine the traditions that surrounded the islands in the west. Several of Yeats's sources had described Tir na nOg in terms evocative of what the last chapter called the lamia motif. "The Enchanted Lake", which Yeats had found in Croker's *Fairy Legends*, might serve as a type of all. In this tale, one of the many to subscribe to the tradition of Tir na nOg as an "underwater land" (*FFT* 179), a young man discovers a beautiful country beneath the waters of a lake in the west of Ireland. The activities of the place center around "fine pleasure-grounds, with an elegant avenue through them, and a grand house, with a power of steps going up to the door" (p. 227). Working on the grounds of the house are all the many young men thought to have drowned in the lake in years past; and as they work they sing songs in praise of the woman who rules the country, songs that describe her as "fair" and "graceful, mild, and pure" (pp. 227, 228). Untouched by the spell of enchantment under which the other young men labor, the most recent arrival then meets the woman, who turns out to be "a powerful fat woman, moving along like a beer-barrel on two legs, with teeth as big as horse's teeth" and "a smile on her face that moved like boiling stirabout" (p. 228). Put off by what he alone is able to see, the young man makes good his escape.

Nothing half this obvious is afoot in Oisin's venturings; but Yeats and Croker none the less share a view of Tir na nOg as lamian, the difference in their stances being that Yeats's reading of the land of the sidhe is by far the more closely thought out. To the poet's eye Niamh and her companions are beautiful, and their beauty is no mask over uncomeliness. But the islands the sidhe inhabit are in their way as delusive as the vanishing islands of legend, in that they appear to promise ultimate satisfactions and then, in the end, fail to satisfy. Looked at from one angle, "The Wanderings of Oisin" is an extended explanation of why it is that they fail.

Like the young boy of "The Stolen Child" or the man of "The Man who Dreamed of Faeryland", Oisin finds himself trapped between pull and counterpull. His love of Niamh draws him out towards Tir na nOg, but after his arrival the lure of earth persistently summons him home. His desire to return to Ireland can only imply that he sees the islands as falling short of the perfection they claim to own, and Yeats reinforces this impression by intimating that the three islands Oisin visits are stopping-off points rather than final destinations, that there is an island beyond the three to which even Niamh is denied access. The 1889 version of the poem obscures rather than clarifies the nature of this fourth fairyland. In the course of their departure from the Island of Victories, Oisin asks his lover:

> 'And Niam, say, of these
> Which is the Isle of Youth?' 'None know,' she said,
> And on my bosom laid her weeping head. (*VP* 46)

Inasmuch as Niamh had earlier identified herself as the daughter of the King of the Young, the ignorance she expresses concerning the whereabouts of his kingdom is an obvious inconsistency.[42] Yeats corrected himself in the first edition of the *Poems* of 1895; he has Oisin ask Niamh which of the islands is the Island of Content, and she gives the same response.

Oisin gives the island its name, but otherwise the poem has nothing to say about the nature of the place; and it cannot be mere happenstance that a number of the more central symbolic figures in the poem come from a place that neither Niamh nor anyone else can locate. Oisin's first sight of them comes as he journeys towards the Island of the Living:

> On, on! and now a hornless deer
> Passed by us, chased of a phantom hound
> All pearly white, save one red ear;
> And now a maid, on a swift brown steed
> Whose hooves the tops of the surges grazed,
> Hurried away, and over her raised
> An apple of gold in her tossing hand;
> And following her at a headlong speed
> Was a beautiful youth from an unknown land. (*VP* 11–12)

Each of their three journeys to the three islands – though not, provocatively, Oisin's solitary ride from the Island of Forgetfulness back to Ireland – is punctuated by an encounter with these four "phantoms" (*VP* 12). They come from an "unknown land"; the only such land in the poem is the Island of Content, and in all likelihood it is to that island that they get them home. If so, then Yeats is suggesting an equation that underlines what he was aiming at in the careful shaping of his arcane romance. To hint that the figures make their homes on the Island of Content is to imply that, for men like Oisin, the true source of contentment is, not the ceaseless gratification of desire, but rather desire itself; for wherever it is that the phantoms dwell, desire is what they stand for.[43] Yeats makes this point in Part III of the poem, when he allows Oisin and Niamh to discern "the immortal desire of immortals" in the faces of "lady and youth", "deer and... hound" (*VP* 47), and makes it still more plainly in the well-known later note:

> In the old Irish story of Usheen's journey to the Islands of the Young, Usheen sees amid the waters a hound with one red ear, following a deer with no horns; and other persons in other old Celtic stories see the like images of the desire of the man, and of the desire of the woman "which is for the desire of the man," and of all desires that are as these (*VP* 153 n.).

Despite the claim that Yeats attributes the image of the hound "vaguely to various... Celtic sources, yet essentially invents it himself",[44] there is little invention going on here, nor are Yeats's sources vague. The "old Celtic stories" that identified the hound with desire were both numerous and direct. Typical examples from known Yeats readings would include Lady Wilde's redaction of the legend about the death of Bran, foremost among the hounds of the Fenians. The tale is a fantasia on sexual desire:

> Bran finally met his death by means of a woman. One day a snow-white hart, with hoofs that shone like gold, was scented on the hill, and all the hounds pursued, Bran leading. Hour after hour passed by, and still the hart fled on, the hounds following, till one by one they all dropped off from weariness, and not one was left save Bran. Then the hart headed for the lake, and reaching a high cliff, she plunged from it straight down into the water; the noble hound leaped in at once after her, and seized the hart as she rose to the surface; but at that instant she changed into the form of a beautiful lady, and laying her hand upon the head of Bran, she drew him down beneath the water, and the beautiful lady and Fionn's splendid hound disappeared together and were seen no more (*AL*, p. 149).

The second volume of O'Grady's *History* had taught Yeats that apples had been symbols of fertility in the works of the ancient Irish bards (p. 169 and note), and in the O'Grady version of Oisin's journey over the seas the sexual implications of the chase are still more apparent than they are in Yeats's poem. Here the youth in pursuit appears with "drawn sword":

"A fawn flew past me, whom two hounds pursued; a fair girl ran by with an apple of gold; a youth with drawn sword pressed behind" (*Hist* I, pp. 36–7). And the folktale variants on this legend of pursuit, tales that left a deep enough impression on Yeats to invite his re-presentation as late as 1914 (*Ex* 57–8), are generally both more fantastic than Wilde's account and more sexually explicit than O'Grady's. Though it appeared in print after the publication of "The Wanderings of Oisin", the translation that came closest to matching the spirit in which the original old tale was told belonged to Hyde. His *Beside the Fire* recounts the story of the "Slender Grey Kerne", a wonderworker who once

> took out a bag from under his arm-pit and he brought out a ball of silk from the bag, and he threw it up into... the firmament, and it became a ladder; and again he took out a hare and let it up the ladder. Again he took out a red-eared hound and let it up after the hare... "I am afraid," said he, "the hound... will eat the hare, and I think I ought to send some relief to the hare." Then he took out of the bag a handsome youth in excellent apparel, and he let him up after the hare and the hound... He took out of the bag a lovely girl in beautiful attire, and he let her up after the hare the hound the youth.

Then:

> "It's badly it happened to me now," says the kerne, "for the youth is going kissing my woman, and the dog gnawing the hare." The kerne drew down the ladder again and he found the youth "going along with the woman, and the dog gnawing the hare," as he said (p. 191).

The refrain of desire here is plain. The pursuing hound, in Yeats's version "all pearly white, save one red ear", is, as Yeats himself implied, a blatant phallic image of "the desire of the man".[45]

Yeats's need to look to folklore sources for the explanation of his four symbolic figures had its motive. Though the youth and lady, deer and hound had also appeared in his most direct model, Comyn's "The Lay of Oisin on the Land of Youth", Comyn had never taken up the question of what they meant. Quite the contrary: Comyn's Niamh explicitly forbids Oisin to speculate about what the figures might signify. Oisin asks:

> 'Who are [those] whom I see,
>   O gentle princess, tell me the meaning,
>   That woman of most beautiful countenance,
>   And the comely rider of the white steed.'

And she answers:

> 'Heed not what thou wilt see,
>   O! gentle Oisin, nor what thou hast yet seen,

> There is in them but nothing,
> Till we reach the land of the "King of Youth."'
> (*TOS* IV, p. 249)

But twice in the 1889 version of Yeats's poem she characterizes the phantoms as "dread" (*VP* 12, 29) and warns Oisin not to speak with them. It is worth asking why the Niamh envisioned by Yeats should be afraid of figures that symbolize desire, since an answer to that question also goes to the heart of an inquiry into why eternal life on the islands can never satisfy Oisin.

Niamh fears desire because, despite her impetuous longing for the company of Oisin, she is incapable of really understanding what desire is. In her home in Tir na nOg, where there are no objects of desire – or, what amounts to the same thing, where all desires are constantly gratified – true desire is impossible. While on the islands, Oisin finds himself in situations in which all of the Living love, and all of them love perpetually; in which battle is constantly joined, with results that are always the same; in which sleep is repose pure and simple, and need never be disturbed. To the islanders whose proper homes these are, all this is as it should be. But to Oisin, who on earth knew bitter as well as sweet, whose mortal soul has battened on variety, actions that invariably produce the same result are actions that are to all purposes empty. As formulated in "The Wanderings of Oisin", the concept of "sorrow" is central to Yeats's meaning. Sorrow is the mood that attends on desires unfulfilled – hence the complacent claim of the sidhe who dwell on the Island of the Living that they never "grow sad" (*VP* 22) – and for Yeats the only kind of joy that qualifies as genuine is that which has sorrow as its near neighbor. It is the possibility that love may be lost that gives human love its depth, a poignancy lacking in the constant loves of the islanders. The chance of defeat, by the same token, lends victory its edge; in the absence of that chance the edge itself must be absent. And where action is non-existent, as it is on the third island, respite from action is pointless.

What Yeats's poem implies, then, is the value of antitheses. What it questions is whether the absolute states of being that man desires – "there are three incompat[i]ble things which man is always seeking," Yeats wrote to Katharine Tynan of his narrative, "infinite feeling, infinite battle, infinite repose – hence the three islands" (*CL1* 141) – deserve their high place in man's estimation. And in the last analysis, the poem's answer to this question is in the negative. The Tir na nOg pictured by Yeats in "The Wanderings of Oisin" functions much as a diapered curtain would later function in his plays: as an unchanging backdrop against which a character can grow, "a scene that only wakes into life when the actors move in front of it" (*UP2* 367). The progress of Oisin from regret to defiance is the yardstick against which any gradations of change in the islands might best be measured. Judged by that standard, the islands emerge as places not of forward movement but of equilibrium, in which any apparent advance – the death of the demon, for instance – must later be negated in order that the original balance may be restored. Deadbeat in the truest sense of the word, the lands Oisin visits with Niamh are in no wise the kinds of places in which his changing mortal heart could find its satisfaction.

The corollary reason for Oisin's reluctance to join the immortal dance is that to do so would be to abjure his strong human will. The strength of that will is apparent in his decisions to leave each of the three islands, and still more so in his declaration that he will go off to fight the devils that Patrick has described to him as invincible. He is clearly the kind of man who insists on his right to control his own actions; but on the enchanted islands this kind of control is impossible, for there the word "will" has no meaning. This idea too had its antecedents in theosophy; Franz Hartmann, for instance, observed that

> the dream of life only differs from the dream after death, that, during the former, we are able to make use of our will to guide and control our imagination and acts, while during the latter that guidance is wanting (*MWB*, p. 154).

Hartmann's description of the difference between the dreams of life and death is a direct gloss on the difference between the attitude Oisin is able to adopt when confronting Patrick and the neutral stance he drifts into during all but a few moments – his discoveries of the lance, the beech bough, the starling – of his stay on the islands. Do what he will, his presence in Tir na nOg affects none of the sidhe but Niamh. In departing her proper sphere to ally her fortunes with those of a mortal, she leaves herself vulnerable to natural shocks; and her increasing sadness as their wanderings continue makes her the first major example in the Yeatsian canon of a Lasting One who loves what passes, the first of the gods by men betrayed (*VP* 275). But Oisin's actions have no bearing on the lives of the other island-dwellers; he appears among them as a human phantom, knocking inaudibly on their stout unresponsive doors. A fairy song accompanies his departure from each of the first two islands, and both songs confirm what by now he must have guessed: that his stay on the islands has made no difference. The lyric that beats time to his farewell to the Island of the Living begins:

> 'Swift are the years of a warrior's pride;
>   It passeth away, and is heard of no longer.
> In honour soon by his master's side
>   Sits a younger and a stronger.
> His toothless hound at his nerveless feet,
>   The warrior dreams in an aged leisure
> Of the things that his heart still knows were sweet –
>   Of war, and the chase, and hunting, and pleasure;
> And blows on his hands in the fire's warm blaze;
>   In the house of his friend, of his kin, of his brother,
> He hath over lingered his welcome; the days,
>   Grown desolate, whisper and sigh to each other.
>
> 'But never with us where the wild fowl chases
>   His shadow along in the evening blaze,

> Will the softness of youth be gone from our faces,
> Or love's first tenderness die in our gaze.'
> (*VP* 26–7)

Though he does not realize it at the time, the task to which Oisin will devote his most passionate energies after his return to Ireland is the refuting of the sentiments expressed by this same song, the demonstrating that the moods of even an aged mortal are more substantial than the dimensionless immortal emotions of the sidhe. Far from dreaming his life away "in an aged leisure", he will bid goodbye to mortality in a spirit of unholy rage. The most singular aspect of his stay on the islands was the lack of emotion he displayed, the yielding of his spirit to the genius of the place. He describes the "joy" he felt on the Island of the Living, but in so doing can do little more than assign to the feeling what seems to him its likeliest name; it was a sensation attained with such ease, with so little personal striving, that he can say of it only that it existed. It does not convince. The recurring encounters with the demon led to neither exultation nor despair, but to the absence of any feeling whatever: "No dreams, no fears,/No languor, no fatigue" (*VP* 44). And his final leavetaking of Niamh: there would be ample reason to expect this moment to mark the emotional high point of Oisin's stay on the islands, inasmuch as he tells Patrick that "even" the saint would have wept had he witnessed Niamh's reaction to the departure of her lover. Oisin himself, on the other hand, not only does not weep but, taking the fallen starling for companion, cuts his beloved loose with words and a wave of the hand.

> Oh, hadst thou seen beautiful Niam wail to herself
>   and blanch,
> Lord of the crosiers, thou even hadst lifted thy
>   hands and wept;
> But, the bird in my fingers, I mounted, mindful only
>   to launch
> Forth, piercing the distance – beneath me the hooves
>   impatiently stept. (*VP* 54)

Suggestive of his impatience to return to the world of men – he is mindful "only" to launch forth – this stanza points still more emphatically to the absence of feeling that had been Oisin's lot from the time of his arrival in the Country of the Young. Like the young boy of "The Stolen Child", he has been moving solemn-eyed through an emotional limbo; and even as the human dreamer missed his chance for happiness in this world because he heard another world beckoning, Oisin cannot be content in Tir na nOg because the only things that stir him deeply during his stay there are his repeated memories of home. His journey back to Ireland is an awaking from long sleep, a breaking out from a bright but brittle shell. The further the Island of Forgetfulness recedes in his wake, the more rapidly do the feelings he had turned his back upon march back through "the gates of [his] heart" (*VP* 57). Sorrow is the first entrant – the vivifier of the soul, and the emotion that had galvanized his departures from each of the three islands (*VP*, 25, 44, 54) – and then, in quick succession, wonder, laughter, scorn, loneliness, pity, pride and defiance (*VP* 57–63). In this last trip over the waters he neither sees nor gives a thought to the figures symbolic of desire that had followed his travels through Tir na nOg. Nor should he: there is no need for surrogate "symbolical representations" of passion in a world in which passions are real. Whatever the beauties of the islands, they cannot offer Oisin more than approximations of the strong and varied emotions of humanity; and what he rediscovers in Ireland are experiences more intense and individualized than any the sidhe can offer. Years after the publication of his poem, Yeats would write that "only the greatest obstacle that can be contemplated without despair rouses the will to full intensity" (*Au* 195). This remark has its bearing on the ending of his early poem. Oisin's coming confrontation with the devils of Christianity is the greatest obstacle he has yet had to contemplate, and he regards it without despair. He has returned to the one world in which true desire is possible, because the objects of desire – the liberation of the Fenians, the leading of them to victory – have yet to be attained. The tone of final certainty that marks his last speech to Patrick makes it clear that the size of the challenge that awaits him has only roused his passionate will to its fullest intensity. Equivocation is at an end. He "will" pray no more; he "will" go to the house of the Fenians; they "will" batter the gateway of brass (*VP* 62–3). For the first time in three centuries, the fact of his existence *will* make a difference to the beings among whom he moves. Oisin as Yeats saw him is a rejecter of eternities, whether the paradise tendered be the everlasting life in Tir na nOg that Niamh would gather him into or the Christian heaven held up to his notice by Patrick. His final lament to the saint, as Yeats noted later on, is "'not for God, but because Finn and the Fianna are not living'" (*Ex* 24). Islands in the stream, clouds in heaven's blue: far havens beckoning vainly, he insists on his humanity.

Notes to Chapter 3

1. Like other writers of the time, O'Kearney – one of whose translations was reprinted by Yeats in *FFT* (275–85) – believed that the legends about the Fenians had a firm basis in fact. Cf. his Introduction to the *Transactions of the Ossianic Society* (1853), Vol. I, pp. 40 and 60–1. He discusses the viability of a different date for the battle in a note to p. 60. For an apt illustration of the mid-nineteenth century's continuing belief in the historicity of the Fenians, cf. James MacKillop's "Finn MacCool: The Hero and the Anti-Hero in Irish Folk Tradition", in *Views of the Irish Peasantry*, p. 87.
2. The alliances reputedly formed were far more numerous than this brief summary would indicate. O'Kearney quotes an old manuscript that names the Clanna Deaghadh of Munster and the Fenians of Alba, Britain and Lochlan as allies of the Clanna Baoisgne; the Connacht Fenians were supported by the household troops of Tara and the forces of Meath and Ulster. Cf. O'Kearney's Introduction, p. 59.
3. Unless otherwise indicated, all subsequent citations are also from the 1889 version of the poem. By 1895 Yeats had moved the opening scene of the poem

from Killarney to Sligo, with Oisin and Niamh meeting on the seaward side of Knocknarea (*VP* 3).

4 Cf. John Rhys, *Lectures on the Origin and Growth of Religion as Illustrated by Celtic Heathendom* (1888), p. 465 n. The phenomenon was known as *grádh éagmaise*, or "love in absence": a love inspired simply by hearing about the beauty of a woman or, in this case, the valor of a man.

5 (*VP* 50). Yeats describes a different kind of bell-branch – the description echoes "The Song of Wandering Aengus" – in his essay on "The Tribes of Danu" (*UP2* 59, 59 n.).

6 Russell K. Alspach gives an extensive list in his "Some Sources of Yeats's *The Wanderings of Oisin*", *PMLA*, Vol. 57 (March 1943), pp. 849-66. Jeffares lists a number of works that discuss possible sources of the poem in *A New Commentary on the Poems of W. B. Yeats*, pp. 429-35.

7 Manannán Mac Lir, the old Irish god of the sea, was both a maker and owner of remarkable swords. The second volume of O'Grady's *History* speaks of the "extraordinary mythical stories" that grew up around the Fraygarta (p. 247 n.). For a description of the sword, which is a "common" feature in Irish legend, cf. Hyde's *Beside the Fire*, p. 182. The reference to Ogham letters does not appear in "The Wanderings of Oisin" until 1895.

8 Though O'Grady's spectre is male, "banshee" (*bean sidhe*, or "woman fairy") is feminine.

The "great eel" was another of the details that Yeats added to the version of "The Wanderings of Oisin" that was published in *Poems* (1895). For another possible source of the image, cf. *Celtic Heathendom*, p. 469, for Rhys's description of Cú Chulainn's fight with the shape-changing Mórrígu. Here too one of the shapes taken is that of a giant eel.

9 Seán Ó Súilleabháin, *Storytelling in Irish Tradition*, p. 16.

10 For the motif at its plainest, cf. Hyde's *Beside the Fire*, pp. 29, 182 n. Jeremiah Curtin's *Myths and Folk-Lore of Ireland* (1890) includes a story that associates the motif specifically with the Fenians; herein Fionn and his followers spend "the first part of [the] night in ease, the second in sport, and the third in a short sleep" (p. 247). The earliest known Yeats source in which the idea appears would be Kennedy's *Legendary Fictions*, p. 264.

11 This concise description of the different musical modes is from P. W. Joyce's *A Social History of Ancient Ireland* (1903) Vol. I, pp. 589-90. Though Joyce's book postdates Yeats's poem, the idea that Irish music owned three distinct styles was widely current when Yeats was writing about Oisin's wanderings; he had come across it in both Gerald Griffin's *Talis Qualis; or, Tales of the Jury Room* (1842?) and Lady Wilde's *Ancient Legends*. Griffin spoke of a music that "sometimes" made those listening to it "weep, sometimes laugh, and at other times... lull[ed] them asleep" (p. 84), while Wilde termed the three styles "the Delightful", "the Sorrowful", and "the Reposing" (p. 276).

Joyce's rendering of *súantraighe* as "lullaby" is perhaps too mild; songs of the kind were supposed to be irresistible and immediately effective, as indeed the sound of the bell-branch is on the Island of Forgetfulness.

12 Ellmann, *The Identity of Yeats*, p. 18.

13 In the 1889 version of the poem, the lance was battered but apparently still intact; the description of it as "broken" first appeared in 1895.

14 As might be expected, Yeats's sources were of a single mind in their praise of Oscar. The first volume of O'Grady's *History* called him "the prime hero of the Fianna" (p. 30). See too O'Grady's second volume, p. 19. Curtin's *Myths and Folk-Lore* subscribed to the same tradition, affirming

that "Oscar, son of Oisin," was "the strongest man of the Fenians of Erin" (pp. 298–9).

15 The transcripts of *The Speckled Bird* suggest that the image of the great vaulted hall of the castle came to the young Yeats in a vision (*VSB* 32).

16 The eye came out at the back of his head, and its baleful gaze was thus turned against the Fomoire themselves. The Tuatha Dé Danaan ostensibly came to power in Ireland after defeating the Fir Bolg in the first battle of Magh Tuiredh. Subsequently they came under the tyranny of the Fomoire, a tyranny they shook off in the battle that Lugh and Balor were a part of.

  To speak of three central pre-Christian eras in Irish history is not to imply neat chronology. The legends allow for an interval of about fifteen hundred years between the overthrow of the Tuatha Dé Danaan and the time of Cú Chulainn and the *Táin Bó Cuailgne*, and not a few heroic tales are set within the period.

17 For these later judgments of the poem by its author, cf. *Ex* 392–3, and see the same volume for Yeats's comment that the idea of progress is "the sole religious myth of modern man" (*Ex* 355).

18 As he does, for instance, in Standish Hayes O'Grady's translation of "The Lamentation of Oisin after the Fenians". Cf. the *Transactions of the Ossianic Society* (1855), Vol. III.

19 For the Yeats version of the Blake letter, see for instance his edition of *The Poems of William Blake*, p. 1. Dated four months before Blake's death in 1827, the letter was to his friend George Cumberland. Yeats's mis-citations of the missive are few and insignificant.

20 Lady Wilde, *Ancient Legends*, p. 276. The proper term is *Rosc-catha*. For a description of the most famous of the old battle odes, cf. Wilde, pp. 133–4.

21 *Transactions of the Ossianic Society* (1853), Vol. I, p. 44.

22 The reference to "sibyl leaves" is in *Zanoni*, p. 48. Blavatsky's own spiritual instructor, Koot Hoomi, had given *Zanoni* his imprimatur; the 1897 edition of Sinnett's *The Occult World* quoted him as saying that Lytton's novel was a "in many respects truthful story" (p. 151). And it was from *Zanoni* that MacGregor Mathers cribbed the idea of the Augoeides (*Zanoni*, p. 71 and note); this was eventually to evolve into the Golden Dawn's concept of "Genius". Mathers was also the author of a remarkable explanation of how Lytton's magus had worked his magic; cf. Vol. IV of Israel Regardie's *The Golden Dawn*, pp. 100–1.

  The members of the Golden Dawn had been urged to read *Zanoni* by no less a figure than Mathers's wife; cf. her comments on "that romance which contains so many valuable hints on Occult study" in Francis King's *Astral Projection, Ritual Magic and Alchemy*, p. 142. Yeats apparently took the advice; cf. his reference to Lytton's work in his 1901 essay on "Magic" (*E&I* 29).

23 Cf. *The Secret Doctrine*, Vol. II, p. 803, and Vol. III of the same work, pp. 268–9. The Rhys reference is on p. 431 of *Celtic Heathendom*, the Hyde reference on pp. 101 ff. in the *Literary History*; cf. p. 104 in particular. The version of the idea put forth by Arbois de Jubainville appears in *The Irish Mythological Cycle* on pp. 191–4.

24 The timid Oisin who appears in this poem jars badly with the heroic image presented by Comyn. Yeats, his sympathies obviously with Comyn, took from the O'Grady translation only specific elements and details. Thus the opening stanza of the "Lamentation" –

  Alas! O Fionn of the Fenians and of the hosts!
  O Oscar of the fights, my son!

> Are ye living, or in what land,
> Whilst Oisin is without action or strength? –

passes into the "Wanderings" as: "In what far kingdom do ye go,/Ah, Fenians, with the shield and bow?" (*VP* 10).

25 Legend had it that he had been killed at Ath-Brea, on the banks of the Boyne, in AD 273.

26 For Blavatsky's description of the "sacred sleep", cf. *Isis Unveiled*, Vol. I, pp. 357–8.

27 *The Secret Doctrine*, Vol. I, p. 203. As used in this chapter, "soul" is a term of convenience; theosophy, which saw man as composed of spirit, soul, and body, would have referred to the principle that survived the death of the body as the Spiritual Monad.

For other references to the moon as the mother of mankind, cf. *TSD* I, pp. 219, 248, 631; *TSD* II, pp. 48, 68, 121, 148, 511; *TSD* III, p. 562. Volume one of Jennings's *The Rosicrucians* held to the same theory (p. 218), as did the popular *The Virgin of the World* (1885), eds Anna Kingsford and Edward Maitland, p. xxviii.

28 The concept of the next world as the complement of this was widespread in Yeats's sources. For some of the clearer formulations of the idea, cf. *The Occult World*, p. 7, and *Magic, White and Black*, p. 181. The author of the latter volume, Franz Hartmann, also gave clear expression to a number of other ideas that Yeats came across as a young man and introduced into his own system later on. *Magic, White and Black*, for instance, affirmed that in "the state after death" the soul "lives on the sum of the impressions accumulated during life", which impressions last "a longer or shorter period until their forces are exhausted" (p. 154). This is a directly Yeatsian hypothesis, as was Hartmann's claim – which Yeats was to echo as late as 1938's *Purgatory* – that all sins "cause effects which have to become exhausted before [the sins themselves] can cease" (p. 251).

29 For Blavatsky's most lucid explanation of Devachan, cf. her *The Key to Theosophy* (1890), pp. 133, 156, 160, 165, 177, 178, 328.

30 *Isis Unveiled*, Vol. I, p. 303, and see the same source, pp. 345, 349, 357.

31 For Johnston's lecture, cf. *The Dublin University Review*, Vol. I, No. 6, pp. 144–6. Though Johnston acknowledged no debt, much of what he had to say was lifted directly from Sinnett; compare, for instance, Johnston's p. 145 with *Esoteric Buddhism*, pp. 115–17.

32 The reference to the Blavatsky manuscript is in the introduction to Volume I of the 1946 edition of *The Secret Doctrine* (Wheaton, Illinois: The Theosophical Press), p. 28. This same volume also helps to fix the date of Yeats's initial meeting with Blavatsky; it asserts that her London residence from May until sometime in September of 1887 was in Norwood (p. 28), and it was in "a little house at Norwood" that Yeats later recalled their first conversation as having taken place (*Au* 173).

When writing the section of his memoirs that dealt with his early involvements with theosophy, Yeats had trouble recalling precisely what he had been up to in the months that followed his first discussions with Blavatsky; but his best surmise – "probably I had been in Sligo where I returned constantly for long visits" (*Au* 174) – was a good guess indeed. He had been in Sligo, and the reason he had gone there was to work on "The Wanderings of Oisin" – particularly on Part III, which was "little more than commenced" (*CL1* 23) when his trail and Blavatsky's first crossed. How direct an influence Blavatsky had on Yeats's poem must remain a matter of informed conjecture, but it is suggestive that

Yeats finished the first draft of the poem in the months immediately following his introduction to the founder of theosophy.

33 Blavatsky's most concise summary of the spiritual evolution idea is in *TSD* II, pp. 190–1. She discusses the concept more fully in *TSD* I, pp. 210–13 and 253, and again in *TSD* II, pp. 197–211. The Blavatsky passages that most closely resemble the descriptions of spiritual evolution put forth by Sinnett and Johnston are in *TSD* I, pp. 203, 211, and *TSD* II, pp. 60 n., 273. For Blavatsky's explanation of the theory of planetary rounds – more obscure than the summary in *Esoteric Buddhism* – cf. *TSD* I, pp. 182–5.

34 For Yeats's comment on his visits to Blavatsky, see *CL1* 96–7. For someone often said to have lacked powers of close observation, Yeats produced a remarkably detailed and accurate sketch of Blavatsky in the *Autobiographies*. Even down to questions of diction, his account is in full accord with the descriptions of Blavatsky – Sinnett's *Incidents in the Life of Madame Blavatsky* (1886), for instance – written by those who had known her both longer and better.

35 *The Key to Theosophy*, pp. 162–3.

36 Ellmann, *The Identity of Yeats*, p. 19. Daniel Albright's comment on the islands seems to catch Yeats's intent more closely: "Each of Oisin's islands is a surrogate for some human need, but is ultimately incapable of satisfying that need; where coitus yields no depression, where battle yields no weariness of human muscle, where sleep yields no regeneration, there is only the emptiness of sterile enchantment." Cf. *The Myth against Myth: A Study of Yeats's Imagination in Old Age* (London: Oxford University Press, 1972), p. 65. Adele M. Dalsimer has advanced an argument much like Albright's; cf. her "W. B. Yeats's *The Wanderings of Oisin*: Blueprint for a Renaissance", *Éire-Ireland*, Vol. 11, no. 2 (Summer 1976), 56–76.

37 The two novels had borrowed their basic narrative thread from the same story. For a reprinting of their common source, cf. *St. Leon*, pp. vii–viii.

38 *FFT* 291. For O'Hanlon's blithe views on Tir na nOg, cf. his *Irish Folk Lore*, pp. 292–3; for O'Grady's, cf. volume one of the *History*, pp. 92, 264; for Lady Wilde's, cf. *Ancient Legends*, pp. 256, 258–9.

39 The tale-type that the Kennedy story most closely approximates is known as "The Adventure of Red-armed Iollann". For a description of its narrative progress, cf. Ó Súilleabháin's *Storytelling in Irish Tradition*, pp. 38–9.

40 All direct citations in this paragraph are from p. 70 of *The Tour*; the materials Yeats paraphrased in the *FFT* paragraph may be found in *The Tour*, pp. 3–4.

The poem by Gerald Griffin that Yeats inserted in this section of *FFT* likewise dealt with "O'Brazil, The Isle of the Blest". Edward O'Shea was, I believe, the first critic to discuss the cuts Yeats made in Griffin's verses, cuts that brought the piece closer in line with his own views of Tir na nOg. Cf. O'Shea's *Yeats as Editor*, p. 24.

41 *A Servant of the Queen*, p. 170.

42 Yeats may have been confusing Tir na mBeo (the Land of the Living) and Tir na nOg – not that there is any real distinction between them in the folklore.

43 Michael J. Sidnell's article on "The Wanderings of Oisin" is the most informed discussion of the poem since Albright's; see "The Allegory of Yeats's 'The Wanderings of Oisin'". Speaking of the theme of desire in the poem, Sidnell argues that Oisin's journey brings him to the discovery "that the longing, not the fulfillment, is the essence" (p. 142). I would agree with that claim,

but cannot agree with Sidnell's observation that the discovery is an "empty" one (p. 142).
44 Bloom, *Yeats*, p. 141.
45 For specific references by Yeats to the legends about women who appeared to the Fenians "in the likeness of hunted fawns", cf. *Ex* 14. For his reference to the "tale that tells how Niamh... came to Oisin as a deer", cf. *E&I* 90. Yeats was using the hound and deer as emblems of desire as late as 1935's *The King of the Great Clock Tower* (*VPl* 992, 993).

[4]

Words of Power, Language of Art

When 1939's "The Circus Animals' Desertion" labelled the islands through which Oisin had journeyed as places of vain gaiety, vain battle, vain repose, Yeats was merely iterating for the last time a view of his early poem that he had literally held from the start. In subsequent years simply "The Wanderings of Oisin", the poem as it appeared in 1889 had a subtitle. Italics included, the first words on the first page of Yeats's first volume of poetry read as follows: "The Wanderings of Oisin/and/*How a Demon Trapped Him*". A phrase like the latter could as easily have served as the subtitle of many of Yeats's early writings on the sidhe; and what it suggests is Yeats's view of Oisin as a man who has been glamoured, baited out of his proper home on earth by a sweet low voice from the west. In his 1898 essay on "The Broken Gates of Death" Yeats confirmed the suggestion, directly numbering Oisin among those whom the sidhe had ensnared:

> when the country men and country women tell of people taken by "the others," who come into the world again, they tell the same tales the old Celtic poets and romance writers told... when they made Oisin sit with Patric [sic] and his clergy and tell of his life among the gods (*UP2* 308).

As the early fairy lyrics had intimated – and "The Wanderings of Oisin" had confirmed – mortals who allowed themselves to heed the call of the other world were destined to find that their involvement with the sidhe resulted in considerably less satisfaction than the propaganda might have led them to expect. Yeats's prose comments on his glamoured Fenian voyager said no less. His 1891 essay on the thoughts and doings of his friend George Russell, for instance, spoke of the ancient Irish vision of "Oisin seeking in vain for three hundred years to appease his insatiable heart with all the pleasures of faeryland",[1] while the versions of the Hanrahan story now called "The Twisting of the Rope" that appeared in the early and mid-nineties referred in like wise to "mightier Oisin, whose heart knew unappeased three hundred years of daemonic love".[2] This same early tale was later to become the showcase for an untitled lyric sung by Hanrahan, and later refined and entitled "The Happy Townland" by Yeats. With its three stanzas – the first describing the apparent joys to be found in the otherworldly townland of the title, the second a series of battles that concludes with those who have been killed "awaken[ing] to life again", the third a drinking bout that ends in sleep – the poem is a thumbnail sketch of the same fabulous territories that Oisin had traversed at full length; and like so many of Yeats's poems, from "The Wanderings of Oisin" in 1889 to 1939's wonderful "News for the Delphic Oracle", it is a poem about a mock paradise, a "high" but "hollow" townland that the "little fox" who speaks in the refrain identifies – slyly – as the "bane" of mankind.[3] From start to finish Yeats poked curiously at traditional models of the transcendent world; and near the end of his life, as at the beginning of his career, he chose Oisin over Patrick, and then declared that the conflict between the worldly and otherworldly realms that the two men represented had been perhaps the "sole theme" of his life's work, and that throughout that work "the swordsman", with the poet's own approval, "repudiates the saint" (*Let* 798).

Yeats's continuing decisions for reality can be accounted for in a number of ways. The chapter to follow will argue that, though the young man was much taken with anti-materialist systems of thought, the young writer was more taken still with warm earthly hearthsides and earth in beauty dressed. Being a writer, Yeats would have argued, he could not have chosen otherwise. The latent connections between a poem like that on Oisin and the writings that center around the symbol of the Rose help explain why it is that, in Yeats's view of the matter, the artist lacks a choice.

"The Wanderings of Oisin" is so characteristically Yeatsian a poem that it is easy to lose sight of the fact that the ostensible author of the piece is, not Yeats, but Oisin. The narrator of the first of the Rose lyrics, "To the Rose upon the Rood of Time", is also a poet, and he joins the Fenian bard in refusing a final union with a world more ethereal than his own. Both men share a common motive: their understanding of the artist's need for a viable subject matter, and their skepticism over whether the transcendent world can furnish the subject matter that they need. Yeats's occult sources had addressed the problem directly. Godwin's *St. Leon*, for instance, acknowledged in its opening pages that the reader might well hesitate before taking up a novel about a man who had discovered the secret of immortality; after all, it might well seem that a story of the kind, "like the history of paradise, or of the future happiness of the blessed", would be a tale "too calm and motionless, too much of one invariable texture and exempt from vicissitude, to excite the attention or interest the passions of the reader" (p. 3). Lytton's *The Coming Race* (1871) resumed the same theme: men being men, it observed, they "would find the happiness of gods exceedingly dull, and would long to get back to a world in which they could quarrel with each other" (p. 54). That comment not only foreshadows the attitude of Oisin, who is plainly much happier swearing at St Patrick than he ever was while dallying with the sidhe, but points to the problem that a writer who would describe a perfect world must face: that perfection can be a barren topic. The narrator of *The Coming Race* walks through a gallery filled with portraits of the members of the tribe, some of the studies dating back thousands of years, others of them more recent; and he notes as he walks that the older the painting, the "higher" its degree of "art". The reason for this, he realizes, is that the utopian clan of the novel's title has been growing steadily more perfect as the years have passed; and

> in proportion as the beauty and the grandeur of the countenance itself became more fully developed, the art of the painter became more tame and monotonous (p. 58).

With these viewpoints Yeats was in wholehearted accord; indeed, his remarks on the matter recall Godwin and Lytton even in his word choice. "Discoveries" (1906), for instance, contends that

> the poet must not seek for what is still and fixed, for that has no life for him; and if he did, his style would become cold and monotonous, and his sense of beauty faint and sickly (E&I 287).

Rather must he

> be content to find his pleasure in all that is for ever passing away that it may come again, in the beauty of woman, in the fragile flowers of spring, in momentary heroic passion, in whatever is most fleeting,... most eager to return in its glory (E&I 287–8).

And the next few sentences in this same passage identify "the unchanging" as the property of "the saint", and "the returning" as the property of "the poet" (E&I 288): this from the artist who would later claim that throughout his work "the saint" had been repudiated by the swordsman bard. In choosing Oisin over Patrick, then, Yeats was affirming that the poet's proper subject matter was the changing world he lived in – the one world in which men like Oisin could give genuine expression to their "momentary heroic passion" – rather than the "still and fixed" world of the supernatural, the world epitomized by the islands to which Oisin had been glamoured. Years later Yeats described the more general problems that he saw places like the islands as posing for the artist, when in his *Autobiographies* he criticized the depiction in Spenser's poetry of "islands" in which certain qualities of beauty, "certain forms of sensuous loveliness were separated from all the general purposes of life" (Au 313). The poet's brief against this kind of versified autism is again reminiscent of Lytton's comment – the more perfect the beauty to be portrayed, the more monotonous the art – about the paintings in the gallery: images of an ideal world, Yeats said, can but "grow in beauty as they grow in sterility" (Au 313).

The basis of these remarks, whether Godwin's or Lytton's or Yeats's, is eminently practical. There was a reason why Homer spent so much of his narrative on the Cyclops and so little on the eaters of the lotus. Be he a painter or a poet, a teller of tales needs a tale to tell; and a world in which change plays no part, or an unchanging perfect face, can be described but once. When Yeats spoke of images of pure beauty as growing in "sterility", he was using the term in its exact sense; images of the kind are "sterile" because they are by nature incapable of begetting fresh images. Arrived at the end of his account of life on, say, the Island of the Living, Oisin is faced with two alternatives: to repeat his barren tale verbatim or to go off in search of something else to talk about. In taking the latter course, he not only proves himself a poet, but proves his creator's belief that a poet must perforce be wary when the transcendent world offers to pose. The prose and lyrics that center on the symbol of the Rose display the same sense of wariness, and for much the same reasons.

Since the Rose poems and stories share a common central symbol, the natural inclination is to begin mining the works in question by asking what the symbol might mean. In this case, however, the natural inclination is the wrong one. The fundamental reason for this – that the Rose cannot be profitably approached in the usual ways in which a reader might approach a literary symbol – will be the subject of a later stage in the discussion. The more immediate reason is that, to the extent that we can treat it simply as a symbol, the Rose has no one meaning: not in the works of Yeats, and less still in the occult sources on which Yeats drew, and least of all in the Order of the Golden Dawn whose rituals evoked the spiritual energies of which the Rose was emblematic.

One need look no further than the comments about the Rose in the *Variorum Poems* to glean an initial impression of how eclectic Yeats took the symbol to be. His claims began quietly enough, when in 1892 he continued the argument advanced in "Apologia addressed to Ireland in the coming days" (now "To Ireland in the Coming Times") by asserting that the Rose had been "a favourite symbol with the Irish poets" (*VP* 798). By 1895 he was referring to "the Eternal Rose of Beauty and of Peace" (*VP* 846), a comment rewritten several years later, with Beauty and Peace becoming "beauty and wisdom" (*VP* 846). In 1899 he offered an observation that ranged more widely still:

> The Rose has been for many centuries a symbol of spiritual love and supreme beauty. The Count Goblet D'Alviella thinks that it was once a symbol of the sun, – itself a principal symbol of the divine nature, and the symbolic heart of things. The lotus was in some Eastern countries imagined blossoming upon the Tree of Life, as the Flower of Life, and is thus represented in Assyrian bas-reliefs. Because the Rose, the flower sacred to the Virgin Mary, and the flower that Apuleius' adventurer ate, when he was changed out of the ass's shape and received into the fellowship of Isis, is the western Flower of Life, I have imagined it growing upon the Tree of Life.

And later in this same passage Yeats resumes his argument for the Rose as an Irish symbol, this in the remarks in which he identifies it as "a religious symbol", and "a symbol of woman's beauty", and "a symbol of Ireland" (*VP* 811). Finally, when at age sixty Yeats looked back over his early career, he came up with his frequently cited observation that

> *The Rose* was part of my second book, *The Countess Cathleen and Various Legends and Lyrics*, 1892, and I notice upon reading these poems for the first time for several years that the quality symbolised as The Rose differs from the Intellectual Beauty of Shelley and of Spenser in that I have imagined it as suffering with man and not as something pursued and seen from afar (*VP* 842).

Yeats chose his words with care here; "quality" denotes nothing specific, and thereby leaves the symbol open to varied interpretations. How varied those interpretations can become Yeats's own words can demonstrate, since what he called his "passion for the symbolism of the mystical Rose" (*UP2* 144) led him to make use of the symbol not only in his poetry, but in plays, stories, essays, letters and private journals besides.

A representative sampling of these references might begin by glancing towards the stories Yeats published in the early and mid-nineties and later collected in *The Secret Rose* (1897). Herein the symbol manifests in a number of guises. It reappears as a symbol of Ireland (*VSR* 207), and as an emblem of desire (*VSR* 179); one of the stories images a "moon which glimmered in the dimness like a great white rose hung on the lattice of some boundless and phantasmal world" (*VSR* 78), and later describes a troop of the sidhe as "rushing together in the shape of a great silvery rose" before they "fade... into the ashen dawn" (*VSR* 81). "Out of the Rose", an early romance in the tradition of *St. Leon* and *Zanoni*, describes the symbol as the "Divine Rose of Intellectual Flame" (*VSR* 17), and as the "Rose of Fire" whence, as with the burning bush of Exodus, the voice of God emerges (*VSR* 22), and as the home of "the Kingdom of God" (*VSR* 23). "Where there is Nothing, there is God" offers a ruby, surrogate for the Rose, as a symbol of God's love (*VSR* 49), while "Rosa Alchemica", the poet's singular tale of the "Order of the Alchemical Rose" (*VSR* 132), pictures a "rose whose every petal is a god" (*VSR* 134), a "living being... of an extraordinary beauty" (*VSR* 146).[4] Published around the same time, 1898's essay on "Symbolism in Painting" affirms that the appearance in a painting of "a winged rose or a rose of gold" will deflect the viewer's attention from the face being portrayed to the archetypal ideas – "Ancestral Beauty", for instance – that the symbols call up (*E&I* 150), and also claims that the rose has been a traditional symbol for profane love as well as divine (*E&I* 147). The private journal of 1901 evaluates the symbol as it appears in tandem with the symbol of the cross. Yeats here describes how, upon awaking from a dream about Christian Rosencreutz – the Father Christian Rosy Cross whose alchemical adventures in AD 1459 were said to have been the basis upon which Rosicrucianism had been built – he found himself thinking of that legendary figure as having "set the rose upon the cross and this by uniting religion and beauty, the spirit and nature – and the union of spirit and nature is magic".[5] The essay on William Morris, "The Happiest of the Poets" (1902), speaks in a similar vein, describing Morris's work as suggesting the possibility of a future marriage between ideal beauty and its natural earthly counterpart, a "last reconciliation when the Cross shall blossom with roses" (*E&I* 64). "Poetry and Tradition" (1907) says of art that "its red rose opens at the meeting of the two beams of the cross, and at the trysting-place of mortal and immortal, time and eternity" (*E&I* 255). And the acting version of *The Shadowy Waters* (1911) both resumes much of what Yeats had already said about his Rose and Rood and adds on new layers of meaning, with Forgael speaking of

> The red rose where the two shafts of the cross,
> Body and soul, waking and sleep, death, life,
> Whatever meaning ancient allegorists
> Have settled on, are mixed into one joy.
> For what's the rose but that? miraculous cries,
> Old stories about mystic marriages,
> Impossible truths? (*VP* 323)

The obvious point to be made here has to do with how wide a field Yeats sees his symbols as traversing. Taken in isolation, the Rose represents Ireland, supreme beauty, Ancestral Beauty, Intellectual Beauty, spiritual love, woman's beauty, profane love, peace, wisdom, the sun, the mother of God, the kingdom of God, God's love, the divine nature and, more generally still, the symbolic heart of things. Taken in combination with the Rood, the Rose comes to stand for reconciliations: of religion and beauty, spirit and nature, ideal and natural beauty, immortal and mortal, eternity and time, soul and body, sleep and waking, life and death and, most generally of all, "whatever" meaning ancient allegorists have settled on. The second point is that, once this crop of references has been gleaned, the reader who has worked the field must face the fact that his labors have largely been in vain. It is natural for the critic to expect that original meanings can be closely approximated, but in this case those expectations will be frustrated. The problem with any attempt to delimit the symbol of the Rose is that Yeats himself made no attempt to circumscribe its meaning, not even at those rare moments when he appeared to be on the verge of lifting the veil. The most striking of those moments comes in his 1898 essay on Althea Gyles, the artist who designed the cover for *The Secret Rose* and whose passion for the symbolism of the Rose was all but the equal of the poet's. Yeats's comments on Gyles's work appear to promise explanation: to understand her drawings, he writes, one must first "understand Miss Gyles' central symbol, the Rose" (*UP2* 135). And to understand this symbol, we must first isolate the symbolic elements of the drawing. The raven poised near the top of the sketch in question is "the desire and will of man". The deep waters over which he hovers are symbolic of "the flesh". He has been sent out of "the ark, the personality of man, to find if the Rose is anywhere above the flood". Having found that it is, he has taken wing to return with it to the ark; but the "sea nymphs" in the drawing, representative of "the spirits of the senses, have bribed him with a ring taken from the treasures of the kings of the world, a ring that gives the mastery of the world, and he has given them the Rose". Finally, then, the exegesis of this "central symbol": the surrender of the Rose by the raven, Yeats says, means that "henceforth man will seek for the ideal in the flesh, and the flesh will be full of illusive beauty, and the spiritual beauty will be far away" (*UP2* 136).[6]

The absence of definition here is indicative. In his most open of moments, Yeats will associate the Rose with terms of a like kind, linking it together with peace or wisdom or love or, as in the Gyles essay, "the ideal" or "spiritual beauty"; but since terms like these themselves resist analysis, such juxtapositions serve only to broaden the connotations of the Rose symbol and defuse still further even the kindlier forms of reductionism. It would be easy to complain of obfuscation here; but the poet's refusal to be pinned down rather shows him as an offspring of the intellectual currents of his time, whether of the serious work that comparative mythologists had undertaken or the underground currents that their work had helped give rise to.

Judged out of context, Yeats's claims for the eclecticism of the symbols of rose and cross seem extreme. But to compare his comments with those offered by other writers of the time is to realize that the young magician had ample precedent for taking his symbols even a good deal further than he did. Thomas De Quincey's "Historico-Critical Inquiry into the Origin of the Rosicrucians and Free-masons" (1824) started things off early in the century, claiming that older arcane writings had depicted "the *rose* and the *cross* as symbols of Alchemy and Cabbalism", and citing the generalized observation of the Rosicrucian apologist Michael Maier (1558–1622) that the Rose was emblematic of the "remote prize" of Rosicrucianism, the cross of the burden to be taken up by a neophyte entering the Brotherhood.[7] Several decades later, Jennings's *The Rosicrucians: Their Rites and Mysteries* offered a discussion of the *crux ansata* of ancient Egypt – a symbol regarded by nineteenth-century occultists as the progenitor of the so-called mundane cross, which was held to have been elaborated in its turn into the Rose and Cross of Rosicrucianism – in which the ansated cross was proclaimed a symbol of the union of male and female (*The Rosicrucians*, Vol. I, pp. 187–8), while the mundane cross that succeeded it was described in veiled terms as a Rosicrucian glyph for the alchemical processes that the wise disciples of Christian Rosencreutz were widely thought to have mastered (Vol. I, p. 101). The crosses are shown in Figure 4.1.

crux ansata   *mundane cross*

Figure 4.1

For Jennings, as for Yeats after him, the Rose was a symbol of the sun (Vol. I, p. 214) – itself no mere heavenly body, if rightly taken, but the "'Golden Sun'" or "Grand Astronomical Central Flame" (Vol. II, p. 231). *Isis Unveiled* agreed with the latter claim – the Rose, it said, was "the Central Spiritual Sun of all the kabalists" (Vol. II, p. 293)[8] – but Blavatsky demurred when it came to relating the symbol to sexuality. Profane writers like Jennings might indeed misinterpret the crucified Rose as representing "the Yoni and Lingam... the female and male principles in Nature" (*TSD* III, p. 296); but the true Rosicrucian, she argued, would find in it a symbol of "the pure ideal of mystic Nature" (*TSD* III, pp. 297). The union of male and female she found instead in the cross (*IU* II, p. 270 n., 392; *TSD* II, pp. 33, 39, 227, 626), which also stood for the "equilibrium of the elements" (*IU* II, p. 87; *TSD* II, p. 576), and the "androgynous dualism of every manifestation in nature" (*IU* II, p. 255), and "the four quarters of the compass" that in turn were emblematic of "the universe" (*IU* II, p. 382; *TSD* II, p. 586), and "the three-fold powers of creation" (*IU* II, p. 539), and "'the foundation and framework of all construction'" (*TSD* I, p. 721) – in brief, the very "key of Heaven" (*IU* II, p. 270 n.). In the *crux ansata* Blavatsky discovered a key to the fall of mankind "into physical male and female generation" (*TSD* II, p. 34) and a symbol of "man, generation, and life" (*TSD* II, p. 634 n.), whereas the mundane cross was better described as a symbol of "pure Pantheism" (*TSD* I, p. 34) that the Rosicrucians had transformed into a "symbol of pregenetic Kosmos" suggestive of "the great mystery of occult generation" (*TSD* I, p. 47) and of "the fundamental principles of light and darkness, *or good and evil*" (*TSD* II, p. 636). Small wonder that this versatile combination of a circle and a cross should be the very "'key of the Kabala'" (*TSD* II, p. 574), the sacred book of Rosicrucianism – and that, as such, the symbol should also admit of being described as "'the basis of the Occultist'" (*TSD* II, p. 587).

Hartmann's *Magic, White and Black* spoke with an enthusiasm all but equal to Blavatsky's. It saw in the cross a symbol of the union of matter with spirit, of the animal with the divine (p. 279), and affirmed that "the *Rose Cross...* is formed by *Wisdom* and *Power*" (p. 6). The Rose and Cross conjoined constituted "the full-grown Tree of Life and of Knowledge, bearing the fruits of salvation and immortality, the dispenser of Life, the protector against evil", while the center of the Cross – the domain of the Rose – served as the dwelling place of that "Reality in which is hidden the jewel of priceless value, the *Truth*" (p. 280). The man "who lives in the light that shines from the centre of the Cross", said Hartmann, is the only true Rosicrucian (p. 241 n.). A. E. Waite's *The Real History of the Rosicrucians* (1887) remained skeptical about how many true Rosicrucians there were to begin with, but joined its voice to the choir in admitting the multifaceted quality of the central symbols of Rosicrucianism. Waite declared that questions about the meaning of the symbol of the Rose "cannot be definitely answered" (p. 10), the reason for this being that neither the manifestos ostensibly issued by the order nor the men who claimed to be order members "have ever given any explanation concerning it" (p. 24); but he did not hesitate to offer explanations of his own. The Rose he associated with things either "celestial or terrestrial" (p. 11): with woman's beauty (p. 11) and spiritual love (pp. 13–14), with Christ and Dionysius (p. 12), with the Virgin Mary and Aphrodite (pp. 17–18).

It was a symbol of "the Logos, the Spirit of Wisdom, and the Spirit of Truth" (p. 11): but then again, Waite noted, Éliphas Lévi had also found in it an emblem of "beauty and life", "love and pleasure", "love refusing to be stifled by the celibate" (p. 23). The cross was equally as protean; it stood for "hidden wisdom", the "life of the world to come", the male sexual organs, "creative and generative energy", and "salvation" (p. 19). Esoterically, it might be taken as a type of Eden (p. 20) or of the four elements (p. 21): no mere earthly sign, then, but "the divine tree", the "tree of the gods", the very "tree of life and knowledge" (p. 20). Given the range that each of these ancient symbols covered on its own, Waite observed, the rose and cross when taken in conjunction were all but beyond explanation; in their union they constitute "either a purely arbitrary and thus unexplainable sign" or, at the very least, a sign whose "significance is to be sought elsewhere" (p. 24).

On the latter count Waite was correct. The significance of the symbol of the crucified Rose is to be sought elsewhere, in this case in the documents and magical workings of the Rosicrucian order that was beginning to stir into life even as Waite's *Real History* was starting to appear in London bookshops. In speaking of the Rose as a symbol of varied aspects, Yeats was following common Golden Dawn practice. If the poet had his Rose of the World, his blossoms emblematic of Beauty or Wisdom or Peace or Battle, his Rose of Fire or Divine Rose of Intellectual Flame, the Golden Dawn could invite its members to meditate on the Rose of Joy (*GD* IV, p. 209) or the Rose of Silence (*GD* IV, p. 209) or the "Fadeless Rose of Creation" (*GD* II, pp. 60, 201, 270) that surmounted the "Immortal Cross of Light" (*GD* II, pp. 201, 270). Following earlier sources, MacGregor Mathers described the cross as a sign of both "the Spirit and the Elements";[9] the Golden Dawn rituals of which he was primary author linked the Rose to the element of air in particular (*GD* II, pp. 34, 159, 248; *GD* III, pp. 86, 207). Those same rituals also associated the symbol with "peace and rest" (*GD* III, p. 50) – a concept likely to have had a bearing on Yeats's "The Rose of Peace" – or, alternatively, with suffering (*GD* III, pp. 255, 258, 267). The Rose Cross too was a symbol of suffering, a suffering said to carry an increased strength in its wake (*GD* II, pp. 212, 226; *GD* IV, p. 161), and of things more esoteric as well. The rituals Yeats studied agreed with Jennings's claim that the central symbol of the Order had its origin in "the Ancient Crux Ansata or Egyptian symbol of Life" (*GD* II, p. 271), then added that later centuries had read the Rose and Cross by their own lights; esoteric Christianity had found therein an emblem of "the Powers hidden in the word INRI" (*GD* II, p. 271), while esoteric Judaism – in terms to be explored later on – had discovered a sign representing "the force of the Ten Sephiroth in Nature" (*GD* II, p. 272). The Rose Cross stood for "Life and Light" (*GD* III, p. 231), and was not only "the symbol for the Microcosm – Man, the Adept" (*GD* IV, p. 40), but the symbol of the macrocosm as well, containing as it did "the affirmation of the principal divisions of the Universe" (*GD* IV, p. 40).

There is, then, nothing uniquely Yeatsian in the poet's assumption that the Rose, whether imaged in isolation or as mounted on the Rood, could support a wide spectrum of specific and general meanings. Indeed, Yeats's oblique remarks about his symbols are couched in precisely the kind of language that the widespread occult subculture of the time was speaking. The reasons it spoke as it did are not far to seek. To the occult way of thinking, it made ready sense that the symbols of rose and cross should signify so widely, and it was only to be expected that the meanings they expressed could at times be contradictory. After all, as Yeats himself observed, "a hundred generations might write out what seemed the meaning" of a given symbol, "and they would write different meanings, for no symbol tells all its meaning to any generation" (*E&I* 148). And if this was true of symbols in general, there were no symbols of which it was truer than the circle, ancient forerunner of the Rose, and the cross upon which it was emblazoned – and this because no symbols reached back as far as those that Rosicrucianism had adopted for its own. The *Real History* was typical in its description of the Rose as a symbol that belonged to the ages, a common property of every major ancient culture. A sigil of the "highest antiquity" (p. 10), it had its origins in nothing less than "the night of time" (p. 23). As universal as it was ancient, it was to be met with "everywhere" (p. 12); it was "'as common a hierogram throughout the vast temples and palaces of the Ancient East as it is in the immense ruins of Central America'" (p. 17). Its most ancient home, Waite felt, might be found in the "far East" (p. 11); but the question of its origins hardly mattered, since it had also surfaced in the symbologies of Greece, Rome, Palestine, Peru, and Mexico (p. 12), and had manifested besides in Persia (p. 13 n.), France (pp. 13–14), Italy (pp. 14–16), England (p. 17), Scandinavia (pp. 17–18) and Germany (p. 18). In turn, the cross could rightly claim to be the "'symbol of symbols'" (p. 20); it was not only of "still higher antiquity" than the Rose but, if possible, even "more universal" (p. 19). *The Secret Doctrine* took a similar view, but went still further than Waite: "The cross and circle", it said, "are a universal conception – as old as the human mind itself. They stand foremost on the list of the long series of, so to say, international symbols" (*TSD* II, pp. 585–6). "The subject is so vast", Blavatsky added, "that it would require in itself alone many volumes" (p. 577).

Whether or not these remarks caught Yeats's specific attention, his familiarity with their content admits of no doubt, since the Order of the Golden Dawn taught the same secret doctrine. Its spokesman in this case is Moina Bergson Mathers, sister of the philosopher, wife of the adept and, as "Vestigia", one of the Order's more eminent members. In her preface to the fourth edition (1926) of her husband's *The Kabbalah Unveiled* (1887), she discussed the Order's view of the cross and the Rose – the latter taking variant forms in different cultures – as the particular archetypes that the student of magic must "inevitably" come to grips with:

> Through all the Sacred Books, be they our Bible, the *Qabalah*, the Egyptian Books, the Vedantic Teachings, the Druidic traditions, etc., the Symbols of the Rose and of the Lily or Lotus and of the Cross, reveal themselves as veritable living images of some great fundamental truth. I am prepared to affirm that any Order, Society, group of

students, etc., forming themselves with the aim of studying the composition and nature of the manifested universe, must inevitably fall under the symbolism of the Rose, of the Lily or Lotus, and of the Cross (p. ix).

What high claims like the above help to demonstrate is that, however exotic the symbol may appear to the casual reader of today, the Rose for which Yeats made such apparently extravagant claims was a bloom that was growing wild in the multihued fields that the occultists of the late nineteenth century had staked out as secret gardens. Nor were their claims as prodigal as they might seem. If the reaction against scientific materialism helped to provide the occult revival with its impetus, it was a continuing widespread interest in comparative mythology that did most to furnish the movement with its symbols. Ever on the lookout for ways to prove that the elements of his work that seemed least traditional were perhaps the most traditional elements of all, Yeats called comparative mythology to witness that, if his red Rose seemed obscure or fanciful, it was only because the modern world had grown forgetful of tradition. In Rhys's *Celtic Heathendom*, he had found what he mistakenly took to be proof that the Rose had once been a standard symbol in the work of the ancient Irish bards (*VP* 812). In the work of the Count Goblet d'Alviella he would find ampler and more legitimate evidence that occultism's stance on the symbols of rose and cross was a stance that more orthodox lines of research could legitimize.

Rhys and Goblet d'Alviella had more than an interest in mythology in common. Both had been Hibbert Lecturers, the former in 1886 and the latter in 1891, and both later elaborated their lectures into books. *Celtic Heathendom* is a familiar title to students of Yeats's work, but the author of the Rose poems was less direct in his reference to the other authority he evoked when discussing his symbol. The only allusion to Goblet d'Alviella in his published work appears in the passage cited earlier in this chapter (p. 129), and even then the context in which the name appears is so vaguely allusive that the reader might well be forgiven for mistaking the man in question for yet another of the unnamed "medieval mystics" whose works Yeats had begun to read even before his first book of poetry was published (*Let* 592). But the work by the Count on which Yeats based so many of his comments about the Rose was going forth in the same years in which Yeats was writing the Rose poems, and was published in 1894 as *The Migration of Symbols*.[10] Here was confirmation.

As ambitious as its title, *The Migration of Symbols* set out to "elucidate the meaning of the principal symbols of the world" (p. 6). What it found was what occultism had found before it: that the cross was one of the two most "widely distributed" symbols of all, the other being the "solar Disk" (p. 33) that, in the view of the *Migration* as in that of magic, eventually came to be symbolized by a rose (pp. 150, 179, 252). Moreover, the *crux ansata*, ancestor of the Rose Cross, was said by the *Migration* to have been one of the two central symbols of the ancient world (p. 82); what Blavatsky had called the key of Heaven (*IU* II, p. 270 n.), the more scholarly work referred to as "the Key of Life" (p. 81). Nor had Yeats exaggerated the tendency of *The Migration of Symbols* to find a kaleidoscope of associations in the symbols it discussed. Even as the poet had claimed, the book proffered the Rose as an emblem not only of the sun but of what Yeats termed "the divine nature"; it also provided him with grounds for his assertions that the Eastern analogue for the Rose was the lotus, and that the lotus had been "imagined blossoming upon the Tree of Life... and is thus represented in Assyrian bas-reliefs".[11] The cross, by the same token, was portrayed by the *Migration* as a central sign in virtually every ancient symbology of East or West, less the holding of any one culture than the kind of imagining that "constitutes a characteristic feature of humanity".[12] Nor was there any real correlation between the number of creeds or cultures that had espoused the symbol and the number of meanings it might come to acquire, since any one group could assign an emblem as many senses as its inclinations could devise. If the early Christians alone could find the image of the cross in "an anchor, a mast and its yard, a standard, a plough, a man swimming, a bird flying, a person praying with outstretched arms, the Paschal Lamb on the spit, and even the human face, in which the line of the nose crosses that of the eyes" (p. 90), and if all cultures and ages could be expected to have worked a similar number of variations on the same symbolic theme, it was no exaggeration to say – as *The Migration of Symbols* said – that "the same image may be used to render the most dissimilar ideas" (p. 95).

In making that last claim, Goblet d'Alviella not only showed himself an unwitting occultist but took his place among the diversified troop of influences, orthodox or esoteric, that helped to shape or reinforce Yeats's developing thought. The heretofore unfamiliar systems of symbolism that had been making their way into England from points east since the end of the eighteenth century had taken hold of the imaginations of apparently disparate groups – comparative mythologists, occultists, poets – and elicited from them a view of symbolism that was in many ways a consensus. Blavatsky would have approved the *Migration*'s claim that dissimilar ideas had a habit of attaching themselves to the same image; in her own eclectic peregrinations through religion, myth, and magic, she too had discovered that "symbols are meant to yield more than one meaning" (*TSD* III, p. 67 n.). And the young Irish poet who had embarked on a similar odyssey had arrived at the same conclusion: to attain "abundance and depth", he wrote, a subjective art like poetry must seek out "ancient symbols", symbols "that have numberless meanings besides the one or two the writer lays an emphasis upon, or the half-score he knows of" (*E&I* 87).

These mutually reinforcing views of the ways in which a true symbol should operate shed light on several of the postures that the Yeats of the nineties adopted. They help to explain his durable insistence on the antiquity of his Rose, since the age and universality of a symbol would in large measure determine the number of meanings that had gathered around it; and the number of meanings a symbol owned would in turn have a direct effect on the "abundance and depth" of the poem in which the symbol appeared. They illumine the grounds of Yeats's conviction that, despite a lack of hard evidence, he ought to be able to identify the Rose as a symbol that had been in use in ancient Ireland (*VP* 812). His occult sources had not only assured him that the symbol was a universal one, but had intimated that the Irish view of the Rose was in accord with that of the Rosicrucians;[13] they told him too that the symbol had "been always in high favour with poets".[14] What more natural, then, than that it should have a place in the works of those "Gaelic poets" (*VP* 812) who had lived in an ancient and isolated Irish countryside where the universal religion had once waxed so strongly that it had never wholly waned? Finally, the views of the symbol put forth by Yeats's sources suggest the first of several reasons why the Rose has for the most part managed to elude traditional modes of analysis, refused to yield all its meaning. The young magician had sent himself to hidden schools, and had learned therein that man's most enduring symbols owned more meanings than man's conscious mind could number. An advancing votary of the Rose Cross, Yeats was banking on the fact that the rose and cross would endure.

When Lytton described *Zanoni* as a work to be regarded in two characters, he was drawing on a standard magical vocabulary. Throughout its history Western occultism had affirmed that its central documents must be taken as parables by the reader who would understand their import – the Rosicrucians in particular were said to have given out "their real doctrines" only "by obscure hint and mystical parable"[15] – and much of the time the occultists who were making the affirmations had spoken their piece in the same words. Thus Robert Fludd (1574–1637), occultist and defender of the Rosicrucian movement that had announced its existence to a skeptical world some two decades before his death: "a wise man reads one thing and understands another", he wrote, and explained that this need for double vision stemmed from the fact that all divine teachings carried a "twofold sense".[16] Thus too Madame Blavatsky, occultist and founder of the Theosophical Society, who declared that "every... Esoteric, half-suppressed teaching... convey[s] a double meaning" (*TSD* III, p. 416). And thus W. B. Yeats, occultist and poet, when in a retrospective glance over his early career he wrote that "I thought that for a time I could rhyme of love, calling it *The Rose*, because of the Rose's double meaning" (*Au* 254). And the drift of comments like these is not that the teachings and symbols in question carry two meanings and no more, but rather that they – like "The Wanderings of Oisin", like "To the Rose upon the Rood of Time" – admit of being read either exoterically or esoterically.

The exoteric meaning of the Rose poems regarded *en bloc* reveals itself in the passage from Yeats cited just above; they are poems about love, addressed (as she herself recalled) to Maud Gonne, though this is more patently true of lyrics like "The Rose of the World" or "The Rose of Peace" than of "To the Rose upon the Rood of Time". This is not to say that the last-mentioned poem neglects the problems faced by the overly worshipful lover. It would not be stretching the point to take the lyric as a gloss on Yeats's ambivalent attitude towards his beloved, the frustrations of his physical desire by his sense of "too great reverence and fear" (*Mem* 127): come near, come near, come near, come not too near.[17] But on the exoteric level the poem's more explicit concern is with the conflict between the opposing lures of the natural and supernatural worlds; and whatever it may suggest about the relationship between Yeats and Maud Gonne, "To the Rose upon the Rood of Time" ultimately comes down on the side of the one world that the poet can effectively take as his theme.

A poem with as many internal resonances as this one is a poem that even a strictly formal analysis can go a fair way towards comprehending. The process of pull and counterpull that was working in the poems about the sidhe, for instance, is clearly operative here as well. The first of the lyric's two stanzas describes the urge towards transcendence:

> Red Rose, proud Rose, sad Rose of all my days,
> Come near me while I sing the ancient ways –
> Cuchullin battling with the bitter tide;
> The druid, grey, wood nurtured, quiet eyed,
> Who cast round Fergus dreams and ruin untold;
> And thine own sadness, whereof stars grown old
> In dancing silver sandalled[18] on the sea,
> Sing in their high and lonely melody.
> Come near, that no more blinded by man's fate,
> I find under the boughs of love and hate,
> In all poor foolish things that live a day,
> Eternal Beauty wandering on her way.

But the second stanza turns away from the transcendent world and grounds its author solidly in the world of the everyday. It locates his subject matter in the properties of earth, whether in the deep soul of humanity or the least significant of living things:

> Come near, come near, come near – Ah, leave me still
> A little space for the rose-breath to fill,
> Lest I no more hear common things that crave,
> The weak worm hiding down in its small cave –
> The field mouse running by me in the grass,
> And heavy mortal hopes that toil and pass,
> But seek alone to hear the strange things said
> By God to the bright hearts of those long dead,
> And learn to chant a tongue men do not know.
> Come near – I would before my time to go,
> Sing of old Eri and the ancient ways,
> Red Rose, proud Rose, sad Rose of all my days.

The same kinds of balancings that characterized "The Man who Dreamed of Faeryland" are again in evidence here. In the first verse, the narrator asks to be rescued into a transcendent state that the image patterns of the poem associate with the sky. The stars sing the sadness of the Rose "in their high and lonely melody"; the narrator sings the "sad Rose" in his poem. The stars are "lonely"; the narrator speaks of being tempted to seek out divine wisdom, and to undertake the search "alone". Gathered into the supernal heavens in which the stars reside, he may at last be set above humanity, be no more "blinded by man's fate". If the symbolism is opaque, the rhetorical thrust of the poem is to this point relatively straightforward. But the second stanza deflects the momentum of the first by setting up a tension between the images that the two verses turn on, a tension through which the poem makes its point. Here the images are of earth rather than sky; the stanza pivots around the "weak worm hiding down in its small cave" and the "field mouse running by me in the grass". In the first stanza, Yeats had glanced towards the transience of all such earth-bound beings, "poor foolish things that live a day". But in the second verse, he identifies with the earth-bound by admitting his own share in mutability; he will sing his song of ancient Ireland "before [his] time to go".

The dilemma is clear. The poet has asked the Rose to rescue him from the limited vision that is man's lot, and has no sooner made the request than he realizes that being gathered into transcendence may come to mean something as bad as being blind. Being set apart from the earth will make him deaf to earth's cries, distant, no longer able to eavesdrop on the cries of desire that emanate from common things that crave. The conflict, in short, is between his strong desire for a vision of and share in the transcendent world and his stronger desire to be a good poet. To attain the transcendent state is to cut oneself off from a subject matter for poetry; for the transcendent world is ineffable, and the poet must deal in words. The second stanza addresses the problem directly. The man who decides to "seek alone to hear the strange things said/By God to the bright hearts of those long dead" will of necessity "learn to chant a tongue men do not know": will, that is, cease to be an artist. Transcendence struck a man dumb: no blessing for a born singer. Better to stretch out with your ear to the ground, and listen hard for the rustlings one can write about.

But none of these remarks reaches down through these strange esoteric verses to the sub-text on which they rest. Talking about transcendent states and the like is all too evidently a different thing from identifying what they are. To make that identification a reader must range outside the perimeters of the poem itself and into the singular occult contexts out of which it grew, the contexts Yeats was inviting the reader to examine when he spoke of his poem's "double meaning".

There is no reason to expect a poem like "To the Rose upon the Rood of Time" to be easy of interpretation, not simply because its symbols are as multifaceted as true occult symbols should be but because Yeats, like a true Rosicrucian, had set out to write a piece that would be not only "symbolic [but] unintelligible to all but the initiated".[19] This kind of discretion was obligatory for the adept. Blavatsky, for instance, only felt at liberty to publish materials never meant for the profane ear because she knew that "Theosophists... alone" would be "able to take in the meaning" (*TSD* III, p. 143), that "Occultists alone" could "understand... fully the sense" in which her statements were made (*TSD* III, p. 516). Here again the language Yeats uses to describe his poetry echoes his occult sources. Having taken pains to disguise his hidden intents, he felt a sense of security akin to Blavatsky's when he went public with poems that masked esoteric meanings; when magical belief was his subject matter, he wrote, it was "probable that only students of the magical tradition will understand me" (*VP* 803). That remark appears in the notes to 1899's *The Wind Among the Reeds*, but it applies with equal force to his earlier verses and stories on and remarks about the Rose; and the words are the words of a custodian, private lore in his grasp, finger to his lips. Sworn to a final secrecy, the voluble Blavatsky emphatically declared that "*no Esoteric truths entirely unveiled will ever be given in public print*" (*TSD* III, p. 490).[20] Yeats had the same motive for reticence, since in writing poems such as "To the Rose upon the Rood of Time" he was giving his readers a window into the temple in Clipstone Street where the Golden Dawn gave out its teachings and worked its hidden rituals.

If Yeats's tendency to regard the Rose as a multivalent symbol had clear antecedents in both prevailing occult theory and the work of men like Goblet d'Alviella, it derived still more directly from the central tenets of the Rosicrucian order that he joined in March 1890. Published between January and September 1892, the Rose poems could not help but reflect the symbols and doctrines that Yeats absorbed and was still absorbing while preparing for the Golden Dawn's Inner Order exams – exams he passed on 21 May of the year when the Rose poems were published.

In brief summary, the Golden Dawn doctrine is a doctrine of correspondences, its base in the cabalistic belief that all things, specific or universal, can be referred to the Tree of Life. There is no need to elaborate this complex theory at length to determine its relevance to Yeats's widespread writings on the Rose. Suffice it to say that the ground of the system is the belief that deity makes itself manifest in a series of emanations, and that in the cabalistic version of this neo-Platonic construct the emanations are ten in number. These emanations, or *sephiroth*, are connected to each other by a system of twenty-two channels, or "paths". Taken together, the *sephiroth* and the paths comprise the Tree of Life: in Yeats's succinct and accurate description, "a geometrical figure made up of ten circles or spheres called Sephiroth joined by straight lines" (*Au* 375). As Figure 4.2 indicates,[21] their being linked by the paths has the effect of making the sephiroth interdependent; each of them not only embodies a force of its own, but partakes to a greater or lesser extent in the forces active in the others. And at the center of all this activity is the *sephira* known as Tiphareth: by virtue of its position, "the receptacle and the centre of the Forces of the Sephiroth and the Paths" (*GD* III, p. 51).

In the abstract, all this has no evident bearing on Yeats's central early symbol; but the Tree of Life had not always been so abstract. Yeats thought that men once "must have thought of it as like some great tree covered with its fruit and its foliage", but that "it had lost its natural form" sometime "in the thirteenth century perhaps, touched by the mathematical genius of Arabia in all likelihood" (*Au* 375);[22] and the Golden Dawn had taken pains to restore to the "geometrical figure" something of its former palpability. The Order imaged the Tree of Life as forming a cross; Tiphareth, the circle at the center of the cross, became the Rose that surmounted it. The reason why this centrality signifies is that, as the heart of the Tree of Life, Tiphareth receives into itself and synthesizes the influences of the other elements of the Tree as well; eight of the twenty-two paths converge therein, for instance, while none of the other *sephiroth* can boast more than five and some own as few as three. A consideration of the associations that group themselves around the other elements of the Tree should suggest the reasons why the associations that crowd in on Tiphareth – the receptacle and center of the forces of the paths and the other nine *sephiroth*, and the symbolical Rose of Yeats's early writings – are, for all practical purposes, infinite.

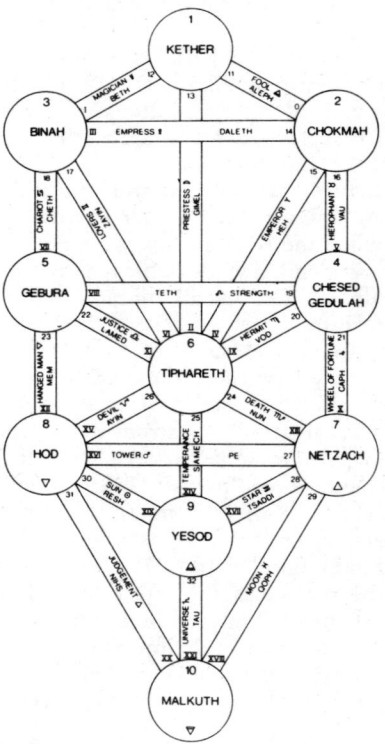

Figure 4.2 The paths on the tree

Whatever their areas of disagreement, students of the history and workings of the Golden Dawn are as one in their view of what made the Order the most important of the many occult societies founded in the West during the past hundred years. Torrens's *The Secret Rituals of the Golden Dawn*, for instance, speaks of the Order's unique success in "bringing together the various occult teachings from many sources" (p. 17), and in "correlat[ing] many of the diverse workings of the past" (p. 21). King's *The Rites of Modern Occult Magic* agrees:

> Much of the Golden Dawn system was not original, for component parts of it can be found scattered through the occult writings of a thousand years of European history. The achievement of... Mathers, or his unknown occult teachers, was to synthesize a coherent, logical system of practical occultism out of these scattered remains of a tradition that had been broken-up by fifteen hundred years of religious persecution (p. 191).

The documents that survived the Order's gradual demise are open invitations to views like these. Occultism's heady claims for the multicultural origins of the symbols of rose and cross were claims that the Order applied to its rites and teachings as a whole, declaring that "the Mysteries of the Rose and the Cross have existed from time immemorial, and that the Rites were practised, and the Wisdom taught, in Egypt, Eleusis, Samothrace, Persia, Chaldea and India, and in far more ancient lands" (*GD* II, p. 216).[23] In fact the Golden Dawn drew on many more, and in many cases more mundane, sources;[24] and it was able to keep its wide-ranging borrowings from becoming mere farrago because, as a cabalistic society, it had in its Tree of Life a means of classifying what it borrowed. Torrens's *Secret Rituals* correctly observes that "the ten circles with their connecting paths are the basis for interpreting all important occult characteristics" (p. 36), and that the Tree provided the Order with "a sublime and wonderful method of co-relating and correcting the various occult teachings given through the ages" (p. 45). *A Garden of Pomegranates* (1932) by Israel Regardie, one-time secretary to Aleister Crowley and prolific historian of the Golden Dawn, draws a prosaic but helpful analogy when it describes how the Tree came to serve the Order as "a convenient method of classification enabling the philosopher to docket his experiences and ideas as he obtains them." Combined, writes Regardie, the ten *sephiroth* and twenty-two paths are "comparable to a filing cabinet of thirty-two jackets in which an extensive system of information is filed" (p. 37).

Figure 4.2 might serve to illustrate what Regardie meant, since each of the paths in the diagram is indeed a source of information. Take, for instance, the path associated with the Hebrew letter Tau, which joins the nethermost *sephira*, Malkuth, to Yesod, the *sephira* directly above it. The Arabic numeral identifies the path as the last of the thirty-two elements of the Tree; the Roman numeral indicates which of the twenty-two Tarot trumps the path is linked with, the card in this case being number XXI, the trump that both the Golden Dawn and Mathers's 1888 book on the Tarot referred to as The Universe.[25] Saturn is the planetary sign; and this combination of letters, numbers, cards, and astrological references is only a beginning, in part because every letter and number and card and sign has its own wide range of significations, and in part because each of the paths owns more associations than this stripped-down diagram of the

Tree would indicate. The Golden Dawn ritual that centered on the path of Tau, for instance, was divided into two parts. The Hierophant of the temple spent the bulk of the first part in naming and explaining to the candidate for advancement the multiple attributions to which the path in question might lay claim. No brief résumé of these arcane materials would be possible;[26] and a longer summary is unnecessary, since the specifics of the ritual do little to illumine the reasons why Yeats regarded the Rose as among the most central of those symbols that have "numberless" meanings. What signifies here is this.

Yeats and the Order to which he belonged were able to take so latitudinal a view of the symbol of the Rose, not simply because the thought of their time tended to do the same, but because a cabalistic system is eclectic of its very nature. Commonplace though it may be, Regardie's comparison of the Tree to a kind of filing cabinet is not inaccurate. With even the lowly path of Tau able to subsume a wide variety of meanings, and with each of the remaining paths and *sephiroth* able to do the same, the Tree of Life had room on its branches for many a rare bird. The candidate who had heard the lengthy explanations of the path of Tau in the first part of his initiation ceremony could not have helped but agree when, in part the second, he was shown the diagram of "the Tree of Life formed of the Sephiroth and their connecting paths" and told that "into its complete symbolism, it is impossible to enter here, for it is the Key of all things when rightly understood" (*GD* II, p. 84). And he would have been still less surprised to learn that Tiphareth, the Rose, located as it was on the Middle Pillar that formed the "point of balance" of the Tree, and itself the "point of balance" on this balancing pillar,[27] had come to be recognized by the Order as a kind of central sea into which the other *sephiroth* poured their rich floods of association through the conduits of the paths.[28] The Order of the Golden Dawn included other kinds of Roses among its magical emblems,[29] but the Rose of the Rose Cross – the Rose that served as model for Yeats's Rose, and for the Order as for Yeats a symbol of "reconciliation"[30] – was the Rose of twenty-two petals that appears in the center of the Rose Cross badge or "Lamen" worn by advanced members of the Order (Figure 4.3).[31] From the inside outwards, its three rings of petals number three, seven, and twelve. These can be interpreted – in a fashion that, as always with the Order, is still more complicated than it already seems – as representing the three central elements of fire, air, and water, and the "old planets seven" of occultism (*VP* 118; *GD* I, p. 101), and the twelve signs of the zodiac (*GD* III, p. 53). Or, in the alchemical formulation of Torrens's earlier *The Golden Dawn: The Inner Teachings*, they "can be used to symbolize the three creative forces or primary divine activities, the seven planetary forces indicated by the basic metals used by the alchemists for transmutation", and "the twelve external forces" that "suggest the mould or cauldron" within which the final transmutation is effected (p. 18). But take them either way, they for a certainty were seen by the Order as referring directly "to the twenty-two Paths" of the cabalistic Tree (*GD* III, p. 51; *GD* II, p. 238); and they thereby formed a vortex that gathered towards itself both the strong secondary forces that traversed the paths and the more powerful originating forces that resided in the *sephiroth* that the paths joined.

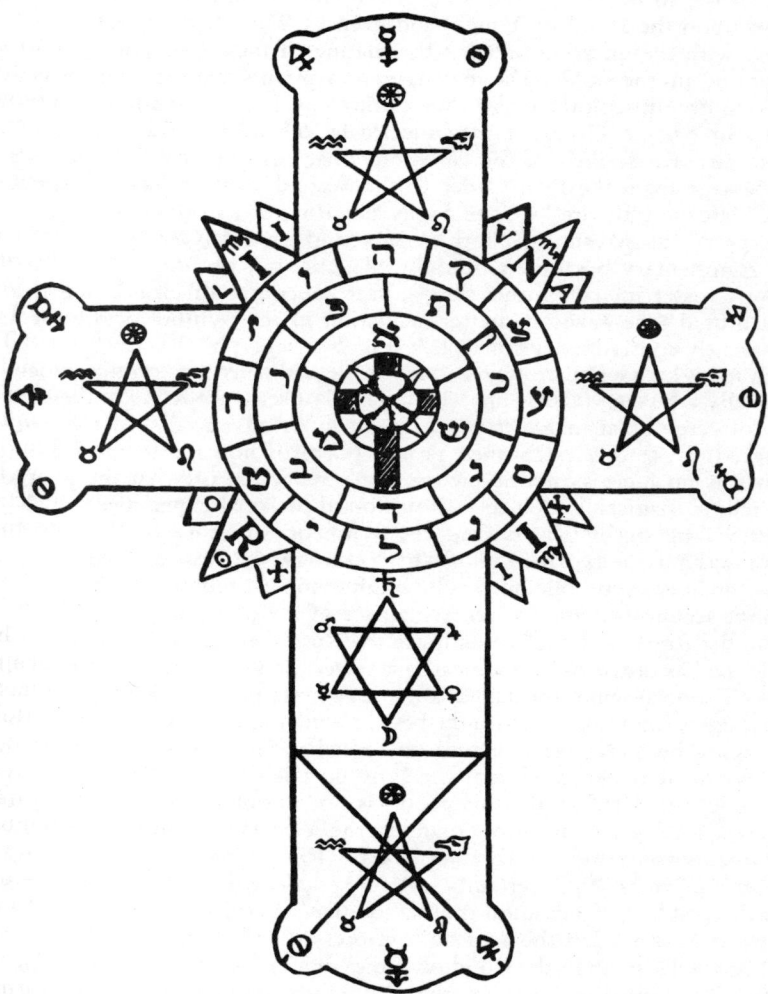

Figure 4.3 The Rose Cross Lamen

As "the central point" between the upper and lower *sephiroth* (*GD* III, p. 54), Tiphareth was "synthetical" (*GD* IV, p. 40); and it is this that most fully accounts for the fact that the Rose was the most synthetic symbol that an Irish poet and an English occult order, both of them bent on synthesis, managed to devise at the moment when their early careers joined paths.

★ ★ ★

The Rose, to be sure, is but one of the two central symbols in "To the Rose upon the Rood of Time"; and even as Waite had capitulated when faced with the question of what the mating of these two potent symbols might mean, the Golden Dawn warned its aspirants that their studies would grow more difficult the closer they came to qualifying for admission to the Inner or Second Order, that of the *Rosae Rubeae et Aureae Crucis*.[32] The Rose Cross described in the ceremony that comprised a candidate's rite of passage from the First Order to the Second was explained as nothing less than the ultimate "Key of Sigils and Rituals", an onerous symbol to interpret, "its Mysteries" both "many and great" (*GD* II, p. 202). In his commentary on these ambitious allegations, Regardie agreed that the Rose Cross Lamen "synthesis[ed] a vast concourse of ideas", and that it constituted "the harmonious reconciliation in one symbol of diverse and apparently contradictory concepts". It is also "a glyph", he went on to add, "of the higher Genius to whose knowledge and conversation the student is eternally aspiring" (*GD* I, pp. 93–4). That last sentence refers to the central rite of ceremonial magic that Yeats and other advanced Order members worked, a rite that establishes Yeats's poem of homage to the Rose and Cross as no mere symbolic picture but a redaction of what the poet and his fellow magicians took to be a profound personal experience.

Prevailing occult theory and the synthetic structure of the cabalistic Tree may join in explanation of why Yeats saw the Rose as uniquely fit to bear whatever symbolic burden he might choose to impose on it; but they cannot account for the sudden reluctance of the narrator of "To the Rose upon the Rood of Time" to embrace the Rose that, up to that point in the lyric, he has urged to "come near" no fewer than five times. It is clear that Yeats is not drawing on standard imagery here; nor, for that matter, is he drawing on anything that might best be understood as a literary symbol. Readying his notes for a lecture on Lionel Johnson, the poet wrote that "above all it is necessary that the lyric poet's life should be known that we should understand that his poetry is no rootless flower but the speech of a man".[33] There are few poems in the Yeatsian canon to which these comments apply more aptly than "To the Rose upon the Rood of Time": its central symbol for a certainty no mere poet's fancy or "rootless flower", but the emblem of a magical transaction that, as he had begun to realize its implications, had left the poet both impressed and wary.

"To the Rose upon the Rood of Time" is another of the many poems in which Yeats tried to draw his central interests together. It deals implicitly with the mixed feelings that his love for Maud Gonne had given rise to, and explicitly with his conviction that an Irish poet must address an Irish subject matter. Latent in that conviction is the belief that the artist's subject matter must come from the world he finds around him, a belief that serves to locate "To the Rose upon the Rood of Time" as a poem that also deals with Yeats's view of the poetic process, with the Rose assuming the place traditionally occupied by the Muse. But the inspiration being sought here is something more than the poetic inspiration of tradition; or rather, since Yeats habitually aimed to balance his central interests instead of distinguishing among them, what he is seeking here are several levels of inspiration at once. On the surface an appeal to a Muse, this lyric is simultaneously a covert address to what the Golden Dawn called the Higher Genius.

As Blavatsky described his powers, the ceremonial magician was capable of both "commanding Elementals who are far lower than himself on the scale of being" – the ability Yeats laid claim to in the second stanza of "Apologia addressed to Ireland in the coming days" – and of "invoking Powers higher spiritually than Man",[34] a power the poet hints at possessing in "To the Rose upon the Rood of Time", since the poem is also meant as an invocation. What Yeats took that term to mean is clear from his *Memoirs*: "My invocations were a form of prayer accompanied by an active desire for a special result, a more conscious exercise, perhaps, of the human faculties" (*Mem* 101). The *Autobiographies* confirms the fact that these stanzas on the Rose were just such a "form of prayer", with Yeats recalling the poem as an instance of the time in his early career when he "prayed" to "the Red Rose" (*Au* 254). The invocation begins in this case with the second line of the poem, since "come" is a word of command in the Golden Dawn's rituals of invocation and, as in "To the Rose upon the Rood of Time", is repeated several times and in rapid succession. The invocation designed to attract "Axir", a lesser angel whom the Order envisioned as a kind of intermediary between the magus who sought divine wisdom and the greater spiritual beings who possessed it, provides a good example of the way in which the word was employed:

> Wherefore come now, thou Angel Axir. Come! Manifest thyself in visible and material form before me, and without delay, from wherever thou mayest be, and make true and faithful answer unto those things I shall have cause to demand of thee. Come thou peaceably, visibly, and affably, and without delay, manifesting that which I desire. Come, I command ye, by all the holy names, by the Archangels above thy kingdom, and by the rulers of thy realm. Come, Axir, come! (*GD* III, p. 204).

And if the initial invocation failed to produce results, the injunction to "come" was repeated shortly thereafter and – as in the opening line of the second stanza of the poem itself – in terms still more emphatic (*GD* III, pp. 207–8). In imploring the Rose to "come near, come near, come near", then, Yeats was dropping clues that confirmed his view of his lyric as a poem with a double meaning, exoteric and esoteric both. But what these clues cannot do is explain precisely what power it is – certainly no strange angel – that Yeats's poem is invoking. As might be expected of a work that deals with the Rose upon the Rood, the beginnings of an answer to this question may be found in the Order's own version of the Rose Cross in abstract: the cabalistic Tree of Life, key of all things when rightly understood.

As already noted, the Tree in its diagrammatic form served Order members as a means of sorting out and reconciling concepts and images from varying occult systems; but its more crucial function was as a kind of grid on which the rites of practical magic worked in the Order were plotted. As with magical workings in general, the central aim of the rites was the rending of the veil, the enabling of the magician to transcend mortal bounds and make contact with the spiritual world beyond. For the Order, the deep source of spiritual "energy" – the phrase is Yeats's[35] – was Kether, the uppermost of the *sephiroth* and hence the acknowledged "Crown" of the Tree (Figure 4.2). There were three basic means of coming in touch with the powerful forces it contained. The first two of these – in Order parlance, the Lightning Flash and the Path of the Serpent – have been described at length in both the documents of the Order and the writings of Yeats,[36] and will come in for discussion later in this chapter. It is the third method that is most relevant here, the method that Order members most frequently employed to arrive at what Regardie has correctly described as the "quintessence of the entire Golden Dawn magical work" (*GD* III, p. ix). This was the so-called technique of the Middle Pillar, and its bearing on Yeats's poem is direct.

Prosaically enough, the Middle Pillar technique was very much what its name implied. Among the several ways of describing it, the Tree of Life might be imagined as consisting of three vertical pillars. That on the left was known as the Pillar of Severity, on the right as the Pillar of Mercy; the middle Pillar, that of Mildness, connected Kether with Malkuth, and it was around this connection that the technique of the Middle Pillar turned. The Order member making use of the technique would picture himself as standing in Malkuth. A series of invocations (*GD* III, pp. 259–65) would attract the force residing in Kether downward along the path called Gimel, uppermost of the Pillar's three connected paths, while the invoker, as Mathers explained it, would "by the use of the Divine Names and aspirations... strive upward by the path of Tau" towards the *sephira* known as Yesod. The magician thus "Rising in the Planes" was urged by Mathers constantly to "look upwards to the Divine Light shining down from Kether upon you". Then, as in Figure 4.2, "from Yesod leads up the Path of Temperance, Samekh, the arrow cleaving upward" and leading "the way to Tiphereth [*sic*]", the "Great central Sun of Sacred Power".[37]

Here again the centrality of Tiphareth in the Golden Dawn schema is insisted on, this time for what the Order would have considered practical reasons. The technique of the Middle Pillar involved a double movement: the ascent of the spirit of the magician along the paths of Tau and Samekh, and the streaming downward of divine force through the canal of Gimel. And the flowing forth of energy from Kether was necessary because the individual spirit could only ascend so far. The three uppermost *sephiroth* on the cabalistic Tree, the "Triad Supernal" that comprised the Tree's most potent centers of spiritual force, were divided from the lower seven by what the Golden Dawn called the Abyss. This was a gulf that not even the advanced adept could cross: hence the impossibility of a direct mounting up of the spirit of the magus from Malkuth to Kether, and hence the necessity of an intermediate point – Tiphareth, the Rose poised in the center of the Tree – where the ascending spirit could meet the "current of the Divine Influx" (*GD* II, p. 66) that its invocations had called down. It is this that accounts for Yeats's description of the Rose as a symbol of "reconciliation" (*E&I* 64). As the point on the Middle Pillar where man could establish contact with the supernatural, Tiphareth was quite literally taken by the magicians of the Golden Dawn to be what Yeats called "the trysting-place of mortal and immortal, time and eternity" (*E&I* 255), the place where "body and soul... are mixed into one joy" (*VPl* 323).

Even as the Rose was central to the Tree, then, the various forms of the technique of the Middle Pillar, being productive of the most important results the magician could hope to obtain, were taken to be the most important rituals he could practice. When Yeats told his fellow magicians that the cabalistic beliefs on which rites of the kind were based comprised the very "essence of our system", and that they furnished a model for the means by which "men come to Adeptship",[38] he was again echoing sentiments that a wide range of occultists shared. Most notable among these was Madame Blavatsky, who had declared that "'communication between the Gods... and those initiated mortals who are spiritually fit to enjoy such an intercourse'" was the "fundamental law and master-key of practical Theurgy" (*TSD* III, p. 57). The Golden Dawn agreed; its rituals described the union of man with the higher spirit as comprising the "Great Work" of magic (*GD* II, p. 214), while its historians asserted that "if one may speak of the Order as having a specific purpose, then that sublime motive is to bring each man to the perfection of his own *Kether*" and, consequently, "to the splendour of the Golden Dawn arising within the heart of his soul" (*GD* II, p. 290).[39] Comments from these same sources also help to illumine the nature of the spirit with which the worker of the Middle Pillar rituals was aspiring to merge. Like a latter-day Plotinus, Blavatsky declared that "every mortal has his immortal counterpart, or rather his Archetype, in heaven"; this spiritual double she referred to as the individual's "Higher Self" (*TSD* III, p. 59). The Golden Dawn had a directly analogous concept in what it called the "Higher Genius", and a direct means of invoking that Genius in its technique of the Middle Pillar.

In its details the Ritual of the Rose Cross (*GD* III, pp. 46–50) is one of the less complex workings that the Golden Dawn devised; but, as its title suggests, it was central to the Order's schema all the same. When Yeats spoke of invocations as "a more conscious exercise... of the human faculties", it may well have been this rite that he had in mind, since the invoker of the Rose Cross was said to be calling upon "another" – and, obviously, higher – "mode of [his] consciousness" (*GD* III, p. 49). That last phrase is pivotal, for really the Ritual of the Rose Cross was a specialized variation on a primary Golden Dawn rite that had as its object the advancement of the magician's "Spiritual Development" (*GD* III, pp. 248–58). The method employed in both these workings was that of the Middle Pillar (*GD* III, p. 257), with the magician seeking both to "draw... down the divine brilliance" from above (*GD* III, p. 253) and to rise upwards "from that lower selfhood which is in me, unto that highest selfhood which is in God the Vast One" (*GD* III, p. 255). This accomplished, the magus who had successfully traversed the paths to Tiphareth would find his or her "lower selfhood" subsumed by its spiritual counterpart: the Higher Self of *The Secret Doctrine*, and the "higher and Divine Genius" (*GD* III, p. 252) invoked by Yeats and his fellow Rosicrucians.[40] This "great transformation", the Spiritual Development rite added, was the magician's "summum bonum" (*GD* III, p. 252).

Inasmuch as Yeats perceived all his central interests as part of a continuum, we need to be wary of distinguishing between Yeats the artist and Yeats the magus. But it is safe to affirm that his magical beliefs and his artistic credo were not always in perfect accord, and that he was sometimes forced to seek a middle ground between them. As a dedicated occultist, he would have agreed with the Golden Dawn's claims about the importance of the Higher Selfhood.[41] But as a no less dedicated artist, he was in the position of having to withhold an unqualified assent to the dictates of practical magic. He had spoken of invocation not simply as an attempt at a more conscious use of man's faculties, but as a prayer that had special results as its object; and the special results produced by invocations that employed the Middle Pillar method serve to explain the hidden reasons why the narrator of this prayer in verse, having invoked the Rose to come near, should shy away from a final union as the moment of union approaches. *Zanoni*'s claim – that "the mirror of the soul cannot reflect both earth and heaven; and the one vanishes from the surface as the other is glassed upon its deeps" (p. 214) – figures directly here. As the commentary on the Rose Cross ritual explains, the rite enables its worker to ascend towards "the Divine White Brilliance" largely by withdrawing him "from the physical" (*GD* III, pp. 50, 49); and while this is a necessary prelude to spiritual union, it is not a step that a poet writing of "common things that crave" would be likely to value highly. Another of the rituals that joined Yeats's poem in centering on the symbol of the Rose Cross – the ceremony for the consecration of the Rose Cross Lamen (*GD* III, pp. 57–61) – spoke of how those who wear the badge were seeking to "lose" themselves in the "Ineffable Light" of Kether (*GD* III, p. 59). And yet another of the Middle Pillar workings (*GD* III, pp. 229–38) explained why the light should be described as Ineffable; the rite successfully performed would bring the magus to divinity's abode in "Silence unutterable" (*GD* III, p. 232). So too the central Spiritual Development ritual, which not only agreed that the attainment of union with one's Higher Genius constituted a leap into worlds that no mere words could capture (*GD* III, p. 257) but, in still stronger terms, affirmed that the invoker who gained his object would be enabled to "dwell in that land which far-off travellers call Naught" (*GD* III, pp. 256–7). This ostensible privilege became possible once the magician had learned "to rise above the planetary darkness wherein I must live, here on Earth" (*GD* III, p. 256) and, "beholding that great Light" that flowed from Kether downward, become "willing to forego all that Earth can offer" (*GD* III, p. 256). Indeed, the lengthy ceremony that initiated Golden Dawn members into the Second Order, that of the Rose of Ruby and the Cross of Gold, pledged that those who performed the "Great Work", attained union with their "higher and Divine Genius", would "at length" become "more than human" (*GD* II, p. 214). The Spiritual Development rite centered on the same aspiration; as the ritual drew towards conclusion, the magician working it invoked his "divine Genius", asking it to help accomplish his request "that I may no more come out to dwell on Earth as mortal man" (*GD* III, pp. 257, 258).

The Order rituals that grouped themselves around the symbols of Rose and Cross and the technique of the Middle Pillar were workings that made large claims, then, and they bear on Yeats's early writings about the Rose in ways both specific and general. Specifically, for instance, they reveal the motive that impels the narrator of "To the Rose upon the Rood of Time" to ask the Rose to "leave" him still "a little space". Since the range of associations that the symbol can carry is effectively limitless, it would be useless to ask what the symbol "means"; nor, for that matter, would phrasing the question thus be in the spirit of the poem in the first place. Rudolf Steiner's remarks on the central symbols of Rosicrucianism serve as reminders of what should be evident to begin with: that worshippers, whether orthodox or heterodox, do not approach their symbols in the spirit of critics. The worker of rites is not seeking to interpret his sigils but, as Steiner emphatically notes, to "*experience*" the occult force that flows through them.[42] So too Yeats in "To the Rose upon the Rood of Time", his invocation of the Rose an appeal for union with his Higher Genius, his poem descriptive of no mere rootless symbol but of a direct experience. And because this is so, the reader of a poem like this one needs to ask, not what its central symbol stands for, but what it is that the force embodied in the symbol *does*, what effect its presence "near" him has on the narrator of the poem. Judged from the viewpoint of the artist, the effect is anything but salutary.

As a magician, Yeats may well have sought to effect that ascent to Tiphareth that, uniting him with his Genius, would ensure "that I may no more come out to dwell on Earth as mortal man". But Yeats as a poet must invert the terms of that proposition, backing down from the union with divinity of which the Rose is emblematic "lest I no more hear common things that crave". The dilemma here is twofold, a problem of ear and tongue. The poet needs to be able to "hear" the cry of common things because he needs a subject matter for his songs; but he also needs a voice to be able to sing in the first place, and if he "seek[s] alone to hear the strange things said/By God to the bright hearts of those long dead", he will perforce lose the voice that he needs. Though Yeats was still studying to pass the Inner Order exams – or had, at best, just passed them – when he was writing the Rose poems, there can be no doubt that these poems are gesturing towards the experience of the advanced adept. Yeats's choice of phrase in the lines cited just above confirms his hidden intent. His later comment on adeptship, for instance, speaks not only of the seer as a man who must "seek alone", but implies – as do both "To the Rose upon the Rood of Time" and 1928's "Blood and the Moon" – that arcane wisdom, the "strange" things "said by God", is the property only of "those long dead": when one "goes his way to supreme Adeptship", he wrote, "he will go absolutely alone, for men attain to the supreme wisdom in a loneliness that is like the loneliness of death".[43] The image of "bright hearts" is equally as revealing. It serves to confirm the fact that the experience alluded to in "To the Rose upon the Rood of Time" is the wedding of man with his Genius,[44] the attaining by the adept of what the above remark by Yeats called "supreme", and the Order called "Higher", wisdom (*GD* III, p. 49). The root principle of all practical magic is the belief in the existence of a system of correspondences between macrocosm and microcosm, the universe and man, correspondences that enable the latter to come into contact with – and in the case of the adept, exert control over – the former. The cabalistic Tree was said to reflect both the Little World and the Great, and its *sephiroth* said to have correspondences in both. As might be expected of the centermost *sephira*, the macrocosmic equivalent of Tiphareth is the sun – hence the reason why the Rose was an appropriate central symbol for an order named the Golden Dawn[45] – and its equivalent in man is the heart. It is this latter correspondence that accounts for the Golden Dawn's concept of the heart as the domain of the Rose, and its injunctions to its members to think of "Tiphareth, whose position answers to the position of the heart, as if the Rose were therein" (*GD* IV, pp. 63, 70) – an image that Yeats gave expression to both in the 1892 lyric called "The Rose in my Heart" and in the same year's "The Two Trees", wherein the beloved is told to "gaze in [her] own heart" because the "holy tree is growing there" (*VP* 134).[46] Hence too the specific recommendations given an Order member who was planning to employ the technique of the Middle Pillar to draw the divine forces down through his body. Kether, he was told, was to be imagined as poised directly over his head. He was to "concentrate first" upon its "whiteness", and thereafter to "concentrate upon [his] Tiphareth, the centre about the heart", and to "draw down into it the White Rays from above". "The Whiteness", the Order document added, "should be brilliant" (*GD* IV, p. 70).

It was this that Yeats had in mind when, in the unfinished rituals written for the Castle of Heroes project, he spoke of the candidate who desired to "see the invisible and become one with it" as having "a bright light in his heart".[47] And it is this that explains God's speech to the bright hearts of the dead as a reference to the divine wisdom to be attained by the adept who, lonely in his workings as the dying, is able to summon the divine brilliance downward towards his heart. The climactic moment towards which the technique of the Middle Pillar was directed, the Great Work, *summum bonum* of the ceremonial magician: yet the narrator of "To the Rose upon the Rood of Time", who has himself set the divine forces in motion through his invocations, stops short at the very moment when the object of his aspirations has finally heeded his words of command, and stops because of his concern that he may "learn to chant a tongue men do not know". Perhaps the most direct gloss on that last line that a Yeats source has to offer comes from *The Secret Doctrine* (Vol. I). "*The speech of the men of the Earth cannot reach the Lords*" of heaven, said Blavatsky, and then went on to imply that the converse also held true: a man and a god, she wrote, "*each must be addressed in the language of his respective Element*" (p. 502, emphasis hers). Early and late, Yeats agreed: not only in his description of the language of divinity as a tongue men do not know, but in his 1913 remarks about spirits who dwelt in "a state of being... where a different relation to time and space has made language, as it is known to us, impossible".[48] And twenty years later still, the earliest draft of what was to become one of the sections of "Vacillation" said that there was no "living speech in heaven's blue" (*Let* 790). No home for artists here: lyric poetry Yeats saw as the living "speech of a man", and Yeats was a lyric poet.[49]

The Middle Pillar workings had, be it said, other attractions to offer. One among them, for instance, promised the seer access to a regard of "eternal beauty" (*GD* III, p. 232), even as the speaker of the poem hopes to arrive at a glimpse of "Eternal Beauty wandering on her way". Yet this proposition too had its drawbacks. The adept actively desired to lose himself in sublimity, and believed that a careful working of his operations would enable him to do just that; but beauty, let the magus climb to it nimbly as he will, was a moving object – in both the possible senses of that phrase – for the poet. There was a dispute brewing here between the narrator who had invoked the Rose and the narrator who later bid it keep its distance, and the results of the debate were to reach down from the Rose poems through the many years of a career that was still aborning when Yeats's early chroniclings of the Rose first saw light.

Yeats first came to magical theory less as a poet than as a man in search of a system of belief; but once magic had joined the company of his other deep interests, his rooted convictions about the poet's need for sincerity made it inevitable that the hidden art should take its place among the subjects of his poetry. It was also perhaps inevitable that, when his occult and artistic interests came into conflict, Yeats should end up favoring the latter. His 1892 letter to John O'Leary, after all, had ranked his central concerns in decisive order; magic was "the most important pursuit of my life", said the poet, "next to my poetry" (*CL1* 303). Written while the Rose poems were going through the press, those remarks not only offer a perspective on why the artist must resist absorption into the Higher Self, but look ahead to the later and similar comments that crop up in Yeats's prose. The best known of these comes with Yeats's claim that the Communicators who spoke to him through his wife in 1917 were less interested in his offer to spend the rest of his life in piecing their occult system together than in furnishing him with "metaphors for poetry".[50] But the more thorough exploration of the tension between the magical and artistic modes had come about years before: in the manuscripts of *The Speckled Bird*, which examined the sometimes conflicting demands of art and magic both.

When Yeats took the Communicators' advice and plumbed their teachings for metaphor, he was enacting in reality what his fictional self-portrait, the "Michael" of the 1900 draft of *The Speckled Bird*, had proposed to do in Yeats's novel. Planning to found an "order of the Grail" – as the novel portrays it, an amalgam of the Golden Dawn and Yeats's projected Castle of Heroes – Michael envisions a magical society that will bring together "young poets and painters, [at] the time when they are looking for their form and substance" (*VSB* 207). The Order, he predicts, will provide them with what they are looking for: "images that come to us in trances and in dreams, will soon begin to make poems and pictures, and so soon as anybody with a little genius comes among us, trances and dreams will give him a strange intensity" (*VSB* 207). This emphasis on the Order as a kind of training ground for young artists was to extend even to its magical symbols, which, "taken from nature", were "to be everything, in short, that one could put into poetry, or into pictorial design" (*VSB* 219). And when "Dunn", who was modelled by Yeats on Mathers, and who is persuaded by Michael to join him in the founding of the Order, speaks of the existence of a grimoire on which the Order might base authentic and powerful rites, Michael responds in terms that no occultist of Mathers's stripe could have accepted. He does "not care much" for books like the one Dunn has described, he says, but admits that the Order has "need of them" in order "to build better books on their foundations" (*VSB* 210, 211).[51]

The row that was preparing in that interchange became a focal point of the 1902 draft of the novel. In a note written into the manuscript, Yeats reminded himself that Dunn, by now renamed Maclagan, "must point out to Michael that his attempts at writing a ritual will not do, as they are too like a play" (*VSB* 222). And several manuscript pages later Maclagan sends Michael a letter that reflects those sentiments precisely, the magician telling his artistically inclined co-worker that

> as we worked on I more and more realized that a wide gulf divided us. You thought all of forms – I of the inner substance. When I was thinking about the gathering into the order of ancient tradition, you were thinking of making it the foundation for patterns. I have come to recognize that you are not a magician, but some kind of an artist (*VSB* 91–2).

The civilities end entirely shortly thereafter, when an artist friend of Michael's tries to persuade Maclagan to let him redesign certain of the masonic jewels Maclagan has introduced into the Order in a way that will give them "beauty"; and the magician, far from accepting the offer, "burst[s] out in a fury against art and artists" (*VSB* 93). But Yeats's point had become plain even before the outburst, and was made still more overtly in an authorial note that appeared but a few manuscript pages earlier:

> The difference of opinion about proper kind of symbolism between Michael and Maclagan must be accentuated. Maclagan had better be quite definitely a disciple of the Rosy Cross as that is embodied in the *Fama*. Michael should as definitely insist on the introduction of such a symbolism as will continue and make more precise the implicit symbolism in modern art and poetry. The antagonism must be made the antagonism between the poet and magician (*VSB* 226).[52]

Though *The Speckled Bird* was a novel in the making, the "antagonism" mentioned here is anything but a fiction. A line from *The Migration of Symbols* might serve as a touchstone in the dispute; therein the author of the introduction to the volume, George Birdwood, asserts that "beauty in decoration ought not to be sacrificed to symbolism" (p. xxii). With that idea Michael would have agreed, and he would have had Yeats's support. In his 1900 comment on the art of Althea Gyles, for instance, Yeats praises her drawings for a "precise symbolism" that none the less "never interferes with" the "beauty" of her design.[53] Put that remark in the passive voice, and it is all but the twin of Birdwood's; and transpose its central terms entirely — beauty of design should never interfere with precision of symbolism — and you have the openly contrary attitude of a pure occultist like Mathers. In his fury against art and artists, Maclagan is not merely acting the philistine. Even the sympathetic Hartmann, whose *Magic, White and Black* had expounded at length upon the ways in which "art and magic are closely related together" (p. 202), felt compelled to insist on the distinction between the "language of art" and that of "power", the language of art being the lesser of the two (p. 273); and it is on that distinction that the antagonism described in *The Speckled Bird* largely rests, since a magical symbol may or may not be beautiful but must, above all, be precise. The pentacle is the classic example. One of the central sigils of white magic when drawn as a five-pointed star, it becomes the tool of the sorcerer when inverted; and lesser deviations than these can be almost as telling. Should a ceremonial magician fail to draw the lines of the figure straight, for instance, the forces invoked through the symbol may be imbalanced; should open spaces be left in the design, malign forces may make their way through the interstices and destroy the harmony of which the center of the pentacle is the symbol. Colors, sizes, their placement in relation to other sigils: all these factors and more have their effect on the way in which a magician's symbols will work. When Maclagan reacts so strongly to the offer of Michael's friend to rework the "ugly" jewels that Maclagan has introduced, his anger is that of a man who knows that to insist that a magical symbol should have "beauty in itself" (*VSB* 93) may render that symbol ineffective or, quite possibly, unsafe. And when Michael, confronted with an argument that a dogmatic occultist could not have helped but consider sound, persists in criticizing Maclagan's magical diagrams as being "without any pattern or any beauty", and continues to insist that "beauty of detail" is to his mind "necessary" (*VSB* 226, 227), he is speaking as a man who speaks the languages of both power and art, but considers the latter the more compelling.

Yeats's diverse portraits of the Rose, then, reflect attitudes that can only be described as central to an understanding of the inner dynamics of his work as a whole. In his poems about the sidhe, in his symbol of the Rose, in the great poems of his middle and later years, he explores the choices open to a man who is conscious of the demands that eternity places on time but who none the less remains "full of tenderness for all life".[54] The preceding chapter argued that Oisin departed the islands in the west because the supernatural world could not satisfy the needs he felt as a man. The beginning of this chapter argued that his further reason for leaving was that the islands also failed to satisfy the needs he felt as an artist; and what this chapter has tried to do since is to suggest that the body of work epitomized by "To the Rose upon the Rood of Time" resumes precisely the same argument that "The Wanderings of Oisin" had advanced. Both are poems about the desiderata of the poet. The narrators of both stop shy of surrender to the lure of the supernal. And, finally, both poems deal with beauty, and debate the question of what kinds of beauty should be the artist's primary concern.

As Yeats saw it, the antagonism between the poet and magician was more than a quibble over the right appearance of magical paraphernalia. The discussion of Oisin as poet centered on the odd paradox that the artist must confront. The purer the beauty of his subject, said Lytton, the "more tame and monotonous" his "art" or, as Yeats had it, the more "cold and monotonous" his "style". These comments give rise to a pair of apparent contradictions. If a flawed art is to be the issue of the quest, then why does the opening stanza of "To the Rose upon the Rood of Time" describe the artist's goal as the discovery of Eternal Beauty? And if the potential rift between the poet and adept is as real as Yeats took it to be, why do the rituals of the Golden Dawn proclaim that the goal of the magician is the same as that of the artist? Here, the likeliest explanation – that, when they spoke of Beauty, the two camps had different kinds of things in mind – is also the most accurate one; and it is these differences in viewpoint that form the ground for the quarrel that *The Speckled Bird* describes.

As already noted, the Golden Dawn grouped its version of the vision of eternal beauty with the rewards to be attained by the adept who managed to unite with his Higher Genius. That union was said to take place in Tiphareth. Mainline cabalistic theory suggests the reason why this particular *sephira* should have been so graced. Each of the ten emanations on the Tree was associated with what might be called a guiding characteristic – Yeats's theory of the Moods owes an obvious debt to the idea – and the guiding characteristic of Tiphareth, the vessel into which the divine splendor was said to pour, was Beauty. Thus Yeats's constant association of the symbol of the Rose with "spiritual" (*UP2* 136) or "Ancestral" (*E&I* 150) or "Ideal" (*VP* 174) or "supreme" (*VP* 811) or "Intellectual" Beauty (*VP* 842): the "Imperishable Rose of Beauty", an early essay in *The Celtic Twilight* called it (*CT* 85), and it appeared as the "Rose of Far-sought Beauty" in a description that dated from early 1893 (*CT* 68).[55] That last phrase is a provocative one. It undercuts Yeats's much-cited 1925 surmise that, as a young man, he had "not" thought of the "Beauty" symbolized by the Rose as "something pursued and seen from afar" (*VP* 842), and thereby suggests that the Rose of the early works had approximated the transcendent symbol envisioned by the Golden Dawn more closely than an older poet had recalled. The Rose lyrics in particular serve to confirm the suggestion.

First published in February 1892, "The Peace of the Rose" (later renamed "The Rose of Peace" to bring its title into line with those of the other Rose poems) is the slightest of the lyrics that group themselves around the symbol; but read for the light it sheds on the tendencies of Yeats's early poetry as a whole, it becomes a poem of no slight interest. Here the symbol is located in a context at once Christian and esoteric. The Christian allusions are self-explanatory; the esoteric context takes its cue from works such as Lévi's *The History of Magic* (1860), which claimed that the rose that blossomed in Dante's *Paradiso* had derived from the hidden tradition, and that in drawing on the symbol Dante had "for the first time manifest[ed] publicly and almost explain[ed] categorically the symbol of the Rosicrucians."[56] Whatever the merits of this opinion, "The Rose of Peace" seems to show the symbol in a different aspect from that which it owned in "To the Rose upon the Rood of Time". No one in these verses is worried lest the Rose not keep its distance:

> If Michael, leader of God's host
>   When Heaven and Hell are met,
> Looked down on you from Heaven's door-post,
>   He would his deeds forget.
>
> Brooding no more upon God's wars
>   In his Divine homestead,
> He would go weave out of the stars
>   A chaplet for your head;
>
> And all folk seeing him bow down,
>   And white stars tell your praise,
> Would come at last to God's great town,
>   Led on by gentle ways;
>
> And God would bid His warfare cease,
>   Saying all things were well,
> And softly make a rosy peace,
>   A peace of Heaven with Hell.

The prospect here is plainly meant as attractive, nor does the poem imply – as do, for instance, the works that describe the homelands of the sidhe – that the prospect is ultimately less attractive than it seems. Yet "The Rose of Peace" has much in common with the fairy poems, since what is ultimately at work in Yeats's writings on both these supernal worlds is a process that might best be termed a sort of metaphysical segregation. The Rose of Peace is indeed a symbol of reconciliation, but it operates as such only on the level of the divine. Within that realm the transcendent symbol can find its proper function; it is comfortable, at home. The analogue here would be with (for instance) the sidhe who inhabit the Island of the Living, their eternal happiness contingent on their never leaving the Island. The unhappy fate of Niamh makes it clear that those who venture out of their proper context, be they gods or men, will eventually come to realize that they should have stayed in place. So with the Rose: supernal Beauty creates and discovers peace within the supernal kingdom. But if it strays beyond those limits, descends to the world of man, it does so to man's detriment. No Rose of Peace, the transcendent force that comes calling in "The Rose of the World" might better be described as the world's bane.

Published a month before "The Rose of Peace", this complementary poem continues the identification of the Rose with a Beauty that, despite the poem's title, ultimately cannot be "of the world". The reasons why it cannot are made clear in several of Yeats's early writings. In his 1899 account of his initial visits to what would later become his own Thoor Ballylee, for instance, he explains that he has already made plans to return to the environs of the tower

> because Mary Hynes, a beautiful woman whose name is still a wonder by turf fires, died there sixty years ago; for our feet would linger where beauty has lived its life of sorrow to make us understand that it is not of the world (*CT* 45).

The 1900 draft of *The Speckled Bird* resumes the same story. Walking near Ballylee, Michael falls in with an old man and, curious because he had "always heard" that Mary Hynes "was very unhappy" (*VSB* 190), asks the man if he knows anything about her. The man confirms what Michael had heard about the woman having "no luck in the world", and blames her beauty: "there is the beauty that's happy in this world, and there are many that have it", he says, "and there is the beauty that's not happy in this world" (*VSB* 190), the beauty of Mary Hynes. "It would have been better for her", he concludes, "if she had been like others" (*VSB* 189). And passages in the 1897 and 1897–8 drafts of the novel not only serve as a gloss on the rationale behind the passages above, but look back directly to the description of Beauty to be found in "The Rose of the World". There were days, laments Yeats's narrator, "when men died gladly for those whom the poets found worthy of their songs" (*VSB* 133), and nations perished for "Helen or for Deirdre" (*VSB* 113). All changed utterly:

> But now all fine beauty in a woman... is beautiful to the few only; and for the one whom it will trouble even to tears, a hundred shall turn away to the first pretty peasant whose rounded body and red and white complexion promise that ready sympathy which is perhaps incompatible with any high distinction of body or of mind; and this loneliness of beauty in the world is the last and most mysterious of its tragedies (*VSB* 133).

"The Rose of the World" is a poem that anticipates all of the excerpts above. Here too Beauty is "lonely" and "mournful"; and the reason for its solitary grief is precisely that it is, as *The Celtic Twilight* had it, "not of the world", and therefore has no better chance of achieving happiness among men than the mortal Oisin had on the islands of the Immortals. As they appear in *The Countess Kathleen and Various Legends and Lyrics*, the first two stanzas of the poem comprise a poem in themselves:

> Who dreamed that beauty passes like a dream?
>   For these red lips with all their mournful pride,
>   Mournful that no new wonder may betide,
> Troy passed away in one high funeral gleam,
>   And Usna's children died.

> We and the labouring world are passing by: –
> Amid men's souls that day by day give place,[57]
> More fleeting than the sea's foam fickle face,
> Under the passing stars, foam of the sky,
> Lives on this lonely face.

Whether the "beauty" of the opening line be taken more as a reference to the supreme Beauty of which the Rose is symbol or as a glance in the direction of Maud Gonne – and it hardly matters, since Yeats saw his reluctant lover's beauty in transcendent terms from the start[58] – what the first stanza is describing is a supernal principle. The phrase that describes it as "mournful that no new wonder may betide" cuts two ways. On the one hand, it refers to heaven's lament over a modern world in which men have "turn[ed] away" from "all fine beauty" because the sense of wonder that beauty once inspired has vanished, "pass[ed] like a dream"; on the other, it serves to underscore the fact that the Beauty of which the Rose is the embodiment, having seen all things on earth from the vantage point of eternity, can take no delight in what men call change but eternity must see as repetition. The second stanza, by contrast, describes a world that, regarded from the more transitory standpoint of man, is so rammed with change that even those of its elements most often thought of as permanent are fickle, passing, giving place. The gulf that divides these two disparate points of view is itself enough to suggest that the mortal and immortal spheres are incompatible, and it is with the image of the neglected "lonely face" that Yeats, as he should have, initially rounded off his poem. But "The Rose of the World" may also be taken as proof that Yeats's problems with Maud Gonne often stemmed less from his compulsion to work her into his life than from his inability to keep her out of it. As Jeffares has noted, George Russell later recalled that Yeats had tacked on what became the third and final stanza of the poem after returning from a long walk in the Dublin mountains with the woman who was his "obsession" (*Mem* 79), a walk that had left her weary and in a gentler mood than usual.[59] Thus the third and concluding stanza:

> Bow down archangels in your dim abode:
> Before ye were or any hearts to beat,
> Weary and kind one stood beside His seat,
> He made the world, to be a grassy road
> Before her wandering feet.

Russell felt that this last stanza had ruined what could have been a fine poem; and his assessment, were it a shade less emphatic, would be exactly the right one. Title his poem what he will, Yeats's first two stanzas had pictured a Rose that was proud and lonely, and had set it apart from a dying world. It is only in the last verse that the title of the poem begins to be justified; and the last verse does not jibe with the lines that preceded it. It describes the Rose as "weary" and "kind", adjectives too sympathetic to serve as fitting companions of pride and loneliness. Beyond that, the stanza hints that the Beauty that of its nature belongs to the other world might none the less have found an easy way open to it on what the poem calls – incongruously, given the description of the world that appears in the second stanza – the "grassy road" of our own. The unlikelihood of that event is made apparent in the poem's opening lines, which catalogue the results of the more notable of Beauty's earlier forays into the kingdoms of man. The grassy road had become scorched earth, broken wall, burning roof and tower, Agamemnon dead; and when "Troy passed away in one high funeral gleam,/And Usna's children died", it was for "Helen and for Deirdre", women in whom the transcendent spirit of Beauty had found a disturbing home on earth, that those ancient nations perished.

The fourth and last of the shorter Rose lyrics displays a similar attitude towards the symbol, though in this case the troubles that attend on Beauty's descent from its proper home visit an individual rather than a nation. Tied to "The Rose of the World" by its specific reference to "red mournful lips", "The Sorrow of Love" is a Rose poem in all but its title; and it not only follows the lead of the lyrics discussed above, but shares a common theme with poems such as "The Stolen Child" as well. Its opening stanza is set within a framework of contented domesticity. The narrator is at home, taking comfort from the noise of the sparrows in the eaves. All the natural world is alive. The moon is full; stars fill the sky; the leaves rehearse a continual song. There are hints that this peace may grow troubled; "quarrel" has an edge to it, and the "loud song of the ever-singing leaves" intimates that the wind is up. But, for the moment at least, the presence of the natural world nearby has enabled the narrator to forget whatever world-sorrows had earlier embittered his soul.

> The quarrel of the sparrows in the eaves,
>   The full round moon and the star-laden sky,
> And the loud song of the ever-singing leaves
>   Had hid away earth's old and weary cry.

The second stanza describes the banishment of content, a banishment effected by the same force that "The Rose of the World" had described as responsible for the destruction of Troy[60] and the deaths of the sons of Usnech:

> And then you came with those red mournful lips,
>   And with you came the whole of the world's tears,
> And all the sorrows of her labouring ships,
>   And all burden of her myriad years.[61]

And the final stanza returns to the underlying theme of "The Stolen Child", the grounded belief that a natural happiness cannot survive the intrusion of a supernatural force. Beyond the more evident contrasts between the two stanzas, the "star-laden sky" of the first verse juxtaposes nicely with "the white stars in the sky" of the third. The latter phrase conveys a growing sense of disintegration that the other images in the stanza support to the full.

> And now the sparrows warring in the eaves,
> The crumbling moon, the white stars in the sky,
> And the loud chanting of the unquiet leaves,
> Are shaken with earth's old and weary cry.

Like its companion image in the first two stanzas of "The Rose of the World", the symbol as it appears here might well be called "The Rose of Discord". In "To the Rose upon the Rood of Time", the narrator had been sufficiently aware of the consuming force embodied in the symbol to insist on a space between. But the narrator of "The Sorrow of Love" is caught unawares; and the Rose, to his sorrow, comes near. The vision of Beauty with which his supernatural visitor presents him forces him, as it forced "The Man who Dreamed of Faeryland", out of all content with the beauties to be found beyond and behind his door.

In sum, then, this most central of Yeats's early symbols had its ultimate origins in a widespread occult and scholarly belief that man's more universal glyphs might – or, more precisely, must – be treated as nexuses of meaning. In fixing the Rose at the center of its Tree of limitless aspects, the Golden Dawn not only continued that idea but carried it to the most extreme form it could reach. Yeats, student of occult systems in general and of the Golden Dawn in particular, was drawn through the wake of both; he evolved his multifaceted symbol with the help of his readings in magic, and drew on his knowledge of magical workings to transform that symbol into an emblem of the union with divinity that the magician sought to attain. That union, the Order held, could part the veil that kept man from a regard of eternal beauty (*GD* III, p. 232); and whatever the shades of meaning that Yeats assigned the symbol in the years after *The Countess Kathleen and Various Legends and Lyrics* was published, the Rose as he had imaged it in 1892 likewise refers to a Beauty not of the world. But for all their mutual promotion of the Rose as a symbol of the transcendent state, Yeats and the Order took radically different attitudes towards the Beauty being symbolized.

For the magician, no poet, the opening of the doors through which the Ineffable Light might flare was not only possible but wholly to be desired. But for a young poet, even a young poet who aspires to adeptship, Beauty is less easy of access. Yeats was at once a dedicated artist and occultist, but his insistent commitments to both camps did not prevent him from recognizing a fundamental difference between them: that the magus ascends to the vision of Beauty by a straight line, the paths of Tau and Samekh, while the poet, badgered by the world – Adam's curse upon him – is forced onto crooked paths. Had a representative work like "To the Rose upon the Rood of Time" been written by a man whose sole interest lay in magical workings, it would have concluded with the narrator of the poem effecting the Great Work, uniting with his Higher Genius, losing himself in the Beauty of which the Rose was emblematic; and the poem would have sounded like any of several minor lyrics by AE. But the subtler of the two young Irish mystics, and the more artistically committed, knew that the poet's limning of Beauty can never be so direct. Let it come gradually or in a sudden rush, the moment of inspiration, the found line, has days of sheer plod as both prologue and aftermath; no sooner does vision call the artist's name than it fades through the brightening air, and the artist who would recapture it is left with a long hunt and, at the end of his toil, a series of approximations. What Beauty he can uncover must be brought up from the obdurate – the later Yeats's "mound of refuse or the sweepings of a street" (*VP* 630), the earlier Yeats's world of common things that crave and all poor foolish things that live a day. Nor does the nature of his trade let him stray from those narrow bounds. For this chapter's purposes, Yeats's most revealing discussion of his chosen vocation – its sedentary toil, its sudden yieldings, its frustrating limitations – comes in his 1917 essay on "Anima Hominis":

> I think that we who are poets and artists, not being permitted to shoot beyond the tangible, must go from desire to weariness and so to desire again, and live but for the moment when vision comes to our weariness like terrible lightning (*Myth* 340).

"We seek reality with the slow toil of our weakness", the passage continues, "and are smitten from the boundless and the unforeseen" (p. 340); and though the reference here is to the experience of the artist, the terms are the Golden Dawn's.

The "slow toil of our weakness" alludes to what the Yeats essay had earlier called "the winding movement of Nature" (*Myth* 340) and what the Order knew as the Path of the Serpent: the twisting course, touching in its upward progress all twenty-two of the paths on the cabalistic Tree, along which the magician effected an arduous rise from the lower levels of the Tree towards the upper. The moment when "vision comes to our weariness like terrible lightning" and leaves the artist struck by "the boundless and the unforeseen" is the Golden Dawn's Lightning Flash: an abrupt influx of Divine Light, a surge of force from above to below that unites the ten *sephiroth* even as the Path of the Serpent links together the paths. These access routes to Beauty Yeats saw as open to both the artist and the magus: rare and sudden moments of revelation their reward for patient laborings. But there was a third method of summoning the divine force resident in the Tree, a method denied the poet:

> Only when we are saint or sage, and renounce experience itself, can we, in imagery of the Christian Cabbala, leave the sudden lightning and the path of the serpent and become the bowman who aims his arrow at the centre of the sun (*Myth* 340).

This is the most direct reference in Yeats's published work to the technique of the Middle Pillar. The sun here is Tiphareth, and the bowman aiming his arrow at its center is the adept who would direct his spirit along the path of Samekh towards magic's version of the vision of Beauty; the Golden Dawn had imagined the paths that linked the bottom quaternary of its Tree as forming a bow (Figure 4.2), and had named "the straight and narrow path of Samekh" (*GD* I, p. 191), Sagittarius its zodiacal sign, "the Path of the Arrow".[62] But to ascend that path was to be "willing to forego all that Earth could offer" (*GD* III, p. 256) – in Yeats's terms, to "renounce experience itself" – and this meant death for the poet. Not being permitted to shoot beyond the tangible, Yeats learned early on that "the fountain of art... is almost wholly experience" (*CL1* 442), and that describing "the realities of experience" was the prime concern of – "above all others" – "the artist" (*UP2* 343).[63] Those remarks, made in 1895 and 1906 respectively, confirm the above-cited 1917 observation that the transcendent world could furnish subject matter only for "saint or sage"; but then Yeats had said the same thing in 1892. The point he made directly in "Anima Hominis" was the same point he had made covertly in "To the Rose upon the Rood of Time": that the vision of Beauty that the Middle Pillar technique produced was not a vision that the poet could draw on, and that "we who are poets and artists" must forgo the wonders open to the "sage" who travelled the path of Samekh, reject a final union with the transcendent Beauty of which the Rose was the symbol. In 1893, Yeats said that "all who sought after beautiful and wonderful things with too avid a thirst, lost peace and form, and became shapeless and common" (*CT* 101). In 1906, he said that the quest after transcendent Beauty would leave the artist's style "cold and monotonous, and his sense of beauty faint and sickly" (*E&I* 287). In 1922, he agreed with Matthew Arnold that a "search" by the artist after "pure beauty" would make for a "'morbid effort'" (*Au* 313). Dividing this man's career into stages is no easy task, nor is it easy to find in the early works an attitude towards the transcendent world that differs from the attitude to be found in the work written later on. The Rose poems had been published in 1892, and served to confirm what Yeats's writings on the sidhe had implied: that the real world was the arena he decided for, and that he made his decision both as man and poet.

Notes to Chapter 4

1 Originally "An Irish Visionary", the story now appears in *The Celtic Twilight* simply as "A Visionary". Citations from *CT* are from the first editions of 1893 and 1902, but page references are to the more accessible paperback reprint. The description of Oisin's "vain" quest is on p. 25 of the 1893 *CT*, on p. 39 of the reprint.

2 In the first edition of *The Secret Rose* (1897), the story was titled "The Twisting of the Rope and Hanrahan the Red"; the line about the "unappeased" heart of Oisin, since deleted, appears therein on p. 142. See too *VSR*, p. 198.

3 Yeats had the glimmerings of the idea for Hanrahan's song as early as the 1897

edition of *The Secret Rose*, but the song did not appear in the Hanrahan stories until 1908's *Collected Works*. It is now more readily available in the versions of those stories that appear in *VSR* (99, 111–13), and the description of the townland as "high" and "hollow" is from that source. "The Happy Townland" (*VP* 213–16) runs parallel to the text from *VSR* in all but a few particulars. Yeats gave his own instructive assessment of this poem on the BBC in October 1937: "I called fairyland 'the world's bane' because I thought of it as that ideal perfection which is the source of all hopeless longing and public tumult." For the passage from which these remarks are taken, see Donald T. Torchiana's *W. B. Yeats and Georgian Ireland*, p. 287 and note.

Arguably the most entertaining of all Yeats's visions of paradise, "News for the Delphic Oracle" begins with a strangely languorous redaction of the Oracle's description of life in the afterworld, and then proceeds to pull the rug out entirely. The craggy rhythms of the third stanza not only help to locate where the poem's real sympathies lie, but to identify the scenes in the first verse – a verse whose ironic singsong beat is identical with that of "MacNamara's Band" – as the humdrum vistas they are. Yeats used monotonic rhythms to the same effect in the final stanza of "John Kinsella's Lament for Mrs. Mary Moore" (*VP* 620–1), his "News for the Catholic Priesthood".

4 All page references in the previous sentences are to *The Secret Rose* (1897) as reprinted in *VSR*. The *Secret Rose* passages that associate the Rose with Ireland, the moon, and the sidhe troop were later dropped by Yeats; the reference to the "Rose of... Desire" appears in a story that Yeats later dropped entirely, but is currently available in *UP1* 392 and *VSR* 179.

5 Cf. Moore, *The Unicorn*, p. 168.

6 Yeats's occult sources offered many an arcane analysis of biblical episodes. The poet was clearly in their debt in this regard; compare his passage on Althea Gyles with (for instance) Franz Hartmann's strikingly similar reading of the Noah story in his *Magic, White and Black*, p. 241. Differing on points of substance, the two commentaries are identical in both vocabulary and approach.

7 A loose translation from German sources, the piece appears in *The Collected Writings of Thomas De Quincey*, Vol. XIII. The reference to the rose and cross as symbols of alchemy and cabalism is on p. 399, that to Michael Maier on p. 416.

8 An assertion repeated in *TSD* II, p. 224. Blavatsky was referring to the *sephira* called Tiphareth rather than the symbol of the Rose, but occultism regarded Tiphareth and the Rose as identical.

9 The comment appears in King's collection of previously unpublished Order documents, *Astral Projection, Ritual Magic and Alchemy*, p. 123.

10 Running this source to ground is made no easier by the fact that Yeats's sole published reference to the volume is in a letter to George Russell, assigned by Wade to March 1898; herein the book is referred to as *The Migration of Symbol* (*Let* 297). The copy of the volume in Yeats's personal library is that published by Archibald Constable and Co. (Westminster, 1894).

11 As the passage cited on p. 129 of this chapter would indicate, Yeats made full use of his readings in the *Migration*. For Goblet d'Alviella's comments on the sun as an emblem of what Yeats called the "divine nature", see particularly pp. 213–18 and 267. The passages in the *Migration* that most closely approximate Yeats's remark about the sun as symbol of the "symbolic heart of things" are on pp. 28 and 189; the book's more specific references to the lotus as the Eastern flower of life, and to its appearance in Assyrian bas-reliefs, are on pp. 154–5. Yeats's paraphrase of the *Migration* is not always precise, but then his

source can itself be confusing; compare, for instance, its remarks about Sacred Trees on pp. 154–5 with those on p. 176. Goblet d'Alviella was also one of the several sources that furnished the poet with background information about the Celestial Tree that ancient mythologies had described as "the pole of the heavens" (*VP* 812); compare those notes from Yeats with the remarks that appear in the *Migration* on pp. 155, 156–8, and 161 ff.

Once he had exhausted the offerings of the *Migration*, Yeats needed to turn elsewhere to justify his description of the Rose as "the flower sacred to the Virgin Mary". One likely source of this assertion is Waite's *The Real History of the Rosicrucians* (p. 17), wherein the poet also found a recounting of how, "in the Metamorphoses of Apuleius, Lucius is restored to his human shape by devouring a chaplet of roses" (p. 12). He had come across the fuller version of the tale of "the flower that Apuleius' adventurer ate" in Pater's *Marius the Epicurean* (1885), pp. 62–4, a work that he had advertised in several early articles; see, for instance, *LNI* 137–42. To be sure, *Marius* had billed the story of Lucius as a "racy, homely satire on the love of magic then prevalent" (p. 63).

12 *The Migration of Symbols*, p. 12, and cf. pp. 13–17 for further discussion of the symbol.
13 In its discussion of the occult significance of the symbol of the Rose, for instance, Jennings's *The Rosicrucians: Their Rites and Mysteries*, Vol. II, had explained that "*Rus*... in Irish signifies 'tree,' 'knowledge,' 'science,' 'magic,' 'power'" (p. 65). Though Yeats could not have known it, Jennings has here conflated three words: *ros* ("wood or copse; point or promontory; bluff or isthmus"); *rús* ("knowledge; history"); and *rós* ("rose"). My thanks to John V. Kelleher and Ronan Murphy for explaining Jennings's mistake.
14 *The Real History of the Rosicrucians*, p. 12. Waite also issues a warning about the effect that "'the sweet breath of [the] beloved Rose'" can have on its admirers (p. 13 n.), a warning that may have had a bearing on the opening lines of the second stanza of "To the Rose upon the Rood of Time".
15 This description of the Rosicrucians appears in the Introduction to *Zanoni*, p. vi.
16 In his chapter on "The Rosicrucian Brotherhood", reprinted in *A Christian Rosenkreutz Anthology*, ed. Paul M. Allen, pp. 379, 366.
17 A candid (and since deleted) passage from the early draft of one of the sections of Yeats's memoirs reveals how deep that frustration was (*Mem* 71–2).
18 The 1892 version of the poem read, incorrectly, "sandaled".
19 De Quincey, "Historico-Critical Inquiry into the Origin of the Rosicrucians and Freemasons", p. 392.
20 Yeats's occult sources were often at odds over the question of how far the veil might be lifted. Troubled by complaints that her *Isis Unveiled* suffered from misstatements and outright omissions, Blavatsky spent much of *The Secret Doctrine* explaining that her earlier work had contained more, and more accurate, information than a first reading might have suggested. Drawing on the standard occult defense against charges of obscurity, she insisted that the obscurities were only apparent: that they had their origins in the fact that the Hidden Wisdom could only be given out gradually, and that the patient student would find all made plain in the end. Yeats, his attitude fostered or at least encouraged by his studies in magic, defended the more mystifying of his early poems in the same terms; see, for instance, his well-known 1901 claim that he needed to leave his "myths and symbols to explain themselves as the years go by and one poem lights up another" (*VP* 847).
21 The diagram pictured here is the frontispiece to R. G. Torrens's *The Secret Rituals of the Golden Dawn*.

22 The belief in an Arabian influence on Rosicrucianism was widespread in the texts that nineteenth-century occultists adopted as their own. C. W. King's *The Gnostics and Their Remains* (1887) is typical in its claim that the Brothers had adapted what Yeats called their "geometrical figure[s]" from Arabian diagrams (p. 315).

23 The rituals of the Golden Dawn underwent changes over the years, particularly after the series of rows that shook the Order around the turn of the century. A different – probably the original – version of this passage may be found in the lecture on "The History of the Rosicrucian Order" written by William Wynn Westcott, one of the Golden Dawn's co-founders (see King's *Astral Projection*, p. 91).

24 King was not exaggerating when he described Mathers as having synthesized the "scattered remains" of the hidden tradition. Among his more anomalous borrowings, Mathers appropriated the prayers of the Elementals from the Abbé de Villars's *Le Comte de Gabalis* (1670); compare, for instance, the prayer of the spirits of fire as it appears in the *Comte* (London: The Old Bourne Press, 1913), pp. 169–71, with the Order's Philosophus ceremony (*GD* II, pp. 151–2). An early parody of the claims of Rosicrucianism (and a work that Pope turned to advantage), the *Comte* was widely held to have been the motive behind the assassination of the Abbé by the Brothers of the Rose Cross; born in 1635, de Villars was (as p. vii of *Zanoni* tactfully puts it) "mysteriously... deprived of his life" while travelling to Lyons in 1673. Mathers obviously considered parts of the book as true coin, and Yeats made it part of his personal library. The Dalkey copy of the volume is that published by William Rider and Son, Ltd (London, n.d.); the bookplate identifies the book as Yeats's. For an intriguing discussion of Yeats and *Le Comte de Gabalis*, see James Longenbach's "The Secret Society of Modernism: Pound, Yeats, Olivia Shakespear, and the Abbé de Montfaucon de Villars" in *Yeats Annual*, Vol. 4 (1986), pp. 103–20.

Though Mathers told his fellow Order members that "in our system of Occultism we are contrary or converse to that taught by the Theosophical Society" (*Astral Projection*, p. 134), his Golden Dawn was often in agreement with Theosophy and in some cases borrowed both ideas and vocabulary from Blavatsky. For some of the more evident resemblances between the two groups, cf. *Astral Projection*, pp. 102, 103, 115, and see the same source for the Order's theosophically oriented views on mediumship (p. 106), the reincarnation of adepts (p. 122), and the realm of "Maya, or illusion" (p. 125).

25 First published as *Fortune-telling Cards. The Tarot, its Occult Significance and Methods of Play* (1888), this modest introduction to the famous pack of cards offers little evidence in support of Mathers's grandiose assertion that the true meanings of "the Tarot attributions" had been revealed to him by "the Secret Chiefs of [the] Order" themselves (cf. his letter to Percy Bullock, cited in Harper's *Yeats's Golden Dawn*, p. 210). In Mathers's defense, it might be pointed out that it was not until a dozen years after the publication of *Fortune-telling Cards* that he made that claim, and he had no doubt done further work on the attributions during the interval. It might also be noted that he had a low opinion of his little book to begin with. In the 1902 draft of *The Speckled Bird*, Yeats pictures "Maclagan" as having "written a sixpenny book on fortune-telling by cards, and a sixpenny dream book." "They have quite a large sale... among servant girls", says Maclagan wistfully, "when I have done a sixpenny book on the language of flowers, and another on chiromancy of the same size, I shall have exhausted the market. To such depths have the arcane sciences fallen" (*VSB* 58).

Long out of print, the sixpenny book is now again available as *The Tarot* (New York: Samuel Weiser Inc., 1969). Mathers's description of the trump called The Universe is on p. 14.

26 It was the Outer Order's ceremony of initiation to the grade of Theoricus (*GD* II, pp. 69–91) that centered on the path of Tau. For the ceremony's description of the attributes of the path, cf. *GD* II, pp. 78–81, or Torrens's *Secret Rituals*, pp. 125–7. Regardie's *A Garden of Pomegranates* gives a briefer précis of the path on its pp. 90–1.

27 These identical phrases are from Torrens's *Secret Rituals*, pp. 116, 42.

28 The importance of Tiphareth in the cabalistic schema is apparent from the sheer number of sources that insist on its centrality. For the more direct and clearer claims, cf. *IU* II, p. 293; *TSD* II, p. 224; Moina Bergson's preface to *The Kabbalah Unveiled*, pp. ix–x; *Astral Projection*, pp. 66, 132; *GD* IV, pp. 231, 241, 288; *Secret Rituals*, pp. 42, 46.

29 Specifically, Roses of five (*GD* III, p. 51), twenty-five (*GD* II, p. 242), and forty-nine petals (*GD* II, pp. 238–40, and cf. Mathers's remarks as cited in *Astral Projection*, p. 123).

30 Compare *E&I* 64 with the *Secret Rituals*, p. 175.

31 The illustration is from *The Golden Dawn*, Vol. III, p. 56. The Order borrowed the basic design for its Lamen from a book called *Secret Symbols of the Rosicrucians of the 16th and 17th Centuries*. First published by J. D. A. Eckhardt at Altona in 1785, this work is now available in *A Christian Rosenkreutz Anthology*, pp. 211–328. The model for the Lamen appears therein on p. 282; the Solomon's Seal that surmounts the badge appears on pp. 318 and 324.

For further discussion of the alchemical aspects of the Rose and the flexibility of the symbol, cf. James Lovic Allen's "Life as Art: Yeats and the Alchemical Quest" (1981), p. 23. Lovic also offers a critical survey of previous writings on Yeats and alchemy on his pp. 20–1 and 29–30.

32 King's *The Rites of Modern Occult Magic* lists the materials that an Inner Order member was expected to have mastered (pp. 63–4). A somewhat more comprehensive version of the same list is available in *Astral Projection*, pp. 28–9.

33 The lecture notes have since been published; cf. Joseph Ronsley's "Yeats's Lecture Notes for 'Friends of My Youth'", in *Yeats and the Theatre*, eds Robert O'Driscoll and Lorna Reynolds (1975), pp. 60–81. The reference to "the speech of a man" is on p. 74.

34 *The Key to Theosophy*, p. 346.

35 From "Is the Order of R.R. & A.C. to remain a Magical Order?", the privately published pamphlet that was Yeats's primary contribution to the internal Order row of 1901. Hard to come by, the pamphlet has since been reprinted in Harper's *Yeats's Golden Dawn*, pp. 259–68; the description of Kether as the source of spiritual energy is on p. 264.

36 For Yeats on the Lightning Flash, cf. *Yeats's Golden Dawn*, pp. 261, 266, and *Myth* 340; on the Path of the Serpent, cf. *Yeats's Golden Dawn*, p. 261, *Myth* 340, *Mem* 103–4, and *Au* 374–5; on the Middle Pillar, cf. *Myth* 340, *Mem* 103–4, and *Au* 374–5. The Middle Pillar makes its presence felt throughout the Order's documents, a latent force in the rituals of the Outer Order, active in those of the Inner; the most succinct description of the Lightning Flash and the Path of the Serpent to appear in the rituals is in *GD* II, pp. 84–5, and see the *Secret Rituals*, p. 130. *GD* I, p. 123, reproduces the Order's diagram of the cabalistic Tree with the Path of the Serpent and the Lightning Flash superimposed thereon. For equally helpful illustrations, cf. the *Secret Rituals*, pp. 238, 251, and cf. the same source

37   for Torrens's brief but accurate summary of the three routes of access to Kether, pp. 43, 144.
37   *Astral Projection*, p. 66.
38   "Is the Order of R.R. & A.C. to remain a Magical Order?", in *Yeats's Golden Dawn*, pp. 260, 265. For a concise example of a ritual employing the Middle Pillar technique, cf. the Ritual of the Rose Cross, *GD* III, pp. 46–50.
39   The historian in this case was "Frater A.M.A.G." (*GD* II, p. 290): Israel Regardie, whose Order motto was *Ad Majorem Adonai Gloriam*.
40   It would be off the point to explore the Order's terminology at length here, but one caveat is worthy of mention. For Order members the "attainment of the knowledge and conversation of [the] higher and Divine Genius" was equivalent to entering "the presence of the Prince of Countenances, the great Angel Metatron, He who bringeth others before the face of God" (*GD* III, p. 252). When Mathers published *The Book of the Sacred Magic of Abra-Melin the Mage* in 1898, he ran these two notions together; and more recent writers on the Golden Dawn have tended to adopt the later set of terms. Thus the reader of, say, Regardie who is looking for references to the Higher Genius is likelier to come across allusions to the Knowledge and Conversation of the Holy Guardian Angel: the vocabulary more elaborate, the basic concept the same. Even as the Golden Dawn could speak of the attainment of the knowledge and conversation of the higher and Divine Genius as "the Great Work" (*GD* II, p. 214), for instance, Regardie could describe "the attainment of the Knowledge and Conversation of [the] Holy Guardian Angel" as "the central operation of all... Magick" (*A Garden of Pomegranates*, p. 156).

    Theosophy too had spoken of the Genius as a kind of presiding angel, and in terms that anticipated the Golden Dawn's technique of the Middle Pillar; cf. Blavatsky's citation of Issac Myer, *TSD* II, p. 122. Virginia Moore offers a diversified listing of the names that the Genius had been known by in systems other than the Golden Dawn's in her *The Unicorn*, p. 132. More recently, James Olney has contributed a splendid recovery of the philosophical sources of the theory of the *daimōn*, a concept that has a clear bearing on the theory of the Higher Genius, in his "Sex and the Dead: *Daimones* of Yeats and Jung"; cf. the Yeats issue of *Literary Imagination*, pp. 43–60. Herbert J. Levine traces the literary antecedents of the *daimōn* theory in the same issue of the same journal; cf. his "'But now I add another thought': Yeats's Daimonic Tradition", pp. 77–84.
41   And did agree: cf. his comments in *Yeats's Golden Dawn*, p. 260.
42   This comment by Steiner (1861–1925), whose idiosyncratic views of Theosophy and Rosicrucianism finally gave rise to his founding of the Anthroposophical Society in 1912, appears in *A Christian Rosenkreutz Anthology*, p. 461; here Steiner adds that "'explanation'" and "'interpretation'" of magical symbols is "quite nonsensical". The sources that the young Yeats was familiar with laid a like emphasis on the primacy of experience over analysis; cf., for instance, *Magic, White and Black*, p. 29, or Hartmann's edition of *The Life of Philippus Theophrastus Bombast of Hohenheim* (1887), pp. 169, 241–2. It was this latter book that Yeats had in mind when he spoke of the beliefs of Paracelsus in the first of his endnotes to 1888's *FFT* (287).
43   "Is the Order of R.R. & A.C. to remain a Magical Order?", in *Yeats's Golden Dawn*, p. 267.
44   The sexual undertones of "To the Rose upon the Rood of Time", most evident in the opening line of the second stanza, both buoy the claim that the Rose poems were written to Maud Gonne and look ahead to Yeats's later description of the union with one's Higher Genius as a "mystic marriage" (*VPl* 323). So

typical a feature in mystical writings, this tendency to speak of the moment of spiritual consummation in physical terms was to remain a characteristic motif in the literature of the Order as well. Regardie's *A Garden of Pomegranates*, for instance, speaks of absorptions into Tiphareth as "mystical nuptials" (p. 96), and of "the supreme moment" during "the Invocation of the Holy Guardian Angel" when "every nerve of the body... is strained in one overwhelming orgasm, one ecstatic rush of the Will and Soul in the predetermined direction" (p. 141, and cf. p. 143).

45 In the Order's rendering of the Tree of Life, Tiphareth was colored rose, the better to symbolize "dawn... and the birth of new life". Cf. Torrens's *The Golden Dawn: The Inner Teachings*, p. 112.

46 "The Rose in my Heart" is now better known as "The Lover tells of the Rose in his Heart" (*VP* 142). The *Memoirs* make it clear that this poem was written to Maud Gonne (*Mem* 78), and a passage from the 1900 draft of *The Speckled Bird* serves as a direct gloss on the thought that enabled the poem; herein Michael writes a letter to Margaret, the Maud Gonne figure in the novel, in which he tells her that it was her "beauty that first filled [his] heart with so much of disquiet with all existing things" (*VSB* 202).

47 As cited in Moore, *The Unicorn*, p. 74.

48 From the unpublished essay, "Preliminary Examination of the Case of E[lizabeth] R[adcliffe]", in which Yeats investigated a case of automatic handwriting. Written in 1913 and revised a year later, the essay is now available in *Yeats and the Occult*, pp. 141–71. The observation cited here appears on p. 169.

49 Regardie's description of the effects of union with one's Higher Genius might be taken as a redaction in prose of the experience described in "To the Rose upon the Rood of Time". Cf. the passage in which Regardie speaks of "the mystical Marriage so often referred to in occult literature", which "comes as a tremendous experience altogether indescribable even to those who are masters of language". The remark pinpoints the artistic dilemma Yeats faced. Cf. *A Garden of Pomegranates*, p. 140.

50 From the Introduction to *A Vision* (1937), p. 8.

51 William H. O'Donnell has since identified the grimoire in question as *The Book of the Sacred Magic of Abra-Melin the Mage* (1898); cf. *VSB* 210, n. 46. Yeats refers to Mathers's rendition of *Sacred Magic*, though not by its full title, in O'Donnell's *Literatim Transcription of the Manuscripts of William Butler Yeats's The Speckled Bird*, p. 392. No text for the neophyte, the *Sacred Magic* could produce sorry consequences. For a description of a case of obsession that afflicted an inexperienced worker of the system, cf. *The Rites of Modern Occult Magic*, pp. 197–200.

52 Published in 1614, the *Fama* referred to in this passage – its full title *The Fama Fraternitatis of the Meritorious Order of the Rosy Cross, addressed to the learned in general and the Governors of Europe* – might best be described as the charter document of Rosicrucianism. Though Yeats's sources were divided over the question of its authorship, it was generally held to be the work of Johann Valentin Andreae (1586–1654), who was also said to be the author of the *Confessio Fraternitatis* (1615) and the controversial *The Chymical Marriage of Christian Rosencreutz* (1616). Yeats would have first read the *Fama* as it appeared in Waite's *The Real History of the Rosicrucians*, pp. 65–84. In a 1915 letter to Ernest Boyd, the poet says that he found "authority for my use of the rose" in "such authors as Valentin Andrea [sic]" (*Let* 592).

53 From Yeats's note on Althea Gyles in *A Treasury of Irish Poetry in the English Tongue* (1932), eds Stopford A. Brooke and T.W. Rolleston, p. 475.

54 From the unpublished 1914 essay in which Yeats recorded his eyewitness observations of the miracle supposedly taking place in the French town of Mirabeau. The essay now appears in *Yeats and The Occult*, pp. 181–9; the remark about a poetry full of tenderness for all life is on p. 187.
55 The 1893 edition of *The Celtic Twilight* refers to the "Rose of Far-sight Beauty" (80), a misprint corrected when the essay containing the phrase next appeared.
56 Éliphas Lévi, *The History of Magic* (1913), p. 346. Though Yeats could not have read the *History* in the original, he found this claim of Lévi's repeated in Waite's *The Real History of the Rosicrucians*, p. 15.
57 In *The Countess Kathleen and Various Legends and Lyrics*, this line incorrectly read "gives place".
58 See, for instance, the revealing description of the Maud Gonne figure in the 1897–8 version of *The Speckled Bird*: "The face of Margaret Leroy was to be always to Michael... a face in a shrine rather than a mortal face, and he was to see it always as he saw it [on the] first day" that they met (*VSB* 133).
59 Like many other background details that are now common knowledge, this fact first surfaced in the 1968 edition of Jeffares's *A New Commentary on the Poems of W. B. Yeats*, pp. 27–8.
60 The reference to Troy is more explicit in the later version of the poem, the second verse of which refers to "Priam murdered with his peers" (*VP* 120).
61 The last line of this verse should have read – and did, when next the poem was published – "all the burden".
62 *Astral Projection*, p. 158. There is an extensive analysis of the image of the adept as bowman in *GD* II, pp. 185–6.
63 A list of all of Yeats's references to personal experience as the foundation of art would be a long one, but it should be noted that the poet was making the claim as late as 1938's "To-morrow's Revolution" (*Ex* 428). For earlier versions of the passage in which Yeats discusses the differences between "saint" and "poet", cf. Joseph Ronsley's "Yeats's Lecture Notes for 'Friends of My Youth'", in *Yeats and the Theatre*, pp. 69, 81.

[5]
Natural Ideals: Yeats and the Walled Garden

Given the complexities of Yeats's probings of the spiritual realm, it was perhaps inevitable that the visionary elements of his work would come to receive so large a share of attention. Yet the early writings themselves habitually focus, not only on the esoteric, but on the worlds of home and nature; and one of Yeats's more exotic lyrics provides a useful starting point for consideration of his less exotic settings. A flawed and generally neglected poem, "The Rose of Battle" not only resumes Yeats's dealings with the world of the spirit but suggests what forms his affections for mundane things were most inclined to take. Herein are the characteristic images of a secured home and a benign natural world that surrounds it: twin images that were to be synthesized, elsewhere in the early work, in the symbol of the walled garden and the varied improvisations – lake-encircled islands, for instance – that Yeats was to work on it. These were homes that were both natural and fast, and emblems that comprised, as Yeats himself would claim, the best description of happiness in the world.

The narrator of "The Rose of Battle" addresses himself to the dissatisfied, the "sad, lonely, the insatiable". He summons them away from their inland lives and bids them join him on the seashore. Ships with unfurled sails wait to take them aboard. As in "The Rose of the World", the rising of the wind described in the first few lines of the lyric hints that a revelation may be at hand; and the poem later reveals that those who gather on the shore are being called out to sea by the sound of "God's bell", buoyed above the waters. Initially all this sounds obscurely positive; but the second stanza implies that when the narrator and his fellow seekers, accompanied by the spirit embodied in the "Rose of all the World", sail out over the waves, it will be but to meet their "fate": to find themselves, in the words of the poem's conclusion, "defeated in [God's] wars".

It is misleading that the narrative progress of this complex poem may be so concisely summarized. For the most part, criticism has avoided "The Rose of Battle",[1] the sound reason for this avoidance being that the poem places major demands on the reader without being good enough to repay the effort spent. The most ambitious of the early Rose lyrics, "The Rose of Battle" is beyond dispute also the least intelligible. In 1892 the poem read thus:

> Rose of all Roses, Rose of all the World,
> The tall thought-woven sails that flap unfurled
> Above the tide of hours, rise on the air,
> And God's bell buoyed to be the waters' care,
> And pressing on, or lingering slow with fear,
> The throngs with blown wet hair are gathering near.
> "Turn if ye may," I call out to each one,
> "From the grey ships and battles never won.
> Danger no refuge holds, and war no peace,
> For him who hears Love sing and never cease
> Beside her clean swept hearth, her quiet shade;
> But gather all for whom no Love hath made
> A woven silence, or but came to cast
> A song into the air, and singing passed[2]
> To smile upon her stars; and gather you,
> Who have sought more than is in rain or dew,
> Or in the sun and moon, or on the earth,
> Or sighs amid the wandering, starry mirth,
> Or comes in laughter from the sea's sad lips,
> And wage God's battles in the long grey ships.
> The sad, the lonely, the insatiable,
> To these Old Night shall all her mystery tell,
> God's bell has claimed them by the little cry
> Of their sad hearts that may not live nor die."
>
> Rose of all Roses, Rose of all the World,
> You, too, have come where the dim tides are hurled
> Upon the wharves of sorrow, and heard ring
> The bell that calls us on – the sweet far thing.
> Beauty grown sad with its eternity,
> Made you of us and of the dim grey sea.
> Our long ships loose thought-woven sails and wait,
> For God has bid them share an equal fate;
> And when at last defeated in His wars,
> They have gone down under the same white stars,
> We shall no longer hear the little cry
> Of our sad hearts that may not live nor die.

Yeats's instincts here betrayed him on several counts, the most immediate being his belief that a poem should give its reader a glass onto the poet's central interests. "The Rose of the World" paid a price for the presence of Maud Gonne; "The Rose of Battle" was to suffer from its author's conviction that an Irish writer not only needed to write on Irish themes, but that it was a "necessity" that he "study the native tradition of expression" as well (*UP1* 378–9). The particular strand of indigenous Irish tradition that Yeats drew on for "The Rose of Battle" was a line that he knew well; it had already engendered many a popular Irish story and poem, laments that had left even the critical eyes of the young Yeats "filled with tears"

(*Au* 102). These were the threnodies of exile, and it is in tales of the kind that "The Rose of Battle" has a good share of its origins. There was, for instance, Lady Wilde's *Ancient Cures*, which Yeats had read and reviewed shortly before his poem was written (*UP1* 170–3). Wilde is describing the departure of emigrants to America:

> Silent and troubled, with the scared, sad look of the hunted deer, they gather on the beach amid the wild cries of their kindred, and sail away in the exile ship, with all its unknown horrors, to the unknown land beyond the sea, as if they were passing to another life through the gates of death (p. 202).

A bleak setting, this, with the exiles described as

> helpless, incoherent masses of ignorant and unorganised men, waifs driven by the storm-winds of despair, with only bitter memories, or vengeful hopes to guide, that, like torches held over an abyss by an uncertain hand, too often lead but to dismay and ruin (p. 203).

The resemblances between the images in passages like these and those in Yeats's poem need no elaboration; and Yeats's derivation of the basic form of "The Rose of Battle" from the form of the emigrant poem was equally as direct. One of the more pervasive forms that the poems that fell into the genre adopted was dialogue, with the seaward crowds passing by an unnamed interlocutor whose task it was to ask them where they were going and why. Shortly before "The Rose of Battle" appeared in print, Yeats had published an article in which he accurately claimed to "know our Irish poets pretty thoroughly" (*LNI* 139); and he was for a certainty familiar with most of the popular poems of which "The Emigrants" by D. P. Starkey (1806–76) might serve as a fit example. Wrote Starkey:

> Behold! a troop of travellers descending to the shore –
> Strong, stalwart youths and maidens, mixed with those in years and hoar;
> With stealth they glide towards the tide, like walkers in their sleep:
> Where are ye going, lonely ones, that thus ye walk, and weep?
>
> No answer: but the lip compressed argues a tale to tell –
> A studied silence seems to hold them bound, as with a spell;
> They pass by me abstractedly, their gaze where, near at hand,
> Rolls through the shade the heavy wave upon the sullen strand.

> Stop – whither go ye? See, behind, e'en yet the landscape smiles –
> The broad sunset illumines yet these pleasant western isles, –
> Why, why is it that none will turn and take one look behind,
> But rather face the billows there, to light and counsel blind?
>
> Peace! questioner – we know the sun upon our soil doth rest –
> Though EMIGRANTS, we have not cast all feeling from our breast;
> But still, *we go* – for through that shade hope gilds the distant plain,
> While round the homes we've left we look'd for nourishment in vain!

Here too the parallels between the Yeats piece and Starkey's lines are clear. In both poems a sad and "lonely" troop descends towards a dark sea, and on or near the seashore meets a solitary man who urges them to "turn" back from the dangers that lie ahead. And in both poems the crowd presses forward – Starkey's impelled by a physical hunger, Yeats's by a spiritual – and in both poems the sounds of their voices are lost as the ship sails on. Starkey:

> Torn is the last embrace apart – the vessel quits the shore –
> They're waving hands from off the deck – we hear their voice no more.

Yeats:

> And when at last defeated in His wars,
> They have gone down under the same white stars,
> We shall no longer hear the little cry
> Of our sad hearts that may not live nor die.

That last phrase echoes yet another poem of exile, a poem even more directly in the spirit of "The Rose of Battle" than was "The Emigrants".[3] Starkey's poem is meant as elegy, a literal account of a leavetaking of Ireland. Yeats's arcane exiles, on the other hand, are bidding farewell to the world, and are doing so because they have been unable to find satisfaction in the common joys – clean swept hearth and quiet shade – of men. James Clarence Mangan (1803–49) had imaged a similar group, cut off from general contentment, lost souls banished, not to America, but to the mind's "Siberia":

> In Siberia's wastes
>   No tears are shed,
> For they freeze within the brain.

Natural Ideals: Yeats's Walled Gardens

> Nought is felt but dullest pain,
>   Pain acute, yet dead;
>
> Pain as in a dream,
>   When years go by
> Funeral-paced, yet fugitive,
> When man lives, and doth not live,
>   Doth not live – nor die.

Yeats knew and admired these verses; he quoted the second of them in his early 1887 essay on Mangan (*UP1* 118), and included the entire poem in his *A Book of Irish Verse* (1895). In the latter case he was paying a just debt, because in 1892 he had transformed the final lines of the Mangan stanzas cited above into the final lines of his own poem about the "sad hearts" of earth's outcasts. Nor was Mangan the only prominent Irish poet to leave his mark on "The Rose of Battle". Yeats did not become an active advocate for Oliver Goldsmith (1728–74) until later on, but he had read the man's works before "The Rose of Battle" was written; in October 1891, for one example, he had said that even though Goldsmith could not fairly be numbered among the national writers of Ireland, his works were "important enough" to merit inclusion among those books that "must be read" by Irishmen (*UP1* 208). That Yeats took his own imperative to heart is clear from a comparison of the diction and imagery of "The Rose of Battle" with their counterparts in "The Deserted Village" (1769–70), wherein Goldsmith offers a description of departing emigrants that directly anticipates the progress of many a later Irish poem of exile, Yeats's not least among them:[4]

> Even now the devastation is begun,
> And half the business of destruction done;
> Even now, methinks, as pondering here I stand,
> I see the rural virtues leave the land.
> Down where yon anchoring vessel spreads the sail,
> That idly waiting flaps with every gale,
> Downward they move a melancholy band,
> Pass from the shore, and darken all the strand.
> Contented toil, and hospitable care,
> And kind connubial tenderness, are there;
> And piety with wishes placed above,
> And steady loyalty, and faithful love. (ll. 395–406)

Yeats does not merely take these lines out on loan, but adapts them to his own purposes. Aside from his more apparent borrowings – the movement towards the shore, the waiting ships, the flapping sails – he takes Goldsmith's triplet of "rural virtues" and makes it show a dark side; "contented toil", "hospitable care", and "kind connubial tenderness" become sadness, loneliness, and insatiability.

The exile poem, then, furnished "The Rose of Battle" with both its basic form and its most central images and, in all likelihood, its metric pattern besides. Though other of Yeats's early poems employ the heroic couplet, its presence in both "The Deserted Village" and "The Rose of Battle", poems that run parallel to each other in so many other respects, argues for a direct influence of the Goldsmith passage on the Yeats. And one other work that made use of the same meter may have had a shaping hand here: the beginning of Book XI of the most famous exile poem of them all.

> Now to the shores we bend, a mournful train,
> Climb the tall bark, and launch into the main:
> At once the mast we rear, at once unbind
> The spacious sheet, and stretch it to the wind:
> Then pale and pensive stand, with cares opprest,
> And solemn horrour saddens every breast. (ll. 1–6)

Yeats's many early references to the work make it clear that he had read the *Odyssey* long before writing "The Rose of Battle", though whether it was Pope's translation he had read as a young man is open to conjecture. Pope is the likeliest candidate: certainly on the strength of personal reputation, and possibly on the strength of John O'Leary's enthusiasm for his work,[5] and mayhap because "The Rose of Battle" echoes Pope's rendering of the Homer. But Pope or no, the *Odyssey* had at least an indirect bearing on the Yeats lyric. As the passages already cited in this chapter indicate, Irish writers who took emigration as their theme tended to portray the departure of the exiles from their native shores, their journeys over seas that concluded on alien strands, as something akin to the passage towards hell. The available evidence suggests that "The Rose of Battle" followed that lead. In Pope's version of it, Homer's Book XI depicted Ulysses and his mournful train as taking sail in "solemn horrour" towards a Hades peopled by an "Unhappy race! whom endless night invades,/Clouds the dull air, and wraps them round in shades" (ll. 19–20). Yeats was familiar with yet another image of "Hades wrapped in cloud"; its source was the Order of the Golden Dawn, and a consideration of the uses to which the Order put the image might help to explain why "The Rose of Battle", a poem that is itself wrapped round in shade, has proved an infernal poem to interpret.

Yeats was generally successful at grafting occult symbols and beliefs onto more traditional stocks. As the opening chapter noted, it was the presence of the theosophical concept of the "pilgrim soul" in "When You are Old" that had helped to generate that poem's most suggestive images; and it was the still more pervasive use of occult theory in "The Wanderings of Oisin" that enabled that poem to suggest that it was gesturing towards things beyond itself. But more to the point, the esoteric elements in these poems did not obtrude. One need not be a student of *The Secret Doctrine* to appreciate "When You are Old" for the love poem that it is, or to read "The Wanderings of Oisin" simply as a romance, and an interesting romance at that. And this is the first count on which "The Rose of Battle" fails. It is not that the poem tries to integrate too many sources, since the models Yeats was drawing on were similar enough in their attitudes to have been able to cohere more or less effectively. Nor is it that the genre he was attempting to adapt to his own purposes was too far out of the common way, since the format of poems of exile would have been familiar to any reader of Anglo-Irish verse. Rather the problem is that in this case the attempted graft did not take. In "When You are Old" and "The Wanderings of Oisin" the occult components were interwoven with the general fabric of the poem; but in the course of "The Rose of Battle" the exoteric and esoteric strands of the poem part company, with the latter asserting themselves at the expense of the former and, in the end, to the detriment of the poem. A retreat into a private system of symbolism, "The Rose of Battle" makes no sense if regarded simply in its exoteric aspect. "When You are Old" is a love poem with occult underpinnings; but "The Rose of Battle" is a magical text that is merely masquerading as a poem of exile. The first poem is accessible to the lay reader on a primary level; the second, too patently not what it purports to be, is not. Nor does the poem fare better if we assume that Yeats was aiming it less at a typical reader than at an audience made up of his fellow magicians. When he spoke of the double meaning that certain of his early poems were meant to convey, he identified his companion "students of the magical tradition" as the "only" readers who would be able to "understand" his intent (*VP* 803); but it is doubtful that even the members of this selective coterie were able to apprehend his hidden level of meaning here.

The least indirect clue to the covert meaning of "The Rose of Battle" may be found in the *Autobiographies*. In the section of that work called "Hodos Chameliontos", Yeats offers a brief recounting of his writing of the Rose poems, more particularly "To the Rose upon the Rood of Time", part of which he cites; and immediately after citing those lines he recalls himself as having been

> plunged without a clue into a labyrinth of images, into that labyrinth that we are warned against in those *Oracles* which antiquity has attributed to Zoroaster, but modern scholarship to some Alexandrian poet: "Stoop not down to the darkly splendid world wherein lieth continually a faithless depth and Hades wrapped in cloud, delighting in unintelligible images" (*Au* 255).[6]

The period of his life that Yeats is recalling here is the time when he commenced the writing of the rituals for the Castle of Heroes, and it postdates the earlier Rose poems by a few years; but it is suggestive that it should have been his recollection of the Rose poems that prompted his comments on being lost in the realm of "Hades wrapped in cloud", that "labyrinth" of "unintelligible images", and all the more suggestive because those phrases describe "The Rose of Battle" precisely. There is, moreover, evidence in both Yeats's own writings and the rituals of the Golden Dawn that this experience of the labyrinth was the Order's equivalent of what Christian mysticism would call the dark night of the soul and, *mutatis mutandis*, of what "The Rose of Battle" calls "Old Night". The lines Yeats cites in the *Autobiographies* passage come directly out of the rituals of the Golden Dawn; and, though they appear in the rites of both the Outer and Inner Orders, it was to the Outer Order member who was still striving towards adeptship that they were most directly addressed.[7] The version of the passage that most closely approximates the citation in the *Autobiographies* appears in the Outer Order ceremony that qualified the neophyte for the relatively advanced grade of Practicus:[8]

> Stoop not down unto the darkly splendid World wherein continually lieth a faithless Depth, and Hades wrapped in clouds delighting in unintelligible images, precipitous, winding, a black ever-rolling Abyss, ever espousing a Body, unluminous, formless and void (*GD* II, p. 101).

These lines were meant to warn the candidate that, as he progressed from neophyte to adept, he would at some point have to undergo a period of deep personal crisis: a span of time, as the Practicus ritual had it,

> when no longer are visible to thee the Vault of the Heavens, and the Mass of the Earth; when to Thee, the Stars have lost their light and the Lamp of the Moon is veiled (*GD* II, p. 102).

This "state of consciousness" Regardie describes as "analogous to that condition described by various mystics as the dark Night of the Soul", an experience that generates

> a sense of intolerable dryness, a dreaded awareness of the fact that all the powers of the soul seem dead, and the mind's vision closed in dumb protest, as it were, against the harsh discipline

of the work required of the candidate seeking to further his spiritual development (*GD* I, pp. 59–60). Inasmuch as this breaking down of the ego is a necessary prelude to the emergence of the new and Higher Self, adds Regardie, the "criterion or hall mark of successful initiation is the occurrence of these or similar experiences", when "the whole universe, under the stimulation of the magical elements and inward analysis, seems to tumble like a pack of cards crazily about one's feet" (*GD* I, p. 56).

The images the Order used to describe this stage in the candidate's development lend support to Regardie's comparison of the experience to the *nox obscura* of mysticism. The ceremony for the grade of Philosophus, highest of the Outer Order's formal grades, spoke of a spiritual enlightenment that could come only after "the Gates of the Land of Night" had been passed, and "the Waters and the Darkness" been subdued (*GD* II, p. 128).[9] Later rituals evoked the same metaphors to express the same meaning: "the knowledge of the Light", said the central Rite of Spiritual Development, comes only "after the formless and the void and the Darkness" (*GD* III, p. 254), a darkness that the Order elsewhere associated with "the Night... wherein is Mystery and Depth unthinkable and awful silence" (*GD* III, p. 230).

Yeats's firsthand knowledge of this state of spiritual aridity is most readily apparent from the 1900 draft of *The Speckled Bird*. At one point in the manuscript he directly anticipates Regardie's later comments about the universe falling like a pack of cards about one's feet, this when the novel's Mathers figure says to Michael: "'It is a tradition of our hidden knowledge, that every one who studies it some day finds that his life falls in ruins about him'" (*VSB* 209). Yeats knew what the man meant; as the *Autobiographies* testifies, he had as a young man "lost" himself, and had done so "periodically for years", in the chaos of the labyrinth (*Au* 376), had found himself all too regularly "astray upon the Path of the Chameleon, upon Hodos Chameliontos" (*Au* 270). In the rituals of the Order, that phrase denoted the period of darkness through which the would-be magician must pass before the golden dawn could break, the temptation of the steadily advancing aspirant by spirits bent on seducing him from the true path, "Demons" that led the aspiring magus astray on the Path of the Chameleon and "never show[ed] true image unto mortal gaze" (*GD* II, p. 102). For Yeats, who so often drew on the vocabulary of magic when discussing the experience of the artist, the phrase came to signify, not simply the dark night of the spirit, but the impotence of the artist who finds himself unable to give shape to the materials of his art. There were times when, "lost... upon Hodos Chameliontos", Yeats "could neither write nor cease to write", and yet was "helpless to create artistic... order" (*Au* 376). Frustrating times, when "image called up image in an endless procession, and I could not always choose among them with any confidence; and when I did choose, the image lost its intensity, or changed" – the aspiring artist being astray on the Path of the Chameleon – "into some other image" (*Au* 270). Times – to come full circle – when, "plunged without a clue into [the] labyrinth", Yeats had stooped down "'to the darkly splendid world wherein lieth continually a faithless depth and Hades wrapped in cloud, delighting in unintelligible images'" (*Au* 255).

It was in the context of a discussion of the Rose poems that the *Autobiographies* cited that formulaic warning from the Order rituals, and because the Rose poem that the formula most closely fits is "The Rose of Battle" – a poem that draws upon the same murky reservoir of imagery – the likeliest conclusion is that this most obscure of the Rose lyrics is Yeats's attempt to approximate the same experience that the formula was intended to describe: the esoteric equivalent of the dark night of the soul. The Order spoke of this stage of magical development as a period of ultimate darkness, when the very "Stars" would lose "their light"; "The Rose of Battle" spoke of "white stars" lost to the sight of ships that had "gone down". The Order located its Land of Night in "the Waters and the Darkness"; the poem does likewise. The Order spoke of a "Night" that shrouds a "Mystery", even as the narrator of the poem promises his fellow questers that "Old Night" will "all her mystery tell". And the Night that the Order imagined was a time of "awful silence": a phrase that finds an analogue in the final lines of the poem, when the seekers who have taken ship cease to be able to hear even the cry of their own "sad hearts". Finally, *The Countess Kathleen and Various Legends and Lyrics* had assigned the poem a borrowed[10] title that was as pessimistic as the poems of exile on which Yeats's poem was partly modelled: "They went forth to the Battle,/but they always fell". Read by these lights, "The Rose of Battle" becomes a description of the magician's progress at its nadir. In the first stanza the seekers are summoned from their native shores by the promise of spiritual revelation – "God's bell" – and are told that, if they follow the summons, "Old Night" will reveal "all" its arcane mysteries. But the second stanza discloses their immediate destination as the waters and the darkness, the dark night that precedes the rising of the light, and finds them "defeated" in their quest. Too far from the earth they left behind to be any longer of it, yet not near enough to their magical goal to be true illuminati, they end their journey in the limbo of a Hades wrapped in cloud, neither dead nor yet fully alive.

A reading of this kind is perhaps too little rarefied for this rarefied poem; yet let the reader come to it armed with the Irish and occult contexts, or with what contexts he will, "The Rose of Battle" does not finally make sense. Nothing can make a poem more coherent than it is, and this Yeats lyric does not happen to cohere. Its narrative pattern overwhelmed by the arcane, the poem suffers besides from too contrived a diction. In "The Rose of Peace", "God's wars" was a straightforward reference to Michael's generalship of the forces of heaven against the armies of hell. But the syntax of "The Rose of Battle" makes the simple phrase ambiguous. When the narrator of the poem calls on his fellow malcontents to come "wage God's battles", he leaves the reader no way of determining who the enemy might be; and the question grows more complex when the second stanza suggests that the antagonist here may be God Himself, that His bell bids men on to a certain defeat – "at last" – and that it does so with the deity's full consent: "God has bid them share an equal fate". So too the phrase that describes "God's bell buoyed to be the waters' care". "Care" cuts two opposite ways here – fittingly, since a buoy both threatens and protects – but the reader is left in the dark as to which of the meanings predominates. To be sure, Yeats may have meant – probably did mean – all these possible readings to be operative at once. If so, the older poet had a lesson to teach the younger. The instruction comes in 1934's fine "The Four Ages of Man", the final couplet of which is "The Rose of Battle" in epigram:

> Now his wars on God begin;
> At stroke of midnight God shall win.

In 1893 Yeats was to criticize the work of Robert Buchanan for its attempt "to make a vague impression of sublimity by piling up indefinite words and pictures" (*UP1* 265). In doing so, he was also pinpointing the central flaw from which his own "The Rose of Battle" had suffered. In the later and better "The Four Ages of Man", a more seasoned poet would not mistake ambiguities for tensions.

For all its failed ambitions, "The Rose of Battle" confirms the fact that the lesser works of a major poet can at times be the clearest beacons onto the thrust of his work as a whole. Yeats's early poetry is possessed of a symbolic geography that is more or less fixed; the symbol of the ocean holds a central place in the complex of images that compose it; and "The Rose of Battle" locates the meaning of that symbol more directly than any other poem Yeats had written or would ever write.[11] With a directness rare in the early work, the reference to "the tide of hours" tells the reader that the ocean stands for time, is symbolic of what Yeats later called – though he could not remember which "neo-platonist" had been his source (*VP* 808)[12] – the "drifting indefinite bitterness of life" (*VP* 808). The primary value of an association of this kind is that it enables other central images to find their fitting place in the overall pattern of the early poems in general. Islands set over the ocean or in the far reaches of a lake generally come to be seen as refuges from the ravages of life, safe places set apart. Less overtly, the seashore, positioned as it is at a median point between the island sanctuary and the less certain life of the inland, becomes a symbol of the intermediate state in which most of the figures in Yeats's early work find themselves. We need only turn the opening pages of *The Poems of W. B. Yeats* to discover how often the early poetry sends its characters down to the water's edge. Scenes are set "by the humming sea" (p. 8) or "along the gleaming/And humming sands" (p. 8), "along the water's edge" (p. 13), by "the lone border of the lake" (p. 15), "by the deep" (p. 16), on the "dim grey sands" (p. 18), in "a field by the river" (p. 20) or "on the pebbly shore" (p. 21). And though there are exceptions to the general rule – as in the overly romantic "The Indian to his Love" – it may none the less be said that the mortals whom Yeats sets to wandering the shores of ocean or lake are almost never happy. In the early writings, contentment comes, not to men and women stationed between island and inland, but to those who live where the shore lies distant: in the walled gardens of the interior, or else on sheltered islands that are themselves types of the walled garden.

Here too "The Rose of Battle" has light to shed: first because it too locates its sad and lonely "throngs" on the seashore, but more crucially for the dispensations that it grants. Whatever its obscurities, the poem was clear on at least one count: that those who had found a sufficient happiness at home – near the "clean swept hearth" – or in nature – "on the earth" – were exempt from the "fate" of the seekers of hidden wisdom. The dedicated occultist was in a position of having to forgo the accustomed pleasures of men. Blavatsky's summary comment on the matter goes to the heart of the contrasts on which "The Rose of Battle" turns. Leaving those who were happy in the world happy where they lay, Yeats's poem numbers only the sad, the lonely, and the insatiable among the elect to whom the keys to the mysteries will be given. So too *The Secret Doctrine*, with its declaration that it is only those

> who have learnt the deceptive value of earthly hopes and the illusive allurements of external nature who are destined to solve the great problems of life, pain, and death (*TSD* II, p. 499).

The rewards promised in that passage, as in "The Rose of Battle", are great; but it remains open to question whether the rewards are greater than the sacrifices – the abandoning of earthly hopes, the cutting oneself off from nature – that they necessitate. As already noted, Mangan's description of men who may "not live nor die" fed directly into "The Rose of Battle"; and Yeats's exegesis of the Mangan lyric suggests that the exiles who appear in both Mangan's poem and his own are people to be pitied, "outlaws cast from the world's soft places for some unknown offence" (*UP1* 118). The corollary to be derived from that observation is that those who have found a sufficient contentment in "the world's soft places" are in a situation to be envied. Yeats's other early lyrics, poems expressive not of a wish to leave the world behind but of a longing to find a happy niche within its confines, testify to the hold that the soft places of the world had on the heart of the young man, the imagination of the young poet.

A clean swept hearth is a soft place, and those who hear "Love sing and never cease/Beside her clean swept hearth" live in the cordial glow of what might be called the domestic ideal. Characters in similar situations appear throughout the early poetry and prose. The lure of the supernatural world could not make a man discontent unless he had had a reason for contentment to begin with; and when the supernatural intrudes in the early works, its targets are most often those who have achieved, or who have an earthly hope of achieving, a state of happy domesticity. The stolen child is glamoured from a warm home; Beauty forces the narrator of "The Sorrow of Love" to forfeit domestic peace, the same sort of domestic peace that his vision of the sidhe prevents the man who dreamed of fairyland from finding in the first place. All three of these early personae are in the same situation as the title character of Yeats's *John Sherman*: the novel, commenced in 1888 and published in 1891, that centered on a young man who was conscious of a "vague something that was dragging him inch by inch from the nook he had made for himself in the chimney-corner" (p. 82). Sherman's vision of what would constitute an ideal existence has nothing to do with otherworldly dreams. He thinks of his fiancée, of

> what he would say to Mary Carton. Now they would be married, they would live in a small house with a green door and a new thatch, and a row of beehives under a hedge. He knew where just such a house stood empty (p. 103).

"I shall be busy with my farm", he tells her. "We will surround ourselves with a wall. The world will be on the outside, and on the inside we and our peaceful lives" (p. 107).

The house that Sherman describes is but one of several such houses in Yeats's writings of the time. In 1887's "How Ferencz Renyi Kept Silent", for instance, his Austrian captor tells the young Hungarian patriot of the title that he must either reveal the whereabouts of the nearby Hungarian rebels or be executed. No adept, Renyi is rather "glad, simple – nay, he sought not mystery", nor "searched the unsearchable" (*VP* 710); and when he is threatened with death, his first thoughts are of the contented life he will have to leave behind. The burden of the image that his mind finds is the same as that of its counterpart in *John Sherman*:

> He a brown farm-house sees,
> Where shadow of cherry, and shadow of apple trees,
> Enclose a quiet place of beds box-bordered, bees,
> Hives, currant bushes. There his kin are. High
> Above, the woods where with the soft mild eye
> Of her he loved fixed on him full of light,
> Often he had bent down some bough all bright
> With berries. (*VP* 710)

So too 1886's *Mosada*, the longish poetic drama that deals with the condemning to death of the young Moorish girl of the title by the monks of the Inquisition. Here the threatening outside force is religious rather than political, but the play is in full accord with the above passage from "How Ferencz Renyi Kept Silent" in its description of Mosada and the man she loves as "lovers/The noisy world divides" (*VP* 700). As she prepares to make good her escape from that world by taking poison just before she is to be executed, her thoughts gravitate in the same direction as Renyi's. Swallows circle "in the dimness" (*VP* 698) beyond her prison window; she thinks of home, and of her "long-lost" lover:

> Oh, swallows, swallows, swallows, will ye fly
> This eve, to-morrow, or to-morrow night
> Above the farm-house by the little lake
> That rustles in the reeds with patient pushes,
> Soft as the whispering of a long-lost footstep
> Circling the brain? My brothers will pass down
> Quite soon the cornfield, where the poppies grow,
> To their farm work; how silent all will be! (*VP* 699)

Of no more than passing interest when taken in isolation, lines like these none the less serve as signposts when replaced in the context of the other early work, inasmuch as they help to locate the source of the impression that the other early writings convey. Whatever may be said about individual works, the early poetry as a whole is indisputably a poetry of longing; the man who wrote these poems was not content; Yeats was in search of a better world, and nothing that can be said can make this less true or less evident. But the primary evidence suggests that his youthful hopes for a better world were centered less in the tantalizing and visionary than in the reality of the small house – John Sherman knew where "just" such a one stood empty – its row of beehives sheltered by the hedge, the house itself hidden off by a little lake, cherry and apple trees serving as its shelter from the noisy world beyond. To be sure, houses like these are not unique in literature, least of all in the Irish novelists whose work Yeats was reading closely in the years when his own early works were being written. Combine the homes described above into a single image, and the domestic ideal emerges in composite. For one thing, the homes this young man imagines are in each case set apart from the noisy world. For another, they are more often than not surrounded by a wall or, in the case of the island, a body of water that serves the same protective purpose. For a third, the natural world is a garden that flourishes near and around them. Finally, they tend to be associated with the image of the tended hearthside: thus "The Stolen Child" with its "kettle on the hob", or "The Rose of Battle" with its "clean swept hearth", or *John Sherman* with its "nook" in the "chimney-corner" or its title character's constant imaginings of the woman he loves sitting by the "fireside" (p. 105). All four of these elements figure in the description of the house that Carleton's *Tales and Stories* had advanced in 1845:

> Down to the left, the river ran between two hanging hills, whose sides were covered with furze, now in full flower and fragrance. Up to our right, immediately on the banks of that blessed stream, stood [a] beautiful and sequestered homestead... , its white walls shining from among the trees, and its chimney sending up a straight column of blue smoke, undisturbed in its symmetry by a single breath of air (*T&S*, p. 376).

Effect a few stylistic changes, and minor changes at that, and that passage might easily be mistaken for its counterparts in *Mosada* or "How Ferencz Renyi Kept Silent" or *John Sherman*. But Yeats's formulation of the image is different from the formulations to be found all through his sources, and the difference consists in this.

What a man sees as threatened is what he holds dear; and that Yeats held his vision of the domestic ideal very dear indeed is most evident from the fact that, when he writes of the small homes in which the ideal found its concrete expression, he writes of places under siege. The sidhe in "The Stolen Child" or "The Man who Dreamed of Faeryland", Beauty in "The Sorrow of Love", the monks of *Mosada* or the Austrian invader in "How Ferencz Renyi Kept Silent", the "vague something" of *John Sherman*: all are forces whose encroachments Yeats repeatedly sees as attempts to come between a man and the sheltered home that was or could have been his. And if it is indicative that the constant target of these assaults should be the life of ideal domesticity, it is equally as indicative that, in Yeats's view, the assaults are destined to succeed. When the smoke has cleared away, the characters in the early works either find themselves cast out from their soft places by the hearthside or, more forcefully, find the home itself in shambles.

The ruined house appears in every period of Yeats's work, even the ultimate; and though the author of *Purgatory* could catch at desolation more forcefully than the young man who wrote *John Sherman*, the image in its early usage has a peculiar force of its own, a force like that of the banshee. It has the unhappy habit of appearing to men in their moments of despair, and leaving them to despair the more with its pledge of a greater woe to come. Mary Carton has just told John Sherman that she will not marry him, and his earlier dream of the walled home they were to share gives way to a vision of an empty home under attack:

> The road under his feet felt gritty and barren. He hurried away from town. It was late afternoon. Trees cast bands of shadow across the road. He walked rapidly as if pursued. About a mile to the west of town he came on a large wood bordering the road and surrounding a deserted house. Some local rich man once lived there, now it was given over to a caretaker who lived in two rooms in the back part. Men were at work cutting down trees in two or three parts of the wood. Many places were quite bare. A mass of ruins – a covered well, and the wreckage of castle wall – that had been roofed with green for centuries, lifted themselves up, bare as anatomies. The sight intensified, by some strange sympathy, his sorrow, and he hurried away as from a thing accursed of God (pp. 109–10).

The felling of the trees is meant to carry a specific burden here, since its trees were the proudest feature of the old Irish estate; indeed, when Yeats later went in search of the image that could most aptly characterize the great houses outside Sligo town – the locale in which the above passage from his novel is set – the images he found were those of "Lissadell among its woods" and "Markree Castle encircled by wood after wood" (*Mem* 77).[13] But it is the linking of the abandoned house with human death – its walls reminding the rejected lover of "anatomies" – and the description of it as "a thing accursed of God" that are more directly responsible for the force of the passage from *John Sherman*, and the force it owns is instructive. The houses described in *Mosada*, "How Ferencz Renyi Kept Silent", and elsewhere in *John Sherman* itself may well be ideal arenas for human happiness, but the language that describes them often skirts too close to the merely sentimental. It is rather when Yeats is faced with describing a house in ruins that his words take on an edge, and their strength is a certain indication of how strongly he wished the house to be whole. The pull of the hearthside is an implicit force in poems like those on the human dreamer or "The Rose of Battle", but *John Sherman* makes it plain: the antithesis of the domestic ideal has a face like that of a death's-head.

Sherman's reaction to the sight of the house – earlier in the novel, his relationship with Mary Carton still intact, he had seen a similarly ravaged home and responded only with a vague regret (p. 57) – is too radical to grow out of other than deep-seated attitudes: profound dread over his apparent failure in love, its wellspring an equally intense need for the security that he saw a reciprocated love as being able to bring about. In this regard Sherman was self-portraiture, since Yeats's fears that domestic content could not survive the onslaught of whatever furies lay beyond the hearthlight ran perilously close to the bone. "The Pity of Love" (1892), for instance, is a brief sketch in paranoia:

> A pity beyond all telling,
> Is hid in the heart of love;

> The folk who are buying and selling,
>   The stars of God where they move,
> The mouse-grey waters on flowing,
>   The clouds on their journey above,
> And the cold wet winds ever blowing,
>   All threaten the head that I love.

Certain imagistic progressions can be traced here: from the world of man to the world of nature and back to the world of man, from the stars above to the waters below to the clouds and winds in between. But whether these images be regarded in isolation or in juxtaposition with each other, it is by no means clear that the things that the images describe should in fact constitute a threat to the narrator's beloved. The one pattern that emerges with consistency is that everything that the speaker of these lines fears is in motion. "The stars of God where they move" might be taken typically, as an image of the passing of time, in which case the other images of movement – "flowing", "journey", "ever blowing" – would take on the same connotations. Opposed to all this flow is the quietistic feeling that the narrator clearly prefers; his pity "is hid", a passive that contrasts effectively with the active forms that dominate the poem and thereby suggests his need to find an atmosphere of rest and stillness in the emotion of love itself. But however tenuous its workmanship, the emotional burden of this brief lyric is unambiguous. The poet was in love; and his pity beyond "all" telling arises from the fact that "all" the world was in conspiracy against him.

The writings examined in the last few pages are part of an evident pattern. In their early stages a dark force glooms just beyond the circle of the hearthlight, and it draws the more near the nearer the work in question progresses towards its end. The existence of this steady undercurrent of menace points to what is perhaps the central emotional goad behind Yeats's writings of the eighties and early nineties. It demonstrates that it would be of little avail to regard these works as if they were divisible into songs of the world on one hand, and songs of the supernatural on the other; and the reason for this is that the elusive writings that center on the supernal worlds of the sidhe or the Rose have their origins in the same state of mind that produced an ingenuous poem such as "How Ferencz Renyi Kept Silent". The nucleus of feeling that generated work after early work was a young man's deep longing for domestic peace and his abiding sense that the peace he was seeking was threatened on all sides. In certain of the early works the outside force is, as it happens, supernatural; in others, as it happens, it is not. But for this young author, the nature of the menace mattered less than his settled conviction that the threat in fact existed, and that whatever frail walls he might raise would be unable to withstand it.

Given the depth of his longings, it is not by chance that some of the more harmonious of Yeats's early poems originated in those moments when he allowed himself to imagine that the fastness he was seeking might be possible of achievement. Even the minor lyrics on the theme show a familiarity with small detail that betrays the poem's subject as a constant daydream:

> Shy one, shy one,
>   Shy one of my heart,
> She moves in the firelight
>   Pensively apart.
>
> She carries in the dishes,
>   And lays them in a row.
> To an isle in the water
>   With her would I go.
>
> She carries in the candles,
>   And lights the curtained room;
> Shy in the doorway
>   And shy in the gloom;
>
> And shy as a rabbit,
>   Helpful and shy.
> To an isle in the water
>   With her would I fly.

Though his revisions of his early work were frequent and often far-ranging, more often than not Yeats had a good sense of when to leave a finished poem alone. The only alteration visited on "To an Isle in the Water" was the changing of a single mark of punctuation. This judgment was the right one, since this slight poem is complete as it stands. It manages the effect that it strives for primarily through its manipulation of images of light. The first stanza shows the woman moving in the circle shed by firelight, her body half in light and half in shadow. The third verse at first sets her face in full light, the encircling halo sent out by the candles she carries, then shortly thereafter locates her in a contrasting darkness, "in the gloom". This working of slight variations on a simple original pattern not only makes for an effective word picture, but lends romance to the least romantic of domestic chores and transforms them into actions that touch chords; a woman setting a table ceases to be a housekeeper and becomes instead the bearer of food and of light.

This is not to say that "To an Isle in the Water" is univocal in its vision. The woman keeps a "pensive" distance between herself and the narrator of the poem; and her lover would not be the first man made uneasy by the sight of a loved woman lost in thought. She is also nothing if not "shy", and the fact that her shyness is like that of a rabbit implies the possibility of imminent flight. Thus the undertrace of anxiousness in these stanzas, the implied concern of a narrator who, content simply to "go" to the island at an earlier point in the poem, speaks instead of wanting to "fly" to it by the time the poem concludes. Yet the woman herself is very much the kind of woman that the young Yeats would have been attracted to. She is neither the unattainable woman of the sidhe, nor even the unholdable coquette to be met with in poems like 1889's "Down by the Salley Gardens", but someone he can at least imagine as a partner in the ideal domesticity that was his heart's desire. Nor is "To an Isle in the Water" the only early poem to yoke together the image of the island and the theme of the domestic ideal. First published in 1890, the most widely known of all Yeats's early lyrics does likewise, and does so from the start.

> I will arise and go now, and go to Innisfree,
>   And a small cabin build there, of clay and
>   wattles made;
>   Nine bean rows will I have there, a hive for the
>   honey bee,
>   And live alone in the bee-loud glade.

The eloquent music of these verses testifies to the power that the image of a secured home had over the young poet's imagination, even if the home life were to be lived "as Thoreau lived": alone (*Au* 72). As many a critic has noticed, Yeats adapted the beginning of his poem from the parable of the prodigal son: "I will arise and go to my father" (Luke 15:18). Though he would later describe his opening phrase as a "conventional archaism" (*Au* 153), there can be few other instances in English literature in which a borrowed line became so tightly worked into the piece for whose sake it was borrowed. The poem on the lake isle is a tonal variation, and its first five words set the key. There are some three dozen accented phonemes in the poem. The biblical phrase contains only twelve of them, yet eight of these same twelve – I will arise and go – account for almost half the sounds in the poem:[14]

> I will arise and go now, and go to Innisfree,
>   And a small cabin build there, of clay and
>   wattles made;
>   Nine bean rows will I have there, a hive for the
>   honey bee,
>   And live alone in the bee-loud glade.
>
> And I shall have some peace there, for peace
>   comes dropping slow,
>   Dropping from the veils of the morning to
>   where the cricket sings;
>   There midnight's all a glimmer, and noon a purple
>   glow,
>   And evening full of the linnet's wings.
>
> I will arise and go now, for always night and day
>   I hear lake water lapping with low sounds by
>   the shore;
>   While I stand on the roadway or on the pavements
>   gray,
>   I hear it in the deep heart's core.

From a musical viewpoint, then, the sounds to be found in the opening phrase of "The Lake Isle of Innisfree" are motifs; and they are also sounds that fit the poem's theme directly. The two most frequent phonemes, "n" and "r", furnish the poem with the necessary sense of peaceful droning. The next most frequent, "i" and "l", lend the setting its stillness. Even a cursory reading of the lyric makes it clear that Yeats set out to depict a setting filled with harmony, but it is careful working on the poet's part to see that the harmony is palpable. When he described the poem as "my first lyric with anything in its rhythm of my own music" (*Au* 153), his remark was both modest and accurate.

The *Autobiographies* indicates that the young man who planned to build himself a cottage on Innisfree – and though the plan was never effected, Yeats was in his mid-twenties before he finally gave it up[15] – meant to spend his time there "seeking wisdom" (p. 72), but this motive plays no part in his poem. The contrast here is not between wisdom and dullness, but between homelessness and home or, more specifically, between London and Sligo. "I was a stranger there", Yeats wrote of his early days in London (*Au* 49); and this is a sentiment that the narrator of "The Lake Isle of Innisfree" shares. The poem imagines him as a man who seems quite literally to have found no home in the city; like the urban wanderer in Synge's "Winter", he confronts the reader beggarlike, standing "on the roadway" or "on the pavements gray". Innisfree stands for the inverse of this situation. As the borrowed line from Luke intimates, the journey back to Sligo would be a lost prodigal's journey back towards being found. Towards home: to what the young Yeats described as his "native place" (*CL1* 102), the "centre" of his "world" (*UP1* 210), the place where he "should like to live... always" (*CL1* 33), and the one place where – like his island-dwelling persona – he could hope to find the "freedom and peace" that he needed (*Au* 256). The home Yeats planned to build on Innisfree, moreover, was as real to him as the island itself; and here it becomes possible to make the essential distinction between the use Yeats makes of the image of the island in a poem like "The Lake Isle of Innisfree" and the uses to which he puts it in a deeply flawed lyric like 1886's "An Indian Song".

Now known as "The Indian to his Love", this poem describes a lover's desire to take his loved one over the seas to what he calls "our isle", and thus appears to anticipate the movement of "To an Isle in the Water"; but a discovery of the difference between the impulses that engendered the two works makes it clear that they have little beyond their narrative progress in common. Apprentice work, the earlier piece relies on images that are caught up in a process of rapid accretion that deprives them of individual value, as for instance when the lover tells the beloved that, "alone of mortals", they will be

> Hid in the earth's most hidden part,
> While grows our love an Indian star,
> A meteor of the burning heart,
> One with the waves that softly round us laugh
>   and dart.

More to the point, the poem – its style since much revised (*VP* 77–8) – remains even in revised form an unfortunate example of why a poetry that flatly beckons a reader towards departure from the world cannot long command the reader's interest. The implied resolution of the lyric – the reaching of the island by the lovers – is no resolution at all, simply because there is nothing to be resolved. The sole reference to the world of man in the poem – "earth's feverish lands" – is simply negative, while the world beyond emerges as a place of perfection pure and simple:

> There dreamy Time lets fall his sickle
> And Life the sandals of her fleetness,
> And sleek young Joy is no more fickle,
> And Love is kindly and deceitless,
> And all is over save the murmur and the sweetness.

"The White Birds" is the only other poem in Yeats's early volumes in which he allows an impossible vision of perfection so thoroughly to dominate his more persistent urge to explore what elements a perfect world might be made of; and like "The White Birds", "The Indian to his Love" derives what little force it has from the single-mindedness of its affirmation. But it is that very single-mindedness that also accounts for the poem's lack of tension and consequent failure. What this lyric has to offer the reader is a young Yeats's version of the neo-Spenserian island alluded to in the last chapter; here again certain forms of sensuous loveliness have been separated from all the general purposes of life (*Au* 313). Late in 1888 Yeats would warn Katharine Tynan that "we should make poems on the familiar landscapes we love not the strange and rare and glittering scenes we wonder at"; "these latter", he added, "are the landscapes of Art", not "of nature" (*CL1* 119). "The Indian to his Love" is just such a landscape of art, a refuge invented rather than imagined, all its details – Time's dropped sickle, Joy unalloyed, Love all kindly and deceitless – fabrication. The shores to which the Indian would tempt his lover are a genial fiction, too remote from life's real purposes to be real, too suprahuman to persuade.

This is the first way in which this poem differs from the other of Yeats's writings that appear to be of its kind. In a sense, all the works discussed in this section draw on the image of the island, whether the image be that of an island out on the waters or a farmhouse surrounded by trees or a small home circled by a wall. But when Yeats turns from fictions about non-existent Eastern utopias to imaginings of an earthly home, his mind inevitably tilts towards the kinds of particulars – a green door, a currant bush, a hive for the honey bee – that are convincing simply because, unlike the isle of the Indian song, they can actually be attained. What Yeats said about another poet applies as directly to himself: "When William Morris describes a house of any kind, and makes his description poetical, it is always, I think, some house that he would have liked to have lived in" (*E&I* 60). Visionary though he was, the young poet turned time and again to the snug homes imaged in the early poems, places where he would have liked to live, dwellings for a woman and a man. "To an Isle in the Water", for instance, takes its cue from a feeling that any young lover would acknowledge as true coin. Unlike his counterpart in "The Indian to his Love", the narrator of the later poem seeks, not to leave his mortality behind, but to safeguard the fragile share of mortal happiness that he sees himself as on the verge of finding. The "curtained room" is already a kind of island, but there is nothing to prevent the noisy world from coming round to knock at the door. John Sherman sought to stave off such visitors by surrounding the small house in which he and Mary Carton were to live "with a wall". The narrator of "To an Isle in the Water", the lake his sheltering moat around the lives of himself and his shy one, is moved by the same human longings for peace, and the same human passion to secure it.

The reasons why the image of what Yeats later called the "small old house" (*Myth* 342) crops up so often in the early work are not far to seek. "It may be that poetry is the utterance of desires that we can only satisfy in dreams" (*UP2* 190), he wrote in 1899; and if his youthful desire for a sheltering home were to be satisfied, it was in dreams and the writings they gave rise to that the satisfaction would have to be found. Enter the figure whom William Murphy's phrase has caught precisely: prodigal father. Increasingly empty of pocket but resolutely footloose of heart, J. B. Yeats moved his family from Dublin to London in 1867, returned them to Dublin in 1880 and back to London in 1887; and these major moves were sporadically interspersed with frequent, if less ambitious, changes of address. There is thus little wonder in the fact that the young poet, who never felt at home when in London, rarely felt at home when at home. "You seem at home and comfortable at all times", he wrote to Katharine Tynan in 1889, "unlike me" (*CL1* 190); and a few years later Lily Yeats's diary would describe her brother as "wandering about" London "like one of the disinherited".[16] There was Sligo, of course, the place Yeats recalled as having "always been my home" (*Mem* 79) and the first in a long series of spiritual lodgings – Coole, the projected Castle of Heroes, Thoor Ballylee – that the poet was to construct. But long or short, his visits to Sligo were visits, and one does not visit the place where one lives; Yeats intimated as much when he wrote that, if Sligo was his home, it was so only "in a sense" (*Mem* 79). Nor was he destined to live there "always" (*CL1* 33); and however the place may have filled the deeper needs of his earlier years, later in life he would speak of the "home that I lacked after I left Sligo".[17]

The early poetry speaks with longing of a solid home life, then, in large measure because the author of these poems lacked anything resembling what his vision of the domestic ideal would allow him to call a home. Nor did Maud Gonne help matters. When they met for the first time in January of 1889, *The Wanderings of Oisin and Other Poems* had just been published. But not a few of the works written after that date are signatures of her influence on Yeats's life, an influence not always benign. It is no secret that, on those rare occasions when the young poet came close to falling in love and perhaps seeing that love reciprocated, as he did with Eva Gore-Booth (*Mem* 78–9) and later with Olivia Shakespear, he inevitably stumbled over his old passion: a fact that may have its bearing on Yeats's inclusion of Beauty among those forces that most relentlessly undermine the life of ideal domesticity. Given Yeats's contradictory longings for both a peaceful life and Maud Gonne, it is perhaps not by chance that the most settled image of the domestic ideal to be found in the early writings is a durable portrait of life lived alone on a lake island, man at one with the natural world. Then again, this kind of image was very much to be expected. "The Rose of Battle" had exempted from its dark quest not simply those who had their residence beside the clean-swept hearth, but those who dwelt content with rain or dew, sun and moon, stars, sea, and earth; and the natural world was Yeats's second place of abode, the alternative home of his youth.

Even as the image of the ruined home had a comment to make on Yeats's felt need for a home life, the clearest indication of the young poet's reliance on nature is the fear he feels at those moments when it appears possible that he will be cut off from the natural world. That fear finds its most direct voicing in the 1886 poem that appeared in *The Wanderings of Oisin and Other Poems* under the title "Miserrimus". But a consideration of that poem, presently titled "The Sad Shepherd", depends upon a prior glance at the poem in which its title character first appeared: 1885's "Song of the Last Arcadian", now known as "The Song of the Happy Shepherd".

The happy shepherd was yet another in the series of voices adopted by Yeats in *The Wanderings of Oisin and Other Poems*. The whole book is marked by an absence of the I-as-narrator, and to that extent is unique in the Yeatsian corpus; though Yeats was to speak through masks throughout his career, from the early nineties onward he would not hesitate to speak in his own voice as well. The poet or, more precisely, the poet-figure that Yeats projected, is the narrator of only three of the lyrics that Yeats later carried over from the first edition of *The Wanderings of Oisin and Other Poems*. All three of these minor verses – their current titles "To an Isle in the Water", "The Falling of the Leaves", and "Down by the Salley Gardens" – rank among the most polished of the early works, but his success with the first person singular failed to persuade the author of the early poems to put it to more extensive use. He preferred at this point to speak through personae, and an uncommon group they are: the old Fenian bard, the Witch Vivien, Kanva the Indian, King Goll, Mosada, the Old Knight of "The Seeker", the Enchantress and the Old Fisherman. The common ground on which these diversified characters stand is that they are all to some extent not of the immediate world, are distanced by years or latitudes from more commonplace modes of existence. Even the peasants: if we were to scratch the surface of one of these seemingly prosaic spokesmen, there would emerge a man or woman in touch with the elemental, living "in a beautiful if somewhat inhospitable world, where little had changed since Adam delved and Eve span" (*UP1* 295).

It is the overlooking of this assumed distance between the reader and a character like the Arcadian that most fully accounts for certain of the more tenuous past readings of "Song of the Last Arcadian". In general criticism has tended to identify the man who "gather[s] by the humming sea" a "twisted, echo-harbouring shell" with the Arcadian himself, the man who "discovers in a sea shell the catalytic agent that makes poetry possible", and to contrast this glad singer with Miserrimus, the sad shepherd who is "no poet" and for whom "the catalyst fails".[18] But despite its enticing symmetry, the contrast does not hold; and the reason why it does not is that "Song of the Last Arcadian" distinguishes among four, not three, types of men, and that the men to whom the Arcadian recommends the use of the shell are not only far from being poets in the making, but are themselves prototypes of the Miserrimus figure, destined to find that the "catalyst" will "fail".

The poem opens with a description of men of worldly action, the "warring kings" who were blind to the permanence of the word. The battles they fought have long since ceased to signify, since the world that appears in this poem is mere illusion, the locus of "many changing things" that prove in the end to have been but "chimaeras". Only the word endures:

> The woods of Arcady are dead,
> And over is their antique joy;
> Of old the world on dreaming fed;
> Grey Truth is now her painted toy;
> Yet still she turns her restless head.
> But oh, sick children of the world,
> Of all the many changing things
> In dreary dancing past us whirled,
> To the old cracked tune that Chronos sings,
> Words alone are certain good.
> Where are now the warring kings,
> Word be-mockers? – By the rood,
> Where are now the old kings hoary?
> They were of no wordy mood;
> An idle word is now their glory,
> By the stammering schoolboy said,
> In the verse of Attic story
> Chronicling chimaeras fled.

Immediately thereafter there follows the warning not to imitate the mistake the warring kings made in giving their lives over to action, and a warning about a second type of men: men of analytic intellect, who in their cold search for fact and consequent rejection of the imagination have perverted the deeper powers of the word. Those who know better are to "seek... no word of theirs". The truth they offer is the "Grey Truth" of the opening lines of the poem, at once objective and insubstantial; for they model their work on that of "the star-gazer" who "knows only the external visible heaven" rather than on that of "the true astronomer", he who "knows two heavens, the external visible and the internal invisible one".[19] The "whirling ways of stars that pass" that they study are one with "the many changing things/In dreary dancing past us whirled", properties of the physical universe alone. The hearts of these misguided astronomers have been "rent... in twain", and this too is a bad sign; for if "there is no truth/Saving in thine own heart", then the truth they have espoused is negligible, fragmented.

> Then nowise worship dusty deeds,
> Nor seek – for this is also sooth –
> To hunger fiercely after truth,
> Lest all thy toiling only breeds
> New dreams, new dreams; there is no truth
> Saving in thine own heart. Seek, then,
> No learning from the starry men,
> Who follow with the optic glass
> The whirling ways of stars that pass –
> Seek then, for this is also sooth,
> No word of theirs – the cold star-bane
> Has torn and rent their hearts in twain,
> And dead is all their human truth.

The "optic glass", or straight and narrow telescope, of the lines above finds its contrasting image below in the twisted shell. These antithetical images anticipate Yeats's subsequent denigration of "the straight road of logic, and so of mechanism", and his concurrent praise of "the crooked road of intuition" (VP 827), the idea he adapted from Blake's declaration that "improvement makes straight roads, but the crooked roads without improvement are roads of genius".[20] More pointedly, the lines also suggest that those who heed the Arcadian's advice and take themselves down to the shore will come to find themselves in the same woebegone state as Miserrimus rather than the privileged state of the Arcadian himself. With the seashore and lakeside functioning as symbols of intermediate states throughout the early poetry, it seems unlikely that Yeats would depart from so consistent a pattern for the sake of one poem; nor does the poem suggest that he does so. No catalyst of poetry, the shell can only transform one's "fretful words a little while", thereby providing a brief respite after which the words will fade in sadness. Its method, moreover, is "guile"; and if the word carries something of the sense of "beguiling", it appears here primarily in its more basic usage, and thus implies that the shell is holding out to the human searchers a promise of consolation that it cannot or will not effect.

> Go gather by the humming sea
> Some twisted, echo-harbouring shell,
> And to its lips thy story tell,
> And they thy comforters will be,
> Rewording in melodious guile
> Thy fretful words a little while,
> Till they shall singing fade in ruth;
> For ruth and joy have brotherhood,
> And words alone are certain good –
> Sing then, for this is also sooth.

There is a clear distinction between this world of compounded sorrow and happiness, "ruth and joy", and the fourth world described in the poem, that in which the "last" Arcadian – the sole true poet to be found here – forms a majority of one. He recommends that his listeners go off to the sea's edge, but he himself goes off to a glade where, presumably, his listeners may not follow. The version of the poem that appeared in *The Wanderings of Oisin and Other Poems* is headed by a stage direction to the effect that the Arcadian "*carries a sea-shell*"; but he clearly uses it only as a prop to carry his point to his audience. Nothing here indicates that he himself has need of the mediation of this or any other catalytic agent; his songs address their audience directly. Nor is there mention of "fretful words"; his singing is presented from the start as "glad" and "mirthful", and is obviously more effective than the song produced by the shell. Orphic in its quality, it verges on being able to restore life itself to the faun that appears in the poem's pastoral conclusion:

> I must be gone – there is a grave
> Where daffodil and lily wave,
> And downy bees have ambuscade,
> And birdly iteration is
> Through all the well-beloved glade.
> Farewell; I must be gone, I-wis,
> That I may soothe that hapless faun
> (Who's buried in the sleepy ground),
> With mirthful songs till rise the dawn.
> His shouting days with mirth were crowned,
> And still I dream he treads the lawn,
> Walking ghostly 'mong the dew,
> Pierced by my glad singing through,
> My songs of old earth's dreamy youth.
> But ah! she dreams not now – dream thou!
> For fair are poppies on the brow:
> Dream, dream, for this is also sooth.

By comparison, the music that comes from the shell is a temporary panacea; and in terms of the poem's fictive context, it is fitting that it should be no more than that. "Song of the Last Arcadian" was originally meant as a speech, the epilogue to *The Island of Statues*. That it was intended to be spoken on the stage helps to explain its cloying repetitions, and also accounts for the distinction the Arcadian draws between himself and those who must seek a lesser satisfaction on the seashore. No poet addressing an audience would assume that his listeners were as much the poet as he. He can point the way to an experience that may briefly approximate the real poetic experience, but true insight into the mystery is afforded only to those initiates who can enter the hidden glade. Miserrimus, to his deep regret, is not among them.

"Miserrimus" resumes where "Song of the Last Arcadian" leaves off. The most wretched man who appeared in prototype in the earlier poem becomes a full-length portrait in the later, with Yeats setting him at the center of the piece in order to explore more fully the reasons for his sorrow. That sorrow has its immediate source in the title character's discovery that his hands must pass through the beauties of the world even as he is trying to lay hold. The adjectives Yeats assigns to the natural world in the poem express this idea precisely. Nature is beautiful; its sands are "gleaming" and "humming", its dewdrops "glistening". But those same busy adjectives reveal a world in flux, elusive of the grasp. There is a telling difference between the troubling world of Miserrimus and the islands through which Oisin makes his way. What seemed to be change in Tir na nOg turned out to be recurrence, and eternal recurrence is at base no different from eternal life; when Oisin follows the sidhe troop on the Island of the Living into the forest, for instance, he finds himself in a place where "tangling creepers every hour/Blossom in some new crimson flower" (*VP* 16). These are not the flowers that grace the world that Miserrimus must inhabit, and "The Wanderings of Oisin" captures the difference between the two worlds succinctly. As the dance of the sidhe goes on, the dancers come to a thicket where "Hung, like meteors of red light,/Damask roses in the night", and

> Sang we softly, "On the dead,
> Fall the leaves of other roses,
> On the dead the earth encloses.
> Never, never on our graves,
> Heaved beside the glimmering waves,
> Shall fall the leaves of damask roses;
> For change and death they come not near us,
> And all listless hours fear us,
> And we never fear the morrow
> Or the wild grey osprey sorrow." (*VP* 21)

As Chapter 3 intimated, it is the rapid and perpetual recurrence of the objects of their desire that enables the sidhe to deride the idea of human sorrow; but Miserrimus dwells in a world of change, and thus is plagued by the leaves of other roses. In the opening lines of the poem, he would vainly have the sea pause long enough to hear his "piteous story"; but its unquiet waves roll along in dreams of their own.

> There was a man whom Sorrow named his friend,
>   And he, of his high kinsman Sorrow dreaming,
>   Went walking with slow steps along the gleaming
> And humming sands, where windy surges wend.
> He called aloud to all the stars to lend
>   Their hearing, and some comfort give, but they
>   Among themselves laugh on and sing alway.
> Then cried the man whom Sorrow named his friend:
> "O sea, old sea, hear thou my piteous story!"
>   The sea swept on and cried her old cry still,
>   Rolling along in dreams from hill to hill.

As in the other early poems, the sea here may be taken as emblematic of time, the "tide of hours": a fitting attribution in the case of this particular lyric, since the sense of the physical world as illusory traces back to the realization that time will surely scatter all. Whatever his dreams or cries, the motion of the waves remains as adamant for Miserrimus as the passing of the hours; and it is his sense of the beauty of nature, coupled with the growing unwelcome knowledge that this beauty passes like a dream, that leads him on to sorrow. His delight in the natural world compels him, paradoxically, to suffer the "persecution of her glory":

> And from the persecution of her glory
> He fled, and in a far-off valley stopping,
> Cried all his story to the dewdrops glistening.
> But naught they heard, for they are ever listening,
> The dewdrops, for the sound of their own dropping.

From the image of the "far-off valley" onward the poem becomes a refashioning of the imagery to be encountered in "Song of the Last Arcadian". The difference between the images of the shell that appear in both poems is a difference only of degree; in the earlier lyric the shell promises brief consolation before failing in the end, while in "Miserrimus" it fails from the start and utterly. But the real contrast between the two poems resides in the distinction between the activities of the Arcadian in his inland glade and the experience of Miserrimus on the seashore. Leaving his audience to their fleetingly successful attempts at creation, the Arcadian goes off to create; he is so much in tune with the natural world that his songs can reach beyond the grave and soothe even nature's dead. The situation in which Miserrimus finds himself is very much the opposite. Both poems draw on a similar complex of images. "Song of the Last Arcadian" has its "whirling ways of stars", its "humming sea", its "well-beloved glade", all of which reappear in the companion poem's laughing stars, "seaways lone", and "far-off valley". But in the later piece Yeats reworks his imagery in a way that makes it lead to different conclusions. Miserrimus finds no satisfaction in the stars, nor will he find any at the sea's edge – so far the poem parallels the Arcadian's song – but neither does he find any in the far-off valley that is his version of the glade, since the dewdrops, "ever listening" for "the sound of their own dropping", heed not a word.

The difference between the two poems, then, is that for Miserrimus nature is implacably narcissistic, so caught up in its own transitory glories that it turns a deaf ear to his cries. Yeats took the basic idea for his poem from "Deirdre" (1876), a long poem by R. D. Joyce (1836–83) on which he was preparing a long commentary – praising it for its "especial excellence", he said it was "by far" Joyce's "finest work" (*UP1* 112, 109) – when "Miserrimus" was first published.[21] In Joyce's version of the legend, Deirdre, sequestered throughout her girlhood with only the old nurse Lavarcum (more generally "Leborcham") for companion, is justly perplexed in her isolation:

> Oh, Lavarcum,
> Come, tell me! – oh, come tell me what I am!
> Did I come here just like the summer fly
> To sparkle in the sun, and then to die?
> I've asked the flies full oft, but murmuringly

> They said they were too filled of present glee
> To give me answer, and they passed away;
> And once unto the streamlet did I say
> "What am I?" for in grove or garden walk,
> I oft feel lonely and perforce must talk
> To all things round that creep, or walk, or fly,
> And well I know their speech. And "what am I?"
> I asked the stream; and it was churlish too,
> And would not speak.

Yeats's lifelong tendency to recast his borrowings in shapes more congenial to his own imagination is evident here, with Joyce's affable conceit becoming the later poet's means towards the realization by Miserrimus that the world he lives in is a passing dream. His subsequent discovery that even the insubstantial world that remains to him has a hard shell around it, that it looks in upon itself and away from his human need, is too harsh to be readily borne. It forces him into an unwilling solipsism, leaves him, in Yeats's own later image, "in futile revery listening to [his] own mind as if to the sounds in a sea shell" (*LNI* xi); it gives him his name.

> And then the man whom Sorrow named his friend
> Sought once again the shore, and chose a shell
> And thought, "To this will I my story tell,
> And mine own words re-echoing shall send
> Their sadness through the hollows of its heart,
> And mine own tale again for me shall sing,
> And mine own whispering words be comforting,
> And lo – my heavy burthen may depart."
> Then sang he softly nigh the pearly rim;
> But the sad dweller by the seaways lone
> Changed all his words to inarticulate moan
> Within her wildering whirls – forgetting him.

To describe the recipient of this pathetic non-revelation as no poet is to miss the frantic increase of the poem. A poet with a forming tale in mind, but lacking the words to tell it, Miserrimus looks to nature as his ally and finds that it has business of its own. The opening of the poem is serene enough, with the man, lost in meditation, "walking with slow steps" along the shore. Then the calling aloud to the stars, the first rebuff, the calls becoming cries, the next rebuff, the slow steps giving way to flight, the fitful vain attempt to tell "all" his story rather than settling for "some" comfort, a third rebuff, the retreat to the site where the anxious quest began, the final rebuff and the lyric's dying fall. A man who was no poet would long since have concluded that this particular game was by no means worth the candle. Miserrimus is rather a failed poet, a kind of Wordsworth *manqué*, cut off from the natural world that he sought as a partner in the creative process and thus unable to create. He does have a story to tell, and does in fact manage to tell it; but he is unable to give it form. And the point to be made here is that, even as Sorrow seeks Miserrimus out rather than vice versa, it is not Miserrimus that fails, but nature that fails him, taking his words and reducing them to an "inarticulate moan" – poet by nature and inarticulate, dweller in a vicious circle of denial.

Like his character, the author of "Miserrimus" had serious doubts about his abilities as a poet. Other of the early writings voice those doubts directly and, in the course of doing so, lay down a broad avenue towards the conclusion of a discussion of Yeats's early views of the natural world and his use of it in his poetry and prose.

Shortly before the publication of *The Wanderings of Oisin and Other Poems*, Yeats wrote to Katharine Tynan, *de profundis*. His primary fear was that, like Miserrimus, he had not been able to get the vision down, had been "inarticulate":

> I am not very hopeful about the book. Somewhat inarticulate have I been I fear. Some thing I had to say. Dont know that I have said it. All seems confused incoherent inarticulate... this book I have no great hopes of – it is all sluggish incoherent. It may make a few friends perhaps among people of my own sort – that is the most. Do what you can for it (*CL1* 93–4).

This same lack of confidence made inroads into the early verse. Aleel, the poet who strays in and out of *The Countess Kathleen*, becomes a figure of defiance in the course of Yeats's several revisions of that play, but was very different in the version that appeared in 1892. Here he was assigned the name of Kevin, and was pictured coming on stage carrying "*a harp with torn wires*" (*VPl* 134). "The crying of these strings grew burdensome", he tells the demonic merchants, "therefore I tore them – see – now take my soul" (*VPl* 136). The image of the broken harp crops up again in 1887's "King Goll", now "The Madness of King Goll", Yeats's unsuccessful attempt to rescue one of the more obscure figures of Irish legend into something like prominence.[22] Goll finds himself in a quandary that in many ways resembles that of Miserrimus. He leaves his royal home in third-century Emain to lead his countrymen against a band of pirates pillaging the coast. During the battle he sees a vision that causes him to break his spear and flee. The precise nature of the vision is not clear, since it takes place in his "most secret spirit"; but in all likelihood it has to do with the attitude or, rather, lack of attitude that he sees revealed in the stars. The stars here are the same stars that appear in the opening lines of "Miserrimus" and, for that matter, in many another early poem: indifferent to the plight of man, emblems of cosmic silence. Goll goes mad at the sight of human death beneath a still sky.

> But slowly as I shouting slew
>   And trampled in the bubbling mire,
> In my most secret spirit grew
>   A fever and a whirling fire.
> I paused – the stars above me shone,

> And shone around the eyes of men;
> I paused – and far away rushed on,
> > Over the heath and spongy fen,
> And crumpled in my hands the staff
> Of my long spear with scream and laugh
> And song that down the valleys rolled.

Having failed as a warring king, Goll becomes a broken haunter of forest solitudes, and one night wanders into a little country town. Yeats's description of the town suggests that only a madman can be concerned with song, and thus with poetry. The residents of the sleeping village have left the harp behind; they dream of their harvest and do not care. The same stanza initiates what will eventually become a direct analogy between Goll's harp and the shell to which Miserrimus tells his story. "Unhuman" here has the force of "suprahuman"; it implies that Goll can contain his sorrow by putting it to song, making it the basis of a work of art:

> Once, while within a little town
> > That slumbered 'neath the harvest moon,
> I passed a-tiptoe up and down,
> > Murmuring a mountain tune
> Of how I hear on hill heads high
> > A tramping of tremendous feet.
> I saw this harp all songless lie
> > Deserted in a doorway seat,
> And bore it to the woods with me.
> Of some unhuman misery
> Our married voices wildly trolled.

And, again like Miserrimus, Goll discovers that the song produced by the harp can provide only temporary comfort. Miserrimus was undone by the natural world, but Goll is still more pathetic; it is he himself who is unable to sustain his song. In later years Yeats was to describe the drawing of Goll that his father had done, with the young poet himself sitting for model, as "a pathetic memory of a really dreadful time" (*Let* 705). This comment is of a piece with Yeats's other retrospective views of his early years: his remark that he remembered "little of childhood but its pain" (*Au* 11), for instance, or his more inclusive description of the "toil of growing up;/The ignominy of boyhood; the distress/Of boyhood changing into man" (*VP* 478–9). "King Goll" shadows forth certain of the more basic reasons behind its author's disquietude, since its title character fails in both of the arenas in which a yet unfledged Yeats dreamt of success. Goll falls short of the mark as both man of action and poet; a crumpled spear and a broken harp are the insignia that convict him. He concludes in madness, a wanderer "by wood and sea", the latter an intermediate site that carries its usual negative connotations:

> And toads, and every outlawed thing,
> > With eyes of sadness rose to hear,
> From pools and rotting leaves, me sing

> The song of outlaws and their fear.
> My singing sang me fever-free;
>   My singing fades, the strings are torn;
> I must away by wood and sea
>   And lift an ulalu forlorn,
> And fling my laughter to the sun
>   – For my remembering hour is done –
> In all his evening vapours rolled.

For all its morbid romanticism, this strained verse describes a figure typical of the characters to be found in the first editions of the early poetry. Oisin is the great exception. Yeats's later verse is filled with defiant men, but the Fenian warrior is the only early persona who comes close to matching their bravura. Towards the end of his life Yeats wondered whether his youthful depictions of "proud, confident people" had not come about as a result of his search for "a cure for my own ailment", compensation for those moments when he had felt himself "much humiliated" (*UP2* 507). Whether this was the case or not, it is suggestive that a motive force of this kind should have occurred to him as a possibility in the first place; and, given the many descriptions of Oisin that had been available to him, it is likewise suggestive that the younger poet should have fixed on the portrait in Comyn and limned its spirit precisely:

> O Patrick! direct me into the place
>   In which Fionn is in hands and the Fianna,
>   And there is not a hell or a heaven there
> That will put them under subjection.
>
> If Osgar my own son be there,
>   The hero that was bravest in heavy conflict,
>   There is not created in hell, or in the Heaven
>   of God
> A host tho' great, that he would not destroy.
>   (*TOS* IV, p. 275)

Here were brawlers, and Yeats took the vehement model for his own. But when he was not caught up by a paradigm, his freedom to invent resulted in self-projections like Kevin, Goll, or Miserrimus, a trio of failures who point in unison towards the poet's own fear of failure. And the fact that these three anxious men live lives that are out of the common way is also indicative, since it was Yeats's own lack of confidence that most fully answers for his early insistence on couching thoughts that were very much his own in the words of characters who, to all appearances, resembled him not at all.

The first-person narratives named above – "To an Isle in the Water", "The Falling of the Leaves", and "Down by the Salley Gardens" – are lyrics that are in no sense controversial; when a reader is told that it was "Down by the salley gardens my love and I did meet", he is not inclined to argue. But a statement against the form of religion that Patrick represents is left in the mouth of Oisin, distanced from his critics by the centuries; and Yeats's belief in reincarnation is voiced by Kanva the Indian, who can hold such a belief unobjectionably.²³ "The Falling of the Leaves" and "Ephemera" are two early poems that, taken side by side, provide an illustration of the way in which the young Yeats will make use of distancings to keep a potentially controversial poem impersonal. The tone and settings of the two are similar enough to be interchangeable; yet "The Falling of the Leaves" is in the first person, "Ephemera" in the third. The reason for this is that the theme of the first poem is the fading of love, while that of the second is reincarnation. Thus the voices that discuss this theme must be other than the poet's own; and Yeats places them at a still further remove from the reader in a series of hypnotic lines that suggest that the voices themselves are disembodied. Purportedly a dialogue, "Ephemera" is rather one of the least populated poems in the language. The setting is an autumn evening, and in the gloom of the woods neither speaker can clearly distinguish the other. The only physical details that either of them can identify are the eyes, eyes that are themselves "half hidden under pendulous lids", and the voice; and when one of the characters addresses the other as "wistful voice" in the opening lines of the poem, the impression left is that there is nothing to be discerned here but a kind of soul's cry. It is smartly worked, this opening effect; there is an intended negation of sexuality at work – the reader has no way of knowing who is speaking in the first ten lines until he arrives at line twelve – and a feeling that the voices are speaking ghostlike from the woods' shade, that they have already passed beyond the physical and are poised between their own dying love and new loves yet to be born. The argument of the poem, as one of Yeats's sources elsewhere summed that argument up, is that

> one life is only one temporary condition among a thousand similar ones through which the character of a man passes in its travels on the road to perfection, and whether he remains a longer or a shorter interval at one station, cannot be of any very serious importance to him.²⁴

Thus the parting lovers in "Ephemera" have the comfort of knowing that, however often leavetakings like this one may have been their lot before, they were but preludes to future unions:

> "Your eyes that once were never weary of mine
> Lie now half hidden under pendulous lids,
> Veiled in a dreamy sorrow for their love
> That wanes." "Ah, wistful voice," replied the other,
> "Though our sad love is fading, let us yet
> Stand by the border of the lake once more,
> Together in that hour of gentleness
> When the poor tired child, passion, falls asleep.
> How far away the stars seem, and how far
> Is our first kiss, and ah, how old my heart!"
> Pensive they paced along the faded leaves,
> While slowly answered he whose hand held hers –
> "Often has passion worn our wandering hearts,

Earth's aliens. Why so sorrowful? Our souls
Shall warm their lives at many a rustling flame."

The effect Yeats was after here was one that he later saw Maeterlinck as having managed to perfection: that of having "set before us faint souls... already half vapour and sighing to one another upon the border of the last abyss".[25] And if the effect calls too much attention to itself to be wholly effective, it none the less comes very close to working; so too do autumn and evening, emblems of the lovers' bodily death, and the specific Yeatsian usage of a site like "the border of the lake", which reinforces the idea of death by locating the wistful voices on the symbolic equivalent of the brink of eternity. Finally, the stars here are the same stars that shine in "Miserrimus" and "King Goll": symbols of the unattainable, too "far away" from the world to hear or care about the faint cries rising from below.

"Miserrimus" also portrayed the natural world as indifferent, but in writing that poem Yeats manages to accomplish what Miserrimus was unable to accomplish: the housing of his own fears in a structure of consolation. The natural world provides the poetry of his youth with as many images as his folklore and occult sources combined – thus the despair of an aspiring artist like Miserrimus, who finds the expected source grown intractable – and it does so with a specificity not to be found in the later works. Criticism has agreed that Yeats lacked an eye for physical detail, and the agreement has been so complete that discussion of the topic usually finds different readers in accord even as regards their choice of terms. Was Yeats an observer? "Yeats was a maker but not... an observer."[26] "His observation of nature emerged through some slight disguise."[27] He describes "a nature stylized and dilute, scarcely at all dependent upon observation".[28] And statements like these find confirmation in Yeats's own frequent claims that the poet should not try to see like a naturalist, that images drawn from nature had value only insofar as they were symbolic of a reality higher than the natural.[29] Yet other comments by Yeats and, more crucially, the early works themselves testify that his attitude towards the natural world was far different in the earlier stages of his career. Was Yeats an observer? The *Autobiographies* speaks deprecatingly of certain of the works of the poet's youth, yet praises even these for their "moments of observation", moments made possible by the fact that the Yeats of the time "still noticed all that passed" (p. 67); nor was he indifferent to physical detail when he

> called upon a cousin towards midnight and asked him to get his yacht out, for I wanted to find what sea-birds began to stir before dawn... I had wanted the birds' cries for the poem that became fifteen years afterwards *The Shadowy Waters*,

he writes, and adds that the play would have been "full of observation" had he "been able to write it when I first planned it" (*Au* 73–4). Remarks made nearer to the years when the early poems were written confirm these hindsights. In 1898, for instance, Yeats recalled that "when I first began to write I desired to describe outward things as vividly as possible" (*E&I* 189); and a decade earlier still he had written a letter to Katharine Tynan in which he equated the leading of a "harmoni[o]us poetic life" with his being "most ardently moved by the more minute kinds of natural beauty" (*CL1* 98). In at least one period of his career, then, Yeats had no objection whatever to looking out on nature through a naturalist's eye. When the early writings plunder the natural world for images, they also pay it the tribute of a keen regard.

Himself no mean eyewitness of the scene, Oliver St John Gogarty has drawn the sharpest distinction between the watchful Yeats of the eighties and the Yeats of the decades to come. "Lady ('Dorothy') Gerald Wellesley has written that Yeats did not appear to notice scenery", he notes, but

> this is the statement of one who merely observed the apparent self-absorption of the latter-day Yeats. Had she read "The Stolen Child", she would have realized how accurate and fitting were the scenes Yeats introduced into that poem, all of them scenes fitted to the poem, all of them from his recollections of Sligo, "where wandering water gushes from the hills above Glen-Car."

"When he was a youth", adds Gogarty, "he took it all in";[30] and the example he chooses to illustrate his point is a nice one. Though it has the ring of a rote phrase,[31] "wandering waters" is also an exact description of the meandering path hollowed out by the waters of Glencar Falls as they flow down towards Glencar Lake; and the small pools that punctuate this rivulet remain even now filled with rushes, scarce able to bathe a star. The lyrics alluded to just above could have illustrated Gogarty's argument more handily still. "Ephemera", for instance, is graced by a neat distinction between the "faded leaves" beneath the feet of the lovers and the "yellow leaves" that continue to fall "like faint meteors in the gloom", while its companion poem provides a more extended, and equally as observant, description of "The Falling of the Leaves". There is no indifference here, either on nature's part or on that of its observer; the poem pays meticulous attention to physical detail, and the care with which it combines its autumn colors is clear ratification of Yeats's youthful tendency to take it all in.

> Autumn is over the long leaves that love us,
>   And over the mice in the barley sheaves;
> Yellow the leaves of the rowan above us,
>   And yellow the wet wild-strawberry leaves.
>
> The hour of the waning of love has beset us,
>   And weary and worn are our sad souls now;
> Let us part, ere the season of passion forget us,
>   With a kiss and a tear on thy drooping brow.

These lines do not impress with their originality. Compositions from color abound in the poetry of the time, as for instance in Wilde's assorted

"Impressions"; and the conclusion of the lyric reaches back further still, glancing as it does towards the Moore of the *Irish Melodies*. But Yeats never works from models, rough or smooth, without refining them; and while "The Falling of the Leaves" is a minor lyric, it is possessed of a coherence and a suggestiveness that were beyond a Moore's reach. Its stanzas are among the very few to escape the blue pencil that their author sooner or later brought to bear on almost all his early works. The reasons for this absence of revision are apparent; if no amount of rewriting could have transformed these verses into a central effort, it is also true that no revision could have left them more perfected than they are. A studious eye is manifest even in the first two lines of the piece, inasmuch as the long leaves of the barley here join with the "long leaves" of the first line to establish a connection between the world through which the saddened lovers move and the natural world inhabited by the mice: the lovers are under the long yellow leaves of the rowan, the mice beneath the long yellow leaves of the barley. The next two lines make it clear that the rest of the stanza is likewise to be a study in yellow, a color that lends its tinge to everything in the poem. The rowan leaves are yellow "above" the man and woman; the "wet wild-strawberry leaves" are yellowing on the vines that trail along the ground below; and the trees and vines taken together thus comprise a kind of frame, with Yeats's description of the lovers as the portrait that the second stanza of the poem will place within it. The choices of rowan tree and strawberry vine show the same kind of care that led to the selection of the barley, since they serve to secure the place of yellow in the poem by establishing the presence of a second color against which it can stand out in contrast. The rowan and the wild strawberry alike blossom in white flowers that give way to red fruit. Yellow and red: rich and autumnal, and colors that lend themselves to a scene that deals with the fading of love.

The stage prepared, the second stanza introduces the characters. The central point to be made about the vagabonds who find a still place in these lines is that they themselves are undergoing the same relentless change that is taking place in nature. All the wood is yellowing, and the poem implies that the death of human love has a like inevitability about it: bodily passion must wane, souls grow "weary and worn". There is a nicely controlled irony in the contrast between the prodigal "season of passion" and the "hour of the waning of love", its curt antidote. The autumnal setting of the poem, moreover, certifies what was all but sure to begin with – that the season of passion was summer – and this equation of human emotions with the seasons of the year effectively forestalls a central question that the reader might otherwise be all but obliged to ask. It is evident that the lovers in question still feel a tenderness for each other: why, then, must they part? The most intriguing aspect of the poem is that it gives no direct answer to this question, but none the less manages to beguile the reader into believing that the parting of the lovers is a given. The first stanza tied the lovers to the natural world by placing them, as the field mice were placed, under a natural canopy. The second stanza reinforced that suggestion by relating their love to the seasons. The parallel images in the last line of each stanza make the equation conclusive; the juxtaposition of "wet wild-strawberry leaves" with "a tear on thy drooping brow" aims at a subliminal acceptance of the idea that love is subject to the same unbending laws that govern nature. Thus does the poem neutralize the temptation to inquire why the lovers must bid one another farewell. The asking of that question becomes tantamount to asking why the seasons change. Summer turns to fall because it must; all true love must die, alter at the best (*VP* 517).

Among their other virtues, the early writings come out of an angular set of mind, a set of mind in many ways as angular as that of the mature poet. It is clear that Yeats's early works propose worlds like those of the sidhe and the Rose as possible models of the transcendent realm. But it is also clear that Yeats, no empiricist in the usual sense of the term, was no idealist either. What he sought to do was to blend these opposing postures into a single beam of perception; and what he became was an empiricist of the spirit. In 1913, while investigating the case of Elizabeth Radcliffe, he told his father that "I have just had a certificate of caution from a well-known American medium who has turned me out of her seances because she says 'nothing ever satisfies' me" (*Let* 584). And when it came to questions about the world beyond the veil, nothing ever did. In work after work, early or late, Yeats refuses an easy acceptance of the supernatural, and fashions instead a series of supernatural test cases; and when he holds them up to the light, he does so less to wonder at their brilliance than to see if they might possibly be flawed.

The paradigms of the supernal that dominate in the early works are Tir na nOg and the sphere of Tiphareth. The prime focus of the early works is on intersections, those crossways where the path of the Immortals – Niamh, for instance, or the Higher Genius – bisects for a time the path of man. The pattern of the early works is to set the two worlds to parleying when they meet, with the seductive representative of the transcendent realm contrasting the beauties to be met with there with their poor homely counterparts on earth. And when all the arguments are in, the sympathies of the early work come to rest more fully with the poor and homely.

Though Yeats rightly insists on the strength of their attractions, the perfect abodes of pure spirits are places that, in his considered view, can satisfy neither a man's need for change and variety nor the artist's need for subject matter. It is on these counts that earthly counterpull has the advantage; and when the author of the early works goes in search of a model of Eden more accommodating to our needs, it is in an earthly garden that he finds it.

Were he suddenly to be "placed among the cold lunar beams of a purely spiritual existence", said J. B. Yeats, he felt that he would find himself "sigh[ing] for the old life with its sins and temptations and its hot sun";[32] and he saw his eminent son as feeling just the same. "Your interest is in mundane things", he wrote to the poet, "and Heaven to you is this world made better, whether beyond the stars or not".[33] On this count father and son were more in accord than we might initially suspect. "Paradise", Yeats wrote to Lady Gregory in 1902, "is happiness, the abundance of earth, the natural life, every man's desire" (*Let* 384). The elements that went to the making of this definition had been preparing for well over a decade, most tellingly in those of Yeats's writings that were directly or indirectly autobiographical. "There is more of myself in it than in any thing I have done", he said of *John Sherman* (*CL1* 245–6); and even as that novel had set up a contrast between the image of the small house with a wall around it and that of a deserted great house whose ancient wall of trees was being felled, so too it juxtaposed the images of sterile and abundant gardens. In the early stages of the narrative, Sherman finds himself a solitary man in London, the rear windows of the house he has rented looking out onto

> a little patch of garden round which the houses gathered and pressed as though they already longed to trample it out. In this garden was a single tall pear tree that never bore fruit (p. 60).

But the passage that follows the description of Margaret Leland's consent to marry him finds the bleak scene transformed. Since renting the house, Sherman has "planted alternate hollyhock and sunflower, and behind them scarlet-runners [that] showed their inch-high cloven shoots" (p. 71). Yet the yard is too small and, says the punning narrator, "this husbandry... too little complex for his affections to gather much round plant and bed" (p. 71); and it takes the promise of an impending domestic content to bring the garden to full bloom. After he "proposed and was accepted", overnight

> there was a new heaven and a new earth. Miss Leland seemed suddenly impressed with the seriousness of life. She was gentleness itself; and as Sherman sat on Sunday mornings in his pocket-handkerchief of a garden under the one tree, with its smoky stem, watching the little circles of sunlight falling from the leaves like a shower of new sovereigns, he gazed at them with a longer and keener joy than heretofore – a new heaven and a new earth, surely! (p. 70).

The point that *John Sherman* seeks to make in its balancing of these passages is a fairly plain one. In the one there is a barren plot with a tree stripped of its fruit. In the other there is the image of Sunday morning, and the twice-repeated image of what Revelation 21:1 called "a new heaven and a new earth": the "holy city, new Jerusalem, coming down from God out of heaven, prepared" – appropriately enough, given the reasons for Sherman's sudden ecstasy – "as a bride adorned for her husband" (21:2). Here is the Garden restored, and this pattern of imagery completes itself – too evidently, but then Yeats was not a novelist – towards the end of the novel, when Sherman, having contrived to break off his engagement with the wealthy ("a shower of new sovereigns") Miss Leland in order to propose to Mary Carton, returns to Sligo, proposes and is refused. He takes leave of the schoolhouse in which she teaches – nearby, not by happenstance, stands a single pear tree whose proper tending Mary Carton sees to (p. 109) – and thinks as he leaves that he had lost the best of all the things he held dear. Twice he had gone through the fire. The first time worldly ambition left him; the second, love. An hour before the air had been full of singing and peace that was resonant like joy. Now he saw standing before his Eden the angel with the flaming sword (p. 109).

The passage that comes next in the narrative is the one in which Sherman, hurrying away from town, sees the skeletal house with its woodcutters (pp. 109–10); and the sequence here is appropriate, since the combined thrust of these passages from *John Sherman* is that a man who has been denied a chance to realize the domestic ideal, and who therefore finds his imagined home in ruins all around him, is a man who has been cast out of what the Yeats of the early works took to be true Eden. The 1900 draft of *The Speckled Bird* draws upon the same complex of images in order to make the same point. On the morning after her arrival, Michael takes Margaret out to the garden behind his home. A concrete illustration of the definition of paradise that Yeats had proposed to Lady Gregory, the garden is both natural – its flowers grow as "wildly" as if they were "in the middle of a great wood" (*VSB* 168) – and abundant to the point of extravagance (*VSB* 167). Within its sheltering confines, moreover, the two young people are happy:

> After breakfast Michael brought her to the garden and neither of them thought of going to see the views from the hills, for they had not outgrown the childish love of little shut-in places and thought that views were uninteresting (*VSB* 167).

The Speckled Bird verges so near to an author's self-description that it seems all but needless to prove that the attitude here ascribed to Michael was shared by Yeats. But if conclusive proof were needed, it could be found in the description of his own early years that the poet set down in 1904:

> Children – or, at any rate, it is so I remember my own childhood – do not understand large design, and they delight in little shut-in places where they can play at houses more than in great expanses where a country-side takes, as it were, the impression of a thought (*Ex* 19).

And for both the author and his character, this shared delight in little shut-in places extended particularly to walled gardens. Michael reflects that "the garden of Eden must have been" much like the one in which he and Margaret find themselves (*VSB* 168); and in a rare tipping of his authorial hand, Yeats reminds himself in a note written into the manuscript that he must "describe the garden carefully", and this because "it is a symbol of the supernal Eden" (*VSB* 242). In advancing that last phrase, *The Speckled Bird* not only joins with *John Sherman* to illustrate its author's hopes of locating an Eden in the world around him, but provides a solid basis for a summing up of the connections the poet saw between a protective world of nature and the peaceful life of home.

Yeats's reference to "supernal Eden" derives from the rituals of the Golden Dawn; and he uses it, as the Order used it, as a symbol of beatitude.[34] But the Order located its version of Eden out of time and space, and it was in this regard that the poet agreed to differ. Seeing Paradise as the abundance of earth, the natural life, every man's desire, he had found a more compelling image of blessedness in a poem by William Morris. "Golden Wings" was a natural draw for a young man who confessed a child's delight in little shut-in places; the Morris that Yeats had known, after all, had made "his poetry out of unending pictures of a happiness that is often what a child might imagine" (E&I 61). And for Yeats, as for Morris, the imagining of that secured happiness ran as follows:

> Midways of a wallèd garden,
> In the happy poplar land,
> Did an ancient castle stand,
> With an old knight for a warden.
>
> Many scarlet bricks there were
> In its walls, and old grey stone;
> Over which red apples shone
> At the right time of the year.
>
> On the bricks the green moss grew,
> Yellow lichen on the stone,
> Over which red apples shone;
> Little war that castle knew.

These "verses ran in my head for years and became to me the best description of happiness in the world", Yeats wrote in 1902, "and I am not certain that I know a better even now" (E&I 60).

If Yeats is worthy of careful consideration, then a confession this direct needs to be weighted most carefully. Of the many portraits of the poet that criticism has offered, one at least has been given too little time at center stage: that of the man who, from his early twenties through his mid thirties,[35] could find no better image of human happiness than many another mortal might have come up with. A life of peace in a place of beauty: whether he be admiring its use in Morris or making use of it himself, the image of the walled garden joins Yeats's abiding love of the natural world that the garden represents to his early longings for a home made sure. His vision of the life of ideal domesticity and his affection for even the more minute kinds of natural beauty are directly interlinked. The early works run through a series of images, all of them evocative of the natural world, through which the poet expresses a deep-felt need for the sort of security that little shut-in places could provide, places where a sheltered hearthlight might survive the drawing near of what threatenings lay beyond. Islands, for instance: both "To an Isle in the Water" and "The Lake Isle of Innisfree" combine an image of a natural fastness with an imagining of what might come to be a home. It is even now too standard a practice to take Yeats's own remarks about the illusory natural world as proof of a limited faith in the tangible. Yet neither Yeats nor his most vehement instructors in the matter ever claimed that the world was plainly false to the touch. What they claimed instead was that it needs must be perceived as such when regarded "from the purely metaphysical view"; and what they freely admitted was that a natural realm that, "regarded from the purely metaphysical standpoint, may be conceived to have no objective reality", could seem very real indeed to a man who regarded it from a viewpoint less sublime.[36] If Yeats's recollections of his early years may be taken as yardsticks, his theories about nature never grew too sublime for his practice. The homes he imagined as alternatives to the home he lacked were all in the natural world.

> One morning I proposed a journey to Lambay Island, and was contemptuous because [my friend] said we should miss our mid-day meal. We hoisted a sail on our small boat and ran quickly over the nine miles and saw on the shore a tame sea-gull, while a couple of boys, the sons of a coastguard, ran into the water in their clothes to pull us to land, as we had read of savage people doing. We spent an hour upon the sunny shore and I said, "I would like to live here always, and perhaps some day I will." I was always discovering places where I would like to spend my whole life (*Au* 59).[37]

Places with something in common, places sheltered by walls or by circling water. Edens, really, places where one could live contented "always":

> Yes, there is an island called Innisfree, and it is in Lough Gill, Co. Sligo. I lived in Sligo when I was young, and longed, while I was still as young as you, to build myself a cottage on this island and live there always.[38]

Little shut-in places, caves perhaps, windbreaks where a fire might rise safe against the wind, places not to be violated by the noisy world, improvised homes:

> A herd had shown me a cave some hundred and fifty feet below the cliff path and a couple of hundred above the sea, and told me that an evicted tenant called Macrom, dead some fifteen years, had lived there many years... Here I stored a tin of cocoa and some biscuits, and instead of going to my bed, would slip out on warm nights and sleep in the cave on the excuse of catching moths... When, however, upon a bank holiday, I found lovers in my cave, I was not content with it again till I heard that the ghost of Macrom had been seen a little before the dawn, stooping over his fire in the cave-mouth. I had been trying to cook eggs, as I had read in some book, by burying them in the earth under a fire of sticks (*Au* 63).

Obsessive images, images now and at all times in the mind's eye. A keen eye could pick out the place. Keen ears would listen:

Natural Ideals: Yeats's Walled Gardens

My father had read to me some passage out of *Walden*, and I planned to live some day in a cottage on a little island called Innisfree, and Innisfree was opposite Slish Wood where I meant to sleep... I could watch my island in the early dawn and notice the order of the cries of the birds (*Au* 71–2).

No one thus bewitched by small details could be anything but a lover; why else speak of Innisfree as "my" island? The early works are self-portraiture, and the portrait is that of a man who, drawn by promises from the world of the spirit, admits the strength of their pull and does not succumb to it. Being a man, it was only to home and to nature that he could turn with his heart still intact: to the world that the hearthlight illumined, and the world where birds' cries bid a measured welcome to the first slow light of dawn.

Notes to Chapter 5

1 But see Frank Hughes Murphy's reading of the poem in his *Yeats's Early Poetry: The Quest for Reconciliation*, pp. 56–60. Murphy rightly notes that the poem ends, "not in the triumph of revelation", but rather in the "failure to achieve" it (p. 59). Yet we can only grasp Yeats's final intent here by showing how he too failed to achieve it; and this is a step that Murphy's otherwise illuminating discussion does not take.

2 In *The Countess Kathleen and Various Legends and Lyrics*, 1. 11 of "The Rose of Battle" read "Besides her clean swept hearth"; 1. 14 read "and singing past". "Besides" became "Beside" in the 1895 *Poems*; "past" became "passed" in the *Collected Poems* of 1933.

3 In bringing a sorrowing Rose down to the seashore, Yeats was also evoking the depiction in exile poems of the spirit of Ireland as a woman keening her departed children by the waves. The opening of T. D. McGee's "Memories", for instance, ran as follows:

> I left two loves on a distant strand,
> One young, and fond, and fair, and bland;
> One fair, and old, and sadly grand, –
> My wedded wife and my native land.
>
> One tarrieth sad and seriously
> Beneath the roof that mine should be;
> One sitteth sibyl-like, by the sea,
> Chaunting a grave song mournfully.

McGee (1825–68) was a prolific writer of emigrant poetry, and Yeats was thoroughly familiar with his work; he included three of McGee's lyrics in the *Book of Irish Verse* (1895). "Memories" was not among them; but the anthology does include "The Banshee" by John Todhunter (1839–1916), with its portrait of the "spectre Erin" sitting on the banks of the Shannon and "keening" her "children exiled and dead". Yeats had high praise for this poem of Todhunter's in a review written in January of 1892 (*UP1* 216–17), the month in which the first of the Rose poems was printed.

4 The question of whether Goldsmith modelled his village primarily on towns he had seen in England or (as seems more likely) on the townland of Lissoy in

Westmeath has never been fully resolved. For the parameters of the debate, cf. Arthur Friedman's preface to the poem in *Collected Works of Oliver Goldsmith*, Vol. IV, pp. 273–7. Yeats included 11. 83–96 and 137–62 of the poem in *A Book of Irish Verse*, but had his doubts about its credentials. "'The deserted village' is Lissoy, near Ballymahon", he wrote in his notes to the volume, "but the feeling and atmosphere of the poem are unmistakably English." Cf. *A Book of Irish Verse* (London: Methuen and Co., 1900), p. 250.

5   For Joseph Hone's remarks on how the young "Yeats used often to ask himself... why O'Leary, who probably cared for no English poet since Pope, should have believed in his talent", cf. *W. B. Yeats, 1865–1939*, p. 53. For the lines from Pope cited here, cf. the Yale edition of *The Poems of Alexander Pope*, Vol. IX, pp. 377–9, 380.

6   Yeats was citing the Chaldean Oracles as the source of this passage as late as 1914's "Swedenborg, Mediums, and the Desolate Places" (*Ex* 57). For his claim that the authorship of the Oracles had traditionally been "attributed to Zoroaster" (*Au* 255), he had for backing not only tradition but a personal acquaintance, William Wynn Westcott, Order co-founder and translator of *The Chaldean Oracles of Zoroaster*. Westcott published this work under his Order motto of Sapere Aude; the preface was written by "L.O.", or Levavi Oculos [Percy Bullock]. Yeats's personal copy of the volume is that published in London by the Theosophical Publishing Society in 1895. George Mills Harper has also noted that Yeats preserved among his personal papers extracts from the translation of the Oracles done by Thomas Taylor (1758–1835); cf. *Yeats and The Occult*, p. 5.

7   The passage appears in the Practicus ceremony (*GD* II, p. 101), the Portal ritual (*GD* II, pp. 193–4), the ceremony for the consecration of the Vault (*GD* II, p. 266), the evocation ritual (*GD* III, p. 196), and the rite of Spiritual Development (*GD* III, p. 249).

Since the language of the passage varies from appearance to appearance, and since the citation in the *Autobiographies* reproduces one version in particular and does so all but verbatim, Yeats probably had the lines about "Hades wrapped in cloud" in front of him as he wrote. In *Yeats and The Occult*, Harper points out that Yeats "had almost a complete study library" for both the Outer and Inner Orders, "including numerous duplicates of rituals" (p. 4). In this case, he could have taken the passage either from his copies of the rituals or from Westcott's *Chaldean Oracles*. As it appears in the copy of the *Oracles* housed in Dalkey, the passage runs thus:

> Stoop not down unto the Darkly-Splendid World; wherein continually lieth a faithless Depth, and Hades wrapped in clouds, delighting in unintelligible images, precipitous, winding, a black ever-rolling Abyss; ever espousing a Body unluminous, formless and void (p. 46).

In its language this passage is identical with the passage in the Practicus ceremony, and its opening is all but identical with the lines cited by Yeats in the *Autobiographies*.

8   For a clear and concise summary of the Order's grade structure, cf. King's *The Rites of Modern Occult Magic*, pp. 56 ff.

9   For Regardie's association of these Order images with the dark night of the soul, cf. *GD* I, pp. 55–6.

10 The title was borrowed from *Ossian* by way of Matthew Arnold. Arnold had used a similar line from *Ossian* to head the series of lectures, delivered in 1866, that became his *On the Study of Celtic Literature* (1867). For a fuller comment on the misunderstandings that Arnold's use of the phrase drew him into, cf.

John V. Kelleher's "Matthew Arnold and the Celtic Revival", in *Perspectives of Criticism* (1950), pp. 197–221.
11   An equally direct phrase – "the waves of time" – appears in 1904's *The King's Threshold* (*VPl* 311).
12   The neo-Platonist in question was for a certainty Porphyry. In later years Yeats would make Stephen MacKenna's translation of Porphyry's *Life of Plotinus* the basis of his "The Delphic Oracle upon Plotinus" (1932) and "News for the Delphic Oracle" (1939). But his 1899 reference to the "drifting indefinite bitterness of life" (*VP* 808) makes it clear that he had read Thomas Taylor's 1817 translation of Porphyry no later than the mid or late nineties, probably in the 1895 reprint of Taylor's *Select Works of Plotinus* edited by G. R. S. Mead. The edition of this work that appears in the Dalkey library belonged to Mrs Yeats; its flyleaf is inscribed "Georgie Hyde Lees, July 1913". But the resemblance between Yeats's language in *VP* and the language in the Porphyry translation confirms the fact that Yeats had read the Mead–Taylor *Plotinus* not long after its publication. Taylor had rendered Porphyry's tribute to Plotinus as follows:

> Oft merg'd in matter, by strong leaps you try'd
> To bound aloft, and cast its folds aside;
> To shun the bitter stream of sanguine life,
> Its whirls of sorrow, and its storm of strife.
> (pp. lxvi–lxvii)

It is typical of Yeats to have forgotten the source but remembered the passage, and it is striking that it should have been this passage that he recalled. A comparison of the Taylor and MacKenna translations serves as further illustration of the fact that the poet's basic interests remained constant over the years. The lines from Taylor that caught his eye in the 1890s describe the journey of Plotinus out towards the islands of the blessed; and when an older Yeats turned to the MacKenna volumes, the lines that impressed him most lastingly – he was numbering them among his touchstones as late as 1931 (*E&I* 409) – were lines that described the same journey. For the MacKenna translation of Porphyry, cf. *Plotinus: The Ethical Treatises* (1917), pp. 1–28. The passage that corresponds with the lines from Taylor cited above is on pp. 22–3.

13   As elsewhere in Yeats's work, the trees here represent the force of old tradition. *John Sherman*'s linking of the image of the ruined house to that of the felling of the trees anticipates by some four decades Yeats's yoking together of the same set of images in 1939's *Purgatory* (*VPl* 1043–4).
14   There are thirty-seven accented phonemes in the poem. In the order in which they appear, the eight noted here are:

aI / , I / , l / , r / , æ / , n / , d / , and / g / .

15   Yeats's accurate recollection was that "I was twenty-two or three before I gave up the dream" (*Au* 72). The initial drafts of the first two stanzas of "The Lake Isle of Innisfree" were written late in 1888 – Yeats's well-known description of the incident that inspired them may be found in both *John Sherman* (p. 92) and the *Autobiographies* (p. 153) – and when he sent these early versions of the opening verses of his poem to Katharine Tynan, Yeats explained that they had had their origins in an "old" daydream of his own (*CL1* 121).
16   Cited in Murphy, *Prodigal Father*, p. 190.
17   Cited in Hone, op. cit. p. 346. The reference is to the "spacious home that I lacked"; but what is telling here is that the poet, a family man in his mid-fifties at the time he made the comment, should still be associating his memory of

Sligo with his sense of what constituted a real home. For a comprehensive summary of "how complex Yeats's emotions were about the state of exile", and by extension the notion of home, cf. George Mills Harper's *'Go Back to Where You Belong': Yeats's Return from Exile* (1973), p. 34. Harper too speaks of how little help J. B. Yeats was in his son's "quest for home" (p. 11), and of the younger Yeats's need for a "spiritual home" (p. 11) in place of the home he lacked. My thanks to Richard J. Finneran for calling my attention to several of the articles and monographs that have a bearing on the arguments of these chapters.

18 Unterecker, *A Reader's Guide to William Butler Yeats*, p. 68. Jeffares recapitulates this line of argument in *A New Commentary on the Poems of W. B. Yeats*, p. 5.

19 Franz Hartmann, *The Life of Philippus Theophrastus Bombast of Hohenheim*, p. 176. The passage cited here comes from Paracelsus rather than Hartmann, though later in the book Hartmann would add that the heavens are "incomprehensible to those who cannot realise the true character of the stars" (p. 238).

20 This Yeatsian touchstone appears towards the end of the "Proverbs of Hell" section of Blake's *The Marriage of Heaven and Hell*.

21 "Miserrimus" first appeared in *The Dublin University Review* for October 1886; Yeats's two-part article on Joyce was published just afterward, in late November and early December issues of *Irish Fireside*. His sometimes inaccurate citation of "Deirdre" appeared in the later essay (*UP1* 111).

22 Actually, the figure described in the version of "King Goll" that appeared in *The Wanderings of Oisin and Other Poems* was at once obscure and very well known indeed, since Yeats's earlier portraits of Goll are conflations of two radically different figures. For a fuller account of the sources of "King Goll", and of the ways in which Yeats's readings of his sources help to illumine the poem's intent, see my "A Source Note on 'The Madness of King Goll'" in *Yeats Annual*, Vol. IV (1986), pp. 189–94.

23 Kanva's argument for reincarnation appeared in "Kanva on Himself" (*VP* 723–4), a poem Yeats dropped after its appearance in *The Wanderings of Oisin and Other Poems*. Even had Yeats been inclined to retain the lyric – not likely, since it was neither remotely Irish nor very good – he would have felt no need to, since the views of reincarnation that the poem puts forth are identical in their substance to those advanced in the more successfully worked "Ephemera".

The other lyric in *The Wanderings of Oisin and Other Poems* that had Kanva as its narrator was "Kanva, the Indian, on God", now "The Indian upon God" (*VP* 76–7). The basic conceit of this lyric, in both its early and revised versions, is that all living things imagine God as a being made in their own image. Inasmuch as Yeats was far along in his theosophical studies when the poem was first published in October of 1886, the second volume of *Isis Unveiled* may well have served him as a primary source. Arguing against the validity of anthropomorphic views of deity, Blavatsky cited an old poem that anticipates "Kanva, the Indian, on God" directly. "If oxen or lions had hands", it reads,

> and could work in man's fashion,
> And trace out with chisel or brush their conception
>   of Godhead
> Then would horses depict gods like horses, and oxen
>   like oxen,
> Each kind the Divine with its own form and nature
>   endowing. (p. 242)

The Yeats lyric concludes with the imaginings of the peacock, and here too the work of Blavatsky may have contributed; in *Isis Unveiled* (Vol. II), the peacock's tail, with its "hundred eyes", becomes a symbol of transcendent knowledge (p. 409). The image is no different in its use in Yeats's poem.

24 Franz Hartmann, *Magic, White and Black*, p. 145.
25 The comment appears in 1898's "The Autumn of the Body" (*E&I* 190). Yeats's remarks on Maeterlinck's characters in the September 1897 issue of *The Bookman* could readily be mistaken for a description of "Ephemera", a poem whose "persons" are, like Maeterlinck's, mere

> shadows and cries. We do not know in what country they were born, or in what period they were born, or how old they are, or what they look like, and we do not always know whether they are brother and sister, or lover and lover, or husband and wife. They go hither and thither by well-sides, and by crumbling towers, and among woods, that are repeated again and again, and are as unemphatic as a faded tapestry; and they speak with low, caressing voices which one has to hold one's breath to hear (*UP2* 52).

26 Louis MacNeice, *The Poetry of W. B. Yeats*, p. 64.
27 Jeffares, *W. B. Yeats: Man and Poet*, p. 28.
28 Ellmann, *The Identity of Yeats*, p. 35.
29 Observations of the kind are too frequent a feature in Yeats's writings to admit of being bundled up in a lone endnote. For a comprehensive early comment on the matter, see the essay on "The Necessity of Symbolism" in the Yeats–Ellis edition of *The Works of William Blake* (1893), Vol. I, pp. 235 ff.
30 Oliver St John Gogarty, *William Butler Yeats: A Memoir*, p. 25.
31 Hone has taken note of Yeats's admission of his early "veneration" of Tennyson in his *W. B. Yeats*, p. 34; and if "wandering waters" has a literary ring to it, it may be because the phrase had earlier appeared in "The Hesperides", wherein "wandering waters unto wandering waters call" (1. 75). For the full text of this early (1832–3) Tennyson lyric, which at any number of points might be mistaken for an early lyric by Yeats, cf. Vol. VI of *The Works of Alfred Lord Tennyson* (1889), pp. 217–20.
32 Cited in Murphy, *Prodigal Father*, p. 522.
33 Cited in Hone, op. cit., pp. 46–7.
34 In the Order rituals, the phrase refers to the transcendent dwelling-place of the Supernal Triad. Cf. Torrens, *The Secret Rituals of the Golden Dawn*, pp. 161, 178. Yeats used the phrase again, and in a context that repays examination, in 1906's "Discoveries" (*E&I* 297).
35 This is a conservative estimate. Yeats prefaced his comments about "Golden Wings" as follows:

> When I was a child I often heard my elders talking of an old turreted house where an old great-uncle of mine lived, and of its gardens and its long pond where there was an island with tame eagles; and one day somebody read me some verses and said they made him think of that old house where he had been very happy. The verses ran in my head for years and became to me the best description of happiness in the world, and I am not certain that I know a better even now (*E&I* 59–60).

The "old great-uncle" was Robert Corbet; the "old turreted house" was Sandymount Castle; and the "somebody" who read the verses to his son was J. B. Yeats, who lived in the Castle briefly during his young manhood. Yeats would have known the Morris poem by his early twenties at the latest; the likelihood is that he knew it much earlier.

36   Blavatsky, *The Secret Doctrine*, Vol. I, pp. 314–15, and cf. pp. 294–5 and 522 for further elaborations of the idea.

37   After their return to Ireland in 1880, the Yeats family lived for several years in the village of Howth, first in "a long thatched house" (*Au* 55) on Balscadden Road, then in "a house overlooking the harbour" (*Au* 61). This second residence – its address, 2 Harbour Road – was and still is known as "Island View", the reason for this being that it looks out towards two prominent islands: Ireland's Eye, which rises just beyond the mouth of the harbour, and Lambay Island, which lies several miles further north. It was the latter of these two that Yeats identified as the place where he "would like to live... always" (*Au* 59).

Unlike "Island View", the long thatched cottage that was the other home of the Yeats family in Howth is long gone. But in the early eighties it was located above Balscadden Bay, just where Balscadden Road ends its brief rise from the harbour of Howth and bends sharply to the left. My thanks to John Loughnane, then of Asgard House, for having located the nineteenth-century surveyor's map that identified this elusive site.

38   Cited in Hone, op. cit., p. 39.

[6]
Aftermaths

One of the surest hallmarks of a major poet is that his work can be as interesting in its flaws as in its masterings; and Yeats's early works, the flawed and perfected alike, are invariably of interest. Had some mistaken angel dropped the sword, the only just recollection of the Yeats who died in 1895 would be that of a great talent whose grasp was in the process of becoming the equal of his reach. For one thing, the early writings staked out an ambitious stretch of ground; by the beginning of his thirtieth year, Yeats was well in evidence not only as poet but as teller of tales in prose, playwright, essayist, editor, critic-reviewer and student of Blake. But more to the point, the complexities of attitude that underlie the later works were already fully present in the works written decades before. The aim of this postscript is to initiate a journey down the corridor that leads towards the later work: first by briefly noting the shifts in use or meaning that Yeats's favored early images underwent in the course of the nineties, and then by exploring the ways in which the concept of the Rose continued to inform the poet's work even after the symbol itself had begun to fade out of his verse.

A reader who knew nothing of Yeats's work but the first editions of his first three collections of poetry would come away from the reading with certain images fixed. These are poems about the fairies, the fairies pictured being for the most part members of the tribe popularly known as the little people; and these are poems about an enigmatic Irish rose. These are poems about nature, marked, many of them, by what their author elsewhere called a "delicate observation" (*UP1* 189);[1] and these are poems about the kind of homes where a soul might find its ease. So things stood as Yeats's ambitious apprentice years drew towards a close. But changes in the poet's life and thought were already preparing changes in his work; and by the mid-nineties all four of the central early foci – sidhe, Rose, nature and home – had either begun to drift out of his writings or, more usually, found themselves being subjected to the sorts of sea changes that would enable the artist of future years to put them to different use.

I

When the naturalist in him died, Yeats himself wrote the obituary. Having noted his early desire to "describe outward things as vividly as possible", he went on to snap the book shut: "And then quite suddenly I lost the desire of describing outward things" (*E&I* 189).[2] The 1898 essay in which these remarks appeared has both a hidden title and a recessed central focus. Ostensibly about "The Autumn of the Body", it could more accurately have been called "The Springtide of the Spirit"; and although the immediate topic of the piece is the symbolist movement and its offshoots, Yeats's real subject is the occult revival that, by reopening the ancient spiritual wellsprings, had in Yeats's view helped to make the symbolist movement possible. Acknowledging that his loss of interest in close observation had made him part of a movement, that "writers are struggling all over Europe... against that 'externality' which a time of scientific and political thought has brought into literature", he none the less insisted that his fellow artists rarely owned "a philosophic understanding of their struggle" (*E&I* 189). Their shift in attitude had been unconscious, he contended, having come from beyond their own minds, like "spray flung up from hidden tides that follow a moon no eye can see" (*E&I* 189); and the hidden tides he had in mind were those of magic, a system of belief that, like symbolism, concerned itself "with the essences of things, and not with things" (*E&I* 193). The resurgence of belief in magic in a few farsighted minds, ran the poet's argument, had drifted down, spray from an unknown source, over the minds of kindred spirits who may well have had no "philosophic understanding" of magic at all.

From a rhetorical point of view, the primary advantage of Yeats's conviction that thought could travel from mind to unsuspecting mind is that it cannot be conclusively refuted. But if his claims for the influence of the magical revival on the symbolist movement cannot be measured precisely, there can be no doubt that magic was the motive force most responsible for Yeats's coming to think like a symbolist. The distinction occultism drew between things and the essences of things was absolute:

> Alone the highest and invisible *originals* emanated from the thought of the Unknown are real and permanent beings, forms, and ideas; on earth, we see but their reflections (*IU* II, p. 158).

This belief, Blavatsky noted, was the "leading metaphysical feature" of occult philosophy (*IU* II, p. 530); and certainly no other tenet holds as central a place in source after Yeatsian source, whether in individual works on the magical tradition or in the Golden Dawn's expression of its conviction that "the whole of nature" was merely "the visible form and vehicle of a spiritual consciousness".[3] The serious occultist, then, needed to make it his business to look, not at nature, but (as it were) through it, to find in shadowy things Below a mirror of their counterparts in the immortal realms Above. "In the glass of things temporal", said *The Secret Doctrine*, "see the image of things spiritual" (Vol. III, p. 400).

That Yeats came to adopt these doctrines as his own needs no proving. The poet who came across the image of the "temporal glass" in *The Secret Doctrine* had already come across a precisely similar image in his admired Blake. The "vegetable glass of Nature", Yeats quoted Blake as having written, had value only insofar as one could discover therein the reflection of "eternal realities"; and, said the Yeats of the nineties, Blake had been wholly right.[4] Putting theory into practice, however, was no easy matter; and when Yeats ceased to see like a realist, his attempts to turn images taken from nature towards a purer use met with uneven results. The 1896 lyric now known as "He bids his Beloved be at Peace" might serve as illustration. When first published, the poem opened thus:

> I hear the shadowy horses, their long manes a-shake,
> Their hoofs heavy with tumult, their eyes glimmering
>   white;
> The North unrolls above them clinging, creeping night,
> The East tells all her secret joy before daybreak,
> The West weeps in pale dew, and sighs, passing away,
> The South would cover them with roses of crimson fire:
> O vanity of sleep, hope, dream, endless desire;
> The horses of disaster plunge in the desolate clay.
>
> (*VP* 154)

What Yeats was attempting here is more interesting than what he achieved. The natural images in the poem are meant to be suggestive of realities beyond themselves, with each of the cardinal points corresponding to one among the immortal moods: North to sleep, East to hope, and so forth.[5] The adjectives associated with those images, moreover, are meant to point through the natural symbol to the greater reality of which the natural symbol is but the reflection. Thus, for instance, Yeats wants "clinging" and "creeping" to be taken as if pausing briefly at the word "night" in order to lend it a kind of non-specific coloring, then passing on through that word to group their connotations around the word for which they are ultimately intended: sleep, the clinging repose whose earthly type is darkness. How far these exotic tactics can take a working poet is open to question, but there can be no question that to approach the natural world thus is to come at it as a symbolist reared in an occult tradition. Yeats's studies in magic had taught him that, since "every form in nature is a symbol of an idea", a regarding of the natural world "with [one's] spiritual eye" could lead a man to "the knowledge of eternal truths".[6] It was but a short step from ideas like these to the poet's own early credo that the task of the symbolist was to set down "words behind which glimmered a spiritual and passionate mood, as the flame glimmers behind the dusky blue and red glass in an Eastern lamp" (*E&I* 190). This kind of revelation, one must add, is more easily spoken of than achieved; and if Yeats's 1901 description of the twofold effect of symbolic art may be taken as a yardstick, then a poem like "He bids his Beloved be at Peace" can be judged no more than one-half a success. The lyric does indeed lead the reader "away from nature", as his experience of occultism had led Yeats himself; but it is by no means clear that, for all its dusky strivings, the poem manages to "bring... us near" to what Yeats called "the archetypal ideas themselves" (*E&I* 102).

II

The image through which the early works expressed the poet's desire for a life of ideal domesticity resurfaced as late as 1937's "What Then?", the retrospective poem in which Yeats, unhappy on other counts, none the less admitted that the most persistent longings of his youth had finally been satisfied: "All his happier dreams came true –/A small old house, wife, daughter, son,/Grounds where plum and cabbage grew".[7] His resurrection of these early touchstones can only be taken as testimony to the strength of their hold on the imagination of a much younger poet; for in the poetry written after the early nineties the image of the garden and small home had for the most part faded from sight. Part of the reason for this was the turning of Yeats's attention from the small house to the great. But little shut-in places had ceased to figure in his work several years before the poet had been absorbed by the ampler vistas of Coole Park and Ballylee; and their cessation was more directly related to a changing view of woman, and a rejection of the "shy one".

However offhand his departure, it is hard to fault Oisin overmuch for taking his leave of Niamh. The bland princess of the sidhe who appears in the first printing of "The Wanderings of Oisin" is far from a realized figure. Yeats describes her at length at the start of the poem, but after that is plainly at a loss as to what precisely to do with her. She is not only one-dimensional but, like all the women imaged in the earlier work, asexual, the kind of idealized image that human flesh denies. When she reappeared in the 1893 version of the poem since retitled "The Hosting of the Sidhe", however, she came in a different guise. Here she occupies the same place Beauty had held in the Rose poems of the year before, that of a force inimical to the peaceful life of home. "Brood no more where the fire is bright", she urges, "filling thy heart with a mortal dream": goodbye to the clean swept hearth, goodbye to happier dreams, and hello to being beckoned out of ease by a Niamh who, with her gleaming eyes and parted lips (*VP* 140), was the prototype of the women who was to enter the spotlight in Yeats's verse up through the turn of the century. With "The Hosting of the Sidhe", the "mild heroines" (*Mem* 86) that Yeats was later to recall as having been in the forefront of his early work were relegated to the wings. With them, inevitably, went the images of the firelit room, the sheltered farm. "One would almost think the house was about to fall upon our heads", says Peter Herne in "Those Who Live in the Storm", the story Yeats published in *The Speaker* in July 1894 (*VSR* 227); and shortly after he says it the hearthfire goes out, despite his attempts to keep it alive (p. 230), and shortly after that the rest of the cottage does indeed collapse, and the members of the Herne family are killed.[8] The neighbors attribute the destruction of the house to the violence of the storm that raged that night; Yeats sees the event as an act of vengeance, the workings of the spirit of a fisherman whom Peter Herne had killed "twelve months ago [that] night" (p. 228). But neither of these explanations has anything to do with the reason why Yeats's imagination should have homed in on this uncommon plot in the first place; and the reason why it did was that a changing view of woman was persuading Yeats towards the extinction of the hearthfire, the destruction of the small house, the phasing out from the poetry of those images of domesticity that had been so prominent only a few years before. Immediately before the roof of the cottage comes down, Peter's sister, Oona, once the lover of the fisherman whom her protective brother had killed, sings a song of welcome as she senses her lover's ghost approaching. Now called "The Heart of the Woman", the song opened thus when it appeared, untitled, in the story in *The Speaker*:

> O, what to me the firelit room,
>   Where I have laughed and spun and played?
> He bade me out into the gloom,
>   And my white breast on his he laid.
>
> O, what to me my mother's care,
>   The milking-place, the sheltered farm?
> The shadowy blossom of my hair
>   Will hide us from the bitter storm. (*VSR* 230–1)

The woman who speaks those lines would not easily be persuaded to carry in the dishes or light the quiet room. Like Niamh in "The Hosting of the Sidhe", Oona anticipates the woman who would come to dominate in Yeats's verse after his sexual initiation by Olivia Shakespear in the winter of 1895–6. Each of the poems he wrote to his married lover in the course of their brief affair has at its center the woman of "passion-dimmed eyes and long heavy hair" (*VP* 155) who drove Yeats out of all content with the ingenuous ideal that easeful hearthlight once embodied; and where he had once imagined his lovers as sheltered by a wall, he now came to see them as breakers of constraints, secret sinners whose illicit loves had made them outcasts from both the common ways of men and the walled gardens he had once conceived as Eden.[9] Yeats never ceased to write about homes; but "the firelit room" and "the sheltered farm" and other scenes of a like kind had disappeared from his poetry by the mid-nineties, banished by a glance from the eyes, dim or gleaming, of women who had turned away from home.

III

And then there were the lesser of the sidhe, the little people who had long been in the habit of rapid disappearance, and who vanished from the sight of Yeats's readers almost as suddenly as they had arrived.

As the Preface suggests and the Appendix (pp. 233–6) confirms, the *Poems* of 1895 was essentially a collection under one cover of revised versions of the poems and play that had been published in Yeats's first two books of verse. But if the only substantial addition to the volume was *The Land of Heart's Desire*, the short play that had opened on the London stage in March 1894, Yeats was to make a good number of deletions. Seventeen of the poems or verse-dramas that had appeared in *The Wanderings of Oisin and Other Poems* were cut, and the bulk of them fall into one of two basic categories. The first category consists of works that are set in foreign or exotic frames, works that would have jarred with the tone of a book that Yeats meant to be Irish and filled with the familiar landscapes he had recommended to Katharine Tynan, not with rare and glittering scenes (*CL1* 119). Thus do *The Island of Statues*, "The Seeker", *Mosada*, "How Ferencz Renyi Kept Silent", "Street Dancers" and *Time and the Witch Vivien* meet their early demise. The second category comprises the fairy poetry or, more precisely, the poems that deal with the *daoine maithe* – literally the "good people", and by extension the "gentry" or the "nobility". Only "The Stolen Child" survived the first edition of *The Wanderings of Oisin and Other Poems*; the untitled "A man has the fields of heaven" vanished like drifting smoke, as did "The Fairy Pedant", "The Fairy Doctor", "The Priest and the Fairy" and "A Lover's Quarrel among the Fairies". The most obvious reason for their eviction is that they are not good poems, or even good children's verse. Yeats was conscious of the inadequacies of these lyrics; no sooner had he completed "The Fairy Doctor" in the summer of 1887, for instance, than he described its stanzas to Katharine Tynan as "trivial verses" (*CL1* 34). Yet he could afford to include that poem, and fairy poems equally as trivial, among the works that appeared in his first volume of poetry; they were not likely to mar the reputation of a writer who, in 1889, had little reputation to speak of. By 1895, however, things had changed.

Fisher Unwin's decision to publish a volume that was, in effect, the *Collected Poems* of a poet just turned thirty evidenced a fine sense of timing as well as a recognition of a real talent. Yeats's formative years rise up like memorials against the horizon of English poetry; a single decade witnessed the deaths of Rossetti (1828–82), Arnold (1822–88), Browning (1812–89), Tennyson (1809–92), and a Hopkins whose fame still lay ahead of him (1844–89). Morris (1834–96) was still on the scene, but had turned his back on the kind of poetry that had earned him his reputation as a poet; Swinburne (1837–1909) continued to publish voluminously, but Yeats saw his work as having turned into a pale imitation of the pyrotechnics of his youth. Housman's (1859–1936) *A Shropshire Lad* (1896) had not yet been published; Hardy (1840–1928) had been writing poetry since the sixties, but was not to collect his work until 1898's *Wessex Poems and Other Verses*. Among writers who were more his contemporaries, Yeats faced competition on a number of fronts, most notably from the members of the Rhymers' Club and from the man whose *Departmental Ditties* and *Barrack–Room Ballads*, reissued by London presses in (respectively) 1886 and 1892, had brought him an immediate popularity on all levels of English society; but Yeats would prove a better poet than any of the rest of the Rhymers, and he knew he would, and a poetry as quickly successful as that of Kipling (1865–1936), he correctly felt, was not a poetry that could earn its author a lasting place in the true processional order.

It was thus that Yeats could stake a claim to a place in the first rank of the living poets writing in English on the basis of two volumes of poetry and a third book that revised and brought into one volume selected poems from the first two. By the mid-nineties, he was in evidence not only on the ambitions and strengths of his own work, but because the most prominent poets of the Victorian period had all but faded from the scene and had not been replaced by names of a like prominence. With the times ripe for a new voice, the publication of his collected *Poems* by a major house was approaching the status of an event. Yeats prepared for it by spending more than three hard months rewriting "almost every thing from the 'Oisin' book & large quantities of the play of 'The Countess Kathleen'" (*CL1* 451); and he was not about to let what he had come to regard as this "new" book of his (*CL1* 458) be marred by the inclusion of fairy verses he had considered "trivial" as many as eight years before. The greater members of the sidhe tribe would have their parts to play in works he would write much further down the line, but not so the little folk. Yeats was entering the fourth decade of a full life. It was time to put away the things of his youth.

IV

The central emblems of transcendence in *The Wanderings of Oisin and Other Poems* are the realms of the sidhe, supernal states that *The Countess Kathleen and Various Legends and Lyrics* had for the most part relocated in the symbol of the Rose. By the time the nineties had drawn to a conclusion, the Rose had been superseded in its turn; and it is with the relegation of that symbol to a lesser place in his poetry that the first full decade of Yeats's career also comes to its close.

Though it would be a while yet before the image faded out of his prose,[10] Yeats had ceased to locate the Rose at the center of his verse by the mid-nineties. Only eight of the thirty-seven lyrics that comprised 1899's *The Wind Among the Reeds* made use of the emblem in any way whatever; and in five of these eight it was an image among other images, another stitch in the embroidery. Of the three lyrics that drew on the symbol in its transcendent aspects, one had first seen print in 1892, Yeats's year of the Rose; the other two had been published in late 1896 and early 1897,[11] and from that point through the end of his life Yeats's uses of his rare bloom in his lyrics were to be both infrequent and sporadic. The coming and going of images in a poet's work is no strange occurrence; but in a poet whose basic themes remained constant from the start of his career to the finish, the question of which images fell by the wayside is perforce of less interest than the question of what images evolved to take their place. When Yeats ceased his heavy reliance on the Rose, he could do so largely because he had been unwinding the skein of a concept that could aptly fill the vacancy.

The last real flowering of *The Rose* came when Yeats used those words as the heading for the first of the two groupings of lyrics in the *Poems* of 1895 (cf. the Appendix, p. 234); and it was immediately before *Poems* appeared that Yeats published his most comprehensive summary of his concept of the Moods.[12] Different readers have traced the source of this theory to similar springs: to Yeats's collaboration with Edwin Ellis on the Blake volumes, to Blake himself, or else to Yeats's readings in Boehme and Swedenborg and to the poet's own visions.[13] And when one is dealing with so eclectic a thinker, it would be unwise to dismiss any of his known sources out of hand. Certainly, for instance, the central works produced by the occult revival had a major part to play here. Yeats's first direct poetic statement about "The Moods" came with the lyric that went by that title. First published in August 1893, the poem finds a direct gloss in passages that had appeared in Hartmann's *Magic, White and Black* and Blavatsky's *The Secret Doctrine* (Vol. III). It was Hartmann who spoke of a benign immortal troop of "self-existent" and "eternal" principles that are "not subject to change":

> Truth, wisdom, justice, beauty, goodness, etc., cannot be changed; it is merely the forms in which they become manifest that can be destroyed. If all the wise men in the world were to die in one moment, the principle of Wisdom would nevertheless exist, and manifest itself in due time in other receptive forms; if Love were to leave the hearts of all human beings, it would thereby not be annihilated, it would merely cease to exist relatively to men, and men would cease to live while love would continue *to be*. Eternal principles are self-existent, and therefore independent of forms, and not subject to change (*MWB*, p. 177).

It was Blavatsky who spoke of a less exalted world than that described by Hartmann, the world of "sentient existence" that in due time would find itself "extinguished... like the flame of a candle burnt out" (p. 400). And it was "The Moods", as it appeared in 1893, that spoke of immortal and changing worlds both:

> Time drops in decay
> Like a candle burnt out;
> The mountains and woods
> Have their day, have their day;
> But, kindly old rout
> Of the fire-born moods,
> You pass not away.

Thus the concept in its general outlines; and Yeats's occult sources had their contributions to make to the particulars of his theory as well. Hartmann, for instance, asked "Whence do the emotions come?" and, having posed the rhetorical question, began his answer with the observation that

> the cosmologies of the ancients express under various allegories the same fundamental truth; that "in the beginning" the *Great First Cause* evolved out of itself, by the power of its own will, certain powers, whose action and reaction brought the elementary forces that constituted the world into existence (*MWB*, pp. 215–16).

These "elementary forces", as Hartmann goes on to argue, are those same universal "emotions" about whose origins he had been inquiring; and, he adds, "they are the active agents of the cosmos" (p. 216). Writing in 1895, Yeats said the same: this when he contended that it was the task of the poet "to bring us into communion with the moods and passions which are the creative powers behind the universe" (*UP1* 380). But which particular "cosmologies of the ancients" had Hartmann had in mind? Any number, according to *Magic, White and Black*:

> These elementary forces are the Devas of the East, the Elohims of the Bible, the Afrites of the Persians, the Titans of the Romans, the Eggregores of the book of Enoch (*MWB*, p. 216).

In his essay on "The Philosophy of Shelley's Poetry" (1900), Yeats granted Hartmann's high claims for "the Devas of the East"; but since he had the axes of Rosicrucianism and Ireland to grind in the bargain, he found his other examples of elementary forces in spirits with whom he was more directly acquainted. In the Shelley piece, his Moods emerge as "ministering spirits who correspond to the Devas of the East, and the Elemental Spirits of mediæval Europe, and the Sidhe of ancient Ireland" (*E&I* 74).[14] The same essay finds Yeats wondering whether Shelley somehow managed to have intuited the theory of the Astral Light, to have

> lit on that memory of Nature the visionaries claim for the foundation of their knowledge; but I do not know whether he thought, as they do, that all things good and evil remain [therein] for ever, "thinking the thought and doing the deed," though not, it may be, self-conscious (*E&I* 74).

And in this case too his language echoes that of Hartmann, who in *Magic, White and Black* had written that, while the spirits he was describing could be either "beneficial or detrimental", they were in any case "not self-conscious rational entities" (p. 216). Finally, there remained the question of how these "Moods" and "ministering spirits" of Yeats, the "emotions" and "elementary forces" of Hartmann, made themselves manifest in the world of man. Hartmann noted that the universal emotions were not themselves "individuals", but that they "may become individualized by finding expression in individual forms" (p. 216); and Yeats, in his 1900 essay on "The Symbolism of Poetry", agreed that "an emotion does not exist, or does not become perceptible and active among us, till it has found its expression" (*E&I* 157). By way of making its point more concretely, *Magic, White and Black* observed that "love and hate, envy and benevolence, lust and greed are not persons, but their shadows may become personified in human... forms", and that it was a man's own bent towards good or evil that determined which of the elementary forms would take up its residence in his soul (p. 216). Yeats too saw the Moods as disembodied, and saw man as their summoner, whether inadvertently or, in the case of the artist or seer, consciously; it was within the power of the poet, he argued, to "call down among us certain disembodied powers, whose footsteps over our hearts we call emotions", and "the more perfect" the art, "the more powerful will be the emotion, the power, the god it calls among us" (*E&I* 157).

However close and numerous these correspondences between Yeats's thought and theosophical theory, the most helpful background on the Moods to be found in Yeats's early known sources appeared in *The Life of Philippus Theophrastus Bombast of Hohenheim* (1887), which from the time it was published was better known as *Paracelsus*. This compendium of and commentary on the writings of Paracelsus was the work of the energetic Hartmann; and as his direct borrowings from the book for his own *Fairy and Folk Tales of the Irish Peasantry* indicate, Yeats first read it sometime between 1887 and the publication of his folklore anthology in 1888.[15] These were the years when his concept of the Moods was in its formative stages,[16] and *Paracelsus* joined with Boehme and Blake and Swedenborg in having instructive models to offer. Early in the volume, for instance, Hartmann defines the Paracelsian concept of the *astra* as

> states of mind, either in the mind of man or in the universal mind. Each mental state in the mind of man corresponds to a similar condition in the mental atmosphere of the world, and as the mind of man acts upon the universal mind, so that mental atmosphere reacts upon him (p. 32).

And later in the book Yeats would find the same concept elaborated by Paracelsus himself:

> Fear, terror, passion, desire, joy, and envy are six states of the mind which especially rule the imagination, and consequently the world of man; and as the mind of man is the microcosmic counterpart of the universal mind, the antitypes of these states are also active in the imagination of the world, and the thoughts of man act upon the latter as the latter acts upon him (p. 140).

What Paracelsus had done here was to take the fundamental hermetic axiom – as above, so below – and rework it in a way that would allow it to be restated: as the Mind of the Universe, so the mind of man. In years to come, this provocative reformulation was to provide Western occultism with a foundation on which to raise the doctrine of the Astral Light, the macrocosmic aura with which – magic having come to think of Mind and mind as correlatives – the practical magician could establish contact at will. It is worth noting here that, when the Yeats of the essay on "Magic" (1901) recalled his introduction to the theory of the Astral Light, he remembered first of all having "read of it in *Paracelsus*" (*E&I* 46), if only because it is a short step from this comment to the hazard that *Paracelsus* might have its light to shed on other areas of the poet's thought as well, most notably on his concept of the Moods.

However intricate the vocabulary that surrounds it, the concept of the Moods prescinds, first from a simple fact, and then from a basic assumption:

that men and women are possessed of emotions, and that one should be able to trace their source. The explanation put forth in *Paracelsus* was that man's more typical feelings – passion, for instance, or joy – had their origins in cosmic antitypes, and that these were located in the universal mind, what the above passage from *Paracelsus* called "the imagination of the world". This is neither more nor less than the theory of the Moods in basic outline – the Moods reside in "the divine imagination", Yeats wrote in 1898 (*E&I* 194) – and *Paracelsus* had also furnished its readers with a model of the mechanism through which man and the Moods came in touch, with "the mind of man act[ing] upon the universal mind" and "that mental atmosphere react[ing] upon him" (p. 32). Thus Yeats as well, when in 1896 he pictured the moment of contact between the human and divine imaginations as a calling forth by man and an answering from the Astral Light: "If you imagine... the semblance of a living being, it is at once possessed by a wandering soul", he wrote, and the "bodiless souls who descended into these forms were what men called the moods" (*VSR* 142, 143).[17]

These "emotions whose beauty has made them eternal",[18] then, had their most immediate source in those same occult studies that furnish the clearest explanation of what Yeats meant by the Moods in the first place. And once clarified, the notion can only be seen as holding a central place in the poet's developing thought. If every human emotion had a divine counterpart, as the doctrine implied, then the artist who wrote of (say) "sexual passion" was also on his way to discoveries about the nature of "divine love" (*E&I* 195); and though his terminology was to change, from the time this central idea struck home Yeats never ceased to make "mortal desires" his vehicles towards revelations about the "immortal moods" (*E&I* 195). But the theory looked back towards his early career as well as ahead to his later, since between the early and mid nineties the Moods had gradually been subsuming the functions that Yeats had once ascribed to the Rose. Both were divine principles, and both permitted man a means of access to divinity; both, moreover, had had a part to play in the shapings of nations, and of Ireland in particular. Like many another occultist, Yeats held that a nation or race came into being largely through the guidance of its tutelary spirit, what Theosophy called its "Watcher" or "Guardian" and what Yeats called its "genius".[19] In 1892 it had been the Rose that had made Ireland's heart begin to beat (*VP* 138); but by 1895 Yeats was referring to "those Immortal Moods which are the true builders of nations" (*UP1* 361) or again to "the builders of peoples, the imperishable moods" (*UP1* 373). The Rose had been a source of inspiration to Irish writers of all ages, or so Yeats had insisted on arguing; but by 1895 he was insisting just as directly that the new literary movement in Ireland had grown out of "the same dominant mood" that had inspired poets such as Ferguson (*UP1* 348), and that the poetry of Allingham had been an expression of "the Immortal Moods, which are so impatient of rhetoric, so patient of mere immaturity" (*UP1* 363), and that the works of Standish O'Grady were "in communion with the moods that have been over Irish purposes" from the start (*UP1* 367).

In brief, then, the Rose faded out of Yeats's verse largely because he was able to let it go; he had found a concept ready to take its place. But what is being traced in these shifts is, not a break in the poet's thought, but a development. Divine in its substance and a conduit towards divinity, a builder of Ireland and inspirer of its artists, the Rose was in a sense the first and, by the poet, most favored of the Moods. Steady conceptual evolutions like this one are perhaps the most characteristic feature of Yeats's work, a body of writing that changed much less than it grew. In 1916 Yeats wrote to Joseph Hone that the house of his thought was "still unfinished", the reason for this being that "there are so many rooms and corridors that I am still building upon foundations laid long ago" (*Let* 605). Remarks like these correctly suggest that the primary source of late Yeats was early Yeats. In 1933, for instance, he observed that he "had in later life worked out with the excitement of discovery" things he had "known in [his] youth" (*LNI* vii). So he had, and not simply in this work or that but in the very centers of his thought. Three weeks before his death in 1939, he told Elizabeth Pelham that he was about to "begin to write my most fundamental thoughts". Seventy-three years: all that labor, all that he had done at his own charge. Knowing "for certain that my time will not be long", he needed a sentence to sum it all up. "It seems to me that I have found what I wanted", he wrote, "when I try to put all into a phrase I say, 'Man can embody truth but he cannot know it'" (*Let* 922). If this were indeed the key, had he some stray intimation as he wrote that the key had been his from very near the start? It was over a half-century earlier that the young student of occultism had learned that "we should not seek to possess the truth, but to let it become manifested in us", and that

> we should be able to feel the truth with our souls, without reasoning about it from an objective standpoint. We should realise the truth by being one with it, and not examine it as if it were something strange and separate from ourselves.[20]

It had all been there as long ago as the eighties: fundamental thoughts to be remembered, if not consciously, then in what the Yeats of the turn of the century called "that unconscious and instinctive memory on which imagination builds" (*UP2* 204). And the man whose final pronouncement was that man can embody truth but not know it was once again working out, with the excitement of discovery, things he had known in his youth, putting the final touches to a house with weathered foundations.

Notes to Chapter 6

1 Yeats made the remark in praise of a passage that appeared in Hyde's *Beside the Fire* (*UP1* 189).
2 From the time his early interest in vivid description of "outward things" had passed, Yeats was constantly to distinguish between the limited results of "observation" and the richer issue of "experience". For illustrations of how sharply he was willing to draw the distinction, cf. *CL1* 442 and *Ex* 160, 196, 428. The earliest of these examples comes from a

piece Yeats wrote in early 1895, the latest from 1938's "To-morrow's Revolution".

3   Descriptions of the natural world as illusory appear throughout Yeats's occult sources. The most emphatic statements on the matter may be found in *Isis Unveiled*, Vol. II, pp. 157–8; *The Secret Doctrine*, Vol. II, p. 280, and Vol. III, pp. 193 n., 404; *The Virgin of the World*, p. 82; and *Paracelsus*, p. 133.

4   Blake's reference to the "vegetable glass of nature" came in a passage that Yeats's 1893 edition of *The Poems of William Blake* grouped among Blake's "Prose Fragments"; in the more easily accessible reprint of that volume (New York: The Modern Library, n.d.), the passage appears on p. 251. Yeats's references to the passage were frequent; for a case in which he cites it in its entirety, cf. 1898's "Symbolism in Painting" (*E&I* 151).

The passage in which Blake spoke of the world of "imagination" as "the real and eternal world of which this vegetable universe is but a faint shadow" was another Yeatsian touchstone. The passage was originally part of the introduction to the fourth chapter of Blake's *Jerusalem*; Yeats included it in *The Poems of William Blake*, pp. 226–7, and cited it at great length in the second of his three 1896 articles on "William Blake and his Illustrations to *The Divine Comedy*". Originally published in *The Savoy* for August 1896, the article containing the Blake citation now appears in *E&I* under the date 1897; the passage about the "vegetable universe" may be found therein on pp. 135–7.

5   In his 1899 note on the poem Yeats observed that he had "follow[ed] much Irish and other mythology, and the magical tradition, in associating the North with night and sleep, and the East, the place of sunrise, with hope, and the South, the place of the sun when at its height, with passion and desire, and the West, the place of sunset, with fading and dreaming things" (*VP* 808).

Symbolic treatments of the four principal points were standard practice in both the Theosophical Society and the Golden Dawn, and a reading of "He bids his Beloved be at Peace" might well begin with a comparison of the poem's description of the cardinal points to the description offered in *The Secret Doctrine* (Vol. III). Herein North is specifically associated with "Winter, Night, Age, Earth", East with "Spring, Morning, Youth, Fire", West with "Autumn, Evening, Manhood, Water", and South with "Summer, Noon, Adolescence, Air" (p. 464). The equivalent formulation in the Golden Dawn comes still closer to the view Yeats proposed in his poem. The Order would have agreed with *The Secret Doctrine*'s association of North with the element of earth, and West with the element of water; but it referred air to the East, and fire to the South, and thereby served as a direct source of the poet's vision of a southern sky filled with "roses of crimson fire". Cf. *The Golden Dawn*, Vol. I, pp. 158–9; Vol. II, pp. 248–9; Vol. III, p. 14; Vol. IV, p. 324.

6   The description of natural forms as "symbols of ideas" may be found in *Magic, White and Black*, p. 271; the reference to nature as a vehicle towards the discovery of "eternal truths" is in *The Secret Doctrine*, Vol. III, p. 261. Views like these were widespread in Yeats's sources. The 1881 edition of *The Occult World*, for instance, spoke of the need "to penetrate behind the veil of matter into the world of primal causes" (p. 102), while *The Migration of Symbols*, with its description of the ancient belief that "the principal phenomena of nature" were nothing more than the outward expressions of the "*numina*" lying behind them (p. 75), catches the intent of "He bids his Beloved be at Peace" to perfection.

Yeats's views on symbolism deepened and shifted throughout the nineties and the early years of this century; Robert O'Driscoll gives a concise summary of their evolution in his monograph *Symbolism and Some Implications of the Symbolic Approach: W. B. Yeats During the Eighteen-Nineties* (1975). O'Driscoll rightly notes that "it seems clear now that [Yeats] found in *symboliste* theory and practice only the corroboration for discoveries he had already made in his study of Blake and the occult" (p. 9), but adds that his essay is not a study in these or other influences (p. 5). For further analysis of the bearing of the doctrine of correspondences on Yeats's theory of symbolism, cf. D. S. Lenoski's "The Symbolism of the Early Yeats: Occult and Religious Backgrounds", in the Yeats issue of *Literary Imagination* (1981), pp. 85–100.

7   As Jeffares has noted, the "small old house" with its garden was no poet's invention; Yeats was thinking of Riversdale in Rathfarnham, his last residence in Ireland. Cf. the *New Commentary on the Poems*, pp. 376, 379.

8   "Those Who Live in the Storm" later appeared in 1897's *The Secret Rose* under the title "The Rose of Shadow". Yeats did not reprint it thereafter. The definitive version of the story is in *VSR* 227–31.

9   Most directly in poems like those now titled "The Travail of Passion" and "The Lover speaks to the Hearers of his Songs in Coming Days". Both these lyrics were published during Yeats's affair with Olivia Shakespear; the adulterous lovers in the former poem are imaged as having to endure the scorn of men, those in the latter as having been banished from heaven. *The Speckled Bird* opens a revealing window onto what Yeats had in mind when he cast his strayed lovers as martyrs, most directly in the passage in which Michael tries to persuade Margaret to leave her husband and "come away" with him: "he knew, he said", that

> it would bring much disgrace upon both her and him, but that was the martyrdom of love. It would be just that martyrdom that would be their glory, and then, the philosophical habit being deep in him, he began to explain how it was right for lovers who broke the social law to suffer their martyrdom gladly and in silence. It was the penalty, the price that they paid for their freedom and for their happiness (pp. 88–9).

Michael goes on to argue that "true lovers were united by their payment to Iseult and to Brünnhilde and to all the saints of passion" (p. 89), a claim that has its echo in both the religious imagery of "The Travail of Passion" and the implied comparison of the lovers in "The Lover speaks to the Hearers of his Songs in Coming Days" to Paolo and Francesca.

10 So Phillip L. Marcus has rightly noted in his *Yeats and the Beginning of the Irish Renaissance*, pp. 48–9.

11 The five lyrics that put the image to incidental use were 1892's "The Lover tells of the Rose in his Heart", 1895's "The Lover asks Forgiveness because of his Many Moods", and 1896's "The Travail of Passion", "He bids his Beloved be at Peace", and "He remembers forgotten Beauty"; the last four of these are poems written with Olivia Shakespear in mind. Of the three poems in which the Rose figures more centrally, "The Poet pleads with the Elemental Powers" was first published in October 1892, "The Secret Rose" in September 1896, and "The Blessed" in April 1897.

12 *Poems* was published in October 1895; Yeats's explication of the Moods appeared in *The Bookman* for August in the same year, as the opening paragraph of the second of Yeats's four essays on "Irish National Literature" (*UP1* 367). Yeats later abstracted the paragraph from the article, titled it "The Moods", and published it as a self-contained piece in 1903's *Ideas of Good*

  and Evil. The paragraph-turned-essay, still dated 1895, is now most readily available in *E&I* 195.

13 Cf. Allen R. Grossman, *Poetic Knowledge in the Early Yeats*, pp. 68–9 and 222 n., and John P. Frayne, *UP1* 366–7.

14 Yeats had been trying to trace a connection between the Moods and the sidhe from early in his career. In his October 1892 article on "Invoking the Irish Fairies", for instance, he wrote that "the fairies are the lesser spiritual moods of that universal mind, wherein every mood is a soul and every thought a body" (*UP1* 247). A year later he was to describe the inconclusive results of one such invocation in the short essay titled "Regina, Regina Pigmeorum, Veni"; herein he describes himself as having asked a queen of the sidhe "whether she and her people were not 'dramatizations of our moods'" (*CT* 70).

  "Regina, Regina Pigmeorum, Veni" is an unusual essay with an unusual title. Yeats hints at the source of the title towards the end of the piece, when he writes that "it were perhaps well for us all if we would but raise the cry Lilly the astrologer raised in Windsor Forest, 'Regina, Regina Pigmeorum, Veni,' and remember with him, that God visteth His children in dreams" (*CT* 70). "Lilly the astrologer" is William Lilly (1602–81), in his day as infamous for his practice of magic as for his political contriving; and the incident Yeats was recalling in *CT* may be found in Lilly's memoirs, though what Yeats was recalling was very different from what Lilly wrote. For one thing, the poet took two entirely separate tales from *William Lilly's History of His Life and Times* and ran them into one; the first of these accounts (p. 229) described "regina pigmeorum veni" [*sic*] as an effective phrase for the calling up of spirits, while the second (pp. 230–1) recounted an act of invocation that had taken place in a forest. For another thing, Yeats got most of his facts skewed. The cry addressed to the queen of the fairies was raised, not by Lilly, but by his friend Ellen Evans (p. 229); and the incident that Yeats locates in Windsor Forest took place in Hurst Wood, and involved neither Lilly nor Evans, but two unnamed acquaintances of the astrologer (pp. 230–1).

  Though the title of Yeats's essay has a literary antecedent, the essay itself grew out of his personal experience; see the late 1892 letter in which he speaks of how he had joined his "uncle" and "cousin" at a "noted" fairy locality, and of their "triumphantly successful" invocation of the sidhe who resided there (*CL1* 323). Yeats's personal copy of W. Y. Evans Wentz's *The Fairy-Faith in Celtic Countries* (1911) serves to identify the uncle and cousin as George Pollexfen and the second-sighted Lucy Middleton. Now in Dalkey, this volume was dedicated to Yeats and AE and personally inscribed "With the author's best wishes to his friend and helper, William Butler Yeats, Esq. Oxford, Nov. 24, 1911". Herein Yeats read that the sidhe "can be seen and their wonderful music heard" on "the strand at Lower Rosses Point" (p. 58); and he underlined *music heard*, and wrote in the margin: "Yes I have heard it – like cathedral bells. LM GP & I heard it." The hearing of the music like cathedral bells is clearly coincident with the experience Yeats recounted in "Regina, Regina Pigmeorum, Veni", the experience he shared with his uncle ("GP") and cousin ("LM"); and Yeats himself was no doubt the source of the claim in *The Fairy-Faith in Celtic Countries* that the music of the sidhe may be heard in Sligo's "Lower Rosses Point". For further details on Yeats's management of his materials in the first editions of *CT*, see my "Hour of Dawn: The Unity of Yeats's *The Celtic Twilight* (1893, 1902)", *IUR*, vol. 13, no. 2 (Autumn 1983), pp. 189–205.

15 Perhaps because of Virginia Moore's doubt that Yeats "ever did more than ruffle the pages" of *Paracelsus* (*The Unicorn*, p. 99), Hartmann's book has been paid

scant heed in studies of the early work. Yet Yeats knew *Paracelsus* intimately enough to be able to borrow from it liberally for the notes to *FFT*. For examples of his indebtedness, see "Armchair Folklore: Yeats and the Textual Sources of *Fairy and Folk Tales of the Irish Peasantry*", *Proceedings of the Royal Irish Academy*, Vol. 83c (1983), pp. 263–4 and 264 n. My thanks to Allen G. Debus for confirming my guess that, when Hartmann's work reached the bookshelves in 1887, it represented the first extended treatment of Paracelsus to appear in English since the seventeenth century.

16 Grossman was perhaps the first reader to note that the concept of the Moods begins to emerge in Yeats's writings as early as November 1886. Cf. *Poetic Knowledge in the Early Yeats*, p. 71; and for the relevant passages from Yeats, see the second of his two early articles on "The Poetry of Sir Samuel Ferguson". It is towards the end of this long essay that Yeats first speaks of his belief in the existence of "universal emotions" (*UP1* 101), and of the "noble sorrows" and "noble joys" that form the central subject matter of those "great legends" that "are the mothers of nations" (p. 104).

17 The source of these sentences is "Rosa Alchemica", which first appeared in *The Savoy* for April 1896 and was afterwards reprinted in 1897's *The Secret Rose*. With the exception of a single change in punctuation, the versions of these sentences that appeared in *The Secret Rose* are identical with those that appear on pp. 142 and 143 of the more widely available *VSR*.

18 At once an indirect reference to and concise restatement of the concept of the Moods, this phrase forms part of a letter that Michael sends to Margaret in the 1900 draft of *The Speckled Bird* (p. 204).

19 The August 1895 article on "Irish National Literature" refers to those "'angels of God'" whose charge it had been to "'set the borders of the Nations'" (*UP1* 367–8). The essay on "The Irish Literary Theatre, 1900", published in January of that year, went on to describe "these angels" as being "each one the genius of some race about to be unfolded" (*UP2* 198–9). Yeats reprinted the passage containing the latter reference as part of his essay on "The Theatre" in 1903's *Ideas of Good and Evil*; the passage is now available, under the date February 1900, in *E&I* 171–2. Yeats's identification of "these angels" with tutelary genii may be found on p. 171.

Like many another Yeatsian hypothesis, the idea that every race and nation had its presiding genius may be traced back directly to the poet's occult sources. Theosophy's reference to the "Watcher" or "Guardian" came in Vol. I of *The Secret Doctrine*, wherein Blavatsky argued that "each people and nation... has its *direct* Watcher, Guardian and Father in Heaven – a Planetary Spirit" (p. 630). Reference to these spirits was frequent in Yeats's readings; for a representative sampling, see Blavatsky's commentary on the planetary "Beings" (*TSD* I, p. 632) known as "Dhyân Chohans" (*TSD* I, pp. 634 n., 654 n., 658, 661, 690, 694, 703 n.). Yeats's comparisons of his genii to angels also had its theosophical antecedents; cf. Blavatsky's remarks on the "Dhyân Chohans or Angels" (*TSD* I, p. 295) or her observation that these "'Watchers'" may be equated with "'the Angels of the Stars of the Christians" (*TSD* II, p. 374).

20 Cf. Hartmann, *Paracelsus*, pp. 131, 140 n.

Appendix

Yeats's constant remaking of his poetry has left us with a volume of collected poems that gives a deceptive impression of what his early career was like. The history of *The Wanderings of Oisin and Other Poems* (1889), *The Countess Kathleen and Various Legends and Lyrics* (1892), and *Poems* (1895) is a history of poems revised, poems deleted, and titles altered. In the tables of contents below, an italicized title belongs to a poem that Yeats abandoned after its appearance in 1889 or 1892. The number assigned each poem upon its first appearance remains the same thereafter, though the title of the poem itself may change: thus "An Old Song Re-sung", no. 26 below, retains that number when it re-emerges as "Down by the Salley Gardens" in *Poems* (1895).

Though Yeats was later to revise many of the individual works therein, the *Poems* of 1895 moved basically unscathed into *W. B. Yeats: The Poems* (1984). *The Countess Cathleen* and *The Land of Heart's Desire* now appear in the *Collected Plays*. The section called "Crossways" appears first in the collected works, "The Rose" second. "Usheen" has become "Oisin" again; and the poem itself now appears towards the end of the collected poems, in the section reserved for works narrative and dramatic. The remaining changes (other than revisions of individual texts) are minor. "The Death of Cuhoolin" (no. 37 below) is now called "Cuchulain's Fight with the Sea". "A Dream of a Blessed Spirit" (no. 32) is now "The Countess Cathleen in Paradise". "To Some I have Talked with by the Fire" (no. 56) now finds its place immediately before "To Ireland in the Coming Times". "Who goes with Fergus?, in 1895 a song in Scene Two of *The Countess Cathleen*, now appears as a lyric poem immediately before "The Man who dreamed of Faeryland". Except for a few changes in capitalization, all other titles were left unaltered, as was the order of the poems themselves.

*The Wanderings of Oisin
and Other Poems* (1889)

1 The Wanderings of Oisin
2 *Time and the Witch Vivien*
3 The Stolen Child
4 *Girl's Song*
5 Ephemera
6 An Indian Song
7 Kanva, the Indian, on God
8 *Kanva on himself*
9 Jealousy
10 Song of the Last Arcadian
11 King Goll
12 The Meditation of the Old Fisherman
13 The Ballad of Moll Magee
14 *The Phantom Ship*
15 A Lover's Quarrel among the Fairies
16 Mosada
17 *How Ferencz Renyi kept Silent*
18 The Fairy Doctor
19 Falling of the Leaves
20 Miserrimus
21 The Priest and the Fairy
22 *The Fairy Pedant*
23 *She who dwelt among the Sycamores*
24 *On Mr. Nettleship's Picture at the Royal Hibernian Academy, 1885*
25 *A Legend*
26 An Old Song Re-sung
27 Street Dancers
28 To an Isle in the Water
29 *Quatrains and Aphorisms*
30 *The Seeker*
31 Island of Statues[1]

Poems
(1895)

56 To Some I have Talked with by the Fire[2]
1 The Wanderings of Usheen
32 The Countess Cathleen
57 The Land of Heart's Desire

The Rose[3]

33 To the Rose upon the Rood of Time
34 Fergus and the Druid
37 The Death of Cuhoolin
35 The Rose of the World
36 The Rose of Peace
53 The Rose of Battle
44 A Faery Song
46 The Lake Isle of Innisfree
47 A Cradle Song
45 The Pity of Love
42 The Sorrow of Love
41 When You are Old
38 The White Birds
54 A Dream of Death
32 A Dream of a Blessed Spirit[4]
48 The Man Who Dreamed of Faeryland
49 The Dedication to a Book of Stories Selected from the Irish Novelists
50 The Lamentation of the Old Pensioner
39 The Ballad of Father Gilligan
52 The Two Trees
55 To Ireland in the Coming Times

Appendix

The Countess Kathleen and Various
Legends and Lyrics (1892)

32 The Countess Kathleen
33 To the Rose upon the Rood of Time
34 Fergus and the Druid
35 The Rose of the World
36 The Peace of the Rose
37 The Death of Cuchullin
38 The White Birds
39 Father Gilligan
40 Father O'Hart
41 When You are Old
42 The Sorrow of Love
43 The Ballad of the Old Foxhunter
44 A Fairy Song
45 The Pity of Love
46 The Lake Isle of Innisfree
47 A Cradle Song
48 The Man who dreamed of Fairy Land
49 Dedication of Irish Tales
50 The Lamentation of the Old Pensioner
51 *When You are Sad*
52 The Two Trees
53 They went forth to the Battle, but they always Fell
54 An Epitaph
55 Apologia Addressed to Ireland in the Coming Days

Crossways[3]

10 The Song of the Happy Shepherd
20 The Sad Shepherd
31 The Cloak, the Boat, and the Shoes
9   Anashuya and Vijaya
7   The Indian upon God
6   The Indian to his Love
19 The Falling of the Leaves
5   Ephemera
11 The Madness of King Goll
3   The Stolen Child
28 To an Isle in the Water
26 Down by the Salley Gardens
12 The Meditation of the Old Fisherman
40 The Ballad of Father O'Hart[5]
13 The Ballad of Moll Magee
43 The Ballad of the Foxhunter

235

Notes

1. The entire play appeared in four numbers of the *Dublin University Review*, April–July 1885. *The Wanderings of Oisin and Other Poems* included only Act 2, Scene 3, the final scene of the play. Thereafter Yeats reprinted only the first fifteen lines of the scene; they became the lyric "The Cloak, the Boat, and the Shoes" in *Poems* (1895).
2. This dedicatory poem, not listed in the original table of contents, and *The Land of Heart's Desire* were the only new additions to the volume.
3. "The Rose" was and is the section heading for the lyric poems that Yeats retained from *The Countess Kathleen and Various Legends and Lyrics*, "Crossways" the heading for the lyrics retained from *The Wanderings of Oisin and Other Poems*.
4. Here an independent lyric, these stanzas had originally appeared in Scene Six of *The Countess Kathleen* in 1892.
5. Yeats moved both this poem and "The Ballad of the Foxhunter" into the "Crossways" section despite their original appearance among the lyric poems of *The Countess Kathleen and Various Legends and Lyrics*.

Selected Bibliography

A Works by Yeats

Autobiographies (London: Macmillan and Co. Ltd, 1955).
The Celtic Twilight. Men and Women, Dhouls and Fairies (London: Lawrence and Bullen, 1893).
The Celtic Twilight (London: A. H. Bullen, 1902).
The Celtic Twilight (New York: New American Library, 1962).
The Collected Letters of W. B. Yeats, Vol. I, eds John Kelly and Eric Domville (Oxford: Clarendon Press, 1986).
The Collected Plays of W. B. Yeats (London: Macmillan, 1960).
A Critical Edition of Yeats's A Vision (1925), eds George Mills Harper and Walter Kelly Hood (London: Macmillan, 1978).
The Countess Kathleen and Various Legends and Lyrics (London: T. Fisher Unwin, 1892).
Essays and Introductions (New York: The Macmillan Co., 1961).
Explorations (New York: The Macmillan Co., 1973).
Four Years (Churchtown, Dundrum: The Cuala Press, 1921).
Ideas of Good and Evil (London: A. H. Bullen, 1903).
"Is the Order of R.R. & A.C. to remain a Magical Order?" (London: n.p., 1901). Reprinted in George Mills Harper, *Yeats's Golden Dawn* (New York: Harper and Row, 1974).
John Sherman; and, Dhoya, ed. Richard J. Finneran (Detroit, Mich.: Wayne State University Press, 1969).
The Letters of W. B. Yeats, ed. Allan Wade (London: Rupert Hart-Davis, 1954).
Letters to the New Island, ed. Horace Reynolds (Cambridge, Mass.: Harvard University Press, 1970).
Literatim Transcription of the Manuscripts of William Butler Yeats's The Speckled Bird, ed. William H. O'Donnell (Delmar, New York: Scholars' Facsimiles and Reprints, 1976).
Memoirs, ed. Denis Donoghue (London: Macmillan, 1972).
Mythologies (New York: The Macmillan Co., 1977).
Poems (London: T. Fisher Unwin, 1895).
The Secret Rose (London: Lawrence and Bullen, 1897).
The Secret Rose: Stories by W. B. Yeats: A Variorum Edition, eds Phillip L. Marcus, Warwick Gould and Michael J. Sidnell (Ithaca, NY: Cornell University Press, 1981).
The Speckled Bird, With Variant Versions, ed. William H. O'Donnell (Toronto: McClelland and Stewart, 1976).
Uncollected Prose by W. B. Yeats, Vol. I, ed. John P. Frayne (New York: Columbia University Press, 1970).
Uncollected Prose by W. B. Yeats, Vol. II, eds John P. Frayne and Colton Johnson (London: Macmillan, 1975).
The Variorum Edition of the Plays of W. B. Yeats, ed. Russell K. Alspach assisted by Catharine C. Alspach (New York: The Macmillan Co., 1966).

The Variorum Edition of the Poems of W. B. Yeats, eds Peter Allt and Russell K. Alspach (New York: The Macmillan Co., 1966).
A Vision: An Explanation of Life Founded upon the Writings of Giraldus and upon Certain Doctrines Attributed to Kusta ben Luka (London: T. Werner Laurie, 1925).
A Vision (London: Macmillan and Co., Ltd, 1937).
A Vision: A Reissue. With the Author's Final Revisions (New York: The Macmillan Co., 1956).
The Wanderings of Oisin and Other Poems (London: Kegan Paul, Trench and Co., 1889).
W. B. Yeats: The Poems, ed. Richard J. Finneran (London: Macmillan, 1984).
The Wind Among the Reeds (London: Elkin Matthews, 1899).

B Works Edited by Yeats

A Book of Irish Verse (London: Methuen and Co., 1895).
Fairy and Folk Tales of Ireland (Gerrards Cross: Colin Smythe, 1977).
Fairy and Folk Tales of the Irish Peasantry (London: Walter Scott, 1888).
Irish Fairy Tales (London: T. Fisher Unwin, 1892).
The Poems of William Blake (London: Lawrence and Bullen, 1893).
Representative Irish Tales (New York: G. P. Putnam, 1891).
Stories from Carleton (London: Walter Scott, 1889).
Ed. with E. J. Ellis, *The Works of William Blake, Poetic, Symbolic, and Critical*. 3 vols (London: Bernard Quaritch, 1893).

C Secondary Sources

Albright, Daniel, *The Myth against Myth: A Study of Yeats's Imagination in Old Age* (London: Oxford University Press, 1972).
Allen, James Lovic, "Life as Art: Yeats and the Alchemical Quest", *Studies in the Literary Imagination*, vol. 14, no. 1 (Spring 1981), pp. 17–42.
Allen, Paul M., ed., *A Christian Rosenkreutz Anthology* (Blauvelt, NY: Rudolf Steiner Publications, 1968).
Allingham, William, *Irish Songs and Poems* (London: Reeves and Turner, 1887).
Alspach, Russell K., "Some Sources of Yeats's *The Wanderings of Oisin*", *PMLA (Publications of the Modern Language Association of America)*, vol. 57, pp. 849–66.
Alspach, Russell K., "Two Songs of Yeats's", *Modern Language Notes*, vol. 61, pp. 395–400.
Ansari, Asloob Ahmad, "Blake and the Kabbalah", in *William Blake: Essays for S. Foster Damon*, ed. Alvin H. Rosenfeld (Providence, RI: Brown University Press, 1969).
Arbois de Jubainville, Henry d', *The Irish Mythological Cycle and Celtic Mythology*, trans. Richard Irvine Best (Dublin: Hodges, Figgis and Co., 1903).
Arnold, Matthew, *On the Study of Celtic Literature* (London: Smith, Elder and Co., 1867).
Bachchans, Harbans Rai, *W. B. Yeats and Occultism* (Delhi: Motilal Banarsidass, 1965).
Ball, Patricia M., *The Central Self: A Study in Romantic and Victorian Imagination* (London: The Athlone Press, 1968).
Blavatsky, Helena Petrovna, "Genius", *Lucifer*, November 1889, pp. 227–33.
Blavatsky, Helena Petrovna, *Isis Unveiled*, 2 vols (New York: J. W. Bouton, 1877).
Blavatsky, Helena Petrovna, *The Key to Theosophy* (London: The Theosophical Publishing Society, 1890).

Selected Bibliography

Blavatsky, Helena Petrovna, *The Secret Doctrine*, Vol. I (Wheaton, Ill.: The Theosophical Press, 1946).
Blavatsky, Helena Petrovna, *The Secret Doctrine*, Vols I and II (London: The Theosophical Publishing Society, 1908).
Blavatsky, Helena Petrovna, *The Secret Doctrine*, Vol. III (London: The Theosophical Publishing Society, 1897).
Bloom, Harold, *Yeats* (New York: Oxford University Press, 1970).
Bornstein, George, *Yeats and Shelley* (Chicago: University of Chicago Press, 1970).
Bowra, C. M., *The Heritage of Symbolism* (New York: The Macmillan Co., 1943).
Bramsbäck, Birgit, *Folklore and W. B. Yeats: The Function of Folklore Elements in Three Early Plays* (Stockholm: Almqvist and Wiksell, 1984).
Bramsbäck, Birgit, "W. B. Yeats and Folklore Material", in *Hereditas: Essays and Studies presented to Séamus Ó Duilearga*, eds Bo Almqvist, Breandán Mac Aodha and Gearóid Mac Eoin (Dublin: The Folklore of Ireland Society, 1975).
Brooke, Stopford A., and T. W. Rolleston, eds, *A Treasury of Irish Poetry in the English Tongue* (New York: The Macmillan Co., 1932).
Bulwer-Lytton, *see* Lytton.
Butler, Samuel, *Hudibras*, ed. Henry Morley (London: Routledge and Sons, 1885).
Byrd, Thomas L., *The Early Poetry of W. B. Yeats: The Poetic Quest* (Port Washington, NY: Kennikat Press, 1978).
Cambrensis, Giraldus, *The Historical Works of Giraldus Cambrensis. Containing the Topography of Ireland, and the History of the Conquest of Ireland*, trans. Thomas Forester (London: H. G. Bohn, 1863).
Cardozo, Nancy, *Lucky Eyes and a High Heart: The Life of Maud Gonne* (Indianapolis and New York: The Bobbs-Merrill Co., 1978).
Carleton, William, *Tales and Sketches, Illustrating the Character, Usages, Traditions, Sports and Pastimes of the Irish Peasantry* (Dublin: James Duffy, 1845).
Carleton, William, *Traits and Stories of the Irish Peasantry*, 2 vols (Dublin: William Curry Jr. and Co., 1830).
Casey, Daniel J., and Robert E. Rhodes, eds, *Views of the Irish Peasantry 1800–1916* (Hamden, Conn.: Archon Books, 1977).
Clark, David R., "Yeats: 'Out of a People to a People'", *Malahat Review*, vol. 22 (April 1972), pp. 25–41.
Clarke, Austin, "Gaelic Ireland Rediscovered: The Early Period", in *Irish Poets in English*, ed. Seán Lucy (Cork: The Mercier Press, 1973).
Clarke, Austin, *The Celtic Twilight and the Nineties* (Dublin: The Dolmen Press, 1969).
Cook, M[abel] C[ollins], *Light on the Path* (Chicago: The Rajput Press, 1911).
Croker, T. Crofton, *Fairy Legends and Traditions of the South of Ireland* (London: John Murray, 1834). The first edition of this work was published by John Murray, 1825–8.
Croker, T. Crofton, *Fairy Legends and Traditions of the South of Ireland* (London: William Tegg, n.d.).
Croker, Crofton, trans. and ed., *The Tour of the French Traveller M. De La Boullaye le Gouz in Ireland, A.D. 1644* (London: T. and W. Boone, 1837).
Curtin, Jeremiah, *Myths and Folk-Lore of Ireland* (New York: British Book Centre, 1975). Originally published by Little, Brown and Co., Boston, 1890.
Daiches, David, "The Earlier Poems: Some Themes and Patterns", in *In Excited Reverie*, eds A. Norman Jeffares and K. G. W. Cross (New York: St Martin's Press, 1965).
Dalsimer, Adele M., "W. B. Yeats's *The Wanderings of Oisin*: Blueprint for a Renaissance", *Éire–Ireland*, vol. 11, no. 2 (Summer 1976), pp. 56–76.

Danaher, Kevin, "Folk Tradition and Literature", *Journal of Irish Literature*, vol. 1, no. 2 (May 1972), pp. 63–76.
De Quincey, Thomas, *The Collected Writings of Thomas De Quincey*, Vols. VII, XIII, ed. David Masson (Edinburgh: Adam and Charles Black, 1890).
Donoghue, Denis, ed., *The Integrity of Yeats* (Cork: The Mercier Press, 1967).
Eddins, Dwight, *Yeats: The Nineteenth Century Matrix* (Alabama: The University of Alabama Press, 1971).
Eliade, Mircea, *Occultism, Witchcraft, and Cultural Fashions* (Chicago: The University of Chicago Press, 1976).
Ellmann, Richard, *The Identity of Yeats* (London: Macmillan, 1954).
Ellmann, Richard, *Yeats: The Man and the Masks* (New York: W. W. Norton and Co., 1979).
Engelberg, Edward, "'He too was in Arcadia': Yeats and the Paradox of the Fortunate Fall", in *In Excited Reverie*, eds A. N. Jeffares and K. G. W. Cross (New York: St Martin's Press, 1965).
Engelberg, Edward, *The Vast Design: Patterns in W. B. Yeats's Aesthetic* (Toronto: University of Toronto Press, 1964).
Evans, E. Estyn, "Peasant Beliefs in Nineteenth-Century Ireland", in *Views of the Irish Peasantry 1800–1916*, eds Daniel J. Casey and Robert E. Rhodes (Hamden, Conn.: Archon Books, 1977).
Ferguson, Sir Samuel, *Congal* (Dublin: Edward Ponsonby, 1872).
Ferguson, Sir Samuel, *Lays of the Western Gael, and Other Poems* (Dublin: Sealy, Bryers and Walker, 1888).
Finneran, Richard J., ed., *Anglo-Irish Literature: A Review of Research* (New York: The Modern Language Association of America, 1976).
Finneran, Richard J., ed., *Recent Research on Anglo-Irish Writers* (New York: The Modern Language Association of America, 1983).
Finneran, Richard J., George Mills Harper and William M. Murphy, eds, *Letters to W. B. Yeats*, 2 vols (New York: Columbia University Press, 1977).
Flanagan, Thomas, "Yeats, Joyce, and the Matter of Ireland", *Critical Inquiry*, vol. 2, no. 1 (Autumn 1975), pp. 43–67.
Flannery, M. C., *Yeats and Magic: The Earlier Works* (Gerrards Cross: Colin Smythe, 1977).
Fraser, G. S., "Yeats and the Ballad Style", *Shenandoah*, vol. 21, no. 3 (Spring 1970), pp. 177–94.
Ginsburg, Christian D., *The Kabbalah* (Prague: Hebrew Publishing Company, n.d. but 1865?).
Goblet d'Alviella, Eugène Félicien Albert, *The Migration of Symbols* (Westminster: Archibald Constable and Co., 1894).
Godwin, William, *St. Leon: A Tale of the Sixteenth Century* (London: Henry Colburn and Richard Bentley, 1832). Originally published by G. G. and J. Robinson, London, 1799.
Gogarty, Oliver St John, *William Butler Yeats: A Memoir* (Dublin: The Dolmen Press, 1963).
Goldsmith, Oliver, *Collected Works of Oliver Goldsmith*, Vol. IV, ed. Arthur Friedman (London: Oxford University Press, 1966).
Gonne, Maud, *A Servant of the Queen: Her Own Story* (Dublin: Golden Eagle Books, 1950).
Gregory, Lady Isabella Augusta, *Cuchulain of Muirthemne* (London: J. Murray, 1902).
Gregory, Lady Isabella Augusta, *Visions and Beliefs in the West of Ireland* (London: G. P. Putnam's Sons, 1920).

Selected Bibliography

Griffin, Gerald, *The Poetical Works of Gerald Griffin* (London: Simms and M'Intyre, 1851).
Griffin, Gerald, *Talis Qualis; or, Tales of the Jury Room* (Dublin: James Duffy, 1874).
Grossman, Allen R., *Poetic Knowledge in the Early Yeats* (Charlottesville, Va: University Press of Virginia, 1969).
Gwynn, Stephen, ed., *Scattering Branches: Tributes to the Memory of W. B. Yeats* (London: Macmillan, 1940).
Hall, James, and Martin Steinmann, eds, *The Permanence of Yeats: Selected Criticism* (New York: The Macmillan Co., 1950).
Hall, Mr and Mrs S[amuel] C[arter], *Ireland: Its Scenery, Character, etc.*; 3 vols (London: How and Parsons, 1841–3).
Hall, Wayne E., *Shadowy Heroes: Irish Literature of the 1890s* (Syracuse, NY: Syracuse University Press, 1980).
Harmon, Maurice, "Cobwebs before the Wind: Aspects of the Peasantry in Irish Literature from 1800 to 1916", in *Views of the Irish Peasantry 1800–1916*, eds Daniel J. Casey and Robert E. Rhodes (Hamden, Conn.: Archon Books, 1977).
Harper, George Mills, *'Go Back to Where You Belong': Yeats's Return from Exile* (Dublin: The Dolmen Press, 1973).
Harper, George Mills, "'Unbelievers in the House': Yeats's Automatic Script", *Studies in the Literary Imagination*, vol. 14, no. 1 (Spring 1981), pp. 1–15.
Harper, George Mills, ed., *Yeats and The Occult* (Toronto: The Macmillan Company of Canada, 1975).
Harper, George Mills, *Yeats's Golden Dawn* (New York: Harper and Row, 1974).
Hartmann, Franz, ed. and trans., *The Life of Philippus Theophrastus Bombast of Hohenheim [Paracelsus]* (London: Kegan Paul, Trench, Trübner, and Co., 1896).
Hartmann, Franz, *Magic, White and Black* (New York: Theosophical Society Publishing Department, 1904).
Hartmann, Franz, *The Principles of Astrological Geomancy* (Boston: The Occult Publishing Company, 1889).
Henn, T. R., *The Lonely Tower* (New York: Pellegrini and Cudahy, 1952).
Hennessy, William H., ed. and trans., *The Annals of Loch Cé*, 2 vols (London: Longman and Co., 1871).
Hereditas: Essays and Studies presented to Séamus Ó Duilearga, eds Bo Almqvist, Breandán Mac Aodha and Gearóid Mac Eoin (Dublin: The Folklore of Ireland Society, 1975).
Hermes Trismegistus, *The Virgin of the World of Hermes Mercurius Trismegistus*, eds and trans Anna Kingsford and Edward Maitland (Minneapolis: Wizards Bookshelf, 1977).
Hinkson, Katharine Tynan, *Twenty-five Years: Reminiscences* (London: John Murray, 1913).
Hirsch, Edward, "'Contention is better than loneliness': The Poet as Folklorist", *Genre*, vol. 12, no. 4 (Winter 1979), pp. 423–37.
Hone, Joseph, *W. B. Yeats: 1865–1939* (Harmondsworth: Penguin, 1971).
Horton, W[illiam] T[homas], *A Book of Images* (London: The Unicorn Press, 1898).
Howe, Ellic, *The Magicians of the Golden Dawn* (London: Routledge and Kegan Paul, 1972).
Hyde, Douglas, *Beside the Fire* (London: David Nutt, 1890).
Hyde, Douglas, *Leabhar Sgeuluigheachta* (Baile Ath Cliath: Clóbhuailte le Gill, 1889).
Hyde, Douglas, *A Literary History of Ireland from Earliest Times to the Present Day* (London: T. Fisher Unwin, 1899).
Hyde, Douglas, *Love Songs of Connacht* (Dublin: Gill and Son, 1893).

Jakobson, Roman, and Stephen Rudy, *Yeats's "Sorrow of Love" through the Years* (Lisse: Peter de Ridder Press, 1977).
Jeffares, A. Norman, *A New Commentary on the Poems of W. B. Yeats* (Stanford, Calif.: Stanford University Press, 1984).
Jeffares, A. Norman, *W. B. Yeats: Man and Poet* (New Haven, Conn.: Yale University Press, 1949).
Jennings, Hargrave, *The Rosicrucians: Their Rites and Mysteries*, 2 vols (London: John C. Nimmo, 1887).
Jochum, K. P. S., *W. B. Yeats: A Classified Bibliography of Criticism* (Urbana, Ill.: University of Illinois Press, 1978).
Johnston, Charles, "Esoteric Buddhism", *The Dublin University Review* (July 1885), pp. 144–6.
Joyce, P[atrick] W[eston], *A Social History of Ancient Ireland*; 2 vols (London: Longmans, Green, and Co., 1903).
Keats, John, *Lamia* (London: Routledge and Sons, 1887).
Kelleher, John V., "Matthew Arnold and the Celtic Revival", in *Perspectives of Criticism*, ed. Harry Levin (Cambridge, Mass.: Harvard University Press, 1950).
Kelleher, John V., "Yeats's Use of Irish Materials", *Tri-Quarterly*, vol. 4, pp. 115–26.
Kennedy, Patrick, *The Banks of the Boro: A Chronicle of the County of Wexford* (Dublin: M'Glashan and Gill, 1867).
Kennedy, Patrick, *Evenings in the Duffrey* (Dublin: M'Glashan and Gill, 1869).
Kennedy, Patrick, *The Fireside Stories of Ireland* (Dublin: M'Glashan and Gill, 1870).
Kennedy, Patrick, *Legendary Fictions of the Irish Celts* (London: Macmillan, 1866).
Kennedy, Patrick, *Legends of Mount Leinster* (Dublin: P. Kennedy, 1855).
Kermode, Frank, *Romantic Image* (New York: Random House, 1957).
Kinahan, Frank, "Armchair Folklore: Yeats and the Textual Sources of *Fairy and Folk Tales of the Irish Peasantry*", *Proceedings of the Royal Irish Academy*, vol. 83c (1983), pp. 255–67.
Kinahan, Frank, "Hour of Dawn: The Unity of Yeats's *The Celtic Twilight* (1893, 1902)", *Irish University Review*, vol. 13, no. 2 (Autumn 1983), pp. 189–205.
Kinahan, Frank, "A Source Note on 'The Madness of King Goll'", in *Yeats Annual*, Vol. IV, ed. Warwick Gould (London: Macmillan, 1986).
King, C. W., *The Gnostics and Their Remains* (London: David Nutt, 1887).
King, Francis, ed., *Astral Projection, Ritual Magic and Alchemy* (London: Neville Spearman, 1971).
King, Francis, *The Rites of Modern Occult Magic* (New York: The Macmillan Co., 1971).
Kingsford, Anna, and Maitland, E[dward], eds and trans, *The Hermetic Works; the Virgin of the World of Hermes Mercurius Trismegistus* (Madras: P. Kailasam Bros, 1885).
Larminie, William, *West Irish Folk-Tales and Romances* (London: Elliot Stock, 1893).
Le Gouz de la Boullaye, François, *The Tour of the French Traveller M. De La Boullaye le Gouz in Ireland, A.D. 1644*, ed. T. Crofton Croker (London: T. and W. Boone, 1837).
Lennhoff, Eugen, *The Freemasons: The History, Nature, Development and Secret of the Royal Art*, trans. Einar Frame (New York: Oxford University Press, 1934).
Lenoski, D. S., "The Symbolism of the Early Yeats: Occult and Religious Backgrounds", *Studies in the Literary Imagination*, vol. 14, no. 1 (Spring 1981), pp. 85–100.

Selected Bibliography

Levenson, Samuel, *Maud Gonne: A Biography of Yeats' Beloved* (New York: Reader's Digest Press, 1976).
"Lévi, Éliphas" (Alphonse Louis Constant), *The History of Magic*, ed. and trans. A. E. Waite (London: William Rider and Son, 1913).
"Lévi, Éliphas" (Alphonse Louis Constant), *The Magical Ritual of the Sanctum Regnum*, ed. and trans. W. Wynn Westcott (London: George Redway, 1896).
"Lévi, Éliphas" (Alphonse Louis Constant), *The Mysteries of Magic: A Digest of the Writings of Éliphas Lévi*, ed. and trans. A. E. Waite (London: George Redway, 1886).
Levine, Herbert J., "'But now I add another thought': Yeats's Daimonic Tradition", *Studies in the Literary Imagination*, vol. 14, no. 1 (Spring 1981), pp. 77–84.
Lilly, William, *William Lilly's History of His Life and Times* (London: Charles Baldwyn, 1822).
Literary Ideals in Ireland (London: T. Fisher Unwin, 1899).
"Loughliagh", *The Dublin and London Magazine* (London: James Robins and Co., 1825), pp. 352–4.
Lover, Samuel, *Legends and Stories of Ireland* (New York: D. and J. Sadlier and Co., 1872).
Lucy, Seán, ed., *Irish Poets in English* (Cork: The Mercier Press, 1973).
Lucy, Seán, "Metre and Movement in Anglo-Irish Verse", *Irish University Review*, vol. 8, no. 2 (Autumn 1978), pp. 151–77.
Lytton, Edward George Earle Lytton Bulwer-Lytton, *The Coming Race* (New York: The Mershon Co., n.d.).
Lytton, Edward George Earle Lytton Bulwer-Lytton, *Zanoni* (New York: The Mershon Co., n.d.).
McAnally, D. R., Jr., *Irish Wonders: the Ghosts, Giants, Pookas, Leprechawns, Banshees, Fairies, Witches, Widows, Old Maids and Other Marvels of the Emerald Isle* (London: Ward, Lock, 1888).
MacCana, Proinsias, *Celtic Mythology* (London: Hamlyn House, 1970).
McGarry, James, *Place Names in the Writings of William Butler Yeats* (Gerrards Cross: Colin Smythe, 1976).
MacKenna, Stephen, trans., *Plotinus: The Ethical Treatises* (London: Philip Lee Warner, 1917).
MacKillop, James, "Finn MacCool: The Hero and the Anti-Hero in Irish Folk Tradition", in *Views of the Irish Peasantry 1800–1916*, eds Daniel J. Casey and Robert E. Rhodes (Hamden, Conn.: Archon Books, 1977).
MacLochlainn, Alf, "Gael and Peasant – A Case of Mistaken Identity?", in *Views of the Irish Peasantry 1800–1916*, eds Daniel J. Casey and Robert E. Rhodes (Hamden, Conn.: Archon Books, 1977).
MacNeice, Louis, *The Poetry of W. B. Yeats* (New York: Oxford University Press, 1941).
Mahony, Christina Hunt, and Edward O'Shea, "A Note on 'The Watch-Fire'", *Poetry* (January 1980), pp. 223–6.
Mangan, James Clarence, *Poems* (New York: P. M. Haverty, 1859).
Marcus, Phillip L., *Yeats and the Beginning of the Irish Renaissance* (Ithaca, NY: Cornell University Press, 1970).
Mathers, S[amuel] L[iddell] MacGregor, trans., *The Book of the Sacred Magic of Abra-Melin the Mage* (Chicago: The de Laurence Co., 1932).
Mathers, Samuel Liddell MacGregor, ed. and trans., *The Kabbalah Unveiled* (London: Kegan Paul, Trench, Trübner, 1926).
Mathers, Samuel Liddell MacGregor, *The Tarot: Its Occult Signification, Use in Fortune-Telling, and Method of Play, Etc.* (New York: Samuel Weiser Inc., 1969).

Meir, Colin, *The Ballads and Songs of W. B. Yeats: The Anglo-Irish Heritage in Subject and Style* (London: Macmillan, 1974).
Melchiori, Giorgio, *The Whole Mystery of Art* (London: Routledge and Kegan Paul, 1960).
Menon, V. K. Narayana, *The Development of William Butler Yeats* (Edinburgh: Oliver and Boyd, 1942).
Meyer, Kuno, ed. and trans., *Cath Finntrága* (London: Oxford University Press, 1885).
Moore, Virginia, *The Unicorn: William Butler Yeats' Search for Reality* (New York: The Macmillan Co., 1954).
Morris, Lloyd R., *The Celtic Dawn* (New York: The Macmillan Co., 1917).
Murphy, Frank H., *Yeats's Early Poetry: The Quest for Reconciliation* (Baton Rouge, La: Louisiana State University Press, 1975).
Murphy, William M., *Prodigal Father: The Life of John Butler Yeats (1839–1922)* (Ithaca, NY, and London: Cornell University Press, 1978).
Nutt, Alfred, ed., with Kuno Meyer, ed. and trans., *The Voyage of Bran Son of Febal*, 2 vols (London: David Nutt, 1895, 1897).
O'Curry, Eugene, *Lectures on the Manuscript Materials of Ancient Irish History* (Dublin: James Duffy, 1861).
O'Daly, John, ed., *Transactions of the Ossianic Society* (1856), Vol. IV (Dublin: John O'Daly, 1859).
O'Donnell, William H., "Yeats as Adept and Artist: *The Speckled Bird, The Secret Rose*, and *The Wind Among the Reeds*", in *Yeats and The Occult*, ed. George Mills Harper (Toronto: The Macmillan Company of Canada, 1975).
O'Donovan, John, ed. and trans., *Annals of the Four Masters*, 7 vols (Dublin: Hodges and Smith, 1851).
O'Driscoll, Robert, *Symbolism and Some Implications of the Symbolic Approach: W. B. Yeats During the Eighteen-Nineties* (Dublin: The Dolmen Press, 1975).
O'Grady, Standis, *The Flight of the Eagle* (London: Lawrence and Bullen, 1897).
O'Grady, Standish, *History of Ireland: The Heroic Period* (London: Sampson Low, Marston, and Rivington, 1878).
O'Grady, Standish, *History of Ireland: Cuculain and his Contemporaries* (London: Sampson Low, Searle, Marston, and Rivington, 1880).
O'Grady, Standish Hayes, ed., *Transactions of the Ossianic Society* (1855), Vol. III (Dublin: John O'Daly, 1857).
O'Hanlon, John ("Lageniensis"), *Irish Folk Lore* (Glasgow: Cameron and Ferguson, 1870).
O'Kearney, Nicholas, ed., *Transactions of the Ossianic Society* (1853), Vol. I (Dublin: John O'Daly, 1853).
Olney, James, *The Rhizome and the Flower: The Perennial Philosophy – Yeats and Jung* (Berkeley, Calif.: University of California Press, 1980).
Olney, James, "Sex and the Dead: *Daimones* of Yeats and Jung", *Studies in the Literary Imagination*, vol. 14, no. 1 (Spring 1981), pp. 43–60.
Orel, Harold, *The Development of William Butler Yeats: 1885–1900* (Lawrence, Kans: University of Kansas Publications, 1968).
O'Rorke, Terence, *History, Antiquities, and Present State of the Parishes of Ballysadare and Kilvarnet, in the County of Sligo* (Dublin: James Duffy, n.d.).
O'Shea, Edward, *A Descriptive Catalog of W. B. Yeats's Library* (New York: Garland, 1985).
O'Shea, Edward, *Yeats as Editor* (Dublin: The Dolmen Press, 1975).
O'Shea, Edward, "Yeats's Revisions in *Fairy and Folk Tales*", *Southern Folklore Quarterly*, vol. 38, no. 3 (September 1974), pp. 223–32.

Selected Bibliography

Ó Súilleabháin, Seán, *Folktales of Ireland* (Chicago: University of Chicago Press, 1966).
Ó Súilleabháin, Seán, *Storytelling in Irish Tradition* (Cork: The Mercier Press, 1973).
Ó Súilleabháin, Seán, and Reidar Th. Christiansen, *The Types of the Irish Folktale* (Helsinki: Academici Scientarium Fennica, 1963).
O'Sullivan, Sheila, "W. B. Yeats's Use of Irish Oral and Literary Tradition", in *Hereditas: Essays and Studies presented to Séamus Ó Duilearga* (Dublin: The Folklore of Ireland Society, 1975).
Paracelsus, *The Hermetic and Alchemical Writings of Paracelsus*, ed. and trans. A. E. Waite, 2 vols (London: James Elliott and Co., 1894).
Parkinson, Thomas, *W. B. Yeats, Self-Critic: A Study of His Early Verse; and The Later Poetry* (Berkeley, Calif.: University of California Press, 1971).
Pater, Walter, *Essays from 'The Guardian'* (London: Macmillan, 1901).
Pater, Walter, *Marius the Epicurean* (London: Macmillan, 1885).
Pope, Alexander, *The Poems of Alexander Pope*, Vol. IX (New Haven, Conn.: Yale University Press, 1967).
Prasâd, Râma, *The Science of Breath and the Philosophy of the Tattvas. Translated from the Sanskrit, with Introductory and Explanatory Essays on Nature's Finer Forces* (London: The Theosophical Publishing Society, 1894).
Raine, Kathleen, *Yeats the Initiate* (London: Allen and Unwin, 1986).
Raine, Kathleen, *Yeats, the Tarot and the Golden Dawn* (Dublin: The Dolmen Press, 1972).
Regardie, Israel, *A Garden of Pomegranates: An Outline of the Qabalah* (St Paul, Minn.: Llewellyn Publications, 1970).
Regardie, Israel, ed., *The Golden Dawn: An Account of the Teachings, Rites and Ceremonies of the Order of the Golden Dawn*, 4 vols (St Paul, Minn.: Llewellyn Publications, 1978).
Reid, B. L., *William Butler Yeats: The Lyric of Tragedy* (Norman, Okla: University of Oklahoma Press, 1961).
Rhys, John, *Lectures on the Origin and Growth of Religion as Illustrated by Celtic Heathendom* (London: Williams and Norgate, 1888).
Ronsley, Joseph, "Yeats's Lecture Notes for 'Friends of My Youth'", in *Yeats and the Theatre*, eds Robert O'Driscoll and Lorna Reynolds ([Toronto]: The Macmillan Company of Canada, 1975).
The Royal Hibernian Tales: Being a Collection of the Most Entertaining Stories Now Extant (Dublin: C. M. Warren, n.d.).
"Sapere Aude" [William Wynn Westcott], ed., *The Chaldean Oracles of Zoroaster* (London: The Theosophical Publishing Society, 1895).
Seiden, Morton Irving, *William Butler Yeats: The Poet as a Mythmaker* (East Lansing, Mich.: Michigan State University Press, 1962).
Shelley, Percy Bysshe, *The Prose Works of Percy Bysshe Shelley*, Vol. I, ed. Harry Buxton Forman (London: Reeves and Turner, 1880).
Sidnell, Michael J., "The Allegory of Yeats's 'The Wanderings of Oisin'", *Colby Library Quarterly*, vol. 15, no. 2 (June 1979), pp. 137–51.
Sinnett, A. P., *Esoteric Buddhism* (London: Trübner and Co., 1883).
Sinnett, A. P., *Incidents in the Life of Madame Blavatsky* (London: George Redway, 1886).
Sinnett, A. P., *The Occult World* (London: Trübner and Co., 1881).
Sinnett, A. P., *The Occult World* (Boston: Houghton, Mifflin, 1897).
Smith, G. Gregory, ed., *The Spectator*, Vol. V (London: J. M. Dent and Co., 1897–8).

Spivey, Ted R., "W. B. Yeats and the 'Children of the Fire': Science, Poetry, and Visions of the New Age", *Studies in the Literary Imagination*, vol. 14, no. 1 (Spring 1981), pp. 123–34.

Stallworthy, Jon, *Between the Lines: Yeats's Poetry in the Making* (Oxford: Clarendon Press, 1963).

Stock, A. G., *W. B. Yeats: His Poetry and Thought* (Cambridge: Cambridge University Press, 1961).

Tate, Allen, "Yeats's Romanticism: Notes and Suggestions", in *The Permanence of Yeats: Selected Criticism*, eds James Hall and Martin Steinmann (New York: The Macmillan Co., 1950).

Taylor, Thomas, *Select Works of Plotinus*, ed. G. R. S. Mead (London: George Bell and Sons, 1895).

Tennyson, Alfred Lord, *The Works of Alfred Lord Tennyson*, Vol. VI (Cambridge: The Riverside Press, 1889).

Thornton, Weldon, "Between Circle and Straight Line: A Pragmatic View of Yeats and the Occult", *Studies in the Literary Imagination*, vol. 14, no. 1 (Spring 1981), pp. 61–75.

Thuente, Mary Helen, *Yeats and Irish Folklore* (New York: Barnes and Noble, 1981).

Torchiana, Donald T., *W. B. Yeats and Georgian Ireland* (Evanston, Ill.: Northwestern University Press, 1966).

Torrens, R. G., *The Golden Dawn: The Inner Teachings* (New York: Samuel Weiser Inc., 1977).

Torrens, R. G., *The Secret Rituals of the Golden Dawn* (Wellingborough: The Aquarian Press, 1973).

Unterecker, John, "Countryman, Peasant, and Servant in the Poetry of W. B. Yeats", in *Views of the Irish Peasantry 1800–1916*, eds Daniel J. Casey and Robert E. Rhodes (Hamden, Conn.: Archon Books, 1977).

Unterecker, John, *A Reader's Guide to William Butler Yeats* (New York: Noonday Press, 1959).

Ure, Peter, *Towards a Mythology* (Liverpool: University Press of Liverpool, 1946).

Villars, Nicolas Pierre Henri de Montfaucon, Abbé de, *Le Comte de Gabalis* (London: The Old Bourne Press, 1913).

Von Reichenbach, Baron Karl, *Researches on Magnetism, Electricity, Heat, Light, Crystallization, and Chemical Attraction, in their Relations to the Vital Force*, trans. William Gregory (London: Taylor, Walton, and Maberly, 1850).

Wade, Allan, *A Bibliography of the Writings of W. B. Yeats*, rev. and ed. by Russell K. Alspach (London: Rupert Hart-Davis, 1968).

Waite, A. E., ed., *Elfin Music: An Anthology of English Fairy Poetry* (London: Walter Scott, 1888).

Waite, A. E., *The Real History of the Rosicrucians* (London: George Redway, 1887).

Waite, A. E., *The Secret Tradition in Göetia. The Book of Ceremonial Magic including the Rites and Mysteries of Göetic Theurgy, Sorcery and Infernal Necromancy* (London: W. Rider and Son, Ltd., 1911).

Waite, A. E., ed., *Transcendental Magic: Its Doctrine and Ritual* (London: George Redway, 1896).

Webster, Brenda, *Yeats: A Psychoanalytic Study* (Stanford, Calif.: Stanford University Press, 1973).

Wentz, W. Y. Evans, *The Fairy-Faith in Celtic Countries* (London: H. Frowde, 1911).

Wilde, Lady Jane Francesca, *Ancient Cures, Charms, and Usages of Ireland* (London: Ward and Downey, 1890).

Wilde, Lady Jane Francesca, *Ancient Legends, Mystic Charms, and Superstitions of Ireland* (London: Ward and Downey, 1888).

Selected Bibliography

Wilde, William, *Irish Popular Superstitions* (Dublin: J. McGlashan, 1852).
Williams, Thomas A., *Eliphas Levi: Master of Occultism* (Alabama: University of Alabama Press, 1975).
Wilson, Edmund, *Axel's Castle* (New York: Charles Scribner's Sons, 1931).
Wilson, F. A. C., *W. B. Yeats and Tradition* (London: Gollancz, 1958).
Yeats, John Butler, *Early Memories: Some Chapters of Autobiography* (Dundrum: The Cuala Press, 1923).
Yeats, Michael, "W. B. Yeats and Irish Folk Song", *Southern Folklore Quarterly*, vol. 31, no. 2 (June 1966), pp. 153–78.

Index

Albright, Daniel xiv
Allingham, William 57–8, 81n., 227
Arbois de Jubainville, Henry d', 100
Arnold, Matthew 163, 212–13n., 222

Ball, Patricia M. 3, 4
"banshee" 89, 121n., 184
Beauty 153, 156, 157–8, 159–62, 163, 191, 209, 220
Birdwood, George 154–5
Blake, William 97, 122n., 194, 215n., 217, 219, 224, 226, 229n.
Blavatsky, Madame 2, 10, 11, 12, 14, 15–16, 18, 20, 26, 31–2n., 32–3n., 34n., 35n., 36n., 39n., 99, 102, 103, 104, 105, 106–7, 124n., 133, 136, 137, 138, 140–1, 147, 149, 164n., 165n., 168n., 181, 214n., 218
  Blavatsky Lodge of the Theosophical Society, 2
  Isis Unveiled, 10, 16, 20, 104, 105, 106, 214–15n.
  The Secret Doctrine, 10, 11, 100, 105, 110, 135, 152, 165n., 176, 181, 218–19, 224, 229n., 232n.
Boehme, Jakob 224, 226
Bottomley, Gordon 1
Bran 96, 115
Browning, Robert 222
Buchanan, Robert 180
Bulwer-Lytton, Edward:
  The Coming Race 127–8, 156
  Zanoni 99–100, 108–9, 112, 122n., 130, 138, 150

Cabalism 132, 162
  Cabalistic Tree, 162
Cairbre 85, 94, 108
Callanan, J.J.: "Cusheen Loo", 57
Cambrensis: *Historical Works* 112, 113
Carleton, William 43, 64
  Tales and Stories of the Irish Peasantry, 48, 49, 54, 56, 69, 74, 76, 79n., 80n., 82n., 184
Carraig Mhic Diarmada 21–2, 24
Castle of Heroes 21–5, 327n., 152, 153, 177, 191
Chaldean Oracles 212n.
changelings 57, 79n.
Chatterji, Mohini 102
Christianity 95, 97, 107, 120
Clanna Baoisgne (Leinster Fenians) 85, 86–7, 92, 93, 94, 95, 96, 97, 107, 120, 120n.

Clarke, Austin 82n.
Comyn, Michael: *Laoidh Oisín ar Thír na nÓg.*, 87, 88, 92, 98, 101, 107, 116–17, 122n., 201
Conchobar Mac Nessa 95
Coole Park 191, 220
Country of the Young *see* Tír na nOg.
critical approach xv–xvi
Croker, Thomas Crofton: *Fairy Legends and Traditions of the South of Ireland*, 41–2, 43, 48, 53, 69, 76, 77n., 80n., 83n., 110, 112, 113, 114
  Tour of the French Traveller. . . , 113
cross, the 132–8, 143
  crux ansíata, 132, 133, 134, 136
  Rose Cross, 134, 136, 138, 144, 145, 146, 154
Crowley, Aleister 143
Cú Chulainn 38n., 89, 95, 121n., 122n.
Curtink, Jeremiah 35n., 43
"Cyclic Pilgrimage" 27–8, 105

Daiches, David xiii–xiv
Dante Alighieri: *Paradiso* 157, 230n.
Davitt, Michael 19–20, 36–7n.
d'Alviella, Count Goblet 129, 136, 137, 141, 154, 164–5n.
Deirdre 95, 158, 160, 197–8
De Quincey, Thomas 132
Devachan 103–4, 106, 107–8, 123n.
Devas 225
"divine nature" 129, 164n.
domestic ideal 182–4, 186, 188, 190–2, 208–9, 211, 217, 220, 221
Dublin Hermetic Society 105
Dublin University Review 105, 123n.

Eddins, Dwight xiv
Ellis, Elwin 224
Ellmann, Richard 9, 91, 124n.
Emain Macha 94, 96, 199
emigrant poetry 173–6, 177, 211n.
Engleberg, Edward xiii

fairies xii, xiv, xv, xvi, 13, 43–9, 70, 71–2, 79n., 80n., 82n., 157, 186, 187, 206, 217, 221–2, 223, 225, 231n.
  beauty of fairyland, 63–4, 110, 120
  "blast", 69, 83n.
  dreamer and, 68–76, 119, 182
  enemies of man, 48–9, 75
  evil spirits, 45–6

Index

fairy demonism, 46, 55–6, 79–80n.
fairy grass, 73–5, 84n.
fairy vengeance, 46–7, 51, 71–2
glamouring, 44–5, 50, 51–2, 54, 55–6, 57–8, 61–2, 63, 70, 71, 80n., 82n., 83n., 126, 128
"happiness" of fairy world, 59–61, 110, 111–12, 117
lamia theme and, 52, 55, 57, 62–3, 75–6, 113–14
maliciousness of, 46–7, 71, 74–5
notorious liars, 60–1, 62
origins of, 47–8, 80n.
sacred wells, 72–3, 84n.
"sociable" and "solitary" fs., 46, 80n.
Tir na nOg (Land of Perpetual Youth), 87, 101, 108, 109, 110–14, 117, 118–20, 196
ultimate fate of, 48, 49–51, 80–1n.
Fama Fraternitatis 154, 169n.
Fenians 85, 99
 Clanna Baoisgne (Leinster Fenians), 85, 86–7, 90, 92, 93, 94, 95, 96, 97, 98, 99, 107, 108, 120n., 121n.
Fergus 95
Ferguson, Samuel 4, 38n., 70, 227
 "The Fairy Thorn", 57, 70, 82n.
 "The Fairy Well of Lagnanay", 57, 70
Fionn 92, 94, 101, 102
Fludd, Robert 138
folk music 90–1, 121n.
folklore xv–xvi, 13, 14, 15, 16–19, 20, 31n., 34–5n., 36n., 39n., 41–3, 51–2, 58, 74, 77n., 78–9n.
 Biddy Hart, 53
 comparisons with magic, 13–19
 f. revival, 42–3
 images of evanescence in, 52–4, 57, 81–2n., 112–13
 lamia theme in, 52, 55, 57, 62–3, 75–6, 113–14
 legends of pursuit, 116, 125n.
 tales about Oisin, 88–9
 Theosophical Society and, 14–15
 Tir na nOg (Land of Perpetual Youth), 87, 101, 108, 109, 110–14, 117, 118–20, 196
 Yeats's f. authorities, 43, 77n., 79n.
Freemasonry 20, 22, 37n.

Gabhra, battle of 85, 86, 92–4, 96, 97, 101, 108
Gaelic Athletic Association 42
Gaelic League 42
Gaelic Union 42
Garnett, Edward 64
glamouring 44–5, 51–2, 54, 55–6, 57–8, 61–2, 63, 70, 71, 80n.
Godwin, William: *St. Leon: A Tale of the Sixteenth Century* 109, 127, 128, 130

Gogarty, Oliver St John 204
Golden Dawn, Order of 9, 13, 26, 31n., 32n., 33–4n., 40n. 100, 122n., 141–4, 146, 147, 153, 156, 161–3, 166n., 167n., 168n., 176, 177–9k, 212n., 215n., 218, 229n.
 doctrines of, 141–5
 founding of, 9
 Higher Genius, 146–7, 149, 150–1, 152, 153, 156, 162, 168–9n., 178, 206
 images of, 178
 Inner Order, 17, 146, 150, 151, 167n., 177
 Lightning Flash, 148, 162, 167n.
 Maud Gonne and, 18, 20–1, 22, 24, 27, 37n.
 Middle Pillar technique, 144, 148–51, 152, 153, 163, 167–8n., 168n.
 Outer Order, 177–8
 Path of Samekh 148, 162–3
 Path of Tau 143–4, 161, 167n.
 Path of the Serpent 148, 162, 167n.
 Practicus ritual 178, 212n.
 Rose Cross Lamen 144–6, 150, 167n.
 Rose symbol and, 129, 134, 135–6, 142–51, 152, 161
 schism in, 23
 Spiritual Development ritual 149, 150–1, 178, 212n.
 Tiphareth, 148–52, 156, 163, 167n., 169n., 206
 Tree of Life and, 141, 142, 143, 144, 146, 147–9, 152, 156, 161, 162, 169n.
 Yeat's initiation into, 2, 29n.
Goldsmith, Oliver 175–6, 211–12n.
Gonne, Maud 1, 2, 6, 8, 17, 29, 113, 138–9, 146, 159, 168n., 169n., 170n., 172, 191, 192
 Castle of Heroes and, 21–5
 first meetings with Yeats and Davitt, 19–20, 36–37n.
 marries John MacBride, 23
 Order of the Golden Dawn and, 18, 20–1, 22, 27, 37n.
 poems written to, 25–8, 138–9
 Scattering Branches, 22–3
 son of, 20, 37n.
Gore-Booth, Eva 191
Gregory, Lady 206, 208
Griffin, Gerald 112, 113, 124n.
Grossman, Allen R. xviiin., 232n.
Gyles, Althea 131–2, 155

Hardy, Thomas 222
Hart, Biddy 53
Hartmann, Franz: *Magic, White and Black* 9, 39n., 110, 118, 123n., 133, 155, 164n., 224–6
 The Life of Philippus Theophrastus Bombast of

250

Hohenheim (Paracelsus) 9–10, 12, 214n., 226–7, 231–2n.
Henley, W.E. 64
"Hermetic Students" 2
Hibbert Lecturers 136
home 68, 171, 182, 183, 190–2, 214n., 217
Homer 128, 176
Hone, Joseph 228
Hopkins, Gerard Manley 222
Horton, W.T. 5
Housman, A.E. 222
Howe, Ellic: *The Magicians of the Golden Dawn* 9
Huxley, T.H. 11. 32n.
Hyde, Douglas 1, 21, 22, 37n., 41–2, 43, 79n., 100, 110, 111, 116
Hynes, Mary 158

imagery/images 67, 171, 176, 189, 197, 198, 207–11, 217, 219–21, 223, 230n.
 broken harp, 199–200
 earth/water i., 64, 65, 66, 68, 74
 Golden Dawn i., 177–80, 209
 in "The Wanderings of Oisin", 92, 95
 island in a lake, 74, 171, 181, 184, 187, 188, 189, 190–2, 209
 natural world, 181, 182, 184, 192, 197, 200, 203, 204, 205–6, 207, 208, 209, 210, 211, 217, 218–19
 ocean, 180–1, 196–7, 213n.
 ruined house, 184–6, 192, 208
 seashore, 181, 194–5, 197, 198, 200, 203
 secured home, xvi, 171, 182, 183–4, 186, 190–2, 207, 208, 209, 210, 217, 220, 221
 shell i., 192–5, 197, 198, 200
 stars 193–4, 197, 198, 199, 203
 symbolic geography, 67, 180–2
 tended hearthside, xvi, 174, 181–2, 184, 192, 209, 211, 220, 221
 walled garden, 171, 181, 182, 184, 190–1, 206–7, 208, 209, 221
Innisfree 61–2, 188–9, 210, 211
Ireland/Irish xv *see also* nationality
 artists, 8
 dramatic movement, 3
 emigrants from, 173–5, 176
 Rose as symbol in, 137–8, 146
 sincerity and, 30n.
islands: in "The Wanderings of Oisin", 86–7, 904, 96, 103–4, 107, 110, 114, 115, 117, 119, 120, 124n., 127, 129, 196
 Innisfree, 61–2, 188–9, 210, 211
 island in a lake image, 74, 171, 181, 188, 190–1, 209, 210 *see also* imagery
 Island of Content, 114, 115
 Island of Forgetfulness, 91, 92, 94, 102, 103–4, 106, 115, 119

Island of the Living, 80n., 91, 92, 93, 94, 96, 103–4, 114, 117, 118, 129, 157, 196
Island of Victories, 91, 92, 93, 94, 98, 103–4, 108, 114

Jeffares, A. Norman 159
Jennings, Hargrave: *The Rosicrucians: Their Rites and Mysteries* 10, 11, 109, 132, 165n
Johnson, Lionel 146
Johnston, Charles 16, 99, 103, 104, 105, 123n.
Joyce, James 4
Joyce, R.D. 197–8, 214n.

Keats, John: *Lamia* 52
Kennedy, Patrick 43, 48, 49–50, 55, 56, 57, 64, 74, 76, 77n., 80n., 89, 111, 112
Kether 148, 150, 167n., 168n.
King, C.W.: *The Gnostics and Their Remains* 10
King, Francis: *The Rites of Modern Occult Magic* 143, 167n.
King, Sir John 21
Kipling, Rudyard 222

lamia theme 52, 54, 55, 63, 64, 75
Land of the Young 86, 114
Land of Virtues 87, 88
Lévi, Éliphas 9, 19, 32n., 36n., 100, 134, 157, 170n.
Lightning Flash 148, 162, 167n.
Lilly, William 231n.
Lissadell 66, 71, 84n., 185
Lough Key 21, 22, 23, 25
Lover, Samuel 43, 77n.
Lugnagall 66, 76, 82–3n., 84n.

McAnally, D.R. 43, 53, 81n., 112
MacDiarmada, Ruaidhri 22
McGee, T.D. 211n.
MacLintock, Letitia 58
Maeterlinck, Maurice 203, 215n.
magic xv, xvi, 2, 6, 8, 10, 11, 12, 13, 16–17, 18, 20, 25–6, 28, 31n., 32n., 33n., 34n., 38n., 155
 comparisons with folklore, 13–15
 magical symbols, 17
 rebirth theories, 38n., 102–3
 "The Wanderings of Oisin" and, 89
 vocabulary of, 138
 Yeats and, 11–14, 152–4, 156, 218, 219
 see also occultism
Maier, Michael 132
Mananián MacLir 89, 121n.
Mangan, James Clarence 174–5, 182
Mannion, Biddy 54, 55, 75, 82n.
Mathers, MacGregor 2, 17, 22, 23, 32n., 122n, 134, 143, 148, 154, 155, 166–7n., 168n, 179

The Kabbalah Unveiled, 10–11, 135
Mathers, Moina Bergson 122n., 135–6
Middle Pillar 144, 148–51, 152–3, 163, 167n., 168n.
Moods, the 156, 219, 224–8, 230–1n., 232n.
Moore, Thomas 205
Moore, Virginia 23, 231n.
Morris, Lloyd R. xiii
Morris, William 130, 190, 209, 215–16n., 222
Murphy, William 191
music 90–1, 121n.

nationality 6, 9, 30n.
natural world 171, 184, 186, 192, 200, 203–6, 208, 209–10, 217, 218 *see also* imagery
neo-Platomism 141, 181
Nirvana 104
Nutt, Alfred: *The Voyage of Bran* 101

occultism xv–xvi, 6, 8, 9, 11, 12–13, 16, 17, 20, 21, 29, 31–2n., 38n., 136, 138, 142, 218–19, 224, 227, 232n.
   afterlife, 108–10
   anti-rational bias of, 11–12, 33–4n.
   Astral Light 225, 226, 227
   folklore and, 13–18, 19, 35n.
   Middle Pillar, *see under* Golden Dawn
   sephiroth 134, 141–2, 143, 144–5, 148, 152, 162, 167
   Seven Lights, 26, 39–40n.
   symbolism and, 136–8, 140, 143–6
   Tiphareth, 141, 144, 145, 148–9, 151–2, 156, 167n., 169n., 206
   Tree of Life, 16–17, 137, 141–7, 148–9, 152, 156, 162, 167n., 169n., 206
   veiled diction of, 99–100, 165n.
   Yeats's enthusiasm for, 12–13, 32n.
   see also magic
O'Donnell, William H. xiv
O'Grady, Standish Hayes 101, 122n., 122–3n.
O'Grady, Standish (James) 76, 80n., 84n., 89, 110, 115–16, 121n., 227
O'Hanlon, John: *Irish Folk Lore* 2, 43, 46, 51, 73, 74, 79n., 90, 110
O'Kearney, Nicholas 85, 101–2, 120n.
O'Leary, John 2, 8, 12, 13, 17, 19–20, 153, 176, 212n.
O'Looney, Bryan 87–8, 101
Oscar 92, 94, 101, 102, 121–2n.
Ossianic Society 77n., 87, 88
   Transactions of, 77n., 101–2, 120n., 122n.

Paracelsus 19, 226
Parkinson, Thomas F. xviin.
Pater, Walter 3, 4, 165n.
Path of the Chameleon 177, 179
Path of the Serpent 148, 162, 167n.

Pelham, Elizabeth 228
Plotinus 149, 213n.
Pollexfen, George 17, 231n.
Pope, Alexander 176, 212n.
Practicus ritual 178, 212n.
primal religion 14–16, 17, 34–5n., 35–6n.
Prometheus 26, 110

Radcliffe, Elizabeth 169n., 206
Red Branch 25, 89, 94, 95
Regardie, Israel: *A Garden of Pomegranates* 143–4, 146, 148, 168n., 169n., 178–9
reincarnation 20, 25, 100–7, 201–2
Rhymers' Club 222
Rhys, Ernest 41
Rhys, John: *Celtic Heathendom* 38n., 39n., 100, 121n., 122n., 136
Riversdale 23, 230n.
Ronsard, Pierre 27
Rosc-catha 98, 122n.
Roscommon 21, 23
Rose, the xv, xvi, 147–8, 155, 164n., 165n., 186, 206, 217, 223–4, 227–8
   Althea Gyles and, 131–2
   beauty and, 129, 130, 131, 133, 134, 153, 157, 159–60, 161, 162, 163, 220
   Count Goblet d'Alviella, 136–7
   cross and, 130–1, 132–6, 138
   eclectic symbol, 129–32, 133–5, 137, 141, 144, 145, 146, 155–6
   emblem of desire, 130, 131
   Irish symbol, 129–30, 131, 137–8
   lotus and, 129, 135–6, 137, 164n.
   occultism and, 136–8
   peace and, 129, 131, 132, 134
   Ritual of the Rose Cross, 149–50, 151
   Rose Cross, 134, 136, 138, 143, 144, 145, 146, 147, 150, 154
   Rosicrucianism and, 130, 132–3, 134, 135
   sun and, 129, 131, 132, 136, 152
   symbol of love, 130, 131, 132, 133, 134
   symbolic heart of things, 129, 131
   Tiphareth, 141–2, 144, 145, 164n.
   Tree of Life and, 129, 137, 141–3, 144, 149
   see also Yeats, W.B.: the Rose Poems
Rosencreutz, Christian 130, 132
Rosicrucianism/Rosicrucians 11, 32–3n., 37n., 100, 130, 132–3, 134, 135, 138, 140, 141, 150, 151, 157, 165n., 166n., 225
Rosses 62, 66, 231n.
Rossetti, Dante Gabriel 222
Russell, George ("AE") 17, 18–19, 37n., 38n., 126, 159, 162

Samekh path 148, 162–3
Scots Observer 50, 61
Seven Lights 26, 39–40n.

Shakespear, Olivia 191, 221, 230n.
Shelley, Percy Bysshe 109, 130, 225
sidhe, the *see* fairies
sincerity 3–9, 25, 28–9, 30n., 153
Sinnett, A.P. 15, 16
  Esoteric Buddhism, 10, 99, 103–4, 105–6, 108
  The Occult World, 10, 16, 99, 103
Sligo 18, 53, 66, 70, 74, 121n., 185, 191, 204, 207, 210, 213–14n.
Spenser, Edmund 128, 130, 190
Spiritual Development ritual 149, 150–1, 178, 212n.
Starkey, D.P. 173–4
Steiner, Rudolph 151, 168n.
Swedenborg, Emanuel 224, 226
Swinburne, Algernon Charles 222
Symbolist Movement 218, 229–30n.
symbols 116–17, 129–38, 176–7, 180–2
  magical, 17
  occult 140, 151, 154, 155, 177–80
  see also imagery and Rose, the
Synge, J.M. 30n., 189

Tarot 143, 166–7n.
Tate, Allen xiii
Tau path 143–4, 161, 167n.
Tennyson, Alfred Lord 215n., 222
The Boston Pilot 8
Theosophical Society 2, 9, 14, 17, 35n., 100, 102, 104, 138, 166n., 229n.
theosophy 9–11, 12, 13, 14, 18, 39n., 106, 123n., 226, 227, 229n.
Thoor Ballylee 37n., 158, 191, 220
Tiphareth 141, 144, 145, 148–9, 151–2, 156, 163, 167n., 169n., 206
Tir na nOg 87, 88, 90, 101, 108, 109, 110–11, 113, 114, 117, 119, 120, 124n., 196, 206
Toberscanavan 66, 72, 83–4n.
Todhunter, John 30n., 211n.
Torrens, R.G.: *The Golden Dawn: The Inner Teachings* 144
  The Secret Rituals of the Golden Dawn, 142–3, 165n., 167n.
Tree of Life 16–17, 39n., 141–5, 146, 147–8, 161, 162, 163, 165n., 169n.
Tuatha Dé Danaan 47, 80n., 95, 122n.
Tynan, Katharine 5, 8, 9, 30n., 58–9, 99, 100, 108, 117, 190, 191, 199, 204, 222
Tyndall, John 11, 32n.

Ulysses 176
"Una Bhán", 21
Unwin, Fisher 64, 222

Waite, A.E. 32n., 133–4, 146
  Real History. . . , 10, 133, 134–5, 165n., 169n.
Wilde, Lady Jane Francesca 15, 63, 110
  Ancient Cures, 18, 45, 52–3, 173
  Ancient Legends, 2, 15–16, 43–9, 55–6, 64, 69, 70, 71–2, 73, 74, 75–6, 79n., 83n., 90, 115, 122n.
Wilde, Oscar 204
Wilde, William: *Irish Popular Superstitions* 43, 45, 47, 48–9, 54, 55, 56–7, 64, 71, 79n.

Yeats, J.B. 3, 4, 5, 7, 10, 30n., 31n., 33n., 191, 200, 206, 214n., 215n.
Yeats, William Butler
  beauty and, 156, 157–62, 163, 191, 209
  Castle of Heroes and, 21–5, 37n., 152, 153, 177, 191
  concept of Moods, 224–8, 230–1n., 231n.
  concept of sincerity, 3–9, 25, 28–9, 30n., 153
  Coole Park, 191, 220
  development as an artist, 2, 163, 228
  domestic ideal, 182–4, 186, 188, 190–2, 208–9, 211, 217, 220, 221
  early work, xiii–xvii, 206, 217–28
  emigrant poetry and, 173–6, 177, 211n.
  fairylore and, 41–3, 58, 61, 63–74, 79n.
  folklore and, 13–17, 31n., 34–5n., 41–3, 58, 61, 77n., 78–9n., 79n.
  folklore authorities, 43, 77n.
  Innisfree, 61–2, 188–9, 210, 211
  Katharine Tynan and, 5, 8, 9, 30n., 58–9, 100, 108, 190, 191, 199, 204, 222
  living in London, 2, 18, 189, 191, 207
  natural world and, 171, 184, 186, 192, 200, 203–6, 208, 209–11
  Olivia Shakespear and, 191, 221, 230n.
  personae adopted, 127, 192–201
  poems written to Maude Gonne, 25–9, 138–9
  rebirth theory and, 102–7, 124n.
  reputation of, 217, 222–3
  Theosophy and, 10, 12, 14, 17, 123–4n.
  see also Madame Blavatsky, magic, Maud Gonne and occultism
Yeats, William Butler: the Rose poems xiii, xvi, 8, 127, 129, 130, 138, 141, 151, 153, 156, 172, 177, 179, 223–4, 227–8
  "The Lover tells of the Rose in his Heart", 68, 152, 169n., 230n.
  "The Rose of Battle", 9, 171–80, 181–2, 184, 185, 192
  "The Rose of Peace", 138, 156–7, 180
  "The Rose of the World", 138, 157–60, 161, 171, 172
  "The Sorrow of Love", 160–1, 182, 184
  "To the Rose upon the Rood of Time", xiv, 127, 138–40, 141, 146–7, 150, 151, 152, 153, 155–6, 157, 161, 163, 168–9n., 177
  see also the Rose

Index

Yeats, William Butler: "The Wanderings of Oisin" xiii, xiv, xvi, xviin., 2, 29, 43, 52, 56, 64, 67, 107, 111, 113, 126–8, 138, 155–6, 158, 176–7, 196, 201, 206, 220
   anti-progress myth, 96–7
   battles in, 85, 86, 92–5
   four phantoms in, 114–15, 116–17, 120
   music in, 90–1, 121n.
   Niamh, 86, 87, 90, 91, 92, 93, 96, 97, 109, 112, 114, 115, 116, 117, 118, 119, 120, 120–1n., 125n., 157, 220
   occultism and, 89, 99–107, 107–10, 123–4n.
   plot of, 85–7
   rebirth theory and, 100–10, 124n.
   St. Patrick, 87, 93, 95, 96, 97–8, 99, 101–2, 118, 119, 120, 127, 128, 201
   sources of, 87–90, 111–16
   structure of, 91–9
   thirds of the night motif in, 90, 121n.
   three islands in, 86, 87, 90, 91, 92, 93, 94, 96, 103–4, 107, 114–15, 117, 118, 119, 126, 127, 128
   value of antithesis, 117–20
   veiled diction in, 99–102
   Zanoni and, 99, 100, 108–9, 112
Yeats, William Butler: works
   A Book of Irish Verse 30n., 175, 211n., 212n.
   "A Lover's Quarrel among the Fairies", 222
   "A man has the fields of heaven", 222
   "Anima Hominis", 162, 163
   Autobiographies, 1, 66–7, 128, 147, 177, 178, 179, 189, 203, 212n., 213n.
   A Vision, 106–7, 153
   "Blood and the Moon", 151
   "Discoveries", 128, 215n.
   "Down by the Salley Gardens", 187, 192, 201
   "Ephemera", 202–3, 204, 215n.
   Fairy and Folk Tales, 13, 19, 42, 43, 46, 47, 51, 54, 57, 58, 59, 62, 69, 77n., 110–12, 226
   "Fergus and the Druid", 25, 38n.
   Four Years [1887–1891], 1
   "He bids his Beloved be at Peace", 219–20, 229n., 230n.
   "He remembers forgotten Beauty", 230n.
   "How Ferencz Renyi kept Silent", 182–3, 184, 185, 186, 222
   "If I were Four-and-Twenty", 6–7
   "Invoking the Irish Fairies", 231n.
   "Irish Fairies, Ghosts, Witches, etc", 53
   Irish Fairy Tales, 43, 46, 47, 77n.
   "Is the Order of R.R. & A.C. to remain a Magical Order?", 167n., 168n.
   John Sherman, 182–5, 191, 207–8, 213n.
   "Kanva on Himself", 201–2, 214n.
   "Kanva, the Indian, on God", 214–15n.
   "Lapis Lazuli", 81n.
   "Magic", 122n., 226
   Mosada, 183–5, 222
   "News for the Delphic Oracle", 127, 164n, 213n.
   "Out of the Rose", 130
   Poems (1895), xviin., 114, 221–3, 230n.
   "Poetry and Tradition", 130
   Purgatory, 82n., 123n., 184, 213n.
   "Regina, Regina Pigmeorum, Veni", 231n.
   Rosa Alchemica", 130, 232n.
   "Street Dancers", 222
   "Symbolism in Painting", 130
   "The Autumn of the Body", 215n., 218
   "The Blessed", 39n., 230n.
   "The Broken Gates of Death", 126
   The Celtic Twilight, 34n., 43, 156, 158, 163n., 170n.
   "The Circus Animals' Desertion", 110, 126, 162
   The Countess Kathleen, 28–9, 199
   The Countess Kathleen and Various Legends and Lyrics, xviin., 27, 130, 158, 161, 179, 223
   "The Cradles of Gold", 62, 82n.
   "The Curse of Cromwell", 82n.
   "The Danaan Quicken Tree", 61–2
   "The Delphic Oracle upon Plotinus", 213n.
   "The Eaters of Precious Stones", 64, 76
   "The Fairy Doctor", 222
   "The Fairy Pedant", 222
   "The Falling of the Leaves", 192, 201–2, 204–6
   "The Four Ages of Man", 180
   The Green Helmet, 82n.
   "The Happiest of the Poets", 130
   "The Happy Townland", 127, 164n.
   "The Heart of the Woman", 221
   "The Host of the Air", 53–4, 81n.
   "The Hosting of the Sidhe", 220, 221
   The Hour-Glass, 76
   "The Indian to his Love", 181, 189–91
   The Island of Statues, 43, 49, 105, 195, 222
   The King of the Great Clock Tower, 125n.
   The King's Threshold, 213n.
   "The Lake Isle of Innisfree", 188–9, 209, 213n.
   The Land of Heart's Desire, 43, 56, 222
   "The Lover asks Forgiveness because of his Many Moods", 230n.
   "The Lover speaks to the Hearers of his Songs in Coming Days", 230n.
   "The Madness of King Goll", 199–201, 203, 204n
   "The Man who Dreamed of Faeryland", 64–6, 85, 114, 139, 161, 182, 184

"The Moods", 224
"The Philosophy of Shelley's Poetry", 225
"The Pity of Love", 185–6
"The Poet pleads with the Elemental Powers", 25–7, 29, 39–40n., 230n.
"The Priest and the Fairy", 49–50, 53, 222
"The Sad Shepherd" ("Miserrimus"), 192–200, 201, 203, 214n.
"The Secret Rose", 230n.
The Secret Rose, 130, 131, 163n., 164n.
"The Seeker", 192, 222
The Shadowy Waters, 131, 203
"The Song of the Happy Shepherd" ("Song of the Last Arcadian"), 192–7
"The Song of Wandering Aengus", 54, 121n.
"The Sorrow of Love", 160, 161, 182, 184
The Speckled Bird, xv, 24–5, 33n., 36n., 40n., 122n., 153–5, 156, 158, 166n., 169n.
"The Stolen Child", xiii, xiv, 44, 57, 58, 59–61, 62–4, 66, 68–9, 114, 119, 160, 182, 184, 204, 222
"The Symbolism of Poetry", 225

"The Travail of Passion", 230n.
"The Twisting of the Rope", 126
"The Two Trees", 25, 39n., 64, 152
"The Unappeasable Host", 82n.
The Wanderings of Oisin and Other Poems, xviin., 49, 50, 58, 59, 99, 191, 192, 195, 199, 214n., 222, 223
"The White Birds", 190
The Wind Among the Reeds, 54, 141, 223
"Those Who Live in the Storm", 220–1, 230n.
Time and the Witch Vivien, 192, 222
"To an Isle in the Water", 187, 188, 189, 190, 191, 192, 201, 209
"To Ireland in the Coming Times", 129, 147
"Vacillation", 153
"What Then?", 220
"When You are Old", 25, 26, 27–9, 40n., 176–7
"Where there is Nothing, there is God", 130
Young Ireland League 18, 36n.